Henry Martyn Dexter

Congregationalism

What is it; Where it is; How it Works

Henry Martyn Dexter

Congregationalism
What is it; Where it is; How it Works

ISBN/EAN: 9783337232528

Printed in Europe, USA, Canada, Australia, Japan

Cover: Foto ©Suzi / pixelio.de

More available books at **www.hansebooks.com**

CONGREGATIONALISM:

What it is; Whence it is; How it works;

WHY IT IS

BETTER THAN ANY OTHER FORM OF CHURCH GOVERNMENT;

AND

ITS CONSEQUENT DEMANDS.

BY

HENRY M. DEXTER,

Pastor of the Berkeley Street Congregational Church, Boston; Editor of the "Congregationalist;" and Associate Editor of the "Congregational Quarterly."

BOSTON:
NICHOLS AND NOYES.
1865.

Entered according to act of Congress, in the year 1865, by
NICHOLS AND NOYES,
In the Clerk's Office of the District Court for the District of Massachusetts.

STEREOTYPED BY W. F. BROWN AND CO

PRESSWORK OF JOHN WILSON AND SON.

TO

ANDREW LEETE STONE;

FOR WHOM

THE EAST AND THE WEST CONTEND

As a Pulpit Orator;

BUT WHOM

NEITHER THE EAST NOR THE WEST HAS YET FULLY COMPREHENDED

IN

The breadth of his Christian sagacity,
The clearness and force of his logical faculty,
And his admirable blending of nearly all of those imperial qualities

WHICH GO TO MAKE UP

A TRUE

Congregational Minister;

THIS VOLUME IS

(WITHOUT PERMISSION)

AFFECTIONATELY INSCRIBED,

BY ONE,

WHO, IN MORE THAN SIXTEEN YEARS OF ALMOST DAILY INTERCOURSE,
HAS HAD BOTH FREQUENT CAUSE AND LARGE OPPORTUNITY
TO KNOW WHAT HE IS AS

A Friend.

Religion is the best thing, and the corruption of it the worst.—JOHN ROBINSON, *Works*, 1 : 33.

We veryly beleeve & trust y⁰ Lord is with us, unto whom & whose service we have given our selves in many trialls; and that He will graciously prosper our indeavours according to y⁰ simplicitie of our harts therin. — ROBINSON AND BREWSTER, TO SANDYS, 15 Dec. 1617.

We are much charged with what we own not, viz. : — Independency, when as we know not any Churches Reformed, more looking at sister Churches for helpe then ours doe, onely we can not have rule yet discovered from any friend or enemy, that we should be under Canon, or power of any other Church ; under their Councell we are. We need not tell the wise whence Tyranny grew in Churches, and how commonwealths got their pressure in the like kind.— HUGH PETER. *Answer of the Elders*, iv.

The Discipline appointed by Jesus Christ for his Churches is not arbitrary, that one Church may set up and practice one forme, and another another forme, as each one shall please, but is one and the same for all Churches, and in all the Essentialls and Substantialls of it unchangeable, and to be kept till the appearing of Jesus Christ. And if that Discipline which we here practice, be (as we are perswaded of it) the same which Christ hath appointed and therefore unalterable, we see not how another can be lawfull ; and therefore if a company of people shall come hither, and here set up and practice another, we pray you thinke not much, if we can not promise to approve them in so doing. — RICHARD MATHER. *Answer of the Elders*, 83.

That Controversies about Forms of *Ecclesiastical Discipline*, concern not the *Essentials* of Religion, but that Good Men may be of various Sentiments about them ; *Salva Fide, et Caritate*, is readily acknowledged. Nevertheless there ought to be a singular Regard unto Truths of this Nature, by us in *New-England*, above what may be affirmed of Men in any other Part of the World, since our Fathers were Persecuted out of their Native Land, and fain to fly into the Wilderness, for their Testimony thereunto : great were the Difficulties and Temptations, and Straits, which they for some time conflicted with, and all upon no other Account, but that so they might enjoy a *pure Discipline and Church state*, exactly conformable to the Mind of *Christ*, revealed in the Holy Scriptures. On which Account, for their Posterity to depart from what their Fathers have with so much Clearness of Scripture Light, taught and practiced, and confirmed with so great Sufferings ; must needs be a greater Sin and Provocation to the Eyes of his Glory, than may be said of any other People on the Face of the Earth. — INCREASE MATHER. *Disq. con. Eccl. Councils*, i.

Some [among us] are great Blessings to the Churches, as inheriting the Principles, Spirit, and Grace of their Fathers and Grand-Fathers ; but many of them do not so. On which account, it is not at all to be wondered at, if they Dislike *the Good Old Way of the Churches* ; yea, if they Scoff at it, as some of them do ; or if they are willing *to depart from what is Ordinarily Practiced in the Churches of Christ in New-England*. For the *Congregational Church Discipline* is not Suited for a Worldly Interest, or for a *Formal Generation* of Professors. It will stand or fall as *Godliness in the Power of it* does prevail, or otherwise. — INCREASE MATHER. *Order of the Gospel*, 11.

Our Fathers fled into this Wilderness from the face of a *Lording Episcopacy* and *Human Injunctions* in the worship of God. Now, if any of us their Children should yield unto, or be Instrumental to set up in this Country, any of the Ways of Men's Invention, such as *Prelacy*, imposed *Liturgies*, Human *Ceremonies* in the Worship of God, or to admit Ignorant and Scandalous Persons to the Lord's Table ; This would *be a backsliding indeed !* It would be a Backsliding to the Things which we and our Fathers have departed from, and have openly testified against, to be not of God. — JOHN HIGGINSON. *Sermon 27 May*, 1663.

It was with regard unto *Church Order* and *Discipline*, that our pious Ancestors, the *Good old Puritan Nonconformists*, transported themselves and their Families, over the vast Ocean to these goings down of the Sun. On which account, a Degeneracy from the Principles of pure *Scriptural*

Worship and *Order* in the Church, would be more Evil in the Children of *New-England*, than any other People in the World. — COTTON MATHER. *Ratio Disciplinæ*, iv.

Consider what will be the latter end of receding or making a defection from the way of Church Government established among us. I profess I look upon the discovery and settlement of the Congregational way, as the boon, the gratuity, the largess of Divine bounty, which the Lord graciously bestowed upon his people that followed him into this wilderness. . . . As for the Presbyterian way of Church Government, it must be confessed that, in the day of it, it was a very considerable step to reformation. The church of God hath been recovered by degrees out of the anti-Christian apostacy. The reformation in King Edward's days was then a blessed work; and the reformation of Geneva and Scotland was a larger step, and in many respects purer than the other; and for my part I fully believe that the Congregational way far exceeds both, and is the highest step that hath been taken toward reformation, and, for the substance of it, is the very way that was established and practiced in the primitive times, according to the Institution of Jesus Christ. . . . And those that would forsake the Congregational, and pass over to the Presbyterian way, because of some differences of notion among our Congregational Divines, or difficulties in the practice and way of the Congregational Churches, shall find that they make but a bad exchange, and that there are as many or more differences, difficulties, and entanglements, in the Presbyterian principles and practice. — PRESIDENT OAKES. *Election Sermon*, 1673.

It is evident indeed, that great Pains are taken to *draw our People*, especially our inconsiderate *young People*, who are too unmindful of the King and God of their Fathers, *from their Love and Attachment to those first Principles of these Churches*; But, as Naboth said to Ahab concerning his Vineyard, in 1 Kings, xxi : 3. *The LORD forbid it me, that I should give the Inheritance of my Fathers unto Thee;* even so it is fit, that we should say to such as would entice us to part with the pure Order of these Churches, *This was our Father's Inheritance :* And GOD forbid, that any should persuade us to give up our inestimable Rights : For the very Thought of parting with them is Shocking. — SAMUEL MATHER. *Apology, &c.* 143.

The exigencies of the Christian Church can never be such as to legitimate, much less render it wise, to erect any body of men into a standing judicatory over the Churches. — PRESIDENT STILES. *Convention Sermon,* 116.

Pilgrim Fathers of New England, victims of persecution, how wide an empire acknowledges the sway of your principles ! Apostles of Liberty, what millions attest the authenticity of your mission ! . . . . . We come, in our prosperity, to remember your trials ; and here, on the spot where New England began to be, we come to learn of you an abiding lesson of virtue, enterprise, patience, zeal, and faith ! — EDWARD EVERETT. *Works,* i : 71.

Spread yourselves and your children over the continent, accomplish the whole of your great destiny, and if it be that through the whole you carry *Puritan hearts* with you, if you still cherish an undying love of civil and religious liberty, and mean to enjoy them yourselves, and are willing to shed your heart's blood to transmit them to your posterity, then will you be worthy descendants of Carver and Allerton and Bradford, and the rest of those who landed from stormy seas on the rock of Plymouth. — DANIEL WEBSTER. *Works,* ii : 524.

There was a State without king or nobles ; there was a Church without a bishop. — RUFUS CHOATE. *Life and Writings,* 1 : 379.

> And still their spirit, in their sons, with freedom walks abroad,
> The Bible is our only creed ; our only monarch, God !
> The hand is raised, the word is spoke, the solemn pledge is given,
> And boldly on our banner floats, in the free air of heaven,
> The motto of our sainted sires, — and loud we'll make it ring, —
> 𝕬 𝕮𝖍𝖚𝖗𝖈𝖍 𝖜𝖎𝖙𝖍𝖔𝖚𝖙 𝖆 𝕭𝖎𝖘𝖍𝖔𝖕, 𝖆𝖓𝖉 𝖆 𝕾𝖙𝖆𝖙𝖊 𝖜𝖎𝖙𝖍𝖔𝖚𝖙 𝖆 𝕶𝖎𝖓𝖌!

PREFACE.

As long ago as in 1859, I was desired by a publisher to recast for a moderately sized volume, an article entitled " Congregationalism — its essential features and inherent superiorities," which, after some previous service as a sermon, had been published in the first number of the *Congregational Quarterly.* I undertook the labor, and the book was announced as in the press, in July, 1860. It so happened, however, that after the copy had been partially prepared and the type-setting begun, circumstances connected with my pastoral charge compelled the temporary relinquishment of the undertaking. Resumed as soon as possible afterwards, the work — thanks to a printer of inexhaustible patience — has been carried on at desultory and often distant intervals, as the pressure of two exacting professions, and other things, would permit. It has thus been written and stereotyped in fragments; since the first fifty pages, one "form" not unfrequently having been completed, before the next page has existed in manuscript.

I mention these facts because they *are* facts — which may explain, though they will not justify, some of the many defects of the volume. If any body sees in it crudities, repetitions, and — in matter and manner — abundant marks of haste; I can only say, with Paul, "I more." Being at last finished, it is now published, because it is an honest — though felt to be a very imperfect — endeavor to discuss, in a practical way, subjects of common concernment; and particularly to make clear to all inquiring minds the simple and efficient processes of Congregationalism. While the wants of ministers, and others who are called upon to discuss Church Polity, have been constantly had in mind, and many notes have been inserted for their eye; the book has yet been especially written for, and to, the intelligent masses of the people, in the deepest conviction that the system of Church order, which it aims to unfold and defend, has special Divine aptitude to bless them, while in the present position of our country this aptitude peculiarly needs to be considered and commended to the general mind; and in the thought that, among other and abler treatises, they might, on some accounts, be grateful for such an one as this.

I have no apology to offer to fellow Christians of other denominations for anything said herein. I have not intended to speak in bitterness or censoriousness, nor otherwise than I would have them speak of my own faith — did facts warrant it — in reversed circumstances. I hold that the most peaceable and useful Christian union is that which is effected by the kindly co-working of denominational bodies, each thoroughly persuaded that it is better than all others, and stimulated to the utmost *esprit de corps;* as that grand army proves most victorious, in which each arm of the service is sure that it is more vital than all others to that success which all, it may be equally, desire, and for which all, under one leadership, contend. If a fellow Christain is an Episcopalian, or a Presbyterian, or a Methodist, I want him to be such with all his heart and soul and mind and strength; and equally I desire an earnest Congregationalism in all who accept the democratic, as, at once, the primitive and the peerless polity. The present crisis in our National affairs demands from every Christian, action of that sagacious, self-denying, and I might almost say strenuous character, which can only be the natural outgrowth of an intelligent, fervid, and untiring inward conviction that *he* has " the mind of Christ."

I have not always cited the most approved editions of the Fathers, and others; because it was more convenient to use those at hand in my own possession, and I had no time to go to the public libraries, and collate passages.

I have remembered that a poor book with a good index is better than a good book with none at all; and having lost countless hours in writing this, for want of tolerable help of that description in many of the volumes which I have had occasion to consult, I have been especially moved to make it in this respect, worthier of the public favor; and I am sure that those who may consult it will not feel that it is over-indexed.

The die on the cover is from the title-page of the late Mr. Joseph Hunter's " Collections concerning the Founders of New Plymouth. London. John Russell Smith. 1854;" being essentially a map, in little, of that locality, " near the joining borders of Nottinghamshire, Lincolnshire, and Yorkshire," which was honored of God as the birth-place of American Congregationalism.

I only add, that the plates of the statistics of pp. 5–7, have been suffered to stand as they were cast five years ago, because it has proved impossible, since the Rebellion, to gain later minute returns from the South, of the character required for those calculations; and that I have introduced — often in the language elsewhere employed — many practical discussions of points of interest to Congregationalists, which have been already published, in one or other of the Journals with which I have editorial connection.

H. M. D.

HILLSIDE, ROXBURY,
5 June, 1865.

ANALYSIS.

CHAPTER I. WHAT CONGREGATIONALISM IS........................pp. 1–7

    Definition... 1
    Fundamental Principles... 2–4
    Number of Congregational churches here and abroad............. 5
    Ratio to other churches here................................... 6
    Very evenly diffused throughout the land....................... 7

CHAPTER II. WHENCE CONGREGATIONALISM IS..................... 8–159

    Sect. 1. *Intimations of Christ on church government.*......... 9–13
    Sect. 2. *Testimony of the Apostles.*.......................... 13–21
    Sect. 3. *Testimony of history to Congregationalism.*.......... 21–25
    Sect. 4. *Proof of the principles of Congregationalism from Scripture and Reason.*............................. 25–159

        1. PRINCIPLE. *Any company of people believing themselves to be, and publicly professing to be, Christians, associated by voluntary compact, on Gospel principles, for Christian work and worship, is a true church.*........................ 25–34

            (1.) A true church is composed of Christians.......... 26–29
                (a.) It is described as holy......................... 26
                (b.) A vital union between it and Christ............ 27
                (c.) Christ's design for it.......................... 27
                (d.) Radically different from the world.............. 27
                (e.) Only believers can rightly receive its ordinances.. 28
                (f.) Unworthy members are to be cut off............. 28
            (2.) Those Christians must be united by covenant....... 29
            (3.) This union must be for Christian work and worship.. 30
            (4.) Every such company is a true church............... 30
                (a.) From scriptural use of the word church....... 31–34
                (b.) The work laid upon the church by Christ and the Apostles consists only with independent bodies... 34

        II. PRINCIPLE. *Such a church, as a rule, should include only those who can worship and labor together, and watch over each other.*... 34–35

        III. PRINCIPLE. *Every member of such a church has equal essential rights, powers, and privileges with every other (ex-*

[xi]

cept so far as the New Testament and common sense make some special abridgement in the case of female members), and the membership together, by majority vote, have the right and duty of choosing all necessary officers, of admitting, dismissing, and disciplining their own members, and of transacting all other appropriate business of a Christian church... 38–43

    (1.) All of its members have equal rights, &c...... 38–40
    (2.) The membership control its action............ 40–43
       (a.) They choose officers....................... 40–41
       (b.) They admit and dismiss members............. 41
       (c.) They discipline and exclude members....... 41–42
       (d.) They transact all other appropriate business.... 43

IV. PRINCIPLE. *Every such church is independent of all outward control, and answerable only to Christ, and is on a level of essential character with every other church on earth*..43–58

    (1.) It is independent, under Christ................. 44–56
       (a.) No Scripture confers control over it upon any.. 44–47
       (b.) No Scripture furnishes evidence of such control... 47
       (c.) Drift of New Testament against it............... 47
       (d.) Arguments for such control do not prove it..... 47–49
       (e.) Texts cited do not prove it.................... 49–55
       (f.) Christ made his churches independent, under himself... 55
    (2.) All such churches on an essential level.......... 56–58

V. PRINCIPLE. *A fraternal fellowship is yet to be maintained between these churches, by advice in Council, &c., &c* 58–67

    (1.) Such fellowship is Scriptural 61–63
    (2.) It is reasonable............................... 63
    Councils are mutual and *ex parte*...................... 64
    They have no *authority* (strictly so called)............ 64–66
    Suppose a church declines such advice ?............. 66–67

VI. PRINCIPLE. *The permanent officers of a church are its Pastor or Pastors, and Deacons, only; to be chosen from its own ranks*.. 67–159

    (1.) *Christ designated but these two classes*............. 68–76
    Apostles, Prophets, Deaconness, &c..................... 69
    Angel of the church.................................. 70
    Evangelists... 71–73
    Miracles, Gifts of Healings, Helps, Governments, &c... 74–75
    Diversities of tongues............................... 76
    (2.) *The first class is Pastors, called also Teachers, Elders, Presbyters, and Bishops*........................ 76–132
       (a.) Testimony of able and candid scholars that these are all names of one office.................... 77–92

Wiclif, John of Goch, Luther, Calvin.................. 77
Cranmer, Melancthon, Coverdale, Polanus, Limborch.. 78
Episcopius, Arminius, Wollebius, Ames, Robinson,
    Lord King, Sclater, Turretin, Stapfer............... 79
Richard Hooker, Milton, Lardner...................... 80
Gibbon, Baxter, Doddridge 81
Owen, Cotton, Davenport, Thomas Hooker, Cotton
    Mather, Chauncy.................................... 82
Wigglesworth, Foxcroft, Dickinson, Walter........... 83
Shepard, Jameson, Wise, Hopkins, Emmons.......... 84
Dwight, Mason, Woods, Guizot, Coleridge, Smyth,
    Bennet... 85
Coleman, Schmucker, Taylor, Sawyer, Breckenridge,
    Pond, Davidson, Punchard, Upham................ 86
Garratt, Vaughan, Hill, Jacobson, Newman, Plumtre,
    Conybeare and Howson.......................... 87
Ullman, Hall, Bacon, Wellman, Athanasius, Cajetan,
    Gualtherus.. 88
Zanchius, Gomarus, Grotius, Brennius, Poole, Henry, Bengel, Macknight, Clark...................... 89
Whitby, Scott, Assembly's Annotations, Bloomfield,
    Baumgarten, Eadie, Hodge, Barnes, Alexander...... 90
Hackett, Mack, Alford, Peshito-Syriac, Michaelis...... 91
(b.) Similar testimony from the Fathers, and from Ecclesiastical history........................... 92–99
    Clement of Rome, Polycarp......................... 92
    Justin Martyr, Irenæus........................... 93
    Clement of Alexandria, Hilary, Jerome............ 94–96
    Chrysostom, Theodoret, Pope Urban............... 96–97
    Mosheim, Waddington, Milner, Campbell, Gieseler,
    Guericke... 97
    Schaff, Kurtz, Killen, Neander...................... 98
    Epistles of Ignatius worthless in evidence............ 99
(c.) Similar testimony from the Scriptures......... 100–110
    (aa.) Examine the words "Pastor," &c., themselves............................... 100–103
    (bb.) Same qualifications demanded of all...... 103–104
    (cc.) Same duties assigned to all.............. 104–107
        (aaa.) To guide......................... 104–105
        (bbb.) To instruct........................... 105
        (ccc.) To administer the ordinances....... 105–106
        (ddd.) To ordain...................... 106–107
(d.) The texts claimed as making the Bishop a superior
    order, fail to sustain the claim............. 107–109
Does the New Testament teach or authorize any such office as that of Ruling Elder ?.................... 110–121
    Presbyterians, Dutch Reformed, &c., hold this..... 110
    Passages supposed to prove it..................... 111
    All turns on 1 *Tim.* v. 17....................... 112

But (1.) these are not *lay* elders................. 112
(2.) they are the same as labor in word and
  doctrine............................. 113
(3.) they can not have ruling for their sole
  function............................. 114
(4.) it is, then, a Congregational text......... 114
  proof of its Congregational sense from
  other texts.......................... 116
(5.) Presbyterian sense of it conflicts with
  the directions of the New Testament.... 117
(6.) *all* elders were to be apt to teach........ 118
Testimony of antiquity, Vitringa, Rothe, Neander,
  Dr. Wilson, &c............................. 118
Calvin invented the office........................ 118
The "Ruling Elder" of our Pilgrim Fathers.... 121-132
Their theory not self-consistent nor useful......... 123
Not a Presbyterian eldership, and soon abandoned.. 132

(3.) *The second class of permanent officers set by Christ in
his churches (for temporalities) is called Deacons.* 132-136
    (1.) Record of the Acts of the Apostles...... 132
    (2.) Epistles prove the same................ 134
    (3.) Early history of the Church proves it.... 134

(4.) *Pastors and Deacons are to be chosen and set apart
by the church from its own membership*......... 136-145
(1.) Every church is to elect its own Pastor and
  Deacons.................................... 136
(2.) Every church is to ordain, or otherwise set
  apart, its Pastor and Deacons............... 136
  (a.) The proprieties suggest some setting
    apart.................................. 137
  (b.) New-Testament theory of ordination
    very simple........................... 138
    Apostles did not "ordain" elders in
    every church, but "secured their elec-
    tion"................................. 138
    Scriptural ground lies in other passages.. 139
    A comely and fit custom............... 140
  (c.) This view supported by our Fathers.... 141
    "Plebeian" ordinations................ 144
    The "six months' notice" plan unscrip-
    tural, uncongregational, needless, in-
    expedient, disgraceful, and disastrous.. 144
    The hierarchal theory of ordination
    false, pernicious, and absurd......... 145
(3.) The Church must elect and set apart these
  officers from its own number............ 146-149
  Duty of a Congregational minister to belong
  to his own church............................ 146
  "Stated supplies"........................ 149-154

   Congregationalism knows such only as exceptions.. 149
   Right of *laymen* to preach if competent........ 150
   The Fathers held that only a Pastor is a minister.. 152
   One may act temporarily as "supply," but only *ad interim*........................... 153
   "Ordination as an Evangelist"............ 154–159
   There is no true ordination but of a church over itself................................ 154
   A *layman* may be authorized by the church to administer the Lord's Supper to it........... 155
   And to baptize, where there is need........... 156
   One who has been ordained as an Evangelist is just as much of a minister as he was before, and no more..................... 157–159

CHAPTER III. How CONGREGATIONALISM WORKS................... 160–235

 Sect. 1. *How to form a church*........................... 160–166
  Is it expedient.. 160
  Number necessary..................................... 161
  Application for letters of dismission, &c. (form)........ 161
  Articles of faith and covenant (form).............. 162–163
  Calling a council where practicable................... 164
  Form of *letter missive*................................. 164
  Action of Council and process of organization.......... 165
 Sect. 2. *How to choose and induct church officers*............. 166–172
  (1.) Choice of lesser officers........................... 166
  (2.) Choice and induction of Deacons 167
  (3.) Choice and induction of Pastor.................... 168
   Co-action of church and society (if one)......... 168
   Form of *call*................................... 168
   Form of *letters missive*........................ 171
   Procedure of Council, &c...................... 171
 Sect. 3. *How to transact the regular business of a church*..... 172–195
  (1.) Standing rules (form)......................... 172–173
  (2.) Rules of order.................................... 174
   (a.) Coming to order............................. 175
   (b.) Motions..................................... 176
   (c.) Amendments................................. 177
   (d.) Privileged motions.......................... 178
    (aa.) The previous question.................... 179
    (bb.) The motion to withdraw the question...... 179
    (cc.) The motion to lay on the table............. 179
    (dd.) The motion to commit.................... 179
    (ee.) The motion to postpone to a fixed date..... 179
    (ff.) The motion to postpone indefinitely......... 179
    (gg.) The motion to adjourn.................... 179

  (e.) Voting.. 180
  (f.) Reconsideration................................. 181
  (g.) Questions of order.............................. 181
  (h.) Committees...................................... 182
    (aa.) Special committees........................ 182
    (bb.) Standing committees....................... 182
    (cc.) Committee of the whole.................... 182
  (i.) Reports... 183
  (j.) Closing a meeting............................... 183
 (3.) Admitting members............................. 183–185
 (4.) Dismissing members (forms, &c.)................ 185–188
 (5.) Disciplining members.......................... 188–195
  (a.) Private offenses when only one individual is
    concerned (forms of complaint, &c.)............ 189
  (b.) Private offenses between two or more............ 192
  (c.) Matters of public scandal....................... 193
  (d.) Violations of the articles of faith and covenant... 194

Sect. 4. *How to vacate church offices*................. 195–206
 (a.) How to vacate lesser church offices.............. 196
 (b.) How to vacate the deaconship..................... 197
 (c.) How to vacate the pastorship..................... 198
  Dismission (forms).................................. 198
  Deposition.. 205

Sect. 5. *Church and parish*............................ 206–213
 (1.) The church standing alone........................ 206
 (2.) The church for all secular purposes acting as a
   parish.. 207
 (3.) Church and parish co-acting...................... 208
  (a.) Organization of a parish........................ 210
  (b.) By-laws of a parish (form)...................... 210
  (c.) Rules for joint action (form)................... 212

Sect. 6. *Councils*..................................... 213–221
 (1.) Who may call a Council........................... 214
 (2.) How a Council is called.......................... 214
 (3.) Letters missive.................................. 215
 (4.) Quorum... 216
 (5.) Organization.................................... 216
 (6.) Scope of business................................ 216
 (7.) Method of business............................... 217
 (8.) Result... 217
 (9.) Force of such a result........................... 218
  No *authority* (purely speaking).................... 219
  Legally (in Mass.): —
   (a.) Of no force until accepted by parties........ 219
   (b.) Justifies the party accepting and acting on it. 219
   (c.) Conclusive as to facts adjudged to be such... 220
   (d.) But the court may revise..................... 220
 (10.) Dissolution..................................... 220

Sect. 7. *Consociation*.................................. 221–225
  A standing Council and not a purely Congregational
    procedure...................................... 222
Sect. 8. *Associations*................................. 225–227
Sect. 9. *Conferences*................................... 227
Sect. 10. *Church extension*.............................. 227
Sect. 11. *Denominational relations*...................... 229
Sect. 12. *How to dissolve a church*................... 230–233
  Where unanimous (form of letter)................... 231
  Where resisted by a minority....................... 232
Sect. 13. *The restoration of offenders*............... 234–235

CHAPTER IV. WHY CONGREGATIONALISM IS BETTER THAN ANY OTHER
  FORM OF CHURCH GOVERNMENT................. 236–296

Sect. 1. *It is more in accordance with the mind of Christ*..... 236–237
  (1.) It is the New-Testament polity.................. 236
  (2.) It is that which Christ has signally blessed......... 237
  (3.) It is that which specially promotes earnest per-
         sonal Christian activity........................ 237
Sect. 2. *It is more practicable in its working than any other sys-
         tem*.. 237–251
  (a.) In the formation of churches..................... 238
  (b.) In the matter of the pastorate................... 241
  (c.) In its methods of worship........................ 248
  (d.) In all church work............................... 249
Sect. 3. *It tends most to promote general intelligence*........ 252–254
Sect. 4. *It tends most to promote piety in its membership*..... 255–259
  (a.) Develops especially individual responsibility....... 255
  (b.) Throws its membership most directly upon the
        Bible, the Spirit, and the Saviour................ 257
Sect. 5. *It most favors true gospel discipline*............... 259–263
Sect. 6. *It has the most favorable influence upon its ministry*.. 263–266
Sect. 7. *Its fundamental principles are more favorable than any
        other to the promotion of the general cause of Christ* 266–267
  (1.) In promoting revivals of religion.............. 267–276
    (a.) In virtue of its freeness of action, and flexibility
          of adaptation................................ 267
    (b.) Its want of reliance upon any thing formal, or
          ritual, for salvation......................... 269
    (c.) The high character of its spiritual demands...... 271
    (d.) Its special training toward dependence upon God. 272
    (e.) Its intense individualism...................... 274
  (2.) In promoting missions.......................... 276
Sect. 8. *It furnishes the most efficient barrier against heresy and
        false doctrine*............................... 277–289
  (1.) Favors the development of error less than others.... 277

    (2.) Furnishes a less favorable shelter for it.............. 280
    (3.) It, in its past history, has actually proved itself a
      safer barrier than any other system......... 281–289
  Sect. 9. It has a kindlier bearing than any other toward a republican form of civil government................... 288–293
  Sect. 10. Its advantages are organic and peculiar to itself, while its disadvantages are incidental to the imperfection of its past development, and so removable.......... 293–295
    The existence of heretical churches Congregationally governed, no proof that these positions are false...................................... 295–296

CHAPTER V. WHAT OUGHT TO BE DONE ABOUT THIS?................. 297
  1. Congregationalists should recognize the fact that Congregationalism is a polity............................. 298
  2. That it is the polity which Christ loves, and would promote...................................... 298
  3. They ought to master it in its grand scope, and minute details..................................... 299
  4. They ought to appreciate the fact that no other polity can be so helpful to this land now as it can be.......... 299
  5. They ought to remember that it is peculiarly the polity of revivals, and work it in that aim, to that end........ 300
  6. They ought to use all honorable means to secure its prevalence.. 301
    (1.) It should be preached as a system from Christ, and which needs to be made clear in what it is, what it is not, and what it demands................... 302
    (2.) Distinctively Congregational missions, home and foreign, should be supported by Congregationalists in preference to all others................... 302
    (3.) Congregationalists should abundantly endow, and thoroughly use, their schools and seminaries..... 303
    (4.) They should purify the practical working of their system of present inconsistencies................ 304
    (5.) They should do justice to its principle of the communion of churches, in more active, and more loving, and more constant fellowship and co-working...................................... 306

INDEX OF SUBJECTS.

Acceptance of a report, 183.
Adjournment, 183.
Adjourn, motion to, privileged, 179.
Adjournment *sine die*, 183.
Admitting members, 183.
Admonition, effect of, 191.
Adoption of a report, 183.
Amendments, 177.
Amend, motion to, may entirely alter and even reverse the meaning of the original motion, 178.
American Congregational Union, 228.
Angel of the Church, what? 70.
Appeal from the decision of the Chair, 182.
Apostles, office, self-limited and temporary, 20.
Apostles assumed no control over the primitive churches, 47.
Apostles threw their influence on the side of popular rights, 19.
Aristocracy, essential, of the Presbyterian system, 291.
Arminianism, in Scotland developed in the Presbyterian Church, 283.
Articles of Faith (form of), 102.
Association, articles of, for a Parish (form of), 210.
Associations, ministerial, what? 225.
Associations, ministerial, error of their attempting to depose from the ministry, 305.
Associations, General, 226.
Authority, properly speaking, none in the decision of a Council, 219.
Baptism, any church, on exigency, may authorize a competent layman to administer, 155.
Barnes, Rev. Albert, case of, illustrates the imperfection of the Presbyterian way of dealing with asserted heresy, 288.
Bishop, what? 102.
Bishop, same as Pastor or Elder, 76.
Bishop, in the Episcopal sense, the offspring of the corruptions of the early Church, 22.
Bishops superior to Pastors; cannot be proved by texts claimed to prove it, 107.
Bishops, American Episcopal, have not the true, untainted Apostolical succession, 245.

"By all means save some," the voice of Congregationalism to each one of her membership, 275.
Call to a candidate to become a Pastor (form of), 169.
Calomel on Mondays, quinine on Tuesdays, and so on, the Episcopal way, 269.
Certificate of good standing should be taken by a travelling Church member (with form), 187.
Certificate of reception from another Church (form of), 186.
Christ placed the sole responsibility of his cause on earth upon the local Churches, 55.
Church, what it is, 1.
Church, composed of Christians, 25, 26.
Church, a true, what is it? 25.
Church, a, must be united by covenant, 29.
Church, a feeble, may be purer than a strong one, 57.
Church, the, a local body, 34.
Church, every, local, independent of all external control, but Christ's, 43.
Church, local, every, on a level with every other, 56.
Church, permanent officers two, only, 67.
Church and Parish, 206.
Church, can it be dissolved by majority vote; opinions on the question, 233.
Church depose their Pastor, when painfully necessary, after advice of Council, 205.
Church, "dropping" from, impossible, 187.
Church extension, 227.
Church extension, early New England way, 228.
Church, how to form, 160.
Church may act without any Parish, 206.
Church may act, for all secular purposes, as a Parish, 207.
Church, how to dissolve, 230.
Church may be dissolved by unanimous vote, 231.
Church, how to proceed where a small minority resist dissolution, 232.
Church work, superior advantages of Congregationalism in, 249.
Church order, why Luther did not reform that as well as Church doctrine, 24.

[xix]

INDEX OF SUBJECTS.

Church of England, has "Calvinistic articles, a Papistical service, and an Arminian clergy," 282.
Churches, at Jerusalem, Antioch, Ephesus, and Corinth, though large, did each meet together in one place for business, 37.
Churches, thirty-five local Congregational, mentioned in the New Testament, 36.
Churches, five primitive, within eye-shot of each other, 36.
Churches, Congregational, proved best on heathen ground, 277.
Churches, more easily formed under Congregationalism than under any other system, 238.
Churches should maintain fellowship, 58.
Churches, voting by, in a Council, the old way, and the best, 216.
Church Courts, faulty and ineffectual working of, 289.
Closing a meeting, 183.
Colenso case, light shed by it upon the utter weakness of Episcopacy to protect itself, 281.
Coming to order, 175.
Committee, motion to commit to, privileged, 179.
Committee, special, 182.
Committee of the whole, 182.
Committee, examining, 184.
Committees, 182.
Committees, standing, 182.
Committees, &c., how to vacate, 196.
Common sense, Congregationalism the religion of, 238.
Complaint against an offender (form of), 190.
Concubinage, spiritual, of the Itinerancy, 265.
Conferences, Church, 227.
Conferences, Church, error of their attempting, or tolerating, any semblance of ecclesiastical or judicial power over the Churches, 304.
Conferences, General, 227.
Confession, 191.
"Conflict of Ages," much read but little received, 280.
Congregational, meaning of the name, 4.
Congregational Church, that at Scrooby the Mother Church of New England, 25.
Congregational Churches, the kind for the foreign mission-field, 277.
Congregationalism, religious democracy, 1.
Congregationalism, a form of Church order, not of faith, 4.
Congregationalism, fundamental principle of, 2.
Congregationalism, six subordinate principles of, 2.
Congregationalism, the necessary outgrowth of the teachings of Christ, 9.
Congregationalism, in a majority, in this country, 6.
Congregationalism has 21 forty-firsts of the Evangelical Churches in this country, 6.
Congregationalism, evenly distributed in the land, 7.
Congregationalism equally adapted to every latitude, 7.
Congregationalism differs from Independency, 2, 60.
Congregationalism, most practicable form of Church government, 237.

Congregationalism most favors the formation of Churches, 238.
Congregationalism, superiority of, in the promotion of general intelligence, 252.
Congregationalism, most practicable in its methods of worship, 248.
Congregationalism, superiority of, in all Church work, 249.
Congregationalism most favors its pastors, 241.
Congregationalism especially favors its ministry, in contrast with other polities, 263.
Congregationalism throws its members most directly upon the Bible, and the Spirit, and the Saviour, 257.
Congregationalism most tends to promote piety in its membership, 255.
Congregationalism most promotes the feeling of individual responsibility for the conversion of men, 255.
Congregationalism most promotes Gospel discipline, 259.
Congregationalism furnishes best barrier against heresy, 277.
Congregationalism casts out a heretic more easily and effectually than any other system, 281.
Congregationalism in England and Scotland, has kept the faith while Presbyterianism has lapsed into heresy, 284.
Congregationalism, most in accordance with the mind of Christ of all Church polities, 236.
Congregationalism most favors the promotion of the general cause of Christ, 266.
Congregationalism most tends to bring on the Millennium, 237.
Congregationalism has been most blessed, 237.
Congregationalism, advantages of, peculiar to itself, 293.
Congregationalism, practical disadvantages of, as sometimes worked, merely incidental to its imperfection of development, and sure to disappear, 293.
Congregationalism, its antagonist systems, in stress of difficulty, obliged to desert their own fundamentals and appeal to its, 294.
Congregationalism, fact that there are many heretical Churches so governed, no fair objection to, 296.
Congregationalism, the mother of this free Republic, 290.
Congregationalism, statistics of, 5.
Congregationalists-Baptists, Unitarians, Universalists, &c., &c., may be, 4.
Congregationalists, ought to recognize the fact that they possess a polity, 298.
Congregationalists, ought to know and feel that they possess the polity which Christ especially loves, and would promote, 298.
Congregationalists, ought to master their polity in its minute details, 299.
Congregationalists, ought to appreciate the fact that no polity can now so bless this land as theirs, 299.
Congregationalists, ought to feel that theirs is the polity for revivals, and work it for that end, 300.
Congregationalists, ought to use all honorable means to extend their polity, 301.
Congregationalists, should preach their system, 302.

INDEX OF SUBJECTS.   XXI

Congregationalists, should especially favor and promote Congregational Missions, Home and Foreign, 302.
Congregationalists, should abundantly endow, and thoroughly patronize, their own Schools, Colleges, and Seminaries, 303.
Congregationalists, should purify their system of all practical inconsistencies, which mar its working, 304.
Congregationalists, should cultivate a spirit of unity, and co-working, 305.
Consociation, 221.
Cousociationism, low-church theory of, 224.
Council, ecclesiastical, what? 213.
Council, theory of a, 63.
Council, who may call, 214.
Council, how called, 214.
Council, organization of, 216.
Council, quorum of, what? 216.
Council, moderator of, best chosen by ballot, 216.
Council, method of business, 217.
Council, scope of business of, 216.
Council, no right to touch any subject not submitted in the Letter Missive, 215.
Council to form a church, procedure of, 164.
Council for settlement of a Pastor, details concerning, 170.
Council, Mutual, to be called for dismissing a Pastor, 200.
Council, Mutual, for dismission, procedure of, 201.
Council, Dismissing, should give suitable credentials to a worthy retiring Pastor (form of), 205.
Council, to dissolve a Church, 230.
Council, to restore a deposed minister, 235.
Council, Mutual, 64.
Council, *ex parte*, 64.
Council, *ex parte*, may be called when a Mutual Council has been refused, 215.
Council, result, 217.
Council, result (form of), 218.
Council, force of result of, 218.
Council, result, force of, in the Massachusetts Courts, 219.
Council, result of, suppose a Church do not accept it? 66.
Council, dissolution of, 220.
Council, dissolved, cannot re-assemble but by a new Letter Missive, and as a new Council, 221.
Council at Jerusalem, 50.
Councils, Ecclesiastical, 213.
Councils, Ecclesiastical, Scriptural, 61.
Councils, Ecclesiastical, reasonable, 63.
Councils, reference to several important ones, 221.
Councils, have no authority, properly so called, 64.
Councils, not to be confounded with Presbyteries, 65.
Courts, revision of results of Councils by, 220.
Credentials, Council should give suitable, to a worthy retiring Pastor (form of), 205.
Covenant, the bond of a Church, 29.
Covenant, form of, 163.
Deacon, what? 132.
Deacon, a temporal office in the Church, 134:
Deacon, office of, testimony of Church History, that it was, in the primitive Church,

the second office in the Church, and for temporalities, 135.
Deacon, is elected by his own Church, 136, 147.
Deacon, to be set apart by his own Church, 136.
Deacons, how to choose and induct, 167.
Deaconess, what the office was, 69.
Deaconship, how to vacate, 197.
Debate may be renewed after the affirmative of a question has been put, 181.
Debating an undebatable question out of order, 181.
Denominational relations, 229.
Deposition of a Pastor, how effected, 205.
Deposition of an unworthy Minister very difficult, if not practicably impossible, in the hierarchal Churches, 247.
Deposition of Pastor, in Consociated Churches, done by Consociation, 225.
Deposed minister, how restored, 234.
Discipline, 188.
Discipline, Episcopalian, futility of, 261.
Discipline, Church, illustrations of the imperfection of Presbyterian, 260.
Discipline, Methodist, imperfection of, 262.
Discipline, Gospel, most favored by Congregationalism, 269.
Dismission, when requested to an unevangelical body, duty concerning, 187.
Dismission, Letters of, should not be valid more than six months or a year, 188.
Dismissing members, 185.
Dissolution of a meeting, 183.
Distrust of our own first principles, danger from, 305.
Diversities of Tongues, 76.
Doubting a vote, 180.
"Dropping" from the Church, impossible, 187.
Duties of Pastor, Elder, Teacher, and Bishop, Scripturally the same, 104.
Earnestness, a great present need of Congregationalists, 302.
Ecclesia, Scripture use of, 31.
Ecclesiastical year, evils of observance of, 268.
Elder, or Presbyter, what? 101.
Elder, lay ruling, Scripture authorizes no such office, 110.
Elder, lay ruling, texts claimed to teach it, teach no such thing, 111.
Elder, lay ruling, Calvin invented the office, 118.
Elder, lay ruling, conceded by eminent Presbyterians to be an office resting on expediency, and not on the Word of God, 119.
Elder, lay ruling, contest about, between Dr. Breckinridge and Dr. Smyth, &c., 121.
Elders, lay ruling, unsupported by a solitary text, 118.
Elders, lay ruling, theory of, conflicts with Scripture theory of Church rule, 117.
Elders who "rule well," the same as those who "labor in word and doctrine," 113.
Ellipsis, Congregational, two foci of, the Independence of local Churches, and their fraternity, 209.
England, Church of, has no fixed doctrine, 286.
England, Church of, helpless against heresy, 286.

Ephesus, Church of, did not have several congregations under one Presbyterial government, 52.
Ephesus, claim that Timothy was Bishop of, absurd, 109.
Episcopacy, American, abandoned "a bulwark of the faith," in her Convention, 282.
Episcopacy, the Colenso case shows how inadequate all its provisions are to secure purity of doctrine, 281.
Episcopalian discipline, futility of, 261.
Episcopalians, had a hard time in getting ministers here in colonial times, 244.
Episcopal Church, first in Boston, became the first Unitarian, 285.
Episcopalians, early American, loose in doctrine, 285.
Episcopacy, in Connecticut, absorbed the Unitarian element, 285.
Epistles of Ignatius, the stronghold of Episcopalians and the Papacy, 99.
Epistles of Ignatius, so interpolated as to be useless for argument, 99.
Error, religious, Congregationalism favors development of, less than any other polity, 277.
Error, religious, less easily sheltered among Congregationalists than elsewhere, 280.
Evangelist, what? 71.
Evangelist, an, ordination as, needless, 154.
Evangelist, an, ordination as, meaningless and uncongregational, 154.
Evangelist, one ordained as, related to the churches precisely as he was before, 157.
Examining Committee, 184.
Excommunication, effect of, 191.
Flexibility, superior, of the Congregational system, 267.
Foci, the two, of the Congregational ellipse, the Independence of the local Church, and the fraternity of those Churches, 299.
Folly of Dr. Woods, and others, who advised Congregationalists to become Presbyterians at the West, seen and acknowledged, 304.
Forms: —
 Articles of Faith, 162.
 Covenant, 163.
 Standing Rules for a Church, 173.
 Rules of joint action of Church and Parish, 212.
 Articles of Association between Church and Parish, 210.
 By-laws of a Parish, 211.
 Complaint to Church, of offending member, 190.
 Certificate of good standing for a travelling Church member, 188.
 Certificate of reception as a Church member, 186.
 Request for letter of dismission to form a new Church, 161.
 Letter, when request for dismission will be probably denied, 162.
 Request for letter of dismission to another Church, 186.
 Letter of dismission from one Church to another, 186.
 Letter of dismission to be given by a dissolving Church to its membership, 231.
 Call to Pastor elect, 169.
 Letter Missive, for Council to form a Church, 164.

Forms (continued): —
 Letter Missive, for Council to settle a Pastor, 171.
 Letter Missive, for Mutual Council for dismissing a Pastor, 200.
 Letter Missive, where the Pastor declines to unite with the Church, 200.
 Letter Missive, for Council in case of difficulty not removing the Pastor, 215.
 Letter Missive for a Council to dissolve a Church, 230.
 Letter Missive for an ex parte Council, 216.
 Result of Council recommending the retiring Pastor, 205.
 Result of Council called to advise in difficulty, 218.
Gifts of healings, what? 74.
Governments, what? 74.
Helps (antilepseis), what? 74.
Heresy, Congregationalism furnishes best barrier against, 277.
Heretic, more easily dealt with under Congregationalism than under other systems, 281.
How to dissolve a Church, 230.
Ignatius's Epistles, the stronghold of the hierarchy, 99.
Ignatius's Epistles, so corrupt as to be useless for argument, 99.
Illustrations of Presbyterian-imperfection in discipline, 260.
Improbability that the "General Assembly" will decide right for the whole Church; Dr. Alexander's sense of, 289.
Independence, superior, of Congregational pastors, 264.
Independency, 2, 60.
Individualism, intense development of, by Congregationalism, 255.
Infidelity, the growth of Presbyterianism in Switzerland, 283.
Intelligence, general, Congregationalism promotes more than any other polity, 252.
Interruption of a speaker, out of order, 181.
Irrelevancies, out of order, 181.
Jefferson, testimony of, to the admirable practical working of Congregational principles, 290.
Judicature, a Consociation, strictly one, and so uncongregational, 223.
"Judicatories," Church, unscriptural, 53.
Layman, a competent, may be authorized by a Church, to baptize, and administer the Lord's Supper, in emergencies, 155.
Letter, receiving members on, from another Church, 184.
Letter for dismission to form a Church (form of), 161.
Letter of request for dismission and recommendation (form of), 186.
Letter of dismission and recommendation (form of), 186.
Letter of dismission to its members by a dissolving Church (form of), 231.
Letter Missive, for a Council to advise with reference to the formation of a Church (form of), 164.
Letter Missive, for a Council to settle a Pastor (form of), 171.
Letter Missive, for calling a Council in case of difficulty in the Church (form of), 215.

INDEX OF SUBJECTS.

Letter Missive, for calling an *ex parte* Council (form of), 216.
Letter Missive, for dismissal of a Pastor (form of), 200.
Letter Missive, for Council to dissolve a Church (form of), 230.
Licensure by an Association, confers no *right* to be a Minister, that was not possessed before, 152.
Lord's Supper, any Church may, in an exigency, authorize any competent layman to administer, to itself, 155.
Malista proves that there is no such thing as a Ruling Elder, in the Presbyterian sense, in the Bible, 113.
Massachusetts Courts have shown progress in their decisions on questions of pastoral difficulty, 203.
Massachusetts way of Church and Parish, 208.
Meeting, closing of, 183.
Members, admission of, 183.
Members, disciplining, 188.
Members, dismissing, 185.
Members of a Church have equal rights and powers, 38.
Members should — as the rule — belong to the Church with which they statedly worship, 185.
Membership, whole, chose original deacons, 15.
Membership, whole, chose apostle in place of Judas, 14.
Membership, whole, chose elders in all the primitive Churches, 16.
Membership, whole, chose delegates, to go with Paul, 15.
Membership, whole, acted in the early Churches in the discipline of offenders, 18, 34.
Membership, whole, ancient, consulted in cases of doubt, 18.
Membership, whole, have the right to admit, dismiss, and exclude members, 41.
Membership, whole, have the right to elect all officers, 40.
Membership, whole, have the right to transact all the business of the Church, 43.
Methodists, troubled in their beginnings here by irregularities rendered necessary by their system, 246.
Methodist discipline, imperfection of, 262.
Minister, New-Testament idea of, that of a *Pastor*, 152.
Ministry, a "standing order," not a doctrine of pure Congregationalism, 151.
Ministry, most favored by the Congregational system, 263.
Ministry, Congregational, have special facilities for usefulness, 265.
Miracles (*dunameis*), what? 73.
Moderator of a church meeting, who? 168.
Moderator, duty to call to order members out of order, 182.
Moderator's decision, appeal from, to the house, 182.
Moderator has no right to refuse to put a vote because he does not like it, 177.
Moderator has no right to refuse to call for the "contrary minds," 177.
Moderator has no right of veto, 176.
Moderator has no right to adjourn the meeting at his pleasure, 177.

Moderator of a Council, best chosen by ballot, 216.
Motion, last made, that for decision, 181.
Motion for the previous question, 179.
Motion to postpone to a fixed time, 179.
Motion to postpone indefinitely, 179.
Motion to commit, 179.
Motion to lay on the table, 179.
Motion to reconsider, 181.
Motion to adjourn, 179.
Motions, privileged, 178.
Napthali, blessing on, Congregationalists have a right to take, 308.
New Light, which is old darkness, not successful among Congregationalists, 280.
Notice, public, should be given of votes of extreme censure, 192.
Offences, private, and concerning only one individual, 189.
Offences, private, where two or more are concerned, 192.
Offences, violations of articles of faith and covenant, 194.
Offences of public scandal, 193.
Offender, complaint against (form of), 190.
Offender, trial of, 191.
Offenders, restoration of, 234.
Offices, Church, how to vacate, 195.
Officers, Church, how to choose and induct, 166.
Order, questions of, 181.
Ordination, New-Testament view of, 138.
Ordination, true Scripture ground of it, not in Acts xiv. 23 and Titus, i. 5, but elsewhere, 138.
Ordination, the act of the Church, proof of, from testimony of the past, 141.
Ordination, hierarchal theory of, untenable, 145.
Ordination, is it for life? 143.
Ordination, without a Council regular, in an emergency, 245.
"Packing" Church Courts, beauty of, in Presbyterianism, 289.
Parish, 206.
Parish, organization of, 210.
Parish, "articles of association" (form of), 210.
Parish, Church may exist without, 206.
Parish, Church may act as, 207.
Parish, By-laws (form of), 211.
Parish and Church, joint action, rules for (form of), 212
Pastor, what the word means in the New Testament, 100.
Pastor to be ordained by his own Church, through a Council, 136.
Pastor, procedure in calling, 168.
Pastor, no longer, no longer a Minister, the early doctrine of New England, 150.
Pastor, strictly, demits his ministry when dismissed, 150.
Pastor, a, should belong to his own Church, 136, 147.
Pastor ought to be ashamed to be afraid to belong to his own Church, 147.
Pastor, suppose the people want him to go, and he won't go? 203.
Pastor, deposition of, how effected, 205.
Pastors, same as Teachers, Presbyters, Elders, Bishops, or Overseers, 67.

INDEX OF SUBJECTS.

Pastors, Congregationalism favors, more than any other system, 241.
Pastorship, how to vacate, 198.
People, the, recognized as the tribunal of last appeal, by the "strong" Church governments, when "any thing breaks," 294.
Piety, Congregationalism more promotive of, than any other polity, 255.
Polity, Congregationalism as decidedly a, as the system of Rome itself, 298.
Postponement to a fixed time, 179.
Postponement, indefinite, 179.
Prayer-meetings, Episcopalian opposition to, 276.
Preach, any competent layman has the right to, 149.
Preaching Congregationalism, a poor and discreditable boast, never to have done it, 302.
Presbyter, what? 101.
Presbyterian law has become so much of a science, that nobody but a lawyer can now understand it, 281.
Presbyterianism in Massachusetts, efforts to introduce it into Congregationalism a failure, 223.
Presbyterianism, non-Republicanism of, 291.
Presbyterianism, powerless as a conservator of doctrine, 283.
Presbyterianism in England, developed into Unitarianism, 283.
Presbyterian Church, first in Boston, settled Dr. Channing as its Pastor, and is now the leading Unitarian Church, 285.
Previous question, 179.
Primitive Church, governed itself, 13.
Profession, receiving members on, 184.
Propounding Candidates, 184.
Public offences, scandalous, 193.
Purity of the Church, most promoted by Congregationalism, 259.
Puseyism, Bishop Eastburn's ineffectual fight against, in Boston, 281.
Qualifications of Pastor, Elder, Teacher, and Bishop, scripturally identical, 103.
Question, debating an undebatable one, out of order, 181.
Quorum of a Council, what? 216.
Rationalism, the outgrowth of "strong" Church governments, in Germany and Scotland, 283.
Reconsideration, 181.
Report, acceptance of, 183.
Report, adoption of, 183.
Reports, 183.
Republic, our, the child of Congregationalism, 290.
Responsibility, individual, more developed by Congregationalism than by any other system, 255.
Restoration of a minister, 234.
Restoration of offenders, 192.
Revivals, Congregationalism specially favors, 268.
Rules of order, 174.
Ruling Elder, lay, an unscriptural office, 111.
Ruling Elder, old New-England theory of, 122.
Ruling Elder, old New-England, founded on a misinterpretation; and a failure, and soon abandoned, 130.

Ruling Elder, old New-England, never an approximation toward the Presbyterian office of that name, 132.
Saybrook Platform, a compromise between Congregationalism and Presbyterianism, 223.
Session, the, the Church, in Presbyterianism, 292.
Shepherd, the Pastor a, 100.
"Six months' notice," unscriptural, uncongregational, needless, inexpedient, disgraceful, and disastrous, 144.
"Six months' notice," under, the vote of Parish to dismiss ultimates the legal relation and terminates all claim for salary, without a Council, 213.
Society, Ecclesiastical (see Parish), 206.
South, the, Congregationalism good for, 240, 299.
Speaker, interrupting one, out of order, 181.
Special Committees, 182.
Standing Committees, 182.
Standing Rules of a Church (form of), 173.
"Stated Supplies," Congregationalism recognizes them only as exceptions, *ad interim*, 149.
Stimulus, Congregationalism gives special to her pastors, 206.
"Strong" government of the Church in England and Scotland, has not kept out heresy, 281, 283.
Strong government of the Roman-Catholic Church has not held it back from heathenism, 282.
Suicide, not the duty of a Church and Parish, 204.
Sum, largest, question on first, 181.
Suspension, effect of, 191.
Synodic way, the old, 306.
Table, to lay on, motion to, 179.
Teacher, what? 101.
Temptation, freedom from, of Congregational Pastors, 263.
Testimony of Commentators to the equality of Bishops and Pastors, &c., 88.
Testimony of eminent scholars to the equality and identity of Bishops and Pastors, &c., 77.
Testimony of Ecclesiastical Historians to the equality and identity of Bishops and Pastors, 97.
Testimony of Fathers, &c., to the equality and identity of Bishops and Pastors, 92.
"*The* Church," not known to Scripture, 81, 49.
Time, longest, question on first, 181.
Timothy, so far from being "Bishop of Ephesus," was an Evangelist, 109.
Tongues, diversities of, 76.
Transfer of Pastors, common in the early days of New England, 143.
Treasurer of a Church should be appointed, 168, 173.
Trial of offence, 191.
Tribble, Rev. Andrew, the means of aiding Jefferson to understand Congregationalism, and thence to shape this Republic, 290.
Unitarianism, would probably have swept and conquered New England but for Congregationalism, 287.
Unitarianism in New England not logically traceable to Congregationalism, 286.

Unitarianism in England grew out of Presbyterianism, 283.
Unitarian Church in New England, first, was the first Episcopal Church, 285.
Unitarian, not a single strictly Congregational Church in England became, 284.
Vacate the smaller Church offices, how to, 196.
Vacate the Deaconship, how to, 197.
Vacate the Pastorship, how to, 198.
Violations of articles of faith and covenant, 194.
Vote, doubting a, 180.

Voting, 180.
Voting, by Churches, in a Council, the old way, and the best, 216.
Waldenses kept the faith pure, 23.
West, the, Congregationalism good for, 299.
West, no longer pre-empted to Presbyterianism, 303.
Whole, Committee of, 182.
Wickliffe, the first modern Congregationalist, 24.
Worship, methods of, superior practicableness of Congregationalism in, 248.

INDEX OF NAMES.

Aaron, 150.
A, B, C, F, M, 228, 277.
Aberdeen, 284.
Abington, 264.
Achaia, 54.
Adams, 244, 290.
Adger, 121.
Ærius, 96.
Agnew, 261.
Agrippa, 113.
Ainsworth, 122, 127.
Alabama, 7.
Alexander, 18, 90, 108, 139, 289, 301.
Alexandria, 37.
Alford, 9, 10, 12, 73, 91, 101, 102, 106, 107, 108, 111, 114, 116, 117, 121, 133, 138, 139, 192.
Allin, 151.
Amesius, 26, 29, 31, 35, 43, 79.
Ambrose, 11.
Ambrosiaster, 97.
American Congregational Association, 207, 210, 221.
American Congregational Union, 228.
American Home-Missionary Society, 228.
Amsterdam. 122, 127, 246.
Ananias, 140.
Anderson. 244, 245.
Andrew, 133.
Andover, 303, 304.
"A Neighbor," 219.
Angel of the Church, 70.
"Anglo-American Church," 267.
Annan, 285.
"Answer of the Elders," 129, 151.
Antioch, 19, 22, 32, 37, 50, 62, 133, 138, 139.
Antioch in Pisidia, 32.
Antiocheans, 99.
Apollos, 54.
"Apostolical Constitutions," 69, 97, 136.
Aquila, 32, 33, 52.
Arabia, 23.
Arabians, 37.
Archbishop of Canterbury, 244, 245.
Archbishop of York, 58, 239, 245.
Aristophanes, 16.
Aristotle, 35.
Arkansas, 7.
Arlington-street Church, 285.
Arminius, 79.
Artemas, 108.
Asbury, 246
Ashton, 131.
Asia, 37.

Asia, Churches of, 36.
"Assembly's Annotations," 90.
"Assembly's Digest," 248, 281.
Athanasius, 74, 88.
Austerfield, 58.
Austin, 233.
Augustine, 11, 96, 98.
Avery, 201. 220.
Babylon, 32.
Bachiler, 125.
Backus, 210, 264.
Bacon, 88, 146, 223, 224, 225.
Badger, 154.
Baker, 207.
Ballantyne, 253, 283.
Balch, 248.
Bancroft, 130, 290, 291.
Bangor, 304.
Baptists, 5, 6, 24, 287.
Barber, 263.
Barclay, 289.
Barnes, 18, 45, 46, 69, 70, 76, 90, 109, 138, 139, 140, 146, 264, 288, 289.
Baronius, 11.
Barrow, 69.
Baumgarten, 14, 18, 30, 50, 90.
Bawtry, 58.
Baxter, 81, 284.
Baylies, 128.
Beatæ Virgini, 99.
Bedford, 201, 202, 219, 220.
Beecher, 226, 289.
Belcher, 24, 291.
Belknap, 285.
Bellamy, 264, 286.
Beman, 289.
Bengel, 45, 46, 74, 89, 121.
Bennett, 29, 34, 38, 85.
Berea, 32.
Bernaldus Constantiensis, 96.
Bernard, 40, 126, 161.
Bethlem, 264.
Beza, 16, 18.
"Biblical Repository," 146.
"Bibliotheca Sacra," 158.
Bilson, 122.
Bingham, 107.
Bishop, 144.
Bishop's Bible, 18.
Bishop of Bath and Wells, 245.
Bishop of London, 243.
Bishop of Peterborough, 245.
Blaikie, 285.
Blanchard, 235.

[xxvi]

INDEX OF NAMES.

Blondelius, 115.
Bliss, 219.
Bloomfield, 90.
Bogue and Bennett, 284.
Bolton, 219.
Bomberger, 87.
"Book of Lutheran Church," 110.
"Book of Middleboro' Church," 132.
Bosheth, 80.
Boston, 143, 151, 155, 222, 223, 226, 232, 239, 243, 285, 306.
Boston Association, 226.
"Boston Recorder," 285.
Bouton, 234, 235.
Bourne, 247.
Bowditch, 284.
Bowman, 122.
Bradford, 58, 122, 127, 128, 145, 228, 277.
Bradshaw, 31, 43.
Branford, 224.
Braintree, 143, 264.
Breckenridge, 86, 120 121.
Brennius, 16, 74, 89, 121.
Brewster, 58, 124, 127, 128, 131.
Brooke, Lord, 129.
Brookfield, 207.
Brookhouse, 204.
Browne, 59, 122.
Brownell, 146.
Brown University, 245.
Duck, 122.
Buckminster, 236.
Budington, 243.
Buffalo, 121.
Bullions, 289.
Bunsen, 100.
Burgess, 235.
Burke, 254.
Burnett, 48.
Burr, 202, 207, 220.
Bushnell, 146.
Butler, 222.
Byram River, 300.
Cajetan, 88.
California, 7, 226.
Callistus, 282.
Calvin, 17, 45, 46, 71, 73, 77, 79, 99, 102, 108, 116, 118, 119, 121, 139, 283.
Cambridge, 151, 221.
Cambridge Association, 225.
Cambridge Platform, 35, 44, 59, 123, 124, 130, 142, 148, 150, 151, 187, 205.
Campbell, 20, 97.
Capellus, Jacobus, 116.
Cape Town, 281.
Cappadocia, 37.
Carpus, 113.
Carter, 145.
Carthage, 87.
Castle of Bayonne, 244.
Catawba Circuit, 250.
Cave, 100.
Ceillier, 100.
Cenchrea, 82, 36, 69.
"Centuriæ Magdeburgenses," 99.
Cesarea, 32.
"Ceylon Mission's Report," 277.
Chandler, 244.
Channing, 285, 287.
Charlestown, 145, 243.
Chase, 69.
Chauncy, 82, 143, 146, 148, 154, 205.

Cheever, 235.
Chelsea, 235.
Chester, 289.
Chilmark, 222.
Cholinus, 73.
"Christian Advocate and Journal," 262.
"Christian Examiner," 146, 209, 210.
"Christian Spectator," 71, 100, 119, 146.
"Christians," 5.
Chrysostom, 14, 20, 96, 97, 107.
Church, 264.
Church of the Advent, Boston, 281.
Church of England in Hebron, 244.
Church of the Pilgrims in Brooklyn, 248.
Church of the Puritans, New York, 221.
"Church Review," 100.
Cilicia, 36.
Claggett, 245.
Clark, 129, 131, 208, 223, 228, 233, 244.
Clarke, 46, 70, 89.
Clement of Alexandria, 94.
Clement of Rome, 92, 96.
Clyfton, 122.
Cobbet, 143.
Coffin, 213.
Cogswell, 235.
Coke, 246.
Coleman, 21, 44, 68, 86, 99, 106, 135, 146, 158, 202, 224, 282.
Colenso, 281, 287.
Coleridge, 85.
Collicott, 125.
"Colonial Records of Connecticut," 222.
"Colonial Records of Massachusetts," 208, 209, 222, 226.
Colosse, 32, 36.
Colton, 71, 244, 281, 282.
Concord, 234.
"Conflict of Ages," 280.
"Congregationalist," 213, 241, 243, 304.
Congregational Methodists, 5.
"Congregational Quarterly," 65, 136, 199, 201, 202, 207, 214, 217, 219, 220, 221, 222, 226, 228.
"Congregational Record," 207.
Connecticut, 222, 223, 224, 225, 226, 285.
"Contributions to Eccles. Hist. Conn.," 223, 224.
Conybeare and Howson, 45, 46, 87, 102, 116, 134, 139.
Cooke, 223.
Cooley, 223.
Cooper, 293.
Corinth, 32, 36, 37, 51, 52.
Cottian Alps, 23.
Cotton, 29, 35, 40, 59, 68, 71, 82, 123, 124, 125, 129, 141, 143, 145, 148, 151, 161, 205, 208, 225, 227.
Council of Trent, 98, 136.
Coverdale, 78.
Crabe, 128.
Craighead, 248.
Cranmer, 18, 72, 78.
Cree Church, 122.
Crete, 107, 108, 138.
Cretes, 87.
Crispus, 106.
Cumming, 289.
Cummings, 155, 192, 220, 221, 235.
Cureton, 99, 100.
Cushing, 175, 177, 178.
Cushman, 128, 131.

INDEX OF NAMES.

Cyprian, 37, 119.
Cyrene, 87.
Daillé, 99, 100.
Dalmatia, 108.
Dalton, 125.
Damascus, 32, 140.
Dana, 224, 264.
Danvers, 221.
Davenport, 29, 30, 35, 40, 42, 60, 82, 123, 141, 143, 148, 205, 222, 223.
Davidson, 16, 17, 21, 29, 33, 44, 50, 52, 61, 68, 71, 75, 86, 114, 118, 119, 134, 146, 157.
Davis, 248, 285.
Dean, 244.
Dedham, 151, 207, 218, 221.
Delaware, 7, 246.
Delft, 151.
Demosthenes, 16, 35.
Denmark, 244.
Derbe, 82.
"Der Deutschen Zeitschrift, 283.
De Tocqueville, 290.
De Wette, 46, 61, 70.
"Dialogue between young and ancient men," &c., 123, 127.
Dickinson, 83.
Diodati, 18.
District of Columbia, 7.
"Divine Right of Church Government," &c., 120.
Doane, 247.
Doddridge, 70, 73, 81.
Dodge, 260, 261.
Dollinger, 282, 284, 286.
Dorchester, 221.
Duffield, 289.
Duke of Aremberg, 178.
Duxbury, 228.
Dwight, 85, 149, 224.
Eadie, 90.
Eastburn, 281.
Easton, 202, 203, 204.
Easter Sunday, 249.
Eastham, 228.
East-Windsor Seminary, 304.
Ebrard, 45.
"Eclectic Review," 146.
Eddy, 132, 146, 213.
"Edinburgh Review," 100.
Edwards, 233, 234.
Egypt, 23, 87.
Elamites, 87.
"Elders, Answer of the," 129, 151.
Ellicott, 70.
Eliot, 145.
Elliott, 223, 255.
Ely, 235.
Embury, 245.
Emerson, 243.
Emmons, 26, 52, 54, 60, 84, 225, 264.
England, 143, 244, 286.
Ephesus, 31, 32, 87, 105, 107, 109, 140.
Epiphanius, 107.
"Episcopal Recorder," 245.
Episcopius, 79.
Erasmus, 16, 18, 73, 101, 139, 156.
Estius, 101.
Ethiopia, 265.
Eusebius, 38, 107.
Evangelist, 71.
Evangelus, 95.
Evagrius, 95, 102.

Exeter, 143, 235.
Fabritius, 157.
Fairchild, 235.
Fairfield, 223.
Fales, 207.
Farmington, 264.
Father Ignatius, 283.
Faunce, 131.
Felt, 129, 131, 208, 220.
Ferris, 246.
Fishback, 290.
Fitch, 219, 224.
Fitchburg, 221.
Fiske, 220.
Flacii Illyrici, 16.
Flint, 226.
Florida, 7.
Fox, 122.
Foxcroft, 83.
Franklin, 264.
Freeman, 285.
French, 235.
Fuller, 129, 155, 156.
Gage, 248.
Gaius, 106.
Galatia, 32, 83.
Galilee, 32, 36.
Gannett, 285.
Garratt, 87.
General Assembly of Presbyterian Church, 290.
Geneva, 283.
"Genevan Version," 18, 72.
Georgia, 7.
Gerhard, 116.
Gibbon, 44, 81, 278.
Gieseler, 21, 97, 118.
Gillett, 245, 289, 294, 295.
Gomarus, 89.
Grafton, 221.
Gray, 200, 228.
Great Eastern, 57.
Green, 288.
Greenwood, 122, 285, 286.
Gregory VII., 11.
Griswold, 276
Grotius, 17, 45, 70, 74, 75, 89, 106, 108, 115, 116, 121, 139, 156.
Groton, 221, 222.
Gualtherus, 73, 74, 75, 88.
Guild, 245, 287.
Guilford, 143, 223.
Gulliver, 285.
Guericke, 13, 97, 100, 135, 158.
Guizot, 85.
Hackett, 60, 91, 108, 139
Hagenbach, 283.
Hale, 223, 283, 290.
Halifax, 249.
Hall, 88, 146, 248, 285.
Hammond, 16, 75, 81.
Hampton, 125, 143.
Hanbury, 40, 44, 59, 122, 148, 151, 161.
"Handbook of Presbyterian Church," 239, 291, 292.
Harker, 248.
Hartford, 224, 225, 226.
Harvard College, 143, 287.
Harworth, 58.
Hawes, 222.
Hawks, 244, 245, 246.
Hawley, 262.

INDEX OF NAMES.

Hebron, 244.
Hellenists, 133.
Hemmenway, 264.
Hening, 244.
Henniker, 209, 210.
Henry, 89.
Henry IV., 11.
Herle, 161.
Hermann, 31.
Hero, 99.
Hertzog, 87.
Heylyn, 74.
Hierapolis, 32, 36.
Higginson, 143, 145.
Hilary, 94, 119.
Hilary of Rome, 97.
Hilary, the deacon, 107.
Hill, 87, 248.
Hitchcock, 233.
Hoadley, 81.
Hodge, 74, 90, 101.
Holland, 122, 239.
Hollister, 245.
Hollis-street Church, 202.
Homes, 222.
Hook, 145, 285.
Hooke, 143, 144.
Hooker, Richard, 80.
Hooker, Thomas, 29, 35, 43, 60, 82, 123, 130, 142, 145, 148, 154, 205, 222.
Hopkins, 84, 264.
Hornius, 192.
Horsley, 75.
House of Commons, 178.
Howard-street Church, Salem, 221, 231, 232, 233, 234.
Hubbard, 145, 264.
Humphrey, 223, 239, 243, 244.
Hunter, 25, 58.
Hyde, 226, 264.
Hutchinson, 124, 125, 129, 131, 144, 205, 206, 254.
Iconium, 32, 138.
Ida, 264.
Ignatius, 37, 99, 100, 136, 145.
Illinois, 7, 226.
Independents, 2.
Indiana, 7, 226.
Indian Territory, 7.
Iowa, 7, 226.
Ipswich, 143, 151, 264.
Ireland, 286.
Irenæus, 34, 93.
Isodore, 136.
Isodore of Seville, 96.
Isle of Poplars, 283.
Jackson, 58.
Jacob, 35, 44.
Jacobson, 87.
James, 107, 109, 145, 243.
Jameson, 84.
Jarratt, 246.
Jefferson, 290, 293.
Jennings, 71.
Jerome, 11, 22, 91, 94, 96, 97, 98, 102, 107, 139.
Jerusalem, 22, 82, 87, 40, 50, 51, 62, 107, 111, 134, 168.
Jessop, 58.
John, 99.
John of Goch, 77.
Johns, 249.

Johnson, 122, 127, 209.
Joppa, 32.
Judea, 36, 87.
Judas, 111.
Junkin, 288.
Justin Martyr, 93, 136.
Kansas, 7.
Kentucky, 7, 248.
Kendrick, 12, 73, 76, 102, 114, 121.
Killen, 76, 98.
King James, 139.
"King James's Version," 72.
King, Lord Peter, 79.
King's Chapel, Boston, 285.
King William Street, 122.
Kirkland, 287.
Kitto, 87, 100.
"Kitto's Journal," 100.
Kniston, 122.
Kuincel, 134.
Kurtz, 98, 135.
Lambeth, 245.
Lamson, 146, 291.
Laodicea, 32, 36.
Laodiceans, 57.
Lardner, 80.
Launcelot, John Paul, 96.
Lawrence, 125, 286.
Lechford, 44, 123, 144.
Lee, 122, 264.
Leicester, 209.
Lesley, 225.
Leyden, 25, 59, 122, 127, 128, 151, 228, 290.
Leyden Church, in Boston, 248.
Lexington, 247, 290.
Liddell and Scott, 16, 105.
Liebetrut, 283.
Lightfoot, 16, 75.
Limborch, 75, 78.
Lincoln, 249.
Lisbon, 225.
Litchfield, 222, 226.
Lombardi Pauperes, 23.
London, 59, 122, 244, 248.
"London Quarterly," 100.
"London Times," 281, 286.
"London and Westminster Review," 24.
Lord Chatham, 282.
Louisiana, 7.
Lucian, 16.
Lücke, 115.
Luther, 16, 23, 77.
"Lutheran Book," 110.
Lybia, 87.
Lydda, 32.
Lynn, 143.
Lyman, 223.
Lystra, 32, 138.
Macedonia, 95, 109.
Mack, 91, 134.
Macknight, 72, 75, 89.
Madison-square Presbyterian Church, New York, 290.
"Madura Mission's Report," 277.
"Magnalia," 130, 143, 151, 222, 227.
Magnesians, 99.
Maine, 227.
Malden, 226, 235.
Maldonatus, 10.
Manchester, 213, 219.
Mann, 233, 286.
Manning, 245, 287.

Marcion, 93.
Marlborough, 222.
Marsh, 283.
Marshfield, 228.
Martha's Vineyard, 155.
Mary, 99.
Maryland, 7, 245.
Mason, 70, 85.
Massachusetts, 129, 130, 206, 207, 208, 210, 211, 212, 213, 216, 222, 223, 226, 227, 230, 232, 285, 286, 287, 290, 301.
Massachusetts Historical Society, 221, 225.
Massuet, 34.
Mather, Cotton, 60, 68, 82, 124, 129, 130, 143, 145, 148, 151, 161, 205, 222, 223, 225, 237.
Mather, Increase, 125, 143, 145, 154, 161, 218, 227.
Mather, Richard, 52, 60, 161.
Mather, Samuel, 142, 157, 192, 205, 218.
Maximus Tyrius, 16.
Mayer, 134.
Mayflower, 128, 290.
Mayo, 125.
M'Clure, 125, 148.
Meade, 243, 245, 247.
Medes, 37.
Medway, 264.
Melancthon, 78.
Mendon, 222, 226.
Mendon Association, 226.
Menochius and Tirinus, 74.
Mesopotamia, 37.
"Message to Ruling Elders," 110, 117.
Metcalf, 202.
"Methodist Book of Discipline," 29, 242, 247, 250, 262, 264, 271.
Meyer, 50.
Michaelis, 70, 91.
Michigan, 7, 226.
Middle States, 7.
Miletus, 103, 105, 107, 109.
Milner, 97.
Milton, 23, 24, 80, 141, 155, 156.
Minnesota, 7, 226.
Mitchell, 206.
Moncta, 23.
Moody, 143.
Moorhead, 285.
More, 246.
Mormons, 117.
Morristown, 288.
Morse, 223.
Morton, 58, 143, 145, 225.
Mosheim, 13, 14, 43, 75, 97, 134, 278.
Mount Seir, 23.
Murdock, 13, 91, 97.
Naomi, 265.
Natick, 154.
Neal, 40, 150.
Neander, 13, 18, 33, 68, 69, 75, 98, 100, 118, 119, 133, 135, 158, 262.
Nebraska, 7, 226.
"Neighbor, A," 219.
Nelson, 225.
Newbury, 143, 264.
New England, 7, 25, 129, 131, 145, 148, 227, 228, 244, 253, 254, 266, 284, 304.
"New Englander," 61, 71, 88, 100, 146.
New Haven, 143, 223, 224, 225, 304.
New Hampshire, 226.
New Jersey, 7, 244.
Newman, 87, 143, 209, 283.

Newport, 264.
Newtown (Cambridge), 145, 208.
New York, 7, 210, 226, 286.
"New-York Observer," 121.
Nicanor, 133.
Nicolas, 133.
Nicolaus Cusanus, 96.
Nicopolis, 108.
Niles, 264.
Nitria, 99.
"Nobis Leyczon," 23.
Noel, 276.
Non-juring Bishops, 245.
"North-American Review," 208.
North Carolina, 7, 250.
Norton, 143, 218, 219.
Norway, 283.
Norwich, 225.
Nott, 213.
Nymphas, 32, 36.
Oceanus, 95.
Œcumenius, 116.
Ohio, 7, 227.
Oliver, 161, 290.
Olshausen, 12, 73, 76, 102, 114, 121, 134.
Onderdonk, 247.
Onesimus, 36.
Ongar, 71.
Ord, 249.
Oregon, 7, 226.
Origen, 37, 119.
Oudin, 100.
Owen, 16, 17, 31, 33, 35, 45, 46, 73, 82, 111, 146, 151, 154.
Pagnini, 16.
Palfrey, 145, 152, 208.
Pamphylia, 37, 138.
Papists, 117.
Park, 225, 252, 255, 279, 286, 287, 290.
Parker, 144, 206.
Parkman, 131.
Parmenas, 133.
Parsons, 237.
Parthians, 37.
Patmos, 71.
Paul of Samosata, 37.
Payson Church, South Boston, 235.
Pearson, 99, 100.
Pelham, 264.
Pennsylvania, 7.
Pepperell, 301.
Pergamos, 32.
Perkins, 122, 148.
Perry, 235, 245.
Persia, 23.
"Peshito-Syriac Version," 91.
Peterborough, 286.
Peter Lombard, 98.
Peters, 244.
Petra, 23.
Phebe, 69.
Phelps, 260, 261.
Philadelphia, 32, 288.
Philadelphians, 99.
Philemon, 32, 36.
Philip, the Evangelist, 71, 133.
Philippi, 10, 32, 90, 95, 102, 134.
Philippians, 99.
Philo, 16.
Phrygia, 37.
Pickering, 200, 201, 202, 203, 204, 207, 220.
Pierpont, 202, 222.

INDEX OF NAMES.

Piscator, 16.
Pisidia, 138.
Pitt, 290.
Plainfield, 209.
Plato, 85.
Pliny, 70, 106.
Plumbe, 262.
Plumptre, 87.
Plymouth, 25, 128, 225, 228, 289, 290.
Plymouth Church, Brooklyn, 210.
Polanus, 78.
Polycarp, 92, 93, 94, 99.
Pond, 60, 61, 68, 71, 86, 207.
"Pontif, Rom, De Ordinat., &c.," 22.
Pontus, 37.
Poole, 16, 70, 74, 89, 116.
Pope Urban II., 90, 98.
Popkin, 285.
Portsmouth, 143.
Porter, 264.
Poughkeepsie, 233.
Powell, 125, 226.
"Prayer-book," 250, 270.
"Presbyterian Banner," 284.
"Presbyterian Book," 49, 51, 52, 53, 54, 110, 111, 121, 239, 242, 250, 260, 261.
Priestly, 283.
Prince, 124, 243.
Princeton, 221, 304.
"Princeton Review," 100, 114, 120, 121, 146, 295.
"Principles of Church Order," 40, 60, 61, 68.
Prochorus, 133.
Provoost, 245.
Priscilla and Aquila, 32, 33.
Prussian Churches, 287.
Ptolemais, 32.
Punchard, 60, 61, 68, 86, 140, 168, 195, 205, 206.
Puritans, 24.
Pusey, 282, 283.
Puteoli, 32.
Quint, 65, 199, 201, 202, 214, 217.
Reading, 220, 221.
"Recollections of Anglo-American Church," 267.
"Records, Massachusetts Colony," 208, 209, 222, 226.
"Records, New-Haven Colony, 222.
Rehoboth, 143, 200, 201, 204, 209, 219, 220.
Reinerus, 23.
"Report of Conference at Constantinople," 277.
"Report of Deputation to India," 277.
"Rheims Version," 18, 72.
Rhode Island, 226.
Rice, 301.
Richards, 235.
Richmond, 249.
"Richmond Religious Herald," 250.
"Richmond Whig," 249.
Rippon, 287.
Robbins, 125, 224, 225.
Robinson, 16, 25, 26, 31, 35, 40, 43, 59, 79, 122, 123, 124, 126, 127, 128, 141, 148, 150, 161, 290.
Rochester, 58.
Rogers, 143.
Rome, 32, 52, 298.
Romans, 99.
Rosencrone, Count de, 244.
Rothe, 118, 119.

Rousseau, 283.
Rowley, 143.
Roxbury, 148, 226.
Rudolphus, 11.
Rumney Marsh, 235.
Russell, 225.
Ruth, 265.
Ryland, 98.
Salem, 131, 143, 145, 220, 221, 223, 231, 232, 233, 243.
Salem Athenæum, 221.
Salisbury, 143.
Samaria, 32, 36, 140.
Sampson, 45.
Sandwich, 202, 207, 220, 221.
Sardis, 32.
Saron, 32.
Savage, 130, 131, 151.
Savoy Confession, 40.
Sawyer, 86, 287.
Say and Seal, Lord, 129, 208.
Saybrook, 222, 223.
"Saybrook Platform," 219, 224.
Scales, 209.
Schaff, 13, 98, 135, 158, 282.
Schmucker, 86.
Scituate, 143.
Sclater, 79.
Scotland, 284, 286.
Scott, 90.
Scrooby, 24, 58, 239.
Scottow, 131, 245.
Seabury, 244, 245.
"Septuagint," 83.
Sharp, 245.
Shedd, 13, 98, 100, 135, 158.
Sheldon, 202, 203, 204.
Shepard, 84, 129, 151, 223.
Shunamite, 265.
Siberia, 265.
Silas, 111.
Simon, 18.
Skelton, 145.
Smith, 16, 31, 36, 87, 122, 233, 235, 283.
Smith and Anthon, 286.
Smyrna, 32, 80.
Smyrnians, 99.
Smyth, 85, 121, 122.
Snell, 223, 226.
Socrates, 35.
Solomon's Porch, 87.
Somers, 264.
South Carolina, 7.
Southern States, 7.
"Southern Presbyterian Review," 121.
Southwark, 122.
"Spirit of the Pilgrims," 71, 114, 210, 221.
Stansbury, 289.
Stapfer, 79.
Stearns, 201, 202, 219, 220.
Stebbins, 221.
Steele, 131.
Stephanas, 106.
Stephen, 133.
Stevens, 242, 246.
Stiles, 44, 218, 222, 225.
Stith, 244.
St. John's Church, Elizabethtown, 243, 244.
St. Nicholas Lane, 122.
Stockbridge, 264.
Storrs, 207, 223, 264.
Street, 143, 144.

Strong, 207.
Stuart, 45, 46, 70, 116.
Studley, 122.
Strype, 122.
Suicer, 16.
Suffolk, North, Association, 225.
Sumner, 156.
Surrey Chapel, 248.
Sweden, 246, 283.
Swedenborgians, 117.
Switzerland, 283.
Syria, 23, 36.
Syrian Convent at Nitria, 99.
Tarsians, 99.
Taunton, 143, 144.
Taylor, 86, 213.
Tennessee, 7, 243.
Tertullian, 12, 29, 31, 37, 106, 156.
Texas, 7.
Thacher, 131, 222.
Theodoret, 91, 96, 97, 107.
Theophilus, 37.
"The Hawaiian Islands," 277.
"The Independent," 285.
"The Panoplist," 221, 223.
"The Presbyterian," 120.
Thessalonica, 32, 117.
Thompson, 121, 146, 200, 201, 204, 220.
Thornton, 254.
Thornwell, 120, 121.
Thurston, 226.
Thucydides, 16, 35.
Thyatira, 32.
"Tigurine Version," 73.
Tigurini, 16.
Timothy, 46, 71, 95, 101, 107, 108, 109, 134, 145.
Timon, 133.
Tindal, 18.
Titus, 71, 107, 108, 109, 138, 139, 145.
Tompson, 52, 161.
Torrey, 13, 98, 100, 135, 233, 235.
Tracy, 140, 168.
Trajan, 106.
Trallians, 99.
Tribble, 290.
Troas, 32, 113.
"The Wesleyan," 263.
Trumbull, 222, 223, 224, 225.
Tucker, 289.
Tudeschus, 96.
Tunbridge Wells, 284.
Turell, 224.
Turner, 46, 101.
Turretin, 79.
Tychicus, 108.
Tyndale, 18, 72.
Tyringham, 201, 220.
Tyre, 32.
Uhden, 44.
Ullman, 88.
Unitarians, 5, 6.
Universalists, 5, 6.
University of Vermont, 233.
Upham, 60, 86, 149, 155, 207, 221, 227.
Usher, 100, 244.

Vaill, 235.
Vane, 208.
Vaudes, 23.
Vaughan, 33, 40, 44, 87, 253.
Vedelius, 99, 100.
Vermont, 226.
Virginia, 7, 245, 247.
Vitringa, 70, 115, 118, 119.
Waddington, 97.
Walch, 77.
Waldenses, 23.
Walker, 155, 156, 210.
Wallingford, 224.
Walter, 83.
Ward, 151.
Wardlaw, 284.
Ware, 287.
Wareham, 213.
Washburn, 209.
Watts, 157.
Webb, 222.
"Weekly Register," 286.
Welch, 225.
Welde, 148.
Wellman, 61, 88, 290.
Wells, 143, 264.
Wesley, 246.
Wesleyans, 5.
West, 264.
Western States, 7.
Westford, 221.
"Westminster Review," 282.
Weymouth, 143.
Whately, 70, 134, 145.
Wheelwright, 143.
Whitaker, 222.
Whitby, 90.
White, 127, 219, 244, 245.
Whitfield, 223, 285.
Whitmore, 200.
Whitney, 204.
Wickliffe, 24, 72, 77.
Wiesinger, 70.
Wigglesworth, 83.
Williams, 284.
Wilmer, 262.
Wilson, 114, 119, 145, 146, 284.
Windham, 225.
Winslow, 128.
Winthrop, 130, 131, 151, 208.
Wisconsin, 7, 220.
Wise, 29, 40, 44, 60, 84, 130, 205, 219, 222, 223, 291.
Wisner, 131, 164.
Withington, 264.
Woodbridge, 143.
Woburn, 145, 226.
Woods, 85, 149, 223, 224, 235, 304.
Wolleblus, 29, 79.
Worcester, 221, 223, 226.
Wordsworth, 10, 70.
Wolstenholme, Sir John, 124.
York, 227.
Young, 123, 127, 128, 129.
Zanchius, 89.

CONGREGATIONALISM.

CHAPTER I.

WHAT CONGREGATIONALISM IS.

A CHURCH is an association of the friends and followers of Christ, for the profession of Christian faith, and the performance of Christian duty.

Every association — or union of persons in a company, for an object — implies a groundwork of organization, with principles and laws; and, therefore, every Church must have such a groundwork.

The working out of these principles and laws in shaping and controlling the life of the organization, constitutes its government; and, therefore, every Church must have some form of government.

All government reduces itself to three pure forms. Its power must be lodged in the hands of some one supreme sovereign, or in the hands of all who are included in the organization, or (somewhere between these two extremes,) in the hands of a privileged order, composed of a greater or smaller number of principal persons. The first, is called the monarchic; the second, the democratic; and the third, the aristocratic form of government.

These forms may sometimes be mingled, in a given case, but every government will naturally be classed under that form of the three, to which it bears the strongest resemblance.

CONGREGATIONALISM is the democratic form of Church order and government. It derives its name from the prominence which it gives to the *congregation* of Christian believers. It vests all ecclesiastical power (under Christ) in the associated brotherhood of each local Church, as an independent body. At the same time it recognizes a fraternal and equal fellowship between these independent churches, which invests each with the right and duty of advice and reproof, and even of the public withdrawal of that fellowship in case the course pursued by another of the sisterhood should demand such action for the preservation of its own purity and consistency. Herein Congregationalism, as a system, differs from Independency; which affirms the seat of ecclesiastical power to reside in the brotherhood so zealously as to ignore any check, even of advice, upon its action. Still, as this difference is only one of the exaggeration of a first principle, it follows that every Independent Church is Congregational, though few Congregational churches are Independent — in this strict and Brownist sense.[1]

Its fundamental principle is the following: — *The Bible — interpreted by sanctified common sense, with all wise helps from nature, from history, from all knowledge, and especially from the revealing Spirit — is the only, and sufficient, and authoritative guide in all matters of Christian practice, as it is in all matters of Christian faith: so that whatsoever the Bible teaches — by precept, example, or legitimate inference — is imperative upon all men, at all times; while nothing which it does not so teach can be imperative upon any man at any time.*

By the application of this primary truth to the Bible, it educes the following subordinate principles, namely: —

1. Any company of people believing themselves to be, and publicly professing themselves to be Christians, associated by voluntary compact, on Gospel principles, for Christian work and worship, is a true Church of Christ.

2. Such a Church, as a rule, should include only those who can conveniently worship and labor together, and watch over each other.

3. Every member of such a Church has equal essential rights, powers and privileges, with every other (except so far as the New Testament and common sense make some special abridgment in the case of female and youthful members); and the membership to-

---

[1] The Congregationalists of England use the term "Independent" as synonymous with "Congregational." And the tenth of the "Principles of Church Order and Discipline" set forth by the "Congregational Union of England and Wales," expressly recognizes the fellowship of churches, and the duty of "separation" from such churches as "depart from the Gospel of Christ."

gether, by majority vote (though, so far as possible to human imperfection, there should never be any *minority* in Congregationalism), have the right and duty of choosing all necessary officers, of admitting, dismissing and disciplining their own members, and of transacting all other appropriate business of a Christian Church.

4. Every such Church, — while it ought meekly and gratefully to receive, and candidly and prayerfully to weigh advice, and, if need be, admonition, from its sister churches — is yet independent of any outward jurisdiction or control, whether from Popes, Patriarchs, Archbishops, Bishops, or other persons assuming to be Christ's officials; from General Conventions, Conferences, or Assemblies; from Synods and Presbyteries, and from Associations, Councils or other courts or convocations; or from other churches; being answerable directly and only to Christ its head. And every such Church, whatever may be the lowliness of its worldly estate, is on a level of inherent genuineness, dignity and authority, with every other Church on earth.

5. A fraternal fellowship should be maintained by these equal and independent churches, with affectionate carefulness for each other's soundness of doctrine, and general welfare — the strong ever eager to aid the weak, as members of Christ's great family. And though every such Church is equal in essential rights and powers with every other, and, by its very constitution, independent of all ecclesiastical control, yet when difficulties arise, or especially important matters claim decision (as when Pastors are to be settled or dismissed, or when any Church itself is to adopt its creed and commence its organic life) it is not only competent but desirable that such churches should, in a fraternal manner, advise each other — assembling by delegation in council for that purpose — such advice being, however, tendered only as one friend counsels another, and subject, in all cases to the final decision of the party asking for it. And, if any Church should seem to its fellow churches wilfully and wrongfully to disregard their advice — by adopting an erroneous creed, or establishing over itself an unsound or unfaithful pastor — those churches would not only have the right, but would be bound in conscience, to withdraw themselves from all complicity with, and responsibility for, such action, by the formal revocation of their existing fellowship with the offending Church, until it should return to what seems to them to be the path of its duty. Such action on their part, however, will in no

way aspire to take the place of *authority* over the Church to which it refers. It will simply be a labor of moral suasion and self-justification, such as might similarly occur among sovereign States, or between families or individuals in private life.

6. The officers which Christ has designated for his churches are of two kinds;—the *first*—indiscriminately called, in the New Testament, Presbyters, Bishops, Elders or Overseers; now usually called Pastors—who preach the word and have the general oversight of the spiritual concerns of the Church; the *second*, Deacons, who attend to the relief of the poor, and the secular affairs of the organization, and aid the Pastor, generally, as they have ability and opportunity. These officers are chosen by the membership from their own number, and the distinctive idea of their office is, that they are to be the servants,—for spiritual and material toil—and not the masters of the Church.

As, by these principles, all the power of the Church on earth is thus held to reside—under the constant oversight of Christ, its ever-living and overruling, though risen, Head—in its *Congregation* of believers, the assembly of the faithful, it is evident that the name CONGREGATIONAL, though neither most compact nor elegant, is yet most apt and forcible, as the distinguishing epithet of those churches which hold this faith.

Since Congregationalism is thus a form of Church order and government, rather than a system of doctrinal faith, it is obvious that—without incongruity or impropriety—it may be held and practiced by those of different religious beliefs. A Church holding an Arminian, or Pelagian creed may adopt and act upon the principle that all Ecclesiastical power is resident in the brotherhood, with as much propriety as a Church holding the Five Points of Calvinism; those who limit Baptism to immersion, with as much success as those who hold that the application of water, in any form, in the name of the Trinity, is Baptism. And, as a matter of fact, though the name "Congregationalists" is popularly associated, as a denominational epithet, mainly with those who hold the Congregational form of Church government in connection with a religious faith represented, for substance of doctrine, by the Catechism of the Westminster Assembly, many other bodies of professing Christians are also Congregational in their Church government. The great Baptist Denomination — with some leanings toward Independency, properly so called — is yet purely Congregational in its principles of Church order and government. The same, for substance, is true also of the Unitarian, Universalist, and "Christian" denominations, and of the Wesleyan, and Independent, or Congregational Methodists.

The number of churches in this country which are essentially Congregational in their form of government, may be approximately estimated, as follows: —

	Churches.
Orthodox Congregationalists,[1]	2,676
Regular Baptists,[2]	12,730
Other Baptists,[3]	5,575
Christians,[4]	1,600
Wesleyan Methodists,[5]	600
Other Congregational Methodists,[6]	200
Unitarians,[7]	246
Universalists,[8]	1,128
	24,755

Add now to these, 2,591 Congregational Orthodox churches in England and her colonies,[9] with 2,000 "Particular,"[10] and some 120 "General" Baptist churches on the same field, and we have — leaving out of the account the large number of essentially Congregational Methodists in the mother country, — a grand total among those who speak the English tongue, of some 29,466 churches whose government is essentially Congregational, as opposed to the aristocratic and monarchic forms of Church government!

The whole number of Christian churches reported in the United States by the last census, was 38,183. Add twenty per cent. for increase, and we have 45,819 as the approximate present number. Comparing with this total the number of churches Congregationally

---

[1] *Congregational Quarterly*, Jan. 1860. p. 139.
[2] *Cong. Quar.*, Oct. 1859. p. 386.
[3] *Cong. Quar.*, April, 1860. p. 222; and American Christian Record. p. 46.
[4] *Cong. Quar.*, July, 1860. p. 305.
[5] *Cong. Quar.* April, 1860. p. 222.
[6] Ibid.
[7] *Cong. Quar.* July, 1859. p. 297.
[8] Ibid.
[9] English "Year Book," 1860.
[10] Appleton's Cyclopedia, Art. "Baptist."

governed on this territory (24,755 less 657, outside the limits of the United States), and we have, in round numbers, a proportion of ²⁴⁄₄₅ths, in favor of Congregationalists as compared with all others; showing that, instead of being, as has often been alleged, a merely Provincial, and peculiarly New England idea, this system of Congregational government for Christian churches, is substantially held and practiced by more than one half of the entire professing Christianity of the land!

Or, if a comparison be desired that shall be confined to churches commonly reputed to be "Evangelical" in their faith; — throwing out of the estimated total of 45,819, ten per cent. for Non Evangelical churches (which would seem to be about what the census would indicate as a fair proportion for them), we have left an "Evangelical" total of over 41,000 churches. Throwing out, on the other hand, from the Congregational total, the 2,974 Unitarian, Universalist, and "Christian" churches, we have left a total of "Evangelical" churches Congregationally governed, of 21,124; thus giving us a Congregational proportion of about ²¹⁄₄₁sts of the entire "Evangelical" Christianity of the nation — still more than one half![1]

As a distinctive form of Church order it is clear, therefore, that Congregationalism leads all others in this country in the number of its adherents, while it has nearly three times as many Evangelical churches, scattered through the length and breadth of the land, as are included in all those Bodies that are Presbyterian in name and form.

Facts show also that the Congregational form of Church order has been found equally practicable and beneficial in all parts of the land. The great majority of the Congregational churches is found out of New England. From the imperfect statistics in our possession, we are

---

[1] The relative strength of several of the prominent Religious Bodies in this country may be hinted at as follows: —

Roman Catholics,	2,834 Churches and Chapels.
Protestant Episcopalians,	2,110 Parishes.
Methodist Episcopalians,	9,423 Ministers.
Presbyterians, (all kinds),	7,954 Churches.
Reformed Dutch,	409 "
Evangelical Lutherans,	2,048 "
German Reformed,	1,013 "
Orthodox Congregationalists,	2,676 "
Regular Baptists,	12,730 "
Other Baptists,	5.575 "
Congregational Methodists,	800 "

able to state that there are 756 churches Congregationally governed in Alabama; in Arkansas, 269; in California, 54; in Delaware, 2; in the District of Columbia, 7; in Florida, 107; in Georgia, 995; in Illinois, 902; in Indiana, 733; in Indian Territory, 45; in Iowa, 388; in Kansas, 44; in Kentucky, 852; in Louisiana, 189; in Maryland, 38; in Michigan, 344; in Minnesota, 97; in Mississippi, 577; in Missouri, 698; in Nebraska, 17; in New Jersey, 120; in New York, 1,239; in North Carolina, 649; in Ohio, 829; in Oregon, 41; in Pennsylvania, 460; in South Carolina, 463; in Tennessee, 644; in Texas, 387; in Virginia, 716; in Wisconsin, 354.

If we arrange these under the grand divisions of the Union, we shall get the following results:—

	Congregational Churches.
New England,	2,977
Middle States,	1,821
Southern States,	4,884
Western States,	6,311

Or, taking the account by States, under each division (counting three territories with the eleven Western States) we have local averages of churches Congregationally governed, as follows:—

In each New England State,	496
" Middle State,	455
" Southern State,	488
" Western State,	450

This shows a remarkable evenness of distribution, and demonstrates that, as a system, Congregationalism has been found to be equally adapted to every latitude and phase of society among us. More complete and later returns would considerably increase these totals.

CHAPTER II.

WHENCE CONGREGATIONALISM IS.

WHENCE did this large number of Christian believers get their faith in this democratic form of Church government; as distinguished from the aristocracy of Presbyterianism, and the monarchy of the Episcopal, Patriarchal or Papal hierarchy?

As a matter of principle, they take it directly from the Bible, interpreted by common sense. As a matter of history, they have received it from a succession of faithful men who gained it from the Bible, illustrated and enforced by the Providence of its benignant Author; and who proved it "in much patience, in afflictions, in necessities, in distresses, in stripes, in imprisonments, in tumults, in labors, in watchings, in fastings; by pureness, by knowledge, by long suffering, by kindness, by the Holy Ghost, by love unfeigned, by the word of truth, by the power of God, by the armor of righteousness on the right hand, and on the left."

A rapid glance over those portions of the New Testament which convey to us the will of Christ concerning his churches — in direct precept, or in the conduct of those who acted under Inspiration from him — will show us how naturally and inevitably the Congregational system of Church order and government grew therefrom, and how necessarily it must ever entrench itself in the hearts of those who look to the Bible simply for their faith.

The Church dates from days described in the book of Genesis. But the *Christian* Church had its origin in the teachings and labors of Jesus. The Gospels contain no record of any prescribed organic plan for its life, yet there were hints dropped from the lips of our Saviour which seem to have been intended to prepare the minds of the disciples for that further revelation of his will, which was subsequently to be made in the preaching and practice of his apostles.

SECTION 1. *The Intimations of Christ in regard to Church Government.*

Without taking space here to gather up all the indirect suggestions and hints which the Gospels contain on this subject, we turn, at once, to three important passages in the record of Matthew.

In the 18th chapter, (*vv.* 15-17,) Christ directs that an offence which cannot be privately settled, be told to the Church, and "if he neglect to hear the Church, [ἐκκλησίᾳ—*ekklēsia*, 'the assembled,' 'the congregation of believers,']¹ let him be unto thee as an heathen man and a publican;" thus suggesting the principle that, so far as internal discipline is concerned, the decision of any associated local body of believers should be final to all under its jurisdiction.

So, in the 20th chapter, (*vv.* 20-28,) when the mother of James and John was an applicant, on behalf of her sons, for some special place of honor in the new "kingdom," and the application had disturbed the other ten, as if the best places in that kingdom were in danger of being surreptitiously taken, Christ, in rebuke and explanation, "called them unto him, and said: Ye know that the princes of the Gentiles exercise dominion over them, and they that are great, exercise authority upon them. But it shall not be so among you: but whosoever will be great among you, let him be your minister [διάκονος—*diakonos*, 'one dusty from running,' 'a runner or waiter']; And whosoever will be chief among you, let him be your servant [δοῦλος—*doulos*, 'bondman,' 'humblest servant']; even as the Son of man came not to be ministered unto, but to minister," etc. So, again, in the 23d chapter, (vv. 8-11,) Christ instructed his disciples: "Be not ye called Rabbi; for one is your Master, even Christ, and all ye are brethren. And call no man your father [spiritual superior] upon the earth; for one is your Father, which is in heaven. Neither be ye called masters, [καθηγηταί—*kathēgētai*, 'leaders of the conscience']; for one is your Master, even Christ. But he that is

---

¹ " τῇ ἐκκλησίᾳ, by what follows, certainly not ' the Jewish Synagogue ' (for how could *vv.* 18-20 be said in any sense *of it*?) but ' *the Congregation* ' of Christians; *i. e.* in early times, such as in Acts iv: 32, the *one* congregation,—in after times, that congregation of which thou and he are members. That it cannot mean *the Church as represented by her rulers*, appears by *vv.* 19, 20,—where any collection of believers is gifted with the power of deciding in such cases. Nothing can be further from the spirit of our Lord's command than proceedings in what are oddly enough called ' Ecclesiastical ' Courts."— *Alford. Greek Test. and Com.* Matt. xviii: 17.

greatest [really greatest] among you shall be your servant," [διάκονος]. These passages seem necessarily to involve, and prepare the way for, the doctrine of the inherent essential equality in rank of all true believers on earth, and to require their subjection only to God as Father, and to Christ as Teacher and Head.[1] And, since every organic body must have *some* government, these precepts — so far as they were left unmodified to mold the future — appear to have been intended to control all ideas of government which might be subsequently proposed for the external development of the Christian Church, and oblige it, under whatever form, to recognize this essential equality among its entire membership, and provide for a ministry of service and not of rule.

We find no record of any counter teaching from our Saviour's lips. The only passage which requires notice, as being even seemingly of different character, is that in the 16th of Matthew, (*vv.* 18–19,) where Christ, in response to Peter's frank and earnest avowal of faith in his Messiahship, says: "thou art Peter [Πέτρος — *Petros*]. and upon this rock [πέτρᾳ — *petra*] I will build my Church; and the gates of hell shall not prevail against it. And I will give unto thee the keys of the kingdom of heaven: and whatsoever thou shalt bind on earth, shall be bound in heaven; and whatsoever thou shalt loose on earth, shall be loosed in heaven." This might, at first glance, look like the conferring of some special function and honor upon Peter, either as an individual, or as the representative of a class. Accordingly we find that the Romish Church has, with short logic, reasoned from this passage thus:[2] 'Peter was the rock on which the Church was built; but a foundation rock must necessarily have existence at least as long as its superstructure, and the promise must therefore have been made to Peter in some sense allowing of succession, and so of permanence; but the Bishop of Rome is the legitimate successor of Peter; therefore this promise of Christ was made to the Bishop of Rome, who, through all time, was thus constituted the earthly head

---

[1] "We have God, in his Trinity, here declared to us as the only Father, Master, and Teacher of Christians; their πατήρ, καθηγητής (= ὁδηγὸς τυφλῶν, Rom. ii: 19), and διδάσκαλος — the only one in all these relations, on whom they can rest or depend. They are all *brethren*: all substantially equal — *none by office or precedence nearer to God than another; none standing between his brother and God.*" — *Alford. Com.* Matt. xxiii: 8–10.

[2] See Maldonatus in Evangelia, in loco; also Chr. Wordsworth's "Four Gospels," in loco.

of the Christian Church — having the power of (the keys) admitting to, or excluding from heaven.

This was not so understood, however, by the Apostles; for, on on occasion,[1] the counsel of James was followed in preference to that of Peter, and Paul once "withstood him to the face, because he was to be blamed."[2] Nor did the early Christian Fathers so understand it.

It is obvious that Christ, when he said "on this rock will I build my Church," either alluded to the declaration of faith which Peter had just made, and meant to say — "upon the rock of *this great truth*, I will build my Church;" or that he turned suddenly from Peter to himself, and meant to say — "upon this rock (of *myself, as the Messiah*,) I will build my Church;" or that he referred directly to Peter, and meant, in some sense, to say — "upon *you, Peter*, I will build my Church." The latter is unquestionably the most natural, and therefore the most probable sense. Nor does it require the adoption of the Romish hypothesis — in itself unnatural and absurd, and unsupported by any shred of other Scripture. We simply need to understand here such a slight play upon words as is very common in the sacred writers,[4] and we get a sound and strong and sufficient sense, without any suggestion of Peter's lordship over God's heritage either for himself, his class, or their successors. "Thou art Peter [Syriac, 'Cephas,' a rock, — so named by Christ himself (John i: 42), because of divine insight into his character] — and upon this rock (this solid fitness — in essential boldness and firmness of character — for service in the difficult work of winning men to the Gospel), I will build my Church; that is, thy labors shall become a foundation stone

---

[1] Acts xv: 7–30.
[2] Gal. ii: 11.
[3] We find among them, indeed, the germs of all subsequent criticism upon the subject. Some few of them regarded the πέτρα of the Church as being Peter; more as the *faith* of Peter; others understood the reference to be to Christ. Augustine changed his view from the former to the latter, as he says, (Retrac. 1: 21). Jerome says, (*Comment on Matt.* vii: 25. — Ed. Basle. A. D. 1536, Vol ix. p. 24), the rock is "Dom. Noster, *Jesus Christus*." Ambrose says, (in Luc. ix. 20), " Petra est *Christus:* etiam discipulo suo hujus vocabuli gratiam non negavit ut ipse sit Petrus, quod de *Petra* habeat soliditatem constantiæ, fidei firmitatem." Augustine (*De peccat. mer. Lib.* ii. *C.* 20. Ed. Antwerp. A. D. 1700), says *Paul* "tanti Apostolatus meruit *principatum.*" So Ambrose declares (De Spir. Sanc. ii: 13), "nec Paulus inferior Petro." Even Gregory VII. (Hildebrand) admitted the doctrine taught last by Augustine, for when he deposed Henry IV., he sent a crown to Rudolphus with the inscription, "*Petra* (Christ) dedit *Petro*, Petrus diadema Rodolpho." — (Vide Baronius, Vol. xi. p. 704.)
[4] See Matt. v: 19; xx: 16, etc.

on which it shall rise.¹ This interpretation is borne out by the fact² that Peter was the first to preach Christ to both Jews³ and Gentiles.⁴ Olshausen seems to lean towards the idea that Peter's enunciated truth was the "rock," yet he says,⁵ "the faith itself, and his confession of it, must *not be regarded as apart from Peter himself personally;* it is identified with him — not with the old Simon, but with the new Peter." And as to "the power of the keys," it is enough to suggest that, so far as the natural idea of opening which attaches to a key is modified by Biblical use, it gets mainly the sense of the power of superintendence with reference to the bestowal of certain privileges,⁶ and its simple use would seem to be to promise to Peter that he shall be made *the instrument for opening the door of the Church to the world;* as he was made after the ascension. And if any idea of vesting power over the Church in Peter, as an individual, or as representing the Apostles, be insisted on in connection with this verse; by turning over to the 18th chapter (v. 18), it will become clear that the same power of binding and loosing was there conferred — and in the same language — upon the whole body of the disciples; the entire Church, as then existing. So that this passage, in no sense, contradicts or modifies those teachings of fraternal equality among his followers, which Christ had before solemnly promulgated.

So far, then, as the Gospels are concerned, it appears to be settled that as Christ was the visible and only head of his Church so long as he remained on earth, and besides him there was no superiority and

---

¹ "The name Πέτρος . . . . . denotes the *personal position of this apostle in the building of the Church of Christ*. He was the first of those *foundation stones* (Eph. ii: 22; Rev. xxi: 14) on which the living temple of God was built: this building itself, beginning on the day of Pentecost by the laying of *three thousand living stones* on this very foundation. That this is the simple and only interpretation of the words of our Lord, the whole usage of the New Testament shows: in which not doctrines, nor confessions, but *men*, are uniformly the pillars and stones of the spiritual building. See 1 Pet. ii: 4–6; 1 Tim. iii: 15; Gal. ii: 9; Eph. ii: 20; Rev. iii: 12." — *Alford. Com. Matt. xvi: 18.*

² "Another personal promise to Peter, remarkably fulfilled in his being *the first to admit both Jews and Gentiles into the Church;* thus using the power of the keys to open the door of salvation." — *Alford. Com. Matt. xvi: 19.*

³ Acts ii: 14.

⁴ Acts x: 34.

⁵ Vol. 1, p. 550. Kendrick's revision.

⁶ Tertullian (de jejuniis adv. Psych. c. 15.) says, — alluding to Paul's permission (1 Cor. x: 25), to eat "whatsoever is sold in the shambles," — "claves macelli tibi tradidit;" — 'Paul has given to you the keys of the meat-market' — meaning free authority to buy and eat whatever is sold there.

no ruling, but all were brethren, equal in rights, however unequal in their performance of service, or their earning of honor; so it was his idea and intention in regard to the practical development of the Christian Church through all the ages, that he should still remain, though ascended, its invisible yet real and only head; and that its membership should permanently stand on the same broad platform of essential equality.

SECTION 2. *The Testimony of the Apostles in regard to Church Government.*

Passing on now to the Acts of the Apostles, we shall see that they bear the most decided testimony that this teaching of Christ was received, and acted upon, by his followers, in the sense which we have put upon it. The Christian Church of the first century — so far as the fifth book of the New Testament conveys its history — was governed, not by Peter, or by any other Apostle, as in Christ's stead; nor by all the Apostles, in their own right, or by any delegation of power from Christ; but by itself, under Christ as its great head; by its entire membership — debating, deciding, doing.[1]

This will be made evident by the examination of those passages which contain a record of Church action. In the appointment of

---

[1] "The essence of the Christian community rested on this: that no one individual should be the chosen, preëminent organ of the Holy Spirit for the guidance of the whole; but all were to coöperate, each at his particular position, and with the gifts bestowed on him, one supplying what might be wanted by another, for the advancement of the Christian life and the common end." — *Neander, Church History.* Torrey's Translation. Vol. 1, p. 181.

"The Jewish and later Catholic antithesis of clergy and laity has no place in the apostolic age. The ministers, on the one part, are as sinful and dependent on redeeming grace as the members of the congregations; and the members, on the other, share equally with the ministers in the blessings of the gospel, enjoy equal freedom of access to the throne of grace, and are called to the same direct communion with Christ, the head of the whole body." — *Schaff. History of the Christian Church*, A. D. 1–311; p. 181.

"The assembled people, therefore, elected their own rulers and teachers, or by their free consent received such as were nominated to them. They also, by their suffrages, rejected or confirmed the laws that were proposed by their rulers, in their assemblies; they excluded profligate and lapsed brethren, and restored them; they decided the controversies and disputes that arose; they heard and determined the cause of presbyters and deacons; in a word, the people did everything that is proper for those in whom the *supreme power* of the community is vested. . . . . Among all the members of the Church, of whatever class or condition, there was the most perfect equality; which they manifested by their love feasts, by the use of the appellations, *brethren* and *sisters*, and in other ways." — *Murdock's Mosheim*, Vol. 1, pp. 68, 69.

"All believers in Christ were called brethren and sisters, and were such in feeling and reality."— *Guericke's Manual.* Shedd's Trans. p. 128.

some one in place of Judas,[1] it appears that an hundred and twenty Church members were present, and Peter, after referring to the fate of the apostate, expressed his conviction of the necessity that some one who was competent, in virtue of a sufficient attendance on Christ's teachings, should [γενέσθαι — *genesthai*, 'be constituted,' or 'appointed'] to be an official witness, with the eleven, of his "resurrection." And they [ἔστησαν δύο — *estēsan duo*, 'stood forward,' or 'selected to stand forward,'] two; and then, recognizing Christ, who had chosen all of the eleven, to be still their Master and Head, and entitled to choose now as before,[2] they prayed him to exercise his choice in the lot by "the whole disposing thereof,"[3] and then 'gave forth their lots,' and the lot fell upon Matthias, who was thenceforth numbered with the eleven Apostles.

Mosheim[4] goes, indeed, so far as to urge that the translation of this phrase "gave forth their lots," [ἔδωκαν κλήρους — *edōkan klērous*] should be 'they cast their votes'— making the passage teach that the suffrage of the one hundred and twenty was exercised not merely — as it confessedly was — in the selection of the two, but also in the subsequent election of the one. And even Chrysostom[5] says: — "Peter did everything here with the common consent; nothing, by his own will and authority. He left the judgment to the multitude, to secure their respect to the elected, and to free himself from every invidious reflection. He did not himself appoint the two, it was the act of all."

Perhaps the real sense of the passage may be cleared by considering the nature of their subsequent action, which it is natural to assume — in the absence of any evidence to the contrary — would be in harmony with what was then done.

We find, then,[6] that when it became needful to appoint deacons to

---

[1] Acts 1: 15-26.

[2] "If any element in the idea of an apostle is clear and well established, it is that of his having been chosen by the Lord himself. (See Luke vi: 13; John vi: 70; xiii: 18; xv: 16, 19; Acts i: 2). Indeed the assembly is so firmly convinced of this prerogative of the Lord in the appointment of an apostle, that they considered the choice of the Lord to have been made already (ver. 24.); so that the lot is only the manifestation of this act of the Lord, which, though secret to them, was already concluded." — *Baumgarten's Apostol. Hist.* Clark's ed. Vol. 1, p. 38.

[3] Proverbs xvi: 33.

[4] *Comment. de Rebus Christ.* pp. 78-80.

[5] *Hom. ad. Act.* 1, p. 25.

[6] Acts vi: 1-6.

aid the apostles in "serving tables," the twelve assembled "the multitude of the disciples," and, having explained the existing necessity, said: "Brethren, look ye out among you [ἐπισκέψασθε — *episkepsasthe*] seven men of honest report, full of the Holy Ghost, and wisdom, whom we may appoint [καταστήσομεν — *katastēsomen*, 'set in place,' 'induct to office,'] over this business. And the saying pleased the multitude [παντὸς τοῦ πλήθους — *pantos tou plēthous*, 'the all of the fulness of people,'] and they chose [ἐξελέξαντο — *exelexanto*, 'selected out,'] Stephen, etc., etc., whom they set before the apostles;" — for what purpose appears from the record of what followed. "And when they [the apostles] had prayed, they laid their hands on them" [the deacons]; not for the purpose of electing them, but by way of solemnly inducting them into the office to which they had been already chosen by the free suffrage of all.

In like manner there is collateral evidence that the whole membership acted in the choice of the messengers or delegates, of the churches, as Paul says [1] in honor of Titus, that it was not only true that his praise was in the gospel throughout all the churches, but that he had also been "chosen [χειροτονηθείς — *cheirotonētheis*, 'appointed by vote of the outstretched hand,'] of the churches to travel" with himself.

So the whole Church appear to have voted in the choice of their presbyters or pastors. The authorized English version indeed says of Paul and Barnabas:[2] "and when they had ordained them elders in every Church, and prayed, with fasting, they commended them to the Lord, etc.," leaving the impression that the elders, or presbyters, or pastors, were put over the churches by Paul and Barnabas, in right of their apostleship; and without any intimation that those churches were even so much as consulted in the matter. But whatever the passage really *does* mean, it is evident that it does *not mean* this. Nothing is said about "ordination" in the Greek. The word upon which the real force of the text hinges is χειροτονήσαντες — *cheirotonēsantes*, which limits and defines the action here described with reference to the elders. That word is derived from two [χείρ — *cheir*, and τείνω — *teinō*,] which signify to 'stretch out,' or 'lift up the hand,' and it is conceded by all that its original use was to de-

---

[1] 2 Cor. viii: 19.   [2] Acts xiv: 23.

scribe the method of voting by 'a show of hands,' in the election of magistrates by the public assemblies of Athens, and hence its primary sense is, to *choose by hand-vote*.[1] It is conceded also that it subsequently took on the secondary sense of *electing* or *appointing in any manner*.[2] The question which must determine its meaning here, is then in which of these senses it was used by the author of the Acts; and, in regard to this, commentators have been divided. Many, most respectable in philological attainments, and eminent for varied learning, have taught that the word was here employed in its primary sense.[3] Others scarcely less eminent, have been equally positive that it is used in a secondary sense, and some would even justify our version in translating it by the word 'ordain.'[4] In this contrariety of opinion, it seems clear that no certainty can be arrived at from the study of the etymology of the word alone, and that the only way of gaining a reasonable security of its intention here is to compare its possible meanings with the circumstances of the case, and settle upon that which best maintains the consistency of the Sacred Record. If we read it "*ordained* them elders in every Church," we strain the sense of the word beyond any secondary meaning which was natural to that time; we assume, without proof, the previous existence of elders (which were now merely ordained) in those churches; we render tautological the account (of seeming public consecration by

---

[1] See Liddell and Scott, Robinson, and Suicer; also Smith's "Dictionary of Greek and Roman Antiquities," art. *Cheirotonia*, p. 271; also Owen's "True Nature of a Gospel Church," works, Vol. xvi, p. 62, where numerous citations are given from Demosthenes, Thucydides, Aristophanes, etc., showing this use; also Colman's "Primitive Church," pp. 59–63.

[2] See quotations from Philo, Lucian and Maximus Tyrius, in Davidson's "Eccles. Pol. of New Test." pp. 201-2.

[3] Vox orta ex more Græcorum, qui porrectis manibus suffragia ferebant. *Beza. in loco.*
"Significat hos suffragiis delectos fuisse." *Erasmus, in loco.*
"Cum suffragiis, sive per suffragia, creassent," is cited by Poole, as the formula in which agree Piscator, and the versions Flacii Illyrici, Tigurina, Pagnini and Piscatoris. — *Poole. Synopsis Crit. in loco.*

[4] See Luther, Brennius, Hammond, etc., *in loco.*
A further idea is suggested by some in connection with this word, which is not without interest, namely: that its chief significance here is in its conveyal of the gift of the Holy Ghost by the imposition of hands. Lightfoot says: "non placet quia in Ecclesiis his recens plantatis ac cosversis nulli adhuc erant idonei ad Ministerium, nisi qui per impositionem manuum Apostolorum Spiritum Sanctum acceperunt." *Chronicon*, 97. And Poole (*Annotations*, Acts. xiv: 23), says the word means "here, to *ordain* to any office or place; which might the rather be done by stretching out, or laying on of the hands of the apostles, because by that means the Holy Ghost (or a power of working miracles) was frequently bestowed, (Chap. viii: 17, 18,) which in those times was necessary to authorize their doctrine to the Infidel world."

'prayer,' 'fasting,' and 'commending to the Lord') which follows; and we throw the narrative out of all natural connection with the system of Church affairs which is elsewhere revealed in the New Testament. If we read it "*appointed* them elders in every Church," we impose this secondary sense upon the verb upon feeble evidence; we commit Paul and Barnabas to a course of policy which is unlike any thing recorded of them before or after; and we make their action exceptional both to the spirit and practice of the time, so far as we can gather them from the inspired narrative. It is admitted that the verb expresses some action of Paul and Barnabas, and the most reasonable supposition is that it asserts that they *superintended the election* of elders by every Church, and then consecrated them with fasting and prayer. This theory does no violence to the verbal integrity of the text, while it brings it into harmony with the general tenor of the action of the early churches. This explanation is that of many ancient and modern scholars,[1] and, we think, justifies itself to every

---

[1] " Populus pastores eligit, sed, ne quid tumultuose fieret, præsident Paulus et Barnabas, quasi moderatores." — *Calvin, Comment, in loco.*

"Solet quidem χειροτονεῖν (*constituere*) sumi de quavis electione, etiam quæ ab uno vel paucis fit. Sed et electioni, de qua agitur, accessisse consensum plebis credibile est, ob id quod in re minori supra habuimus, vi: 2, 8." — *Grotius, Comment, in loco.*

"In all other places on such occasions, the apostles did admit and direct the churches to use their liberty in their choice. (Vide Acts, xv: 22, 25; 1 Cor. xvi: 3; 2 Cor. viii: 19; Acts, vi: 3.) If on all these and the like occasions, the apostles did guide and direct the people in their right, and use of their liberty, as unto the election of persons unto offices and employments when the churches themselves were concerned, what reason is there to depart from the proper and usual signification of the word in this place, denoting nothing but what was the common practice of the apostles on the like occasions?"—*Owen.* "*True Nature of a Gospel Church.*" Works. Vol. xvi: p. 63.

"The spirit of similar transactions and the general tenor of the New Testament, forbid the supposition [that Paul and Barnabas acted without the concurrence of the churches]. Even in appointing an apostle, the company of the believers took a prominent part. The apostles did not complete their own number of themselves. The popular will was consulted. So, too, in the case of deacons. Hence it may be fairly inferred that the appointment of elders here recorded was not made contrary to the wish of the disciples."—*Davidson.* "*Eccl. Pol. of New Text.* p. 205.

"But even though in its later usage χειροτονεῖν may have acquired the general signification of the supreme investiture of officials, yet, in its original acceptation, it signified an election, by holding up of the hands; and this signification is clearly established by 2 Cor. viii: 18, 19, to be still surviving in the phraseology of the New Testament. Besides, the transition from the original to the secondary signification of the word was brought about by the course of political development, whereas in the Church not only did there exist no such ground for the later usage, but, on the contrary, an opposite influence might be supposed to be at work. Accordingly, we must allow that Rothe is right, when, with regard to the passage before us, he maintains that the most natural interpretation of χειροτονήσαντες αὐτοῖς, is assuredly the one which

candid mind, as that best fitting all the exigences of the case, while distinctly affirming the participation of the entire membership in the choice of those who were thus put over them in the Lord.

Evidently, also, the whole Church acted in the discipline of offending members — as Christ had commanded,[1] — for Paul says [2] to the Church at Corinth, of a certain offender, "put away from yourselves that wicked person." And afterward [3] he says — apparently referring to subsequent action of theirs (caused by his advice) in the same case — "sufficient unto such a man is this punishment, which was inflicted (ὑνο τῶν πλειόνων — hupo tōu pleionōn), 'of the many,' *i. e.* the brotherhood of the voting Church.

It is equally clear that the whole membership was consulted in cases of doubt and difficulty. This was done in regard to Peter,[4] when there was a question whether he had done right in preaching

---

adheres the closest to the original acceptation of the word: 'they — the two apostles — allow presbyters to be chosen for the community by voting.'" — *Baumgarten. Apostolic History*, vol. i. p. 456.

See also *Neander. Geschichte der Pflanz. u. Leit.* 1, 203, and *Simon, die Apostolische Gemeine-und Kirchenverfassung*, S. 27.

Dr. Alexander, himself a Presbyterian — whom all students of the New Testament Greek will respect as a sound critic — says of this transaction: "the use of this particular expression, which originally signified the vote of an assembly, does suffice to justify us in supposing that the method of election was the same as that recorded (Acts vi: 5, 6), where it is explicitly recorded that the people chose the seven, and the twelve ordained them." — *Alexander on Acts*, vol. ii. p. 65.

Albert Barnes, also a Presbyterian, says on this passage, "probably all that is meant by it is that they (Paul and Barnabas) presided in the assembly when the choice was made. It does not mean that they appointed them without consulting the Church, but it evidently means that they appointed them in the usual way of appointing officers, by the suffrage of the people." — *Barnes' Notes on Acts*, p. 211.

It is, moreover, a curious fact that the old English Bibles long retained, both in their text and margin, the recognition of a popular vote in this election of elders. Matthew Tindal says: (*Rights of the Chr. Church asserted*), "We read only of the apostles constituting elders by the suffrages of the people, which, as it is the genuine signification of the Greek word used, so it is accordingly interpreted by Erasmus, Beza, Diodati, and those who translated the Swiss, French, Italian, Belgic, and even English Bibles, till the Episcopal correction, which leaves out the words 'by election,' as well as the marginal notes, which affirm that the Apostles did not thrust Pastors into the Church through a lordly superiority, but chose and placed them there by the voice of the congregation."

Tyndale's translation (A. D. 1534) reads, "And when they had ordened them elders *by election* in every congregacion*," etc. Cranmer's (A. D. 1539), "And whan they had ordened them elders *by election* in euery congregacion," etc. The Genevan (A. D. 1557), "And when they had ordeined them Elders *by election* in every Churche," etc. This recognition disappears in the Bishop's Bible (1568), (for obvious reasons), and from the Rheims version (1582), and found no place in the authorized one, dated 1611.

[1] Matt. xviii: 17. [2] 2 Cor. ii: 6.
[3] 1 Cor. v: 13. [4] Acts xi: 1-18.

the Gospel to the Gentiles, and, after they had heard the evidence in the case, "they ("the Apostles and brethren,") held their peace and glorified God, saying: then hath God also to the Gentiles granted repentance unto life." So when the question arose[1] whether to require Gentile converts to be circumcised, we find that Paul and Barnabas "were received of the Church and of the Apostles and elders," and stated the case; after which "it pleased the Apostles and elders, *with the whole Church*, to send chosen men of their own company to Antioch," etc. They accordingly chose Judas and Silas — who were neither Apostles nor elders, but only "chief men among the brethren" — to go to Antioch, and sent a letter by them, beginning: "the Apostles and elders *and brethren*, send greeting," etc. When this committee reached Antioch, they called not the officers of the Church, merely, together, but τὸ πλῆθος — *to plēthos*, 'the multitude,' and delivered *them* the Epistle, "which when *they* had read, *they* rejoiced for the consolation." Thus the whole book of the Acts is veined by like democratic reference to "the brethren," as the court of ultimate appeal, and the last residence of the power that was in the Church. This same chapter goes on (v. 33) to tell us significantly, that after Judas and Silas had tarried a space at Antioch, "they were let go in peace, *from the brethren*, unto the Apostles."

The Apostles were, from the specialty of their position, exceptional to all rules, yet they seem always careful to throw the weight of their influence on the side of popular rights. They counted themselves "less than the least of all saints," and their language to the masses of the Church was, "ourselves your servants for Jesus' sake." They never claimed supreme authority over the Church because they were Apostles, and they taught those chosen of the Church whom they inducted into office, that it was not their function to be "lords over God's heritage," but "ensamples to the flock." They indeed exercised, in the beginning, some practical control over the infant churches — just as our missionaries do among the heathen now — but it appears to have been *pro tempore*, and to have ceased so soon as those churches were in circumstances to enter upon the normal conditions of their life. They addressed the membership of the churches as "brethren" and "sisters," and when remonstrating with them for

---

[1] Acts xv: 4-31.

any irregularity, it was still with them as "brethren." They treated the churches as independent bodies, capable of, and responsible for, self-government. They reported[1] their own Apostolic doings to them, as if they considered themselves amenable to them.

They addressed in their Epistles the *whole body of believers;* especially when they spoke of matters requiring action. Paul's Epistle to the Church at Philippi, begins: "Paul and Timotheus, the servants of Jesus Christ, *to all the saints in Christ Jesus* which are at Philippi — with the bishops [that is, pastors] and deacons." They recognized the right of the churches to send out messengers and evangelists. They consulted with the churches, and the result of the discussion about circumcision was published in the name of "the Apostles *and* elders *and* brethren." They advised the churches to settle their own difficulties,[2] never assuming to adjust them because they were Apostles. They laid the whole matter of electing officers and disciplining offenders upon the churches — functions whose very nature involved in this action of theirs the most radical and convincing testimony that they believed the membership of the Church to be, under Christ, the ultimate residence of Ecclesiastical power. They appear even to have devolved the administration of Christian ordinances upon the pastors of the individual churches. Paul thanks God that he personally baptized very few. Peter did not, himself, baptize Cornelius, or his companions.[3]

The Apostles, clearly filled a peculiar, self-limiting and temporary office. They had the oversight of the planting of churches, and the care of them in their first immaturity. Paul speaks of himself as burdened — not with the bishopric of some particular territory, but with "that which cometh upon me daily, the care of *all the churches.*" The same appears to have been true of his brethren, all — separately and together, wherever Christ might call, and however Christ might guide — laboring "for the perfecting of the saints, for the work of the ministry, for the edifying of the body of Christ." Chrysostom says,[4] "the Apostles were constituted of God first-men ['overseers,' 'leaders'] not of separate cities and nations, but *all* were entrusted *with the world.*" When they died, they left the churches to go on in

---

[1] See Acts xi: 1-18; xiv: 26, 27, etc.
[2] 1 Cor. vi: 1-8.
[3] Acts x: 48.
[4] As cited by Campbell, Lec. p. 775.

this line of democratic life which they evidently felt that Christ had prompted, and which they had, clearly, labored to promote.

Placing this now by the side of those deductions from our Saviour's teachings which we have already made, we seem to get very clear and sufficient evidence that the Christian Church, as it went forth from the immediate impress of the Saviour and his inspired followers, on its divine mission of preaching the Gospel to every creature, was essentially democratic, or Congregational, in form — recognizing no power of ruling above its membership below Christ still its Great Head; its few and simple offices being offices of service and not of mastership; and its presiding and controlling spirit one of fraternity, simplicity, and universal responsibility.

SECTION 3. *The Testimony of History in favor of Congregationalism.*

As this Church of churches went abroad on its holy mission, it would naturally go in the spirit of its founders, and repeat everywhere the model of its original in its earliest home. Gieseler[1] says, "the new churches out of Palestine formed themselves after the pattern of the mother Church in Jerusalem," and all the earliest and most trustworthy authorities which have come down to us confirm his words, and indicate that the democratic platform continued to be characteristic of the Church until it was modified, in the second and third centuries after Christ, by the invasion of alien elements. It is not our purpose here to anticipate the full discussion of particulars, which is subsequently proposed under their separate heads. It is sufficient, at this stage of the discussion, to quote the testimony of one every way competent to form a judgment, who has studied the subject of Christian Antiquities, in their bearing upon Church government, with more tireless zeal and exhaustive research, than perhaps any other living man,[2] and who sums up the result, under this head, as follows: — "These [early Christian] churches, wherever formed, became separate and independent bodies, competent to appoint their own officers, and to administer their own government, without reference or subordination to any central authority or foreign power. No

---

[1] Davidson's Translation, v. 1. p. 90.   [2] Rev. Lyman Coleman, D. D.

fact connected with the history of the primitive churches is more fully established or more generally conceded."[1]

It was not till the latter half of the second century after Christ, when the fervor of the piety of the Apostolic age had began to cool, that the office and title of bishop,—in any sense correspondent to any thing now suggested by that name—begin to show themselves in the history of the Church, and then they appear to have come in as the choice between two evils.[2] The formation of a sacerdotal caste, claiming for themselves prerogatives and authority like those of the Jewish priesthood, followed; until the people were stripped of the right of the election of their pastors,[3] ecclesiastical officers were multiplied, and, by the desire of ambitious men among the clergy to acquire power—favored by the fact that their superior culture necessarily gave them great influence over a comparatively illiterate Church membership—the order of the Church was gradually swayed from the simple democracy of Jerusalem and Antioch 'clean over' to the monarchic abominations of the Papacy.

Neighboring churches were first consolidated into one bishopric, then aggregated bishoprics grew into a vast hierarchy, which overcame all popular resistance, and settled itself securely for centuries at Rome, giving birth there to those monstrous and malignant heresies of doctrine, and those mournful and miserable immoralities of life, which, raying out gloom upon the general mind and heart, brought on the long night of "the dark ages."

---

[1] "Ancient Christianity exemplified." Chap. vi. sec. 4. p. 95.

[2] Jerome (lived A. D. 331-420) suggests that the idea of a standing officer, called a bishop, was resorted to as an expedient to quell the unchristian dissensions which had arisen among the clergy. He says:—

"Idem est ergo presbyter, qui episcopus; et antequam diaboli instinctu, studia in religione fierent, et diceretur in populis; ego sum Pauli; ego, Apollo, ego autem Cephæ, communi presbyteriorum consilio ecclesiæ gubernabantur. Postquam vero, unusquisque eos, quos baptizaverat suos putabat esse, non Christi, in toto orbe decretum est, ut unus de presbyteris electus superponeretur cæteris, ad quem omnis ecclesiæ cura pertineret et schismatum semina tollerentur."—*Comment. on Tit.* i. 5. *Opera. tom.* ix. fol. 245.

[3] It is remarkable that a trace of this original Congregationalism, even to this day, maintains and justifies itself in the very ritual of the Papal system; since the Bishop is made to say, while ordaining a priest: 'it was not without good reason that the fathers had ordained *that the advice of the people should be taken in the election of those persons who were to serve at the altar;* to the end that, having given assent to their ordination, they might the more readily yield obedience to those who were so ordained.' ["Neque enim frustra a patribus institutum, ut de electione illorum qui ad regimen altaris adhibendi sunt, consulatur etiam populus," etc.].—*Pontif. Rom. De Ordinat. Pres. fol.* 38.

The fact was long unknown to the world, yet there seems to be good evidence that in the valleys of the Cottian Alps, a little band, known since the twelfth century as 'the Waldenses,' successfully resisted this invasion of Papal corruption, and maintained their position against all persecution.[1] They were the faithful ones to whom Milton makes such stirring reference in his thirteenth Sonnet: —

> "Avenge, O Lord, thy slaughtered Saints, whose bones
> Lie scattered on the Alpine mountains cold;
> Even them who kept thy truth so pure of old,
> When all our fathers worshipped stocks and stones,
> Forget not: in thy book record their groans,
> Who were thy sheep, and in their ancient fold
> Slain by the bloody Piemontese that rolled
> Mother with infant down the rocks. Their moans
> The vales redoubled to the hills, and they
> To Heaven. Their martyred blood and ashes sow
> O'er all the Italian fields, where still doth sway
> The triple tyrant; that from these may grow
> A hundred fold, who, having learned thy way,
> Early may fly the Babylonian woe."

But, with this exception, "darkness covered the earth, and gross darkness the people," until the Reformation dawned upon a world that — largely Christian as it was, in name — resembled that Christian world on which the Apostles closed their dying eyes scarcely so much as the bittern-haunted solitudes of the wilderness of Mount Seir to-day resemble that magnificent Petra which dwelt so proudly in the clefts of the rocks, centering the caravans of Arabia, and Persia, and Egypt, and Syria, and overflowing with the wealth of the Orient.

Moreover, Luther and his immediate coworkers in this Reformation were so engrossed by the consideration of the *religious* errors of Romanism, as a system of personal salvation for guilty and lost men, and so intent upon restoring the doctrine of justification by faith alone

---

[1] They claim to have inherited their religion, with their lands, from the primitive Christians. The '*Nobla Leyczon*' (A. D. 1100); Moneta, '*Contra Catharos et Valdenses,*' Lib. v. p. 405, (A. D. 1240); and Reinerus, '*De Sectis Antiquorum Hæreticorum,*' c. 4. *Bib. Patr.* Vol. iv. (A. D. 1250) bear witness that the sect which they call "Vaudès," and "Lombardi Pauperes," and which was beyond question identical with those whom we call the Waldenses, made the same claim, six and seven hundred years ago, which they now make, of direct descent from the primitive Church without alloy from the Papacy.

to its ancient and Scriptural place before the people, that they seem, for a time, to have overlooked the fact that the organic constitution of the Church had been changed from its original simplicity quite as much as the great doctrines of faith; with the related fact that those very errors of doctrine had come in through the door opened for them by those organic modifications. Nor ought we to forget that the first Reformers were so dependent upon the coöperation and protection of the secular arm of kings, princes, and nobles, who would have frowned upon any attempt to introduce radical reform into the outward structure of the existing Church, that they may readily have felt that, if any effort in that direction were desirable, the time had not yet come when it could be wisely attempted. It was only when further experience had taught the truly pious that a hierarchy *with* the doctrine of justification by faith could be just as tyrannical as a hierarchy *without* it, and that any comfortable and equitable enjoyment of the individual right of thought and action was beyond hope so long as the working processes of the Church remained what they were; that the philosophy of the connection between the outward form and the inward life of religion began to be reasoned out, and men, reading their Bibles anew with this point specially in mind, at length made the startling discovery that the genuine Church of the New Testament — that pure and simple democracy which Christ gathered about himself, and which the Apostles nurtured, and which both bequeathed to the future as the instrument of its regeneration, — no longer had visible existence among men.

From the day of Wickliffe — in Milton's words, " honored of God to be the first preacher of a general Reformation to all Europe," and since Milton's day affirmed to be " the modern discoverer of the doctrines of Congregational dissent "[1] — there were persons in England seeking this great truth, if haply they might feel after it and find it. The Baptists[2] date the origin of their existence as a denomination, among those days, and those investigations. There can be little question, however, that this discovery was most fully made by the English Puritans. Attempting to organize their own religious life in accordance with it, at Scrooby and elsewhere, the English hierarchy drove them out with violence. They cast about for a country where

---

[1] *London and Westminster Review.* No. 1. 1837.   [2] Belcher's "Religious Denominations."

they might reproduce the Apostolic model, and attempt to bring men back to its understanding and imitation. Fourteen years before the company which John Robinson had trained and sent forth from Leyden with his blessing, landed on the rock of Plymouth, they had banded themselves together into a Congregational Church,[1] — the mother Church of New England — on those principles, hinted at in the previous chapter, which have given so much of vitality and of victory to the reformed religion in this land, and which, gradually leavening the lump of modern Society, have inwrought themselves into the religious life of the age to that extent which has been indicated in the statistics already given.

SECTION 4. *Proof from Scripture and Reason of the Truth of the Essential Principles of Congregationalism.*

Having thus glanced at the teachings of Christ and his apostles, and the history of the churches founded by them, and so taken preparatory notice of the general drift of the four Gospels, and the Book of the Acts, and the state of the facts, in the direction of the cardinal doctrines of Congregationalism, we are now prepared, more intelligently, for a more rigid inquiry how far its essential and distinguishing features bear the complexion of common sense, and of that word of our God which is to stand forever?

We may safely take the seminal Congregational principle — that the Bible, rightly interpreted, is our only and sufficient guide — for granted, and proceed to test those doctrines which, under the guidance of that principle, the system announces as imperative upon men. In doing so, it will be convenient to follow the order in which they have been already announced — (pp. 2, 3, 4).

I. ANY COMPANY OF PEOPLE BELIEVING THEMSELVES TO BE, AND PUBLICLY PROFESSING THEMSELVES TO BE CHRISTIANS, ASSOCIATED BY VOLUNTARY COMPACT, ON GOSPEL PRINCIPLES, FOR CHRISTIAN WORK AND WORSHIP, IS A TRUE CHURCH OF CHRIST.

Here are four distinct points, namely:

1. A true Church must be composed of those who believe themselves to be, and publicly profess to be, Christians.

---

[1] Hunter's "Founders of new Plymouth." p. 89.

2. To constitute a true Church, these professedly Christian persons must be united together, on Gospel principles, by voluntary compact, or covenant.

3. That covenant must be for purposes of Christian work and worship.

4. Every such company of professing Christians, united by such a covenant, for Christian work and worship, is a true Church of Christ.

1. *A true Church must be composed of those who believe themselves to be, and publicly profess to be, Christians.*[1]

They must believe themselves to be Christians, or their movement toward a Church estate becomes stamped at once with hypocrisy or total misapprehension. They must profess themselves to be Christians — and do so publicly — because the very idea of a Church involves the idea of confessing Christ before men;[2] of letting the light of their piety shine before men, that God may be glorified. That such hopeful piety in its members is essential to the existence of a true Church, will appear to be true from the testimony of several classes of passages.

(1.) *From those texts which describe the Church as being a holy body.* Such as:—

Heb. xii: 23. The General Assembly and Church of the first born, which are written in heaven.

Acts ii: 47. And the Lord added to the Church daily such as should be saved.

---

[1] "Now how marvellous a thing is it, and lamentable withal, that amongst Christians, any should be found so far at odds with Christian holiness, as to think that others than apparently holy, at the least, deserved admittance into the fellowship of Christ's Church, and therewith of Christ! Do, or can, the gracious promises of God made to the Church, the heavenly blessings due to the Church, the seals of divine grace given to the Church, appertain to others than such?"—*John Robinson. Works.* Vol. iii. p. 66.

"Both the Scriptures, and common reason teach, that whomsoever the Lord doth call, and use to, and in any special work or employment, he doth in a special manner separate and sanctify them thereunto. And so the Church, being to be employed in the special service of God, to the glory of his special love, and mercy in their happiness, and to show forth his virtues, must be of such persons, as, by and in whom, he will, and may thus be worshipped and glorified."— *Ibid.* Vol. iii, p. 127.

"*Est societas fidelium*, quia idem illud in professione constituit Ecclesiam visibilem, quod interna et reali sua natura constituit Ecclesiam mysticam; id est *fides.*" *Amesius, Medull. Theol. Lib. Prim. Cap.* xxxii. sec. 7.

"By a visible Church, we are to understand a society of visible *saints.*"— *Emmons.* Vol. v. p. 444.

[2] Matt. x: 32; Luke xii: 8; Matt. v: 16, etc.

Rom. ii: 29. But he is a Jew which is one inwardly; and circumcision is that of the heart, in the spirit, and not in the letter; whose praise is not of men, but of God.

(2.) *From those which describe the vital union between Christ and the Church.* Such as: —

John xv: 5. I am the vine, ye are the branches, etc.

1 Cor. vi: 15. Know ye not that your bodies are the members of Christ?

Eph. i: 22, 23. And hath put all things under his feet, and gave him to be the head over all things to the Church, which is his body, etc.

Eph. ii: 20–22. And are built upon the foundation of the Apostles and prophets, Jesus Christ himself being the chief corner stone; in whom all the building fitly framed together groweth unto an holy temple in the Lord: in whom ye also are builded together, etc.

(3.) *From those which announce the design which Christ has in regard to the Church.* Such as: —

Titus ii: 14. Who gave himself for us, that he might redeem us from all iniquity, and purify unto himself a peculiar people, zealous of good works.

"Eph. v: 25, 26. Even as Christ also loved the Church and gave himself for it; that he might sanctify and cleanse it... that he might present it to himself a glorious Church, not having spot, or wrinkle, or any such thing; but that it should be holy and without blemish.

(4.) *From those which affirm a radical distinction between the Church and the world.* Such as: —

2 Cor. vi: 14–18. For what fellowship hath righteousness with unrighteousness? and what communion hath light with darkness? and what concord hath Christ with Belial? or what part hath he that believeth with an infidel? and what agreement hath the temple of God with idols? for ye are the temple of the living God . . . wherefore come out from among them, and be ye separate, saith the Lord, etc.

Eph. v: 11. Have no fellowship with the unfruitful works of darkness, but rather reprove them.

2 John: 10, 11. If there come any unto you, and bring not this doctrine, receive him not into your house, neither bid him God-speed: for he that biddeth him God-speed is partaker of his evil deeds.

(5.) *From those which require such preparation for the reception of Church ordinances as only believers can have.* Such as:—

Acts ii: 38. Repent and be baptized.

1 Cor. v: 8. Let us keep the feast, not with old leaven, neither with the leaven of malice and wickedness; but with the unleavened bread of sincerity and truth.

1 Cor. xi: 27-29. Wherefore, whosoever shall eat this bread, and drink this cup of the Lord, unworthily, shall be guilty of the body and blood of the Lord. But let a man examine himself, and so let him eat of that bread, and drink of that cup. For he that eateth and drinketh unworthily, eateth and drinketh damnation to himself, not discerning the Lord's body.

(6.) *From those which require the discipline of unworthy members.* Such as:—

1 Cor. v: 11-13. But now I have written unto you not to keep company, if any man that is called a brother be a fornicator, or covetous, or an idolater, or a railer, or a drunkard, or an extortioner; with such a one, no, not to eat. . . . Therefore put away from among yourselves that wicked person.

2 Thess. iii: 6. Withdraw yourselves from every brother that walketh disorderly.

Tit. iii: 10. A man that is a heretic, after the first and second admonition, reject.

To these might be added, also, that great class of texts which represent the Church as the Christianizing element in human society; as the 'salt of the earth,' the 'light of the world,' the 'pillar and ground of the truth,' etc. But it is hardly necessary to multiply proofs of so plain a point. If the Church is appointed to be peculiarly a holy body, if its members are to be united to Christ by the bond of a living faith, if Christ's design for the Church involves holiness in its membership, if it is to be radically distinguished from the world, if only believers can rightly partake of its ordinances, and if the unworthy in its ranks are to be cut off; it becomes very clear that only those who believe and profess to be Christians have any right to its privileges, or any share in its promises. The worldly-minded man, however correct in outward morality, has no place there. His salt is without savor. The light that is in him is darkness. The idea that all persons who live a life outwardly reputable, or who have great respect for Christian things, or who — to use the language of the Methodist "Discipline,"[1] — have merely a "desire of salvation," may rightly belong to the Church, was not an Apostolic, as it is not a Scriptural idea,[2] but was begotten in the day when the Church and the world began to fraternize.

2. *To constitute a true Church, these professedly Christian people must be united together by voluntary compact, or covenant.*[3]

The necessity for this arises out of the very nature of things. A Church is an organization. But every organization must have some organizing bond. The very act of associating implies a purpose, and the act of associating for a purpose implies some mutual understanding of, and agreement in, that purpose, and such understanding and agreement is a covenant — express or implied; written, verbal, or of inference.

God bound his people to himself and to each other, in the olden time, by covenants, references to which are scattered along the pages of both Old Testament and New.[4] And there are many Biblical principles and precepts which imply that it is God's will for his chil-

---

[1] "Doctrines and Discipline of the Methodist Episcopal Church." Ed. 1856, pp. 27, 28.

[2] "A Church, consisting of the indiscriminate mass of a nation, where the great majority have no semblance of Christian character, would have astounded the early fathers; though their successors were by degrees familiarized, but not always reconciled, to the mischievous perversion of terms." — *Bennett. "Theol. of Early Church."* p. 142.

"There is no evidence in the New Testament of the term *Ecclesia* ever being applied to a visible baptized society consisting of a mixed multitude, godly and ungodly." — *Davidson. "Eccl. Pol. of the New Test."* p. 130.

[3] "That whereby the Church is as *a city compacted* together, is the Covenant." — *John Davenport's "Power of Congregational Churches asserted and vindicated."* p. 37.

"Mutuall covenanting and confoederating of the Saints in the fellowship of the faith according to the order of the Gospel, is that which gives constitution and being to a visible Church." — *Hooker's "Survey of the Summe of Church Discip."* p. 46.

"For the joyning of faithfull Christians into the fellowship and estate of a Church, we finde not in Scripture that God hath done it any other way then by entering all of them together (as one man) into an holy Covenant with himselfe." *John Cotton's "Way of the Churches."* p. 2.

"Corpus sumus de conscientia religionis, et disciplinæ divinitate, et spei fœdere." — *Tertullian. Apol.* 39. This is misquoted by John Wise, who adds "whereas such a body, or religious society, could not be united but by a covenant; he (Tertullian) calls it a covenant of hope, because the principal respect therein was had unto the things hoped for." — *John Wise's "Vindication."* p. 8, Ed. 1772.

"Vinculum hoc est *fœdus*, vel expressum, vel implicitum."—*Amesius, Lib.* 1. *Cap.* xxxii: 15.

"Materia Ecclesiæ, sunt tum communiter vocati, et in *fœdus* gratiæ recepti. *Wollebius, Lib.* 1. *Cap.* xxv: 10.

[4] Gen. xvii: 7; Exod. xxxiv: 27; Deut. iv: 13, ix: 11, xxix: 12; Josh. xxiv: 16-25; Neh. ix: 38; Ps. cliii: 18; Rom. ix: 4; Gal. iii: 17, iv: 24; Eph. ii: 12; Heb. viii: 7, etc.

dren to become united, as a covenant, only, would unite them. His Church is a 'city,' a 'house,' a 'body fitly joined together and compacted;' a 'body' in which there should be no 'schism.' Its acts are directed to be such as imply the union of its members in covenant; otherwise it could not 'withdraw' itself 'from every brother that walketh disorderly,' nor 'love the brotherhood,' nor 'walk by the same rule,' nor 'mind the same thing.'

3. *This covenant must be for purposes of Christian work and worship.*[1]

Good people affiliated for good purposes are not a Church, unless those purposes are distinctively *Church* purposes; that is, unless they aim directly at the promotion of the worship and service of God on Earth. This is evidently true in itself, and it finds proof in all which the Scriptures say of the churches of Christ. Turning to the first admission of members to the Christian Church after the ascension,[2] we see that they 'that gladly received the word' were baptized and 'added to the Lord;' that they 'continued steadfastly in the Apostles' doctrine and fellowship, and in breaking of bread and in prayer.' So the uniting one's self to the Church is called [3] 'confessing Christ before men,' that is, publicly pledging one's self to personal faith in Christ, and a life of obedience to him. It is laid down as the duty of the members of the Church,[4] to 'consider one another, to provoke unto love, and to good works; not forsaking the assembling of themselves together.' All which (coincident with the whole tenor of the Gospel) goes to show that when men form a Church or join themselves to one, they enter into a covenant for sacred purposes; — the maintenance of all Christian doctrines, the practice of all Christian duty, the salvation of men and the glory of God.

4. *Every such company of professing Christians, so united by covenant for Christian work and worship, is a true Church of Christ.*[5]

---

[1] "Christ, believed on and confessed, is the rock whereupon a particular visible Church is built."— *John Davenport.* "*Power of Congregational Churches vindicated.*" p. 10.
[2] Acts ii: 41-46.
[3] Matt. x: 32.
[4] Heb. x: 24, 25.
[5] "This we hold and affirm, that a company, consisting though but of two or three, separated from the world — whether unchristian or anti-christian — and gathered into the name of Christ

This will be seen to be true from two considerations.

(1.) *From the Scriptural use of the word 'Church.'* The Greek word ἐκκλησία — *ekklēsia*, is derived from a verb meaning 'to call out,' and hence, 'to assemble,' and is the word that had been long in use at Athens to signify the general assembly of the citizens, in which they met to discuss and determine upon matters of public interest; — regularly about four times a month, and, on occasions of sudden importance, whenever summoned by express for that purpose.[1] The word is used in three senses in the New Testament.

(*a.*) *It sometimes has this primary meaning;* as in the account of the tumultuous gathering at Ephesus, where the 'town clerk' says:[2] "if ye inquire any thing concerning other matters, it shall be determined in a lawful *assembly*," "and he dismissed the *assembly.*" Stephen seems to have used it in much the same general sense of 'a gathered multitude,' where he said of Moses,[3] "this is he that was in the ἐκκλησία, in the wilderness, with the angel," etc.

(*b.*) *It is sometimes used to describe the general assembly of Christian people on earth — the Church universal.* Thus, in these passages: —

"God hath set some in the *Church*, first apostles, secondarily prophets," etc.[4]

---

by a covenant made to walk in all the ways of God known unto them, is a Church, and so hath the whole power of Christ." — *John Robinson. Works*, Vol. ii. p. 132.

"And for the gathering of a Church I do tell you, that in what place soever, by what means soever, whether by preaching the Gospel by a true minister, by a false minister, by no minister, or by reading and conference, or by any other means of publishing it, two or three faithful people do arise, separating themselves from the world into the fellowship of the Gospel, and covenant of Abraham, they are a Church truly gathered, though never so weak," etc. — *Ibid.* Vol. ii. p. 232.

"Every congregation or assembly of men, ordinarily joined together in the worship of God, is a true visible Church of Christ." — *Bradshaw's "English Puritanism."* *Neal*, Vol. i. p. 428.

"A congregation, or particular Church, is a society of believers joined together by a special band among themselves, for the constant exercise of the communion of saints among themselves." — *Amesius, Medull. Theol.* Cap. xxxii. Sec. 6.

"The visible Church state which Christ hath instituted under the New Testament, consists in an especial society, or congregation of professed believers." — *John Owen. Works*. Vol. xv. p. 262.

"Sed ubi *tres*, Ecclesia est, licet laici." — *Tertullian. De Exhor. Cast.* Sec. 7.

[1] See Article *Ecclesia*, in Smith's "Dictionary of Greek and Roman Antiquities." p. 439. Also Hermann's "Political Antiquities," Sec's 125, 128.

[2] Acts xix: 39-41.   [4] 1 Cor. xii: 28.
[3] Acts vii: 38.

"I persecuted the *Church* of God, and wasted it," etc.[1]

"Head over all things to the *Church*."[2]

"The general assembly and *Church* of the first born, which are written in heaven," etc.[3]

(*c.*) *Its most distinct and frequent sense is, however, that of an assembly of Christians in a particular place:* that is; a local Church. Thus we read of: —

"The *Church* which was at Jerusalem."[4]

"A whole year they assembled themselves with the *Church* [in Antioch] and taught," etc.[5]

In like manner we find mention of the *Church* at Cenchrea,[6] that at Corinth,[7] and those at Ephesus,[8] Laodicea,[9] Thessalonica,[10] Smyrna,[11] Pergamos,[12] Thyatira,[13] Sardis,[14] and Philadelphia.[15]

We find, also, the same use of the word in its plural form in many passages;[16] such as, "the *churches* had rest throughout all Judea, and Galilee, and Samaria," etc.,[17] "the *churches* of Galatia,"[18] "the *churches* of Macedonia,"[19] "the *churches* of Asia,"[20] and, indefinitely, "the *churches* of the Gentiles."[21]

So, again, we have mention made of "the Church," in "the house" of Priscilla and Aquila;[22] that in the "house" of Nymphas;[23] and that in the "house" of Philemon.[24]

There is no record of the use of this word ἐκκλησία by Christ himself, except upon two occasions. One was when he said to Peter,

---

[1] Gal. i: 13.
[2] Eph. i: 22.
[3] Heb. xii: 23.
[4] Acts viii: 1, xi: 22.
[5] Acts xi: 26.
[6] Rom. xvi: 1.
[7] 1 Cor. i: 2; 2 Cor. i: 1.
[8] Rev. ii: 1.
[9] Rev. iii: 14.
[10] 1 Thess. i: 1; 2 Thess. i: 1.
[11] Rev. ii: 8.
[12] Rev. ii: 12.
[13] Rev. ii: 18.
[14] Rev. iii: 1.
[15] Rev. iii: 7.

[16] A local Church is also clearly implied, though not mentioned by name, in Samaria (Acts viii: 5), Damascus (Acts ix: 10–19), Lydda (Acts ix: 32), Saron (Acts ix: 35), Joppa (Acts ix: 36–38), Cesarea (Acts x: 44–48), Antioch in Pisidia) Acts xiii: 14–50), Iconium (Acts xiv: 1–4, 21–23), Lystra (Acts xvi: 2), Derbe (Acts xvi: 1, 2), Philippi (Acts xvi: 12–40), Berea (Acts xvii: 10–14), Troas (Acts xx: 5–11), Tyre (Acts xxi: 4), Ptolemais (Acts xxi: 7), Puteoli (Acts xxviii: 13, 14), Rome (Acts xxviii: 14–16), Colosse (Coloss. 1: 2), Hierapolis (Coloss iv: 13), and Babylon (1 Pet. v: 13).

[17] Acts ix: 31.
[18] 1 Cor. xvi: 1, Gal. i: 2.
[19] 2 Cor. viii: 1.
[20] 1 Cor. xvi: 19.
[21] Rom. xvi: 4.
[22] Rom. xvi: 3, 5, 1 Cor. xvi: 19.
[23] Col. iv: 15.
[24] Phil. v: 2.

"upon this rock will I build my *Church;*"¹ and the other where he instructed his disciples, if one of his followers should have cause of complaint against another, and other suitable efforts to remove the difficulty should fail, to "tell it unto the *Church,* and if he neglect to hear the *Church,* let him be unto thee as an heathen man, and a publican."² On the first of these occasions he clearly referred to the Church universal, and to his great work of human redemption. On the second, he, as clearly, could not have referred to the Church universal, and the only natural inference is that — looking forward to the time when his followers on earth should be crystallized into local churches — he framed this law to meet their necessities in those churches, through all coming time, and meant for them to take the comfort of his gracious promise: "where two or three are gathered together in my name, there am I in the midst of them."³

The weight of New Testament authority, then, seems clearly to decide that the ordinary and natural meaning of the word ἐκκλησία is that of a local body of believers associated for the enjoyment of Christian privileges, and the performance of Christian duty.⁴ If this

---

¹ Matt. xvi: 18. ² Matt. xviii: 17. ³ Matt. xviii: 20.
⁴ "The word *Ecclesia* [in the New Testament] signifies, either the whole Christian Church — the total number of believers, forming one body under one head; or a single Church, or Christian society."— *Neander.* "*Planting and Training of the Christian Church.*" Amer. edit. p. 92, note.

"The term 'Church' signifies a number of believers habitually assembling for the worship of God in one place. . . . The word uniformly bears this signification when applied to any of the separate assemblies of Christ's servants on Earth."— *Davidson.* "*Ecclesiastical Pol. of New Test.*" pp. 59, 60.

"These things being so plainly, positively, and frequently asserted in the Scripture, it cannot be questionable unto any impartial mind but that particular churches or congregations are of divine institution, and consequently that unto them the whole power and privilege of the Church doth belong; for if they do not so, whatever they are, churches they are not."— *John Owen.* "*Inquiry into the original, etc., of Evangelical Churches.*" Works. (Edit. 1851) Vol. xv. p. 277.

"Its use [the word *Ecclesia*] as signifying the ministers of religion in distinction from the people, or as embracing all the persons professing Christianity in a province or nation, is unknown in the sacred Scriptures. We read in the New Testament of *the Church at Jerusalem,* of *the Church in the house of Priscilla and Aquila,* and of *the churches in Judæa* and *the churches in Galatia;* but we meet with no such phrase as the Church of Judæa, or the Church of Galatia. This application of the term was reserved until the time when Christianity became established as a 'part and parcel' of the kingdoms of this world."— *Vaughan.* "*Causes of the Corruption of Christianity.*" p. 403.

"The Greek word *Ecclesia,* which the New Testament, after the Septuagint, employs, and which we translate *Church,* was adopted by the Latins, who derived sacred terms, as well as ideas, from the Greeks. To them the word being in familiar use, was known to signify a *con-*

be so, then any company of believers so associated, have a right to hold themselves to be an ἐκκλησία — a true Church of Christ, in the place of their abode.

(2.) *This view is confirmed and established by the obvious consideration that the precepts enjoined upon the primitive churches, and the functions assigned to them by Christ and his apostles, were such as implied, and could only consist with, the action of independent local bodies.*

The Scriptural exhortations to Christian fidelity, and usefulness, imply such free opportunities for labor, as local and independent churches only can furnish. The responsibilities that are set forth, are such as could rightly rest only on the members of such churches.

It is easy to see that the method of discipline for offenders which our Saviour prescribed would be both unnatural and absurd, if attempted to be carried out in any Church having any form other than that of a local associate body of believers; while it is plain that, in such a body, it becomes most sensible, suitable, and sufficient.

So also of the elective franchise. When we come, further on, to consider the fact that the Divinely ordained method of Church action is for *the whole brotherhood* to cast their votes for Church officers, and in regard to the management of all Church affairs, we shall be able to set in a strong light the unscripturalness of any theory of the Christian Church, which does not involve the direct and responsible participation of all of the brotherhood in its affairs.

We conclude, then, that any company of professing Christians, associated by voluntary covenant, on Gospel principles, for Christian work and worship, is thereby constituted a true Church of Christ.

II. SUCH A CHURCH — AS A RULE — SHOULD INCLUDE ONLY THOSE WHO CAN CONVENIENTLY WORSHIP AND LABOR TOGETHER, AND WATCH OVER EACH OTHER.[1]

---

gregation. This idea pervades all the earliest Ecclesiastical writings, though translations have frequently misled their readers." — *Bennett.* "*Theology of the Early Church.*" p. 133.

Irenæus, as late as the fourth quarter of the second century (Contra Hæreses, Lib. 2, Cap. xxxi. Sec. 2), uses the word in this sense; speaking of the Church "κατὰ τόπον," or, as the Latin translation gives the phrase, "ea, quæ est in quoquo loco." — *Opera.* (*Massuet's Edition*, A. D. 1734.) Vol. i. p. 164.

[1] "We, on the contrary, so judge, that no particular Church under the New Testament, ought

This accords with what we shall find to be one prominent element in the manifestation of the divine idea of the constitution of the Church on earth, namely, that of an organization which shall place each individual believer in direct contact, on the one hand (in the way of responsibility), with his ascended Lord, and on the other (in the way of labor), with that practical every-day work for the salvation of men and the glory of God, which the Church must perform in order to be 'the salt of the earth,' and 'the pillar

---

to consist of more members than can meet together in one place." — *John Robinson. Works.* Vol. iii. p. 12.

"The Church must not exceed the quantity and compass of one congregation. For the Church must meet ordinarily together with their officers," etc. — *John Davenport.* "*Power of Cong. Churches vindicated.*" p. 56.

"Such cohabitation is required, which is necessary for the dispensation of God's ordinances, the administration of Church censures, for otherwise, the end of the covenant would be made frustrate, and the benefit of the whole prejudiced." — *Hooker's* "*Survey.*" p. 49.

"Neque est ecclesia hæc a Deo instituta proprie Nationalis, Provincialis aut Diœcesana (quæ formæ fuerunt ab hominibus introductæ ad exemplar civilis regiminis, præsertim Romani) sed Parochialis, vel unius congregationis, cujus membra inter se combinantur, et ordinarie conveniunt uno in loco ad publicum religionis exercitium." — *Amesius. Medull. Theol.* Cap. xxxix. Sec. 22.

"To such a body" — a particular Church — "how many members may be added, is not limited expressly in the word, onely it is provided in the word, that they be no more than that all may meet in one congregation, that *all may heare, and all may be edified.* For the Apostle so describeth the whole Church as meeting in one place. 1 Cor xiv: 23. But if all cannot heare, all cannot be edified. Besides the Apostle requireth, that when the Church meeteth together for the celebrating of the Lord's Supper, *they shall tarry one for another,* 1 Cor. xi: 33, which argueth the Church indued with onely ordinary officers, should consist of no greater number then that all *might partake together of the Lord's Supper in one congregation,* and therefore such Parishes as consist of 15,000, though they were all fit materialls for Church fellowship, yet ought to be divided into many churches, as too large for one. When the hive is too full, bees swarme into a new hive; so should such excessive numbers of Christians issue forth into more churches. Whence it appeareth to be an error, to say there is no limitation or distinction of Parishes, meaning of churches (*jure divino*), for though a precise quotient, a number of hundreds and thousands be not limited to every Church, yet such a number is limited as falleth not *below seven,* nor riseth above the bulke of *one congregation, and such a congregation wherein all may meete, and all may heare, and all may partake, and all may be edified together.*" —*John Cotton.* "*Way of the Churches.*" pp. 53, 54.

"Wherefore, no society that doth not congregate, the whole body whereof doth not meet together, to act its powers and duties, is a Church, or may be so called, whatever sort of body or corporation it may be." — *John Owen.* "*Inquiry,*" etc. *Works.* Vol. xv. p. 270.

"I appeal to all authentic Greek writers — Thucydides, Demosthenes, Plato, Aristotle, Socrates, etc., — out of whom plentiful allegations may be brought, all of them showing that this word *Ecclesia did ever signify only one assembly, and never a dispersed multitude, holding many ordinary set meetings in remote places,* as diocesan and larger churches do. Now according to these, and other Greeks, living 'n the Apostle's days, do the Apostles speak." — *Henry Jacob's* "*Attestation.*" (A. D. 1613.) p. 209.

"The matter of the Church, in respect of its *quantity,* ought not to be of greater number than may ordinarily meet together conveniently in one place, nor ordinarily fewer than may conveniently carry on Church work." — *Cambridge Platform.* Chap. iii. Sect. 4.

and ground of the truth.' Unless each Christian is a member of a Church which naturally draws him into direct connection with all its services, so as to lay upon him his share of accountableness to the Great Head for every vote that is taken, and of participation in every labor that is attempted; that idea cannot be reached, and that highest degree of development of the Christian life, which is inseparable from it, cannot be realized.

We have seen that this is the most prominent suggestion of the term ἐκκλησία (*ekklēsia*). In more than sixty instances this word is used in the New Testament under circumstances which naturally imply a single congregation of believers.

Moreover, as many as *thirty-five* different churches are — directly or indirectly — referred to by name in the New Testament, in addition to the general mention of churches 'throughout all Judea, and Galilee, and Samaria,'[1] 'through Syria, and Cilicia,'[2] the 'churches of Asia,'[3] etc. When we consider how soon after Christian churches began to be formed at all, this language was used, we are naturally led to the conclusion that the apostles and their colaborers were accustomed to organize a Church in every place where they found believers enough to associate themselves together for that purpose. This inference gains force when we consider that some of these churches were undoubtedly sufficiently near each other to have readily permitted their fusion into one, if it had not been thought essential to include in a single Church no more believers than could regularly and conveniently unite together in the enjoyment of its privileges and the performance of its duties. For example, Cenchrea was the port and suburb of Corinth, yet there were churches at both places. Hierapolis was visible from the theatre of Laodicea, and Colosse was near — some think directly between — them;[4] while Nymphas[5] appears to have lived in, or near, Laodicea, and it is almost certain that Philemon was a resident of Colosse.[6] So that there is the strongest probability that these five churches — at Hierapolis, Laodicea, Colosse, and those in the houses of Nymphas and Philemon — were all situated within a very few miles, probably within eye-shot, of each other;

---

[1] Acts ix: 31.   [2] Acts xv: 40, 41.   [3] 1 Cor. xvi: 19.
[4] See Dr. William Smith's Dictionary of the Bible. Art. "*Hierapolis.*"
[5] Coloss. iv: 15.
[6] Philem. v: 10; Coloss. iv: 9. Onesimus was a Colossian, and the obvious presumption is that they belonged to the same place.

near enough, at least, to demonstrate, by the fact of their individual existence, that it was the aim of the Apostles to include within a given Church only those who could conveniently and regularly assemble together to share its duties.

We are, of course, aware that it has been objected to this view that the churches at Jerusalem, Antioch, Ephesus and Corinth must have been too large to be gathered into any one room. But, although many thousands of Jews believed at Jerusalem, a very large proportion of them were converted at the time of the Pentecost, which assembled the representatives of the entire nation in the metropolis, so that we are without information as to the number of residents of Jerusalem who became Christians, while we are expressly told that the multitude that heard were 'out of every nation under heaven,'[1] — 'Parthians, and Medes, and Elamites, and the dwellers in Mesopotamia, and in Judea, and Cappedocia, in Pontus and Asia, Phrygia, and Pamphylia, in Egypt, and in the parts of Lybia about Cyrene, and strangers of Rome, Jews and proselytes, Cretes and Arabians;'[2] and it is settled by Inspiration that the resident Church at Jerusalem did meet 'all with one accord in Solomon's porch,'[3] and did act Congregationally together; — in the choice of deacons, in hearing delegates from Antioch, and sending 'chosen men' thither. So we find that Saul and Barnabas 'assembled themselves with the Church'[4] at Antioch during 'a whole year,' and that when Saul and Barnabas returned from the missionary journey on which they had been sent from Antioch, 'they gathered the Church together,'[5] and 'rehearsed all that God had done with them.' And, at a later period, when the delegation from Jerusalem went down to Antioch, 'they gathered the multitude'[6] of the Antiochean Church 'together,' before they 'delivered the Epistle.'[7] With regard to

---

[1] Acts ii: 5.   [3] Acts v: 12.   [5] Acts xiv: 27.
[2] Acts ii: 10.   [4] Acts xi: 26.   [6] Acts xv: 30.

[7] "Antioch, the capital of Syria, where the disciples of Jesus, attracting by their numbers the public attention, were first called Christians, is shown by the letters of Ignatius, to have had, in the second century, but one congregation of the faithful. It was still one in the days of Theophilus. When its bishop, Paul of Samosata, was, towards the end of the second century, deposed, he refused to resign the churches' *house* — not *houses*. Carthage was a kind of African Rome, and enjoyed the services of the most eminent men; but both Tertullian and Cyprian speak of only one congregation, which chose its bishop, Cyprian, by public acclamation, in the third century. Alexandria, an immense city, the seat of what may be called the first Christian university, contained, in Origen's time, but one congregation It was not till the end of the third century that we read of Christians in the extreme suburbs of a city in Egypt, having sep-

Ephesus, we find no hint in Paul's Epistle to that Church that it differed, in this respect, from other churches, but many precepts which would be most natural if it did not so differ; and, as to the Church at Corinth, it is clear that Paul twice recognizes it as one homogeneous body when he says: — "when ye come together, therefore, into one place," etc.,[1] and "if, therefore, the whole Church be come together into one place," etc.[2]

When we add to these considerations the remembrance of the fact that it would be always inconvenient and unnatural, and often impossible, to carry into effect Gospel discipline in any Church, or to elect its officers and carry on its government by the action of the whole body, unless it is of that size that all of its members can meet to discuss its affairs and decide upon them; we have sufficient evidence that the Scriptural theory of a Church is of one composed only of so many members as can conveniently act together in the performance of its functions.

III. EVERY MEMBER OF SUCH A CHURCH HAS EQUAL ESSENTIAL RIGHTS, POWERS, AND PRIVILEGES, WITH EVERY OTHER (EXCEPT SO FAR AS THE NEW TESTAMENT AND COMMON SENSE MAKE SOME SPECIAL ABRIDGMENT IN THE CASE OF FEMALE AND YOUTHFUL MEMBERS); AND THE MEMBERSHIP TOGETHER, BY MAJORITY VOTE, HAVE THE RIGHT AND DUTY OF CHOOSING ALL NECESSARY OFFICERS, OF ADMITTING, DISMISSING, AND DISCIPLINING THEIR OWN MEMBERS, AND OF TRANSACTING ALL OTHER APPROPRIATE BUSINESS OF A CHRISTIAN CHURCH.

Here are two points: —

1. Every member of a Congregational Church has equal essential rights, powers, and privileges with every other member.

2. The membership, by majority vote, have the right and duty of choosing all necessary officers, admitting, dismissing, and disciplining members, and transacting all other appropriate business of a Christian Church.

1. *Every member of a Congregational Church has equal essential*

---

arate places, not called churches, but συναγωγαί, *synagogues;* and not for meetings on the Lord's day, but on Wednesdays and Fridays, when they convened for prayer, [*Eusebius, lib.* vii. c. 30] or held prayer-meetings. — *Bennett.* "*Theology of the Early Chr. Church.*" p. 139.

[1] 1 Cor. xi: 20.
[2] 1 Cor. xiv: 23.

rights, powers, and privileges with every other member. This is the dictate of reason in regard to the membership of a body constituted as the Church is. Its members—however diverse in natural powers, or in point of intellectual attainments, or social position—all come into it upon the same conditions, make the same promises, and seek the same ends. All stand upon an equality before God as to their need of salvation, as to the way of salvation, and as to the duties of salvation. The king and the beggar must alike 'repent and be converted' before they can offer themselves as suitable candidates for admission to the Church—both passing into it through the same 'strait gate.' And, when entered, both must depend with the same humility upon the same grace, for daily sustenance in the divine life. Of the two, indeed, the king will be apt to need most grace, and be in greatest danger of falling, because of the sorer temptations which, from his position, will be likely to 'beset him behind and before.' So that there will be nothing in the fact that, in one aspect of his life, he is a king, to give him any preëminence in the Church over his brother, who, in one aspect of *his* life, is a beggar. They stand before God together there as sinful *men* for whom Christ died, to be comparatively estimated not by their worldly station, but 'according as God hath dealt to every man the measure of faith.' And if this will be true of them, it will be true of all.

The same conclusion follows from the voluntary, associate, character of the Church, considered as an organization. It is expressly confederated on the basis of equality among its members; and on that basis every member—as the rule—must necessarily have the same rights, powers, and privileges as every other.

This view the Scriptures confirm. They nowhere hint any reason for, or Divine intention of, any inequality of privilege in the Church. But they expressly state that the 'multitude'[1] was accustomed to gather together for action on business requiring action, and that it was when it 'seemed good'[2] to 'the whole Church'—being 'assembled with one accord'—that action followed.

The only exception to this is the express curtailment, by Paul, of some portion of the prerogatives of females; with such practical modification as good sense may suggest in the case of very young and in-

---

[1] Acts vi: 5, xv: 12, xxi: 22.   [2] *Ibid.* xv: 25.

experienced members — which exceptions will be subsequently considered in another connection.¹

2. *The membership, by majority vote, have the right and duty of choosing all necessary officers, of admitting, disciplining, and dismissing members, and transacting all other appropriate business of a Christian Church.*²

This follows inevitably from the very theory and constitution of the body, and is abundantly established by Scriptural authority.

(1.) *The right and duty to choose all necessary officers.* The right of an equal voice in the election of the officers of the body, is one of the inherent rights of the membership of every such voluntary association as — in one aspect of it — every Church is. And if we turn to the New Testament, we find that the membership of the primitive

---

¹ See Chap. iii.

² "Christ hath given this power to receive in, or cut off, any member, to the whole body together of every Christian congregation, and not to any one member apart, or to more members," etc.—*Confession of Low County Exiles.* Hanbury, Vol 1. p. 95.

"Every particular society of visible professors agreeing to walk together in the faith and order of the Gospel, is a complete Church, and has full power within itself to elect and ordain all Church officers, to exclude all offenders, and to do all other acts relating to the edification and well-being of the Church."—*Savoy Confession.* Neal, Vol. ii. p. 178.

"Nor may any person be added to the Church as a private member, but by the consent of the Church," etc. *Ibid.* p. 179.

Cambridge Platform says Church power is in the hands of the "brethren formally and immediately from Christ." Chap. v. Sect. 2.

See, also, an eloquent passage — too extended to be quoted here — in John Robinson's answer to Bernard. *Works,* Vol. ii. pp. 140, 141.

"The subordinate ordinary power of acting Church affairs, in the order appointed by Jesus Christ, for attainment of the ends of Church communion, is given by Christ to a visible congregation of confederate believers, as the first and proper subject of it."—*John Davenport,* "*Power of Congregational Churches,*" etc. p. 90.

"Wee do not carry on matters, either by the *overruling power of the Presbytery,* or by the consent of the *major part* of the Church, but by the generall and joynt consent of all the members of the Church; for we read in the Acts of the Apostles, the Primitive Church (which is a pattern for succeeding ages) carried all their administrations, ὁμοθυμαδόν, that is, with one accord, Acts ii: 46, as becometh the Church of God; which ought to be of *one heart,* and *one soul,* of *one mind,* and *one judgement,* and all to speak the same thing. Acts iv: 32; 1 Cor 1: 10; Phil. ii: 2, 3." *John Cotton's* "*Way of the Churches.*" p. 94.

"A particular Church or congregation of saints, professing the faith, taken indefinitely for any Church (one as well as another), is the first subject of all the Church offices, with all their spirituall gifts and power, which Christ hath given to be executed amongst them," etc. *John Cotton's* "*Keyes of the Kingdom,*" etc. p. 67.

"The people, or fraternity, under the gospel, are the first subject of power."—*John Wise.* "*Vindication of the Government of New England Churches.*" (Ed. 1772.) p. 44.

"The administrative power in each Church is the voice of its majority, from which there is no appeal, except by the consent of both parties, and even then simply in the spirit of arbitration." — *Vaughan's* "*Congregationalism; or the Polity of Independent Churches viewed in relation to the state and tendencies of Modern Society.*" London. 1842. 2d Edit. p. 3.

churches held and exercised this right. The Church at Jerusalem chose a twelfth apostle to be the successor of Judas;[1] and this was done by vote of the whole brotherhood, as we have before shown.[2] In like manner we have seen that the brotherhood chose the seven deacons;[3] their presbyters or pastors;[4] and the messengers to Antioch.[5] In fact there is no record in the New Testament of any other method of electing Church officers than by vote of the whole brotherhood, nor do we know of any precept, or even hint, looking in any other direction.

(2.) *The right to admit and dismiss members.* Somebody, and somebody who has intelligence, time, and opportunity, must have this right, or that fundamental principle that they only are entitled to membership who give credible evidence of piety, could not be maintained; nor could transfers be made from one Church to another. And from the democratic form of the Church, this power would naturally inhere in the entire membership. Furthermore, the power of choosing officers, which are the greater; involves and includes the power of choosing private members which are the less. It is clear, moreover, that it was not enough[6] for Barnabas to be satisfied of Paul's worthiness; but the fears of 'the brethren' had to be allayed concerning him, before he could enter into fellowship with them. And, in the presence of the strong presumption in favor of the residence of this power of admission in the hands of the membership, and the absence of all hint of its residence elsewhere, we think that the matter is made Scripturally clear by the fact — which will be presently set forth — that the power of casting out of the Church is expressly lodged in the body of covenanted believers. It is a familiar, and a sound maxim — *ejusdem est potestatis aperire et claudere, instituere et destituere ;*[7] and its application in this case would settle the question that as the membership are expressly commanded to act in excision, with them must lie the power of admission, as well.

• (3.) *The right to discipline and exclude members.* Here the Scripture is so explicit, and even minute in its directions, that there is room for no reasonable doubt as to the divine intention. As we have already seen,[8] Christ most expressly committed the duty of discipline in every Church to its members, and made their decision final.[9] And

---

[1] Acts 1: 15–26. [3] See page 15. [5] See page 19.
[2] See page 14 [4] See page 15. [6] Acts ix : 26–30.
[7] "The same power that can open, can shut; that can set up, can set down."
[8] See page 9. [9] 1 Cor. v : 13 ; 2 Cor. ii : 6.

we find many passages which were evidently intended to stimulate the membership to the performance of this disagreeable and most solemn duty, in some of its lighter or severer aspects. Such is the following; — " Now I beseech you, brethren, mark them which cause divisions and offences, contrary to the doctrine which ye have learned, and avoid them."[1] So the passage,[2] directing the Corinthian brethren not to 'company' with certain offenders, saying "do not ye judge them that are within," (that is, in the Church), and closing "therefore put away from among yourselves that wicked person," is in point. So is that,[3] beginning "now we command you, brethren, in the name of our Lord Jesus Christ, that ye withdraw yourselves from every brother that walketh disorderly," etc., and that in the Epistle to Titus;[4]—"A man that is an heretic, after the first and second admonition, reject," etc. It will not be denied that all these precepts are addressed to 'the brethren' of the churches — and not to any Bishop, or other Church officer, nor to any Session, Presbytery, or other Church court — and the conclusion becomes inevitable, that the whole right and duty of that form of Church action which is contemplated by and provided for in them, is solely with 'the brethren.' Paul — as if to remove any lingering doubt that the responsibility was upon the membership, and upon them *all*, — distinctly says,[5] it must be, when they "*are gathered together*," that they "deliver such a one unto Satan for the destruction of the flesh, that the Spirit may be saved in the day of the Lord Jesus." This, Paul elsewhere [6] calls "a punishment inflicted [ὑπὸ τῶν πλειόνων — *hupo tōn pleionōn*] of the many," or, as we familiarly say, 'by the crowd.'— "Thus," says John Davenport,[7] upon this passage, "he establisheth their power to bind, and teacheth them how to use it; and, in like manner, he exhorteth them, upon the man's repentance, to turn the key, and to open the door of Christian liberties to him, and to loose him from the former censure, by forgiving him, in a legal, or judicial sense."

Thus Christ's minute commands, with Apostolic precepts, and the obvious practice of the Primitive churches, unite to put beyond a doubt the fact that the power of 'the keys' in discipline — to its last results — is vested in the brotherhood of the Church.

---

[1] Rom. xvi: 17. [3] 2 Thess. iii: 6. [5] 1 Cor. v: 1-5.
[2] 1 Cor. v: 9-13. [4] Titus iii: 10. [6] 2 Cor. ii: 6.
[7] "*Power of Congregational Churches asserted and vindicated.*" p. 101.

WHENCE CONGREGATIONALISM IS.

(4.) *The right to transact all other appropriate business of a Christian Church.* This right to transact all business that is incidental to the functions of Church life — being subordinate to those rights which are vital to that life — must follow from them. If the membership are empowered to admit, dismiss and discipline their own members, and to elect their officers, they must have the lesser right to do all other needful things. And the fact of the actual exercise of such subordinate rights by the membership, is Scripturally shown by cases already referred to,[1] where the entire body was consulted by the Apostles themselves, in cases of doubt and difficulty.[2]

IV. EVERY SUCH CHURCH IS INDEPENDENT OF ANY OUTWARD JURISDICTION OR CONTROL — WHETHER FROM POPES, PATRIARCHS, ARCHBISHOPS, BISHOPS, OR OTHERS ASSUMING TO BE VICEGERENTS OF CHRIST; FROM ANY ASSEMBLIES, SYNODS, PRESBYTERIES, CONVENTIONS, CONFERENCES, ASSOCIATIONS OR COUNCILS, ASSUMING TO SPEAK IN THE NAME OF 'THE CHURCH'; OR FROM OTHER CHURCHES — BEING ANSWERABLE DIRECTLY AND ONLY TO CHRIST ITS HEAD: AND EVERY SUCH CHURCH IS ON A LEVEL OF INHERENT GENUINENESS, DIGNITY, AND AUTHORITY WITH EVERY OTHER CHURCH ON EARTH.[3]

---

[1] See pages 18, 19.   [2] Acts xi: 1-18, xv: 4-31, etc.

[3] " Although all the churches were, in this first stage of Christianity, united together in one common bond of faith and love, and were, in every respect, ready to promote the interest and welfare of each other by a reciprocal interchange of good offices, yet, with regard to government and internal economy, every individual Church considered itself as an independent community, none of them ever looking beyond the circle of its own members for assistance, or recognizing any sort of external influence or authority. Neither in the New Testament, nor in any ancient document whatever, do we find any thing recorded from which it might be inferred that any of the minor churches were at all dependent on, or looked up for direction to, those of greater magnitude or consequence." — *Mosheim. De Rebus Christ. Sæc* i. Sec. 48.

" Christus vero sic instituit Ecclesiam, ut a sese semper pendeat, tanquam a capite."—*Amesius. Medull. Theol.* Lib. i. Cap. xxxii. Sec. 25.

" Christ has not subjected any Church to any other superior ecclesiastical jurisdiction than that which is within itself." — *Bradshaw's "English Puritanism."* Chap. ii. Art. 4.

" The Lord Jesus is the king of his Church alone, upon whose shoulders the government is, and unto whom all power is given in heaven and earth." — *John Robinson. Works.* Vol. ii. p. 140.

" The truth is, a particular congregation (Church) is the highest tribunall. . . . If difficulties arise . . . the counsell of other churches should be sought to clear the truth, but the power . . . rests still in the congregation, where Christ placed it."—*Hooker's "Survey."* Part iv. p. 19.

" Every particular ordinary congregation of faithful people . . . is a true or proper visible Church, *jure divino*, — by right from God. Every such congregation here, and everywhere, is

Here are two main points:—

1. Every Congregational Church is, by divine right, independent of all control from without, except that of Christ its Head.
2. Every Congregational Church is on a level of inherent genuineness, dignity, and authority, with every other Church on earth.

1. *Every Congregational Church is, by divine right, independent of all control from without, except that of Christ its head.*

(1.) There is no Biblical precept conferring any control over the local Church upon any man or body of men. Those directions which Paul gave with reference to subjection to 'principalities and powers,'[1] have sometimes been twisted in that direction, as if the Apostle were then persuading Church members to submit to a Bishop or a Pope, rather than admonishing citizens toward a due subordination to the laws of the land. And the two precepts in the last chapter of the Epistle to the Hebrews (vv. 7, 17), have been claimed, by Papists and others, as establishing the right of a hierarchy to the obedience

---

endued with power immediately from Christ, to govern itself ecclesiastically, or spiritually."—*Henry Jacob's "Reasons for Reforming Church of England."* Hanbury. Vol. i. p. 222.

"Every Church hath power of government in, and by itselfe; and no Church, or officers, have power over one another but by way of advice or counsalle."—*Lechford's "Plain Dealing."* Mass. Hist. Coll. Third Series. Vol. iii. p. 74.

"A Congregational Church is, by the institution of Christ, a part of the militant visible Church."— *Cambridge Platform.* Chap. ii. Sec. 6.

"Christ's gospel churches in their fraternities are not such cyphers as they stand in some men's accounts; but are really and truly proper bodies, full of powers, and authorities, for the government of themselves, and all their concerns, as all democracies are."—*John Wise. "Vindication of Government of New England Churches."* (Ed. 1722.) p. 56.

"Neither were they [the early churches] *subordinate to one another.* No example of this subordination has yet been adduced from the New Testament. Even those called mother-churches, such as were at Jerusalem and Antioch, did not claim exclusive power over others. *All were distinct independent Societies.*"—*Davidson. "Eccl. Pol. New Test."* p. 136.

"The churches constituted on this strictly voluntary principle, and thus wholly spiritual in their character, were churches possessing each a separate and *independent* character."—*Vaughan. "Causes of the Corruption of Christianity."* p. 408.

"Independence and equality formed the basis of their [the churches] internal constitution."—*Gibbon. "Decline and Fall of the Roman Empire."* Smith's Edit. Vol. ii. p. 191.

"The exigences of the Christian Church can never be such as to legitimate, much less to render it wise, to erect any body of men into a standing judicatory over them."—*Pres. Stiles. "Convention Sermon,"* (A. D. 1761.) p. 91.

"Nothing in the history of the primitive churches is more incontrovertible, than the fact of their absolute independence, one of another. It is attested by the highest historical authorities, and appears to be generally conceded by Episcopal authors themselves."—*Coleman's "Apostolical and Primitive Church."* 3d Edit. 1853. p. 50.

"The several churches are altogether independent of one another."—*Uhden's "New England Theocracy."* p. 68.

[1] Titus iii: 1.

of the churches. But those precepts clearly refer to the relation of the members of a Church to its own Christian teachers, and not to its subordination to any external authority — whether of one or of many.

The first (*v.* 7): — "Remember them that have the rule over you," is explained by the clause succeeding: " who have spoken unto you the word of God; *whose faith follow*, considering the end of their conversation." The words translated " that have the rule over you," [τῶν ἡγουμένων ὑμῶν — *tōn hēgoumenōn humōn*], rather mean 'your teachers or leaders in faith,' and the reference — involved in the word 'remember,' — apparently is to those who were already dead, whose example was to be had in constant and affectionate imitation, as both a stimulus and a guide.[1] So that there is not here the remotest reference to any 'rule' over the Church at all; as our translation (prepared by prelates) wrongly suggests.

The other verse (*v.* 17), unquestionably does make allusion to rul-

---

[1] " He first sets before the Jews the example of those by whom they had been taught; and he seems especially to speak of those who had sealed the doctrine delivered by them, by their own blood," etc. — *Calvin. Comment. in loco.*

" Sanctitatem in omni vita exhibuerunt, et in ea perstiterunt ad mortem usque.... Hanc sanctitatem per fidem acceperant atque servaverant; quare videte eandem fidem retineatis, ut par sit et vester exitus." — *Grotius. Comment. in loco.*

" By the description following, it is evident that the Apostle here intends all that had spoken or preached the word of God unto them, whether apostles, evangelists, or pastors, who had now finished their course," etc. — *John Owen. Comment. in loco.*

" That is, calling to mind the peaceful and happy death of those religious teachers among you, who gave you instruction respecting the word of life, imitate their faith; that is, persevere in your Christian profession, as they did, to the very end of life." — *Stuart. Comment. in loco.*

" Here dead teachers are intended; as appears from the word Μνημονεύετε, from the past tense of ἐλάλησαν, and especially from the following part of the sentence..... The reference seems to be to those holy preachers of the gospel, like Stephen and James (Acts vii: 59, 60, xii: 2), who died for Christ: 'remember them and consider their deaths, in order to imitate their steadfastness in the faith.'" — *Sampson. Comment. in loco.*

" We shall have to understand a reference to such men as Stephen, James the son of Zebedee, and James the younger, who was stoned in a tumult, A. D. 62, — men whose death was known to the readers, and whom they even *now* doubtless acknowledge as ἡγούμενοι." — *Ebrard. Comment. in loco.*

" Innuit ergo doctores ex primis Christi testibus et apostolis, eorumve discipulis et sociis, qui paulo ante *decesserant*, vel jam jamque decessuri erant." — *Bengel. Gnomon. in loco.*

" Remember them that were your leaders, who spoke to you the Word of God; look upon the end of their life, and follow the example of their faith." — *Conybeare and Howson.* (*New translation.*) "*Life and Epis. St. Paul.*" First 4to Edit. Vol. ii. p. 547.

" The sentiment here is, that the proper remembrance of those now deceased who were once our spiritual instructors and guides, should be allowed to have an important influence in inducing us to lead a holy life." — *Barnes. Comment. in loco.*

ing *in* the Church, but not to ruling *over it*. Our translation says, "obey them that have the rule over you, and submit yourselves; for they watch for your souls, as they that must give account, that they may do it with joy, and not with grief; for that is unprofitable for you." But here again, "them that have the rule over you," is τοῖς ἡγουμένοις ὑμῶν [*tois hēgoumenois humōn*], signifying, as before, simply *the spiritual teachers, or guides*, of the Church, whose proper authority over them 'in the word and doctrine,' its members are bound to recognize and respect.[1] That those ordinary ministers of religion who labor in, and with, a Church, are here intended, and not any hierarchy without, is made evident by the declaration that the 'guides' referred to, are those which 'watch for souls,' which 'watching' was assigned to Timothy,[2] as a part of his work as an Evangelist; and they are to 'watch' not as those who are to reign over the Church and

---

[1] "Doubly foolish are the Papists, who from these words confirm the tyranny of their own idol : ' the Spirit bids us obediently to receive the doctrine of goodly and faithful Bishops, and to obey their wholesome counsels; he bids us also to honor them.' But how does this favor mere apes of Bishops?"—*Calvin. Comment. in loco.*

"The rulers, or guides, here intended, were the ordinary elders, or officers of the Church, which were then settled among them."—*John Owen. Comment. in loco.*

"Obey your leaders and be subject to them; for they watch over your souls, as those who must give an account."— *Stuart.* (*New translation.*) *in loco.*

"Proper attention and obedience to spiritual guides is here inculcated," etc.— *Turner. Comment. in loco.*

"Doctoribus defunctis *memoriam* præstate (v. 7,) viventibus *obedientiam*..... Obedite in iis, quæ præcipiunt vobis tanquam salutaria ; *concedite*, etiam ubi videntur plusculum postulare..... Auditores debent ductoribus suis *obedire* et *concedere*, ut cum gaudio," etc. — *Bengel. Gnomon. in loco.*

"In the former verse the Apostle exhorts them to remember those who had been their leaders, and to imitate their faith ; in this he exhorts them to obey the leaders they now had, and to submit to their authority in all matters of doctrine and discipline, on the ground that they watched for their souls, and should have to give an account of their conduct to God. If this conduct were improper, they must give in their report before the great tribunal with grief; but *in* it must be given: if holy and pure, they would give it in with joy. It is an awful consideration that many pastors who had loved their flocks as their own souls, shall be obliged to accuse them before God for either having rejected or neglected the great salvation."—*Adam Clarke. Comment. in loco.*

"Render unto them that are your leaders obedience and submission ; for they, on their part, watch for the good of your souls, as those that must give account ; that they may keep their watch with joy and not with lamentation ; for that would be unprofitable for you."— *Conybeare and Howson.* (*New translation.*) Vol. ii. p. 548.

"Gehorchet *euren Führern* und folget ihnen ; denn sie wachen über eure Seelen, als die einst Rechenschaft geben sollen," etc. — *De Wette's translation, in loco.*

"The reference here is to their religious teachers, ... and the doctrine is, that subordination is necessary to the welfare of the Church, and that there ought to be a disposition to yield all proper obedience to those who are set over us in the Lord."—*Barnes. Comment. in loco.*

[2] 2 Tim. iv : 5.

call *it* to an account, but as themselves 'they that must give account' to the Great Head, for the faithfulness with which *they* have led and fed their flock 'like a shepherd.'

So that, rightly read, neither of these precepts suggests any ruling over a Church from without, except that of Christ, in his Word and by his Spirit, ever shaping that ruling that is within it, to the praise and the glory of his name.

(2.) *There is no evidence furnished by the Scriptures of the exercise of any outward control over the primitive churches.* We have already seen (pp. 19, 20), that the Apostles neither claimed nor exercised such control over those churches which they had founded. There is no record of the assumption, or exercise of such control by any other man or body of men. And we shall more clearly see how adverse the supposition of any such control is to the facts in the case, when we come to the particular consideration of those texts which are urged — as indirect evidence — on its behalf.

(3.) *The whole drift of the New Testament is in a direction opposite to any theory of control over the individual Church.* Not only did the individual churches, in obedience to Apostolic counsel, and under the Apostolic eye, perform untrammelled all the functions of their Church life; but the sole responsibility of their life and labor was laid and left upon them by Christ and his Apostles, who everywhere recognized the right and duty of 'the brethren' to make final decision upon all matters. Men, from reading the New Testament alone, could hardly be led to conceive of any supremacy, whether of one or many, over that local *Ekklesia*, whose 'works' and 'labor' and 'patience' had — among others — this praise; — "thou hast tried them which say they are Apostles and are not, and hast found them liars."[1]

(4.) *The general arguments of the advocates of some external jurisdiction over the local churches do not sustain that doctrine.* A late earnest writer in the interest of the Papacy, has argued that since the Church must have some government, and Christ does not himself visibly preside over it, he must have delegated his power either to some one man, to an order of men, or to the whole Church collectively. The former and latter suppositions he throws out as insufficient for the

---

[1] Rev. ii: 2.

duties to be performed; inconsistent with His rights as the founder of the institution, and incompatible with the end intended; and then draws the conclusion that the power of the Church was actually vested, by its Great Head, in "several offices, in due subordination to each other," all centering in the occupant of the Papal chair.[1] But this argument is most evidently founded upon a low view of the power of truth over the minds of men, and a complete ignoring of the possibility of that constant influence by Christ himself over the affairs of his kingdom on earth, which his own words, 'Lo I am with you alway,' entitle his people to expect. It is kindred to that old assumption of despots that men cannot be trusted to govern themselves, without forts forever frowning upon them, and an omnipresent police peering into their affairs. Self-government is inconceivable to many minds, as a system that can be trusted to be a regulator of human conduct; and many even who accept it as sufficient in civil affairs, distrust it still in regard to spiritual things. But, if there were only one man on earth, and he loved God, and 'willingly walked after the commandment,' doubtless he could be governed by the influence of Christ through the Word, and the Spirit, without a Pope. It is difficult to see why, if there were two such men, the same might not be true of them; and so of ten, or one hundred. It is difficult, indeed, to see why, on these conditions, the same might not be true of any number of men up to the whole of the race. So that to deny that the Congregational theory — that Christ committed the government of the Church to its own members, under His constant supervision — is adequate to the performance of all that the nature of the case demands, is to deny the sufficiency of truth to do its work, or the omnipotence of Christ in the superintendence of that work, or both. And all reasoning toward the Papacy as a necessity that the Church on earth may be suitably governed, is, in the face of the facts, as baseless and impertinent, as the assumption would be in regard to civil matters, that there can be no just and suitable order, and subordination, without absolute monarchy everywhere.

The same, for substance, is true of the assumptions of the prelacy of the Episcopal Church, and of the aristocracy of Presbyterianism;

---

[1] "*The Path which led a Protestant Lawyer to the Catholic Church,*" by P. H. Burnett. New York. 1860. pp. 61-107.

all practically denying that Christ can procure the proper government of his Church on earth without some hierarchal help.

(5.) *The texts cited by the advocates of some external jurisdiction over the local churches, in proof of its Scripturalness, do not sustain that doctrine.* We have already seen[1] how baseless is the Papal assumption that Christ, in the 16th of Matthew, committed the government of the Church to the hands of Peter, as future Bishop of Rome, to be administered in the line of Episcopal succession from him.

The Episcopal arguments for the supremacy of 'the Church' over all local congregations and all individual believers, are mainly founded upon such an interpretation of the word 'Church' as sanctions their claim. But we have seen[2] that the Scriptural usage of the word ἐκκλησία (*ekklēsia*) does not countenance such an interpretation, and that those functions which Christ appoints to his churches[3] do not comport with it.

The central idea of the Presbyterian theory — which places the board of Elders, the Presbytery, the Synod, and the General Assembly, over the local Church — is that "the several different congregations of believers, taken collectively, constitute one Church of Christ, called emphatically *the Church;* — that a larger part of *the Church,* or a representation of it, should govern a smaller, or determine matters of controversy which arise therein; — that, in like manner, a representation of the whole should govern and determine in regard to every part, and to all the parts united; that is, *that a majority shall govern:* and consequently that appeals may be carried from lower to higher judicatories, till they be finally decided by the collected wisdom and united voice of *the whole Church.*"[4] But we have already seen[5] that this fundamental assumption is erroneous, and that the *local Church* is the only one known to the New Testament; whence it follows that all arguments founded on the theory of any other Church, must be without warrant from the word of God. The same conclusion will be inevitable if we examine those texts which are specially relied on to sustain this assumption. The main passage

---

[1] Pages 10, 11. [2] Pages 31–33. [3] Page 34.
[4] "*The Constitution of the Presbyterian Church in the United States of America.*" Form of Government. Book I. Chap. 12, note.
[5] Pages 31–33.

quoted, for that purpose, in the "Book of Discipline," is Acts xv: 1–29. By turning to that passage, our readers will see that certain Judeans had insisted, in the Church at Antioch, that all Christian believers from the Gentiles should be circumcised. A discussion arose. Paul and Barnabas participated in that discussion, but made no attempt authoritatively to decide it. The Church finally sent Paul and Barnabas, with several lay delegates, to Jerusalem, to consult about the matter. It is stated that they were sent 'unto *the Apostles and Elders* about this question.' But that this language was not used to exclude, but rather to include (by specifying its most prominent persons)[1] the *whole* Church at Jerusalem, is made evident by the fact that (*v.* 4) 'when they were come to Jerusalem they were received *of the Church*, and of the Apostles and Elders,' and declared their errand. 'And the *Apostles and Elders* came together for to consider of this matter,' and when they had fully considered it, 'it pleased the Apostles and Elders, *with the whole Church*,' to send a delegation to Antioch with their reply, and *they* wrote letters by them, after this manner: 'The Apostles and Elders *and brethren* send greeting, etc. . . . It seemed good *unto us, being assembled with one accord*, to send,' etc. And the delegation went to Antioch with this epistle, and 'when they had gathered *the multitude*' of the Church at Antioch together, they delivered it, etc.

We submit that nothing can well be plainer than that this was a Congregational, rather than a Presbyterian procedure. The entire membership of the Church at Antioch send delegates to the entire membership of the local Church at Jerusalem, to ask their advice on the question whether circumcision is still a rite in force upon them. The entire membership of the local Church at Jerusalem — under the guidance and counsel of the Apostles — meet those delegates, consider

---

[1] "Now the Apostles and Elders are mentioned first and foremost as members in this assembly. But that we ought to think of this assembly as an universal one, is implied as self-evident; 'for,' as Meyer says, 'the deliberation of the Apostles and Presbyters took place in the presence and with the coöperation of the whole assembled Church, as appears from *v.* 12, compared with *v.* 22, and most distinctly from *v.* 25.'"— *Baumgarten's "Apostolic Hist."* Vol. ii. p. 13.

"The *brethren* were also present at the meeting. In this respect it was unlike modern Synods, from which the people generally are excluded as members."— *Davidson.* "*Ecclesiastical Pol. of New Test.*" p. 323.

"The Apostles and Elders are mentioned on account of their rank, not as comprising the entire assembly. It is evident from *v.* 23, that the other Christians at Jerusalem were also present, and gave their sanction to the decrees enacted."— *Hackett on Acts, in loco.*

the matter, and send a reply, which the Church at Antioch receives, and is comforted. We do not see how any man who does not read this chapter through a Presbyterian glass darkly, can, by any possibility, distort it into any semblance of support of the Ecclesiastical judicatories which belong to the Presbyterian system.

Equally fruitless are other attempts to graft that system upon the honest sense of the New Testament. The "Book" says,[1] "The Church of Jerusalem consisted of more than one." It then cites, in proof, the following passages:

Acts vi: 1. "When the number of the disciples was multiplied, there arose a murmuring of the Grecians," etc.

Acts ix: 31. "Then had the churches rest throughout all Judæa," etc.

Acts xxi: 20. "Thou seest, brother, how many thousands of Jews there are which believe," etc.

Acts ii: 41, 47. "The same day there were added unto them about three thousand souls. And the Lord added to the Church daily such as should be saved."

Acts iv: 4. "Many of them which heard the word believed; and the number of the men was about five thousand."

We can find in these passages no assertion, nor even hint, of more than one Church at Jerusalem. There were other churches in Judea. And, beyond doubt, thousands of those who were converted at Jerusalem were foreign Jews come up to the feast. And even if all were residents, and all remained, there is still no particle of evidence that they were associated into more than one Ecclesiastical body. We have seen[2] that they all met together in one place for business, apparently as other churches met; which is the clearest proof that they, however numerous, were but one Church.[3] And the attempt which

---

[1] Book I. Chap. 10, note.   [2] Page 37.

[3] "The entire multitude of the Christians [were called together] not the one hundred and twenty. (Acts I: 5.) That the Christian community in Jerusalem was divided into seven distinct churches, each of which assembled by itself and chose a deacon (as some assert, *i. e.*, Mosheim, Kuinoel) is untenable and improbable. The difficulty of apprehending how many thousand Christians could have assembled in one place, is lessened by the probability of the fact that many of them had left Jerusalem, where they were present merely on account of the feast." — *De Wette, in loco.*

So, of the Church at Corinth, the following thoughts are worthy of consideration:

"The place (1 Cor. xiv: 23) that speaks of the whole Church coming together into one place, doth unavoidably prove (for aught we can discern) that Corinth had their meetings, and not by way of distribution into several congregations, but altogether in one congregation: and

the "Book" makes, to prove that there were several churches in Jerusalem which had a practical Presbyterial union for purposes of business, by first assuming that there were so many believers there that they could not all have belonged to one Church, and then quoting such passages [1] as speak of the Church action at Jerusalem as being that of one body, which they say must then have been a Presbytery, is a begging of the very question in debate, which no man would tolerate, for a moment, in a secular argument.

Equally absurd seems to us the attempt of the "Book," to prove from the burning of the books of those 'which used curious arts' at Ephesus, taken in connection with other passages which speak of Paul's 'tarrying at Ephesus until Pentecost,' and of 'a great door and effectual' as being opened to him there, etc.,[2] that "the Church of Ephesus had more congregations than one, under a Presbyterial government."[3] Unquestionably there was a time when there was more than one Church in Ephesus. The first fruits of Paul's preaching there, appear to have been gathered into a Church in the house of Aquila. Subsequently, on his second visit, converts so multiplied that a new assembly was gathered elsewhere. But when Aquila removed to Rome,[4] the Church that had been in his house appears to have coalesced with the other assembly, and thenceforth we hear only of 'the Church' at Ephesus; as in Acts xx: 17 (A. D. 58), Rev. ii: 1 (A. D. 67, or as some think, A. D. 96), without any added incidents, upon which the liveliest imagination could hang the Presbyterial theory.[5]

It is indeed wonderful with what calm assurance the Presbyterian "Book" attaches its code to Scripture references which have not

---

doth also answer your reason drawn from the variety of teachers and prophets in that Church; for it is plain from that very chapter, that the Church of Corinth had many prophets: *let the prophets speak two or three, and let the rest judge* (v. 29); and many that spake with tongues, who must speak by course two or three, and one interpret (v. 27); yea every one generally had a psalm, or a doctrine, or a revelation, or an interpretation (v. 26): as indeed they came behind in no gift (1 Cor. 1:7); and yet for all their variety of gifts and gifted men, prophets, interpreters, speakers with tongues, and the like, both they and the whole Church also, even women and all, used to come together into one place." — "*Modest and Brotherly Answer*," etc., *by Richard Mather and William Tompson.* London: 1644. 8vo. p. 37.

[1] Acts xv: 4, xi: 22, xxi: 17, 18, etc.
[2] 1 Cor. xvi: 8, 9, 19; Acts xviii: 19, 24, 26, etc.
[3] Book i. Chap. 10, note.
[4] He was there in A. D. 57, when Paul wrote the Epistle to the Romans. Rom. xvi: 3–5.
[5] See the subject well and thoroughly discussed by Dr. Davidson. "*Eccl. Pol. New Test.*" pp. 98–112.

even the semblance of remotest possible connection with the subject. The vivid imagination which led the ancients to picture an *ursa major* in the northern heavens, on the strength of a cluster of stars that much more decidedly suggests to the less poetic modern mind the form of a humble kitchen utensil, was feeble in comparison with it. For example, we learn [1] that " three ministers, and as many elders as may be present belonging to the Presbytery, being met at the time and place appointed, shall be a quorum competent to proceed to business," from Acts xiv: 26, 27, compared with Acts xi: 18; passages which declare that when Paul and Barnabas "had gathered the Church together, they rehearsed all that God had done with them, and how he had opened the door of faith unto the Gentiles," and that "when they heard these things, they held their peace and glorified God, saying, then hath God also to the Gentiles granted repentance unto life!"

So all the proof adduced by the "Book," from Scripture, in support of the power of Church 'judicatories,' over the churches and their membership, is [2] those passages in the 18th of Matthew (*vv.* 15–20), which record Christ's confiding of all matters of discipline *expressly to the hands of the Church itself*, and the direction of Paul (also to the *Church itself*,) when 'gathered together,' to cast out the unworthy! We are also referred for proof [3] that "the Church session consists of the pastor or pastors, and ruling elders, of a particular congregation," solely to the same direction of Paul,[4] " in the name of our Lord Jesus Christ, when ye are gathered together, and my spirit, with the power of our Lord Jesus Christ," etc. So we find [5] the position that the Church session "have power to inquire into the knowledge and Christian conduct of the members of the Church," educed from one single passage, and that the following, in the Old Testament: [6] — "the diseased have ye not strengthened, neither have ye healed that which was sick, neither have ye bound up that which was broken, neither have ye brought again that which was driven away, neither have ye sought that which was lost; but with force and cruelty have ye ruled them,"—a text which, it seems to us, would prove any thing else, at least, equally as well! So the power of the

---

[1] Book I. Chap. 10, Sec. 7, note.
[2] Book I. Chap. viii. Sec. 2, note.
[3] Book I. Chap. ix. Sec. 1, note.
[4] 1 Cor. v: 4, 5.
[5] Book I. Chap. ix. Sec. 6, note.
[6] Ezek. xxxiv: 4.

Presbytery[1] to "issue and receive appeals from Church sessions," to "examine and license candidates for the holy ministry:" to "ordain, instal, remove and judge ministers;" to "resolve questions of discipline;" to "condemn erroneous opinions;" and, in general, to "order whatever pertains to the spiritual welfare of the churches under their care;" is wholly rested — so far as Scriptural authority is concerned — upon those passages which narrate the discussion at Jerusalem in regard to circumcision;[2] the exhortation of the brethren in Ephesus to the disciples at Achaia to receive Apollos;[3] the separation of Barnabas and Saul to the work whereunto God had called them;[4] the address of the twelve apostles to the Church at Jerusalem in regard to the choice of the seven deacons; and Paul's advice to the Ephesians,[5] to pray "always with all prayer and supplication in the spirit, watching thereunto," etc.; and to the Philippians[6] to "be careful for nothing, but in everything by prayer and supplication, with thanksgiving, let your requests be made known unto God!" Our Presbyterian friends regard these passages as so overwhelming in demonstration of the Scripturalness of their views and of the unscripturalness of all opposing ones, that they calmly, say, on proceeding to speak of Synods and of the General Assembly:[7] "as the proofs already adduced in favor of a Presbyterial assembly in the government of the Church, are equally valid in support of a Synodical assembly, it is unnecessary to repeat the Scriptures to which reference has been made, or to add any other." We find it easy to agree with them on the point of the *equal* validity of *such* texts in support of Synods — and we might add, of Ecumenical councils, and of the whole system of the Papacy, as well — but we can hardly concur in their conclusion that nothing more is needed to establish their system as the natural outgrowth of the Bible. However those who take Presbyterianism first for granted, and then go to the Bible with both the expectation and determination to find there the evidence of its truth — or, if not that, at least not to find there the evidence of its errors — may regard these 'proof texts;' it seems to us abundantly clear that they who take the Bible for granted, and go meekly, pray-

---

[1] Book i. Chap. x. Sec. 8.
[2] Acts xv: 5-24.
[3] Acts xviii: 24, 27.
[4] Acts xiii: 2, 3.
[5] Eph. vi: 18.
[6] Phil. iv: 6.
[7] Book i. Chap. xi, note.

erfully, and studiously, to its pages to find out what form of Church government will be the simple and unforced outgrowth of its records, and its precepts ; could by no ordinary possibility educe from it the Presbyterian theory.

(6.) *Christ, by his own voice, and through that of his Apostles, placed upon the local Church the sole and final responsibility of its affairs — under himself.* That he did this in respect to the discipline of members, we have already seen.[1] We have seen also that he did it in regard to the election of Church officers.[2] We have seen that he did it in reference to all other necessary business of a Christian Church.[3] This ought to decide the matter.

He never hinted to his churches that they were to carry their work to others to be done, or their troubles to others to be settled, or their trials to others to be borne; but he directed *them* to 'fight the good fight of faith,' and to 'endure hardness' for him. And in the extremest case of difficulty and discipline, he did not instruct Paul to assume to interfere — either for himself, or for the twelve apostles — as being officially authorized to settle it; nor to advise or command the Church to lay the matter before Presbytery, Synod, or any other tribunal, but directed him rather to inform those interested, that the painful act of excommunication that had become necessary, would be properly done if done 'in the name of our Lord Jesus Christ,' by them, when 'gathered together.' He charged them to remember the words which their martyred teachers had spoken to them while they were yet present with them, and to obey the pious counsels of the living who were breaking to them the bread of life; but he never commanded them as churches to 'give place by subjection' to any power but his own; — 'no, not for an hour · that the truth of the gospel might continue with them.'

But, if Christ laid the direct responsibility of all their affairs upon the local churches; and if the texts cited by the advocates of some external jurisdiction over these churches are guiltless of any such suggestion; and if the general arguments of those advocates for such jurisdiction are equally baseless; and if the whole drift of the New Testament is in a direction opposite to that of any theory of control over the individual Church ; and if there is no evidence furnished by

---

[1] See pages 9, 41, 42.   [2] See pages 14-18, 40.   [3] See pages 18, 19, 43.

the Scriptures that any such jurisdiction was even attempted over the churches planted by the Apostles; and if there is no Biblical precept whatever, conferring the control of the local Church upon any man or body of men — it is an easy and inevitable inference that every true Christian Church is, and ought to be, inherently independent of any jurisdiction from without, except that of Christ its Head; who, though ascended 'unto his Father and our Father, and to his God and our God,' is yet never 'far from every one' of his churches, which 'in him live, and move, and have their being.'

2. *Every true Congregational Church — whatever may be the lowliness of its outward estate — is on a level of essential genuineness, dignity and authority, with every other Church on earth.* This is a necessary consequence of the obvious fact that a true Church of Christ gets its vitality, and value, not from the number of its members, or their wealth, or honorable position in human society; nor from the magnificence of its temple, or the splendor of its worship; nor from its affiliation with some wide-reaching and imposing hierarchy; but from its living union to its great Head. Since it is Christ's life,— rooted in him, branching in them — that must be the life of every true Church; and his wisdom and power, flowing from him through them, that must be their wisdom and power; it follows that wherever 'two or three' truly gathered in His name, have Him 'with them alway,' their wisdom may be — and, if they are faithful to their possibilities, will be — *Christ's* wisdom, and their dignity will be the dignity of Christ 'in the midst of them,' and their authority, the authority of Christ acting and speaking through them; while the largest and most imposing organization cannot have any wisdom that is wiser than that, nor any dignity that is more august than that, nor any strength that is stronger than that, nor any authority that is more imperial than that.

The function of a Church on earth is to let its "light shine before men,"[1] to be "the pillar and ground of the truth,"[2] — by "manifestation of the truth," to commend itself "to every man's conscience in the sight of God."[3] To do this, fidelity to the truth is the main essential. The 'little candle' that throws its beams afar —

"So shines a good deed in a naughty world;" —

---

[1] Matt. v: 16.   [2] 1 Tim. iii: 15.   [3] 2 Cor. iv: 2.

if it is only always burning, may be even more useful as a guide to the benighted traveller, than if it were a bonfire dazzling his vision by the brief brilliance of its blaze, only to make the night afterward darker around him, by the contrast. The little pilot-boat, that seems hardly more substantial than a cockle-shell on the heaving bosom of the sea, if it only know the way, may go before and pilot an Indiaman safe up the windings of the channel, to her wharf, even better than the Great Eastern could do in its place. And no Church can be so small in numbers, or so feeble in its pecuniary resources, or so humble in all its outward seeming, that — if it live the life of Christ — it may not safely 'bring unto their desired haven' all those around it who 'labor and are heavy laden,' and who seek the way to that 'rest that remaineth to the people of God.'

Moreover, a Church that is few in numbers, and feeble in its temporalities, is, by those very circumstances, thrown the more on its sense of dependence upon the strength of Christ, and is therefore the more likely to be in quick and constant sympathy with him. Driven to look to his Providence for its daily bread, it is not exposed to that temptation which proved too much for the Laodiceans,[1] and its religion will almost necessarily be more pure and fervent and effectual, than if its outward circumstances should seduce it to say 'I am rich, and increased with goods, and have need of nothing;' the fact being that this very worldly prosperity had blighted its spiritual life, until, with all its outward seeming of thrift, in the eye of God it is 'wretched, and miserable, and poor, and blind, and naked.' Piety is both the strength and the dignity of a Church of Christ. And piety is nurtured by the feeling of dependence for temporal, as well as spiritual blessings. There is often most prayer where there are fewest to pray; and there can be no doubt that many a log cabin on the Western frontier, which rudely shelters 'two or three' devout men, in the overlooking eye of Heaven lifts itself under the Sabbath sun with a loftier glory, than the proudest cathedral pile whose towering summit flushes with that sun's earliest and latest kiss. The voice of Christ will be just as true, just as wise, just as imperative, when it speaks through the conscience (enlightened by the Spirit, and the Word) of a little company of farmers in the back-woods, as when it utters itself

---

[1] Rev. iii: 14-22.

through the medium of the 'influential' and 'cultivated' membership of a thronged city Church; while reason and observation suggest that the obstacles to the pure deliverance of that voice, will be many more in the latter case, than in the former.

That little handful of North of England men — William Bradford, and George Morton, and Francis Jessop, and Richard Jackson, and Robert Rochester,[1] and their humble associates — as they used to steal along the green lanes between Austerfield, and Harworth, and Bawtry, toward the manor-house of the Archbishop of York, in Scrooby — then tenanted by William Brewster, who, as they "ordinarily mett at his house on ye Lord's day . . . with great love entertained them when they came, making provision for them to his great charge"[2] — to take sweet counsel together, and shake off the "yoake of antichristian bondage, and as ye Lord's free people, joyn themselves (by a covenant of the Lord) into a Church estate, in ye felowship of ye gospell, to walke in all his wayes, made known, or to be made known unto them, according to their best endeaours, whatsoever it should cost them, the Lord assisting them;"[3] were not only a true Church, but we might almost claim, — though so few, and, in outward seeming, so feeble and unprophetic of great results, — were the truest Church at that moment existing on the earth; having more of Christ's authority than any other, and concentrating within themselves — since the germs of American Christianity, and American missions, and even of American freedom, were there — more irresistible and more benignant might than any other. So it has again and again come true, that God hath "chosen the foolish things of the world to confound the wise; and God hath chosen the weak things of the world to confound the things which are mighty; and base things of the world and things which are despised, hath God chosen, yea, and things which are not, to bring to nought things that are; that no flesh should glory in his presence."

V. A FRATERNAL FELLOWSHIP IS YET TO BE MAINTAINED AMONG THESE INDEPENDENT CHURCHES, AND, WHEN INSOLUBLE DIFFICULTIES ARISE, OR SPECIALLY IMPORTANT MATTERS CLAIM

---

[1] Hunter's "Founders of New Plymouth," pp. 102-129.
[2] *Bradford's* "*Plimoth Plantation.*" (Ed. 1856.) p. 411.   [3] *Ibid.* p. 9.

DECISION (AS WHEN A PASTOR IS TO BE SETTLED OR DISMISSED, OR A CHURCH ITSELF IS TO ADOPT ITS CREED, AND COMMENCE ITS ORGANIC LIFE), IT IS PROPER THAT THE ADVICE OF OTHER CHURCHES SHOULD BE SOUGHT AND GIVEN, IN COUNCIL; SUCH ACTION IN NO CASE HOWEVER (EVEN WERE ADVICE THUS GIVEN TO BE SO REJECTED, AS TO NECESSITATE A TEMPORARY WITHDRAWAL OF FELLOWSHIP), BEING ANY THING MORE THAN A LABOR OF FRATERNAL SUASION, OR SELF-JUSTIFICATION.[1]

---

[1] Even Robert Browne — with all his Brownism — held to "a joining or partaking of the authority of elders, or forwardest and wisest, in a peaceable meeting, for redressing and deciding of matters in particular churches, and for counsel therein." — "*Points and Parts of all Divinity.*" (A. D. 1582.) *Def.* 51. *Hanbury.* Vol. i. p. 21.

John Robinson held that the elders of the churches should be called in council upon doubtful matters, and gave (A. D. 1624) as a reason why he had not earlier answered a letter sent to his Church at Leyden, from the Congregational Church in London, that "he conceives it not orderly that the bodies of churches should be sent to for counsel, but only some choice persons," etc. — *Works.* (Ed. 1851.) Vol. iii. p. 382.

"Though the Church of a particular Congregation, consisting of Elders and Brethren, and walking with a right foot in the truth and peace of the Gospel, be the first subject of all Church power needfull to be exercised within itself; and consequently be independent from any other Church or Synod in the use of it; yet it is a safe, and wholesome, and holy ordinance of Christ, for such particular churches to joyn together in holy Covenant or Communion, and consultation amongst themselves, to administer all their Church affairs (which are of weighty and difficult and common concernment), not without common consultation and consent of other churches about them. Now Church affairs of weighty and difficult and common concernment, wee account to be *the election and ordination of Elders, excommunication of an Elder,* or any *person of public note* and *employment — the translation of an Elder* from one Church to another, or the like. In which case we conceive it safe and wholesome, and an holy ordinance to proceed with common consultation and consent." — *John Cotton.* "*Keyes of the Kingdom.*" (Ed. 1852.) p. 102.

"When the matter is weightie, and the doubt great on both sides, then (with common consent) wee call in for light from other *churches;* and intreat them to send over to us such of their Elders, or Brethren, as may be fit to judge in such a cause; upon their coming, the Church meeting together in the name of Christ, the whole cause, and all the proceedings in it, are laid open to them; who by the help of Christ, pondering and studying all things according to the rule of the Word, the truth is cleared, a right way of peace and concord discovered and advised, and the spirits of the Brethren on all parts comfortably satisfied." — *John Cotton.* "*Wayes of the Churches.*" (Ed. 1645.) p. 96. See also pp. 105–107.

"Although churches be distinct, and therefore may not be confounded one with another; and equal, and therefore have not dominion one over another; yet all the churches ought to preserve Church communion one with another, because they are all united unto Christ, not only as a mystical, but as a political head, whence is derived a communion suitable thereunto. This communion is exercised sundry ways; (1.) by way of mutual care; (2.) by way of consultation one with another; (3.) by way of admonition; (4.) by way of participation; (5.) by way of recommendation; (6.) by way of relief and succor in case of need," etc. — *Cambridge Platform.* (A. D. 1648.) Chap. xv.

"Intireness of Church-government, in a particular Church compleated with its officers, *in re propria,* will well consist with that communion of churches which the Scripture establisheth. The reason is, because both are the Ordinances of Christ, and Christ's Ordinances do

As was said in the beginning (p. 2), Congregationalism differs from Independency, by its recognition of this practical fellowship be-

not interfere. . . . . . Therefore Church-communion must be only in a way of Brotherly association, for mutuall helpfulness, in matters of this nature, but not in way of subordination or subjection of one Church to the Ecclesiastical Government, whether of another Church, or of the Elders of several churches assembled in classes or synods," etc. — *John Davenport.* "*Power of Congregational Churches asserted and vindicated.*" p. 140.

"Their determinations (*i. e.*, those of Councils,) take place, not because they concluded so, but because the churches approved of what they have determined. For the churches sent them, and therefore are above them; and therefore may send others if they see fit, who may vary in their judgements, and alter their sentences if they see fit." — *Hooker.* "*Survey.*" Part iv. p. 47.

"The decree of a Council hath so much force as there is force in the reason of it." — *Richard Mather.* "*Church Government.*" (A. D. 1643.) p. 66.

"As all Protestant writers of note (Grotius only excepted,) approve of the Necessity and Usefulness of Ecclesiastical Councils, so do those of the Congregational Discipline. It has ever been their declared Judgment, that when there is Want of either Light or Peace in a Particular Church, it is their Duty to ask for Council, with which Neighbour Churches ought to assist by sending their Elders, and other Messengers, to advise and help them in their Difficulties. And that in Momentous Matters of common Concernment, Particular Churches should proceed with the concurrence of Neighbour Churches. So in the Ordination of a Pastor, much more in the deposing of one. Thus it has ever been in the Churches of New England." — *Increase Mather.* "*Disquisition concerning Ecclesiastical Councils.*" (A. D. 1716.) p. ix.

"The Synods of New England know no *Weapons* but what are purely spiritual. They pretend unto no *Juridical Power;* nor any significancy, but what is meerly *Instructive* and *Suasory.* They are nothing but some Wise and Good Men meeting together to advise the Churches how to observe the rules of the most Inoffensive *Piety.* When they have done all, the Churches are at Liberty, to judge how far their Advice is to be followed. They have no *Secular Arm* to enforce any *Canons;* They ask none; They want none." — *Cotton Mather.* "*Ratio Disciplinæ.*" (A. D. 1726.) p. 173.

"It is entirely consistent with *Reason and the Revelation of God's mind* in His Word, that there should be *Councils and Synods* called upon requisite Occasions. . . . . But there is great Danger, lest such Meetings should be *hurtful to the Principles and Liberties of particular Churches,* and so *degenerate from the good Ends* which ought to be designed and pursued in them. . . . . Wherefore it is to be hoped, that *the Brethren* in these Churches *will always maintain their Right to sit and act in Councils and Synods;* but yet that they will *never think of placing any juridical power* in them, but will *always continue to assert the Powers and Privileges of Particular Churches, which are sacred Things, by no means to be slighted and undervalued, nor to be left at the Mercy of any Classes or Councils, Synods or General Meetings.*" — *Samuel Mather.* "*Apology for the Liberties of the Churches in New England.*" (A. D. 1738.) pp. 109, 128.

See also John Wise's "Churches' Quarrel Espoused," *passim.*

"All the present disputes about Councils mutual, and ex-parte Councils, in respect to their *authority,* are vain and useless: because they have no divine authority at all. . . . . The human device of giving *power* to Associations, or Consociations, or Councils, to decide in Ecclesiastical causes, has been a fruitful source of Ecclesiastical injustice, tyranny, and persecution." — *Dr. Emmons. Works.* (Ed. 1860.) Vol. iii. pp. 584, 586.

"It is an acknowledged principle in respect to Councils, that they possess only advisory powers; in other words, their decisions are addressed to the understandings and consciences of men, and are enforced solely by moral obligations. They are considered by the churches as interpreters or expositors of what is right, expediency, and duty, in the particular cases submitted to them. Their proper business is to GIVE LIGHT." — *Upham.* "*Ratio Disciplinæ.*" p. 185.

tween the churches. Such fellowship, we believe to be both Scriptural and reasonable.

1. *We hold it to be Scriptural, as being involved in Scriptural principles, and substantially enjoined by Scriptural precept and example.* The unity of the visible Church,[1] and the family relation

---

"Councils may be called, and may give advice; but this advice may be accepted or rejected." — *Dr. Pond.* "*The Church.*" (Ed. 1860.) p. 83.

"They believe that it is the duty of Christian churches to hold communion with each other, to entertain an enlarged affection for each other, as members of the same body, and to co-operate for the promotion of the Christian cause: but that no Church, nor union of churches, has any right or power to interfere with the faith or discipline of any other Church, further than to separate from such as, in faith or practice, depart from the Gospel of Christ." — "*Principles of Church order,*" etc., *of Congregational Union of England and Wales.* Sec. 10.

"This, then, I suppose to be the doctrine of ancient and modern Congregationalists: — In cases of difficulty, a Church, or the aggrieved members of a Church, may call for the advice of a council of sister churches; and this advice the Church is bound respectfully to consider and cheerfully to follow, unless manifestly contrary to what is right and Scriptural; but of this, the Church has an undoubted right to judge; and to act in accordance with its deliberate judgment." — *Punchard.* "*View of Congregationalism.*" (Ed. 1860.) p. 117.

"In a multitude of counsellors there is safety. Whatever wisdom be centered in a single Christian society, cases will arise in which it may be benefited by the counsel of others. Yet it is not wise to resort to them [Councils] too often. Their assistance may be sought far too frequently. Matters comparatively trifling, which might be adjusted in another way, may be brought before such tribunals. This is not judicious. There must be a felt, urgent necessity for councils. They ought not to be lightly summoned, or hastily appealed to. Nothing but unusual difficulty or injustice should bring them into being." — *Dr. Davidson.* "*Ecclesiastical Polity of the New Testament.*" p. 341.

"The communion of churches with each other, and especially of 'neighbor churches' in mutual recognition, mutual helpfulness, and mutual responsibility, is not something forced into the Congregational system, *ab extra*, by the pressure of experience; a merely empirical expedient borrowed from Presbyterianism; a new piece of cloth sewed upon an old garment; but is an essential element of the system, as laid down in all the ancient platforms, and as explained and defended by the Congregational fathers more than two hundred years ago, on both sides of the ocean." — "*New Englander.*" Vol. xiv. (1856.) p. 22.

"Councils often assume authority which they do not possess. The style of language which they use in their *results* is often exceedingly objectionable. When called, for instance, to *advise* a Church with regard to dismissing its minister, the Council not unfrequently takes the business entirely into its own hands, and, after hearing a representation of the case, of its own authority *pronounces* the minister *dismissed.* 'And hereby,' they say, '*he is dismissed.*' Other assumptions of authority, equally glaring and equally inconsistent with the fundamental principles of Congregationalism, are frequently made by Councils; and there are reasons of the most imperative nature why every practice of this kind should be at once corrected..... An Ecclesiastical Council should always make the impression, both by their demeanor and their language, that their work is *advisory* or *persuasive;* or, as in the case of their actually ordaining a minister, that they act simply as *the servants of the Church*, performing the work of its members for them, and only at their request. It should not only be understood, but it should be more distinctly and formally acknowledged than it usually is, both by the ordaining Council and the members of the Church, that the ordaining power is vested in the Church, and not in the Council." — *Wellman's* "*Church Polity of the Pilgrims.*" (Ed. 1857.) p. 114.

[1] 1 Cor. xii: 13; Eph. iv: 4; John xvii: 20-22.

subsisting between its branches,[1] make it at once a natural and proper inference that a constant fellowship between those branches, should conserve that unity.

So the general suggestions — "with the well-advised is wisdom,"[2] "he that hearkeneth unto counsel is wise,"[3] "where no counsel is, the people fall; but in the multitude of counsellors, there is safety,"[4] "without counsel, purposes are disappointed; but in the multitude of counsellors they are established,"[5] are calculated (and no doubt intended) to suggest to churches, as forcibly as to individuals, the value of advice and sympathy in cases of doubt and difficulty. Moreover, those precepts which make it the duty of all Christians to "walk by the same rule," and "mind the same thing,"[6] to "have fellowship one with another,"[7] to be "fellow-helpers to the truth,"[8] to be "fellow-workers unto the kingdom of God,"[9] to be "kindly affectioned one to another, with brotherly love,"[10] to be "likeminded one toward another, according to Christ Jesus,"[11] to "be of one mind," and "live in peace,"[12] to "keep the unity of the Spirit, in the bond of peace,"[13] to "walk in love, as Christ also hath loved us,"[14] to "stand fast in one spirit, with one mind striving together for the faith of the Gospel,"[15] to "love one another with a pure heart, fervently,"[16] to "withdraw yourselves," and "admonish as a brother, him that walketh disorderly,"[17] neither to "bid him God speed"[18] who bringeth not Christ's doctrine; to "come out from among them" who touch the "unclean thing,"[19] — all involve those duties for all individual churches, as truly as for all individual Christians, and require, for their proper exercise, such a theory of natural Church communion, and watchfulness, and counselling, as distinguishes Congregationalism from Independency, properly so called.

Add to this the direct force of the example recorded in the 15th chapter of the Acts, where counsel was asked of the Church in Jerusalem, by the Church at Antioch, in its difficulties — even while the Apostles still remained, and still retained the authority of inspiration

---

[1] 1 Thess. iv: 9, 10; Heb. xiii: 1; 1 Pet. i: 22, ii: 17; 1 John iii: 11-23, iv: 7-21.
[2] Prov. xiii: 10.
[3] Prov. xii: 15.
[4] Prov. xi: 14.
[5] Prov. xv: 22.
[6] Phil. iii: 16.
[7] 1 John i: 7.
[8] 3 John: 8.
[9] Col. iv: 11.
[10] Rom. xii: 10.
[11] Rom. xv: 5.
[12] 2 Cor. xiii: 11.
[13] Eph. iv: 3.
[14] Eph. v: 2.
[15] Phil. i: 27.
[16] 1 Pet. i: 22.
[17] 2 Thess. iii: 6, 15.
[18] 2 John: 10.
[19] 2 Cor. vi: 17.

within reach of the Church — and there seems to be clear warrant from the Bible, for the custom of Councils called by churches, in the Congregational manner.

2. *Being Scriptural, we hold that manner to be also reasonable.* It is founded upon the facts: — that all Congregational churches stand upon the same grace of God in the regeneration of the individuals of whom they are composed; upon the same platform of Bible doctrine as the foundation and rule of their life; upon the same Holy Spirit as their Comforter and Guide; and upon the same Jesus Christ as the Saviour of their individual members, and the Great Captain and Head of their associated host. Having the same nature, need, and temptations, the same salvation, the same origin and end, the same rule and aim, the same stimulus and reward, the same love and life; being thus one in all their constituent elements and aspirations; it is reasonable for them to befriend each other, to watch each other's progress as they march side by side along the 'king's highway,' and fraternally to say: —

> "We'll bear each other's loads, for we,
> Neighbors in aim, in toil should be.
> So shall our wayfare easier hold —
> More long for peace, more short for pain;
> Such kindness yields a thousand fold
> In blessings sown and reaped again."

As separate members of the one body of Christ, it must always be true of all the churches, that "whether one member suffer, all the members suffer with it; or one member be honored, all the members rejoice with it;" or one member be perplexed, all the members sympathize and consult with it — and this is all which the Congregational doctrine of Councils involves.

It is proper to add here a word in regard to their details — though they will be discussed more fully in another place.[1]

The theory of a Council always is, that the Church desiring advice, asks that advice of such of its sister *churches* as it may select for that purpose. And as those churches cannot respond, and tender the desired counsel *en masse*, they send a delegation of their membership — usually headed by their pastors — to act in their stead. By con-

---

[1] See Chap. iii.

sequence, it is the *churches*, constructively, that are present and form the Council; and the pastors, and other delegates, are not there by any official or individual right, but simply because they were *sent* by bodies which could not attend in person, and which therefore act through them.

Councils are of two kinds — *mutual* and *ex-parte*.

A mutual Council is one in the calling of which, all parties to the difficulty, or perplexity concerning which relief is sought, unite. An ex-parte Council is one which is called by one of those parties, after every proper effort to induce all interested to call a mutual Council, has failed; and no ex-parte Council has a right to proceed to the consideration of the case before it, until it has satisfied itself that every reasonable endeavor to secure a mutual Council has been tried, and failed, and until it has offered itself as a mutual Council to all parties, and been rejected as such. This grows out of the simple principle that advice for the relief of perplexity, and the healing of difficulty, should be founded upon the full and candid consideration of *all* related facts, — which implies the coöperation of *all* concerned; while such advice will be the more likely to produce a salutary effect, the more fully all parties have previously presented their views of those questions on which it is sought. Where Christian principle fully governs all those minds which are interested in the matter in debate, an ex-parte Council can never be necessary; for a mutual Council can always be agreed upon by those who are sincerely desirous of finding the path of duty, and honestly willing to follow wherever it may lead. But, as Christian principle sometimes loses its hold upon Christian professors, "it must needs be that offences come," which will sometimes require an ex-parte Council for their adjustment.

Councils have no *authority* whatsoever — properly so called. They are invited to give advice, and it is *advice* which they give; which the parties inviting them, may accept or reject, according to their own conscientious conviction of their duty to God in the matter. Yet there is a moral and spiritual weight in their decisions, growing out of the facts: — that when good men, the representatives of Christian churches, meet, and in the fear of God, and with invocation of the wisdom of the Spirit, prayerfully investigate a point, and deliberately make up their minds concerning it, there is great inherent probability that they will be right; and that since this way of Councils is Christ's appointed way out of difficulty for the local Church, it is reasonable to hope and expect that his special guidance — as its Great Head — will make itself appear in their decisions, when reached as carefully, humbly, thoughtfully, patiently, and prayerfully, as they always ought to be. So great, therefore, is the weight of probability in favor of the rightness of the advice of such a Council, and so strong the presumption that it ought to be followed by those to whom it is given, that nothing but the clearest evidence of its being in error, can justify the honest followers of Christ in failing to comply with it.

Presbyterians who have become Congregationalists — or who act as Congregationalists, without becoming such — are very apt to confuse our Councils with their own judicatories; and, finding it difficult to imagine how we can live without somehow being governed from without, are apt to conceive of Councils as bodies having authority, and set, like the centurion, to say 'unto one, Go, and he goeth; and to another, Come, and he cometh; and to its servant, Do this, and he doeth it.' And — partly from the presence of those trained in Presbyterianism, and partly from the forgetfulness of many Congregationalists of their own first principles, favored by that love of control which is natural to man — our Councils have not unfrequently assumed, or seemed to assume, in their 'results,' the language of power, rather than that of persuasion; decreeing, rather than dissuading from the wrong; enacting, rather than exhorting toward the right.

But, as it is one of our fundamental principles,[1] that no Church has, or can have, any authority over any other Church, and as the members of all Councils have their seats in them only as representatives of their churches — which can communicate to their delegates no authority which they do not themselves possess; it is plain that no Council can have any Scriptural right to do any thing more than advise those who have called it together. And as Christ has placed upon every local Church, the sole responsibility of its own affairs, it would have no right to submit itself to the authority of any Council, if any authority were assumed by one.

The whole truth is tersely stated thus, by one of the ablest of our younger writers:[2] — "The Congregational doctrine of the authority

---

[1] Pages 44-56.   [2] Rev. A. H. Quint, in *Cong. Quarterly*, Vol. ii. pp. 63, 64

of Councils, therefore is this: Councils come into being by the call of parties inviting. They have power to organize; power to examine credentials — with no power to enlarge or diminish their number; power to examine the subject specified in the 'Letters Missive,' but no other subject; power to hear evidence; power to deliberate on the proper course to be taken in reference to that subject; power to advise the parties inviting them what to do in the matter — with no power to *direct* or *order* any particular course, or to reverse individual Church action; and — with power to pray a good deal more for Divine assistance than many Councils have done — they have power to dissolve."

It may be asked, in case a Church should decline to adopt the advice of Council, is there any remedy; and is there any good of that Council? We reply that there is at least this good of that Council — if it has done its work as it ought to do it; namely, its result has placed in a clear light before that Church, and the world around it, that course of duty which it is morally bound to pursue; and as passion cools, and those unchristian elements which have warped it from its better judgment by and by subside, that advice of Council, by the silent appeal of its justness, will constrain the Church to its adoption. It is no small matter to have a comparatively impartial community looking on and justifying such a result, and condemning such a Church. In the end, that which ought to be done will be done, and that supremacy of Christian principle over the community which is temporarily imperiled by the aberration of the offending Church, will be meanwhile maintained by that Christian result of Council, representing the moral force of the Church universal there, and saying to all concerned, 'this is the way, walk ye in it.'

Technically, there is no remedy for the refusal of a Church to follow the advice of Council; that is, the Council has no power to enforce its advice — for it ceased to exist, as a Council, and became resolved into its constituent members, as soon as its advice was given. The case may indeed be conceived of, where — in case the non-following of advice of Council involves the fellowship of the churches, or some breach of morality, or heresy of doctrine — the churches whose delegates had composed the Council, might feel themselves compelled to suspend fraternal intercourse with the offending Church, during its aberration from the commonly received path of duty; but they would take such action on the merits of the main question, and not because the advice of their delegates in Council had not been followed; standing, in all respects, in the same position with other sister churches which had not been invited to send delegates to the Council, but which are moved to unite together in this cessation of fraternity, on the Scriptural ground of 'withdrawing' from those who 'walk disorderly.'

Thus the Congregational doctrine of Councils — like other of our doctrines — throws us back immediately upon the Saviour, and compels us to exercise a quick and living confidence in him, and his watchful care over those churches which he has 'redeemed unto God by his blood.' We are not suffered to rest in the decrees — easily obtained, however dull may be our perceptions of truth, and however sluggish our faith in Christ — of any human tribunal; but we are perpetually driven to clarify our sense of Divine things, and quicken our hold upon the Spirit, and deepen our consciousness of dependence upon Him who is 'head over all things' to us, by that ever and everywhere recurring motto of our system, which has as real a meaning to us in things Ecclesiastical, as in the matter of our personal salvation — "*we walk by faith, not by sight.*"

VI. THE PERMANENT OFFICERS WHICH CHRIST DESIGNATED FOR HIS CHURCH, ARE OF TWO, AND ONLY TWO CLASSES; THE FIRST, — FOR THE CARE OF ITS SPIRITUAL CONCERNS — PASTORS (INDISCRIMINATELY STYLED, IN THE NEW TESTAMENT, PASTORS AND TEACHERS, PRESBYTERS OR ELDERS, AND BISHOPS OR OVERSEERS,) THE SECOND, — FOR THE CARE OF ITS TEMPORAL CONCERNS — DEACONS; BOTH TO BE CHOSEN BY THE MEMBERSHIP FROM THEIR OWN NUMBER.

Here are four points for proof: —

1. Christ — by the precept and example of his Apostles — designated only two classes of permanent officers for a Christian Church.

2. The first class — for the care of its spiritual concerns — are indiscriminately styled, in the New Testament, Pastors, Teachers, Presbyters or Elders, and Bishops or Overseers.

3. The second class — for the care of its temporal concerns — are called Deacons.

4. Both are to be chosen and set apart by the Church, from its own membership.

1. *Christ designated only two classes of permanent officers for his churches.*[1] The following, it is believed, are all the titles which have been supposed to be associated with office in connection with the churches of Christ in the New Testament; namely: Apostles,[2]

---

[1] "It remaineth therefore, that the ordinary Officers of the Church which are to continue to the comming of Christ Jesus, are either Elders (whom the Apostle calleth also Bishops, Tit. i: 5, 7; Acts xx: 17-28) or Deacons," etc. —*John Cotton.* "*Way of the Churches.*" p. 10.

"Finding the first Epistle to Timothy passing from the Directions for the good Conduct of *Bishops*, immediately to those for that of *Deacons*, without any mention of *Presbyters* distinct from them, is it not as evident as a Noonday Sun can make any thing in the world unto us, that there are only those Two *Ordinary Officers* instituted by the LORD for the Service of His Churches, and that there is no Institution for any other *Bishops*, but the *Pastors of Particular Congregations?*—*Cotton Mather.* "*Some Seasonable Inquiries.*" (A. D. 1723.) p. 2.

"When we look at the settled state of the churches, after charisms had generally ceased — when the minds of Christians were no longer elevated and enlightened by extraordinary influences of the Spirit — when all that remained of the gifted brethren appeared in the elders — men favored with less remarkable manifestations; we shall find no other office-bearers besides them, than those attending to the secular affairs. Bishops and Deacons were intended to continue in the churches of Christ; other offices were temporary." — *Davidson's* "*Ecclesiastical Polity of the New Testament.*" p. 153.

"The original and ordinary officers of the Church consisted of two classes; the first, known by different names, ἐπίσκοποι — *overseers, superintendents, bishops; πρεσβύτεροι — presbyters, elders; διδάσκαλοι — teachers; ποιμένες — pastors*, etc.: the second, διάκονοι — *servants, deacons.*" — *Coleman's* "*Ancient Christianity.*" p. 127.

"All the distinction we can admit between bishops and presbyters then, is that the latter was particularly the name of dignity, the former the name designating the function, or particular sphere of activity. . . . Besides these, we find only one other Church office in the Apostolic age — that of Deacons."—*Neander.* "*History of the Christian Church.*" Vol. 1. pp. 186, 188.

"Can any thing be made more plain, by Scripture testimony, than the correctness of this doctrine of Congregationalism, that elder, pastor, bishop, are different titles of the same Church officer? . . . . If this be an admitted fact, and the soundness of the first principle of Congregationalism be allowed — that the Scriptures are our safe and only guide in respect to Church polity — then it must follow, that no distinction should now be made between elders and bishops. This is Congregational doctrine. Deacons are the only other permanent Church officers recognized by Congregationalists." *Punchard's* "*View.*" pp. 97, 98.

"We come back, then, with entire confidence upon what we conceive to be the doctrine of the New Testament, that there are but two distinct *orders*, or *classes* of officers in the Church of Christ; the one having charge of the *spiritual* concerns of the Church, the other of its *temporal* concerns: the one commonly denominated *bishops* or *presbyters*, the other *deacons.*" — Dr. Pond's "*The Church.*" p. 71.

"They believe that the only officers placed by the Apostles over individual churches, are the bishops or pastors, and the deacons; the number of these being dependent upon the numbers of the Church; and that to these, as the officers of the Church, is committed respectively the administration of its spiritual and temporal concerns — subject, however, to the approbation of the Church." — "*Principles of Church Order.*" *Congregational Union of England and Wales.* v.

[2] Luke vi: 13; 1 Cor. xii: 28; Eph. iv: 11, etc.

Evangelists,[1] Prophets,[2] Pastors,[3] Teachers,[4] Presbyters or Elders,[5] Bishops,[6] Angels of the Church,[7] Deacons,[8] and Deaconesses.[9]

Of these it will probably be conceded at once that the *Apostles* and *Prophets*, having been divinely endowed and commissioned with miraculous gifts for a special work in connection with the early days of Christianity, are to be regarded as extraordinary laborers, having no successors in the peculiar relation which they sustained to the churches.[10] The office of *Deaconess* seems also to have had relations so peculiar to the condition of women in the East in the early times of the Church, — by rigorous social usage, nearly inaccessible to the helpful visitation of the male functionaries of the Church — as to have become outgrown in that onward march of society which Christianity has caused, by which the condition of women has been raised to a level with that of the other sex; so that — in the absence of any precept for its continuance — this too may be classed among extraordinary offices, the supply of which has ceased — and was intended to cease — with the demand.[11]

---

[1] Eph. iv: 11; Acts xxi: 8; 2 Tim. iv: 5.   [2] 1 Cor. xii: 28; Eph. iv: 11; Acts xiii: 1.
[3] Eph. iv: 11.   [4] Eph. iv: 11; Acts xiii: 1; 1 Cor. xii: 28.
[5] Acts xi: 30; xiv: 23; xv: 2, 4, 6, 22, 23; 1 Tim. v: 17; Tit. i: 5; James v: 14, etc.
[6] Phil. i: 1; 1 Tim. iii: 1, 2; Tit. i: 7.   [7] Rev. i: 20; ii: 1, 8, 12, 18; iii: 1, 7, 14.
[8] Acts vi: 1-7; Phil. i: 1; 1 Tim. iii: 8, 10, 12, 13.
[9] Rom. xvi: 1; 1 Tim. iii: 11.

[10] "The Apostolical office, as such, was personal and temporary; and therefore, according to its nature and design, not successive or communicable to others in perpetual descendence from them. It was, as such, in all respects extraordinary, conferred in a special manner, designed for special purposes, discharged by special aids, endowed with special privileges, as was needful for the propagation of Christianity, and founding of churches." — *Barrow.* "*Pope's Supremacy.*" *Works.* (Ed. 1845) Vol. iii. p. 115.

"This office, [the Apostle's] from its nature, was temporary, and was confined to those who had been with him [the Saviour] during his public ministry, and whom he had specially called for this purpose, with Matthias, who was chosen to fill the vacated place of Judas, and Paul, who was called to the *special* work of the Apostleship among the Gentiles, and permitted to see the Saviour in a miraculous manner, after his ascension, *in order* that he might have the appropriate qualification of an Apostle .. There is no evidence whatever that the office of 'prophet' was intended to be permanent." — *Barnes.* "*Apostolic Church.*" pp. 191, 196.

[11] "Phebe our sister," was a διακονον — *deaconess* [*servant*] "of the Church, which is at Cenchrea." Neander (*Pfl. u. Leit.* Ed. 4, pp. 265—267) proves that the deaconesses, of whom Phebe was one, ought not to be considered as identical with the "widows" of 1 Tim. v: 3-16. The "Apostolical Constitutions" settle it that, when they were written, there was no identity between the two, for it is commanded that the deaconesses be selected from among the virgins, but when this could not be, they must, at least, be widows. (See Chase's "*Apos. Con.*" p. 374.) The reason for their appointment comes out in *Book* iii. Chap. xv. "*Apos. Con.*" where it is commanded: — "Ordain also a Deaconess, who is faithful and holy, for the ministrations to the women. For sometimes thou canst not send a Deacon, who is a man, to the women in

The precise meaning of the term *Angel of the Church*, as used in the Apocalypse,[1] has been the subject of some controversy. The word ἄγγελος (*aggelos*) literally means 'one who is sent,' 'a messenger,' and perhaps its most natural sense in this connection would be to understand it as referring to the pastor of the Church as the messenger of God to it for instruction, and its messenger to God in the offering of worship. At any rate it is clear that no hint is given in the New Testament of any other officer of the Church who might more appropriately bear the name, and the weight of critical authority[2] is altogether in favor of such an exposition of the phrase as

---

certain houses, on account of the unbelievers. Thou shalt therefore send a woman, a Deaconess, on account of the imaginations of the bad."

Pliny, in his celebrated letter to Trajan, says "necessarium credidi, ex duabus ancillis quæ *ministræ* dicebantur, quid esset veri et per tormenta quærere;"—"I deemed it necessary to put two maid-servants, who are called *deaconesses*, to the torture, to ascertain the truth." The "even so must *their wives* be grave," etc., (1 Tim. iii: 11) most probably refers to this order of female officers. Literally it is " Even so must γυναῖκας — [*the women*] be grave," etc. Alford says (*Com. in loco.*) that these are *deaconesses*: — " In this view the ancients are, as far as I know, unanimous. Of the moderns, it is held by Grotius, Michælis, De Wette, Wiesinger, and Ellicott."

[1] Rev. i: 20; ii: 1, 8, 12, 18; iii: 1, 7, 14.

[2] " Certain it is, ἄγγελος signifieth no more than is common to all ministers, namely, to be God's messengers, and move upon his errand." — *Poole's Annotations, in loco.*

" By ἄγγελος we are to understand the messenger or person sent by God to preside over this Church, and to him the epistle is directed, not as pointing out his state, but the state of the Church under his care. *Angel of the Church* here answers exactly to that officer of the synagogue among the Jews, called *sheliach tsibbur*, the messenger of the Church, whose business was to read, pray, and teach in the synagogue." — *Adam Clarke, Comment. in loco.*

" And to the angel, *or minister*, of the Church which is in Smyrna, Pergomos," etc.—*Doddridge's "Family Expositor," in loco.*

" He holds in his hand the seven stars which are the angels, *or ministers*, of the churches." —*Wordsworth " On the Apocalypse."* p. 139.

" By Angels of the Churches must be here understood those *rulers of the Christian Church*, whose office it was to offer up public prayers in the Church, to manage sacred concerns, and discourse to the people."—*Vitringa.* "*Anakr. Apoc.*" p. 25.

" As the Gospel is preached only by *men*, this 'angel' who has it to preach to 'every nation and kindred and tongue and people' must be *the symbol of a human ministry.*"—*Dr. J. M. Mason. Works.* Vol. 2. p. 147.

" The word [angel] designates here the *leading teacher*, or *religious instructor* in the Asiatic Churches."—*Stuart. Comment. in loco.*

" The conclusion, then, to which we have come, is that the 'angel of the Church' was the pastor or the presiding presbyter in the Church; the minister who had the pastoral charge of it, and who was therefore a proper representative of it."—*Barnes. Comment. in loco.*

Archbishop Whately refers the term 'angel' here to the pastor of the Church, but supposes him to have been nominated by the Apostles, and so an ἄγγελος in virtue of being sent by *them*. He says:—" It seems plainly to have been at least the general, if not the universal, practice of the Apostles, to appoint over each separate Church a single individual, as a chief Governor, under the title of ' Angel,' (*i. e.* Messenger, or Legate from the Apostles"), etc. —"*Kingdom of Christ.*" (Carter's Ed.) p. 44.

takes it out of the catalogue of separate functionaries ordinary or extraordinary, and makes it but another special synonyme for the chief permanent officer of the Church.

The term *Evangelist*[1] occurs three times in the New Testament. It literally means 'a messenger of good tidings.' Such were Philip the deacon, Timothy and Titus. Evangelists seem to have corresponded almost precisely with what are known in our day as *missionaries* — whose business it is to preach the Gospel in 'the regions beyond' the already Christianized part of the world. Some indeed have supposed that they were temporary laborers,[2] whose special duty ceased with the age of the Apostles and of miracles; but whether this be so or not, it is generally agreed that, as their function was a peculiar one, leading them out where churches did not exist, they

---

Those who wish to study the subject thoroughly, are commended to an article in the *Bibliotheca Sacra*, for April, 1855, from the pen of Rev. Isaac Jennings, of Ongar, England, who gives nine different previous expositions of the phrase, and then proposes two more. That which he favors is a reference of the word *angel* to its literal sense, understanding it of delegates or messengers sent by the seven churches to visit John in Patmos, and bearing thence these epistles to the respective bodies which sent them. This he thinks "meets the *exigentia loci*; is perfectly natural in itself; meets and removes various difficulties, and is open to no fair grammatical, logical, or theological objection." (p. 343.)

[1] Acts xxi: 8; Eph iv. 11; 2 Tim iv: 5.

[2] "Apostles, Evangelists, and Prophets were bestowed on the Church for a limited time only, — except in those cases where religion has fallen into decay, and evangelists are raised up in an extraordinary manner, to restore the pure doctrine which had been lost." — *Calvin. Comment. Eph. iv: 11.* (*Calvin Translation Society's translation.*)

"But for the continuance of this office of an Evangelist in the Church, there is no direction in the Epistles either to Timothy or Titus, or any where else in Scripture." — *John Cotton.* "*Keyes*," etc. p. 78.

"Although the office of Evangelist corresponded with that of a modern *missionary*, it may be fairly inferred that it was *temporary*, being so connected with the Apostolic functions, that when the latter ceased, *it* necessarily ceased at the same time. There are no Apostles in the present day to send forth Evangelists on special errands; neither do men possess the extraordinary gifts which belonged to the primitive Evangelists. Paul makes no mention of them along with bishops and deacons, in his directions to Timothy. The office in question, like that of an Apostle, was not confined to one Church; whereas, no office-bearers intended to be permanent in the Christian dispensation belong to *more than one* Church. Modern missionaries, improperly said to be *ordained* before their departure to heathen lands, sustain no *office*. They do not become office-bearers till a Christian Church invite them to take oversight of them in the Lord, and they accept the call." — *Dr. Davidson*. "*Eccles. Pol. of New Test.*" p. 145.

"If all are not agreed that this office [of Evangelist] was *temporary*, they are agreed that it does not belong essentially to the structure of a local Church." — *Art.* "*Church Offices.*" *Spirit of the Pilgrims.* Vol. iv. (1831), p. 136.

See an excellent article on "Evangelists," by Dr. Pond in the *New Englander*, (1844), Vol. ii. pp. 297–303.

See also an article, of an opposite tenor, by C. Colton, in the *Monthly Christian Spectator*, (1828), Vol. x. pp. 292–296, 337–340, 393–398.

cannot — whether intended to be temporary or not — properly be considered as a class of permanent officers in the churches.

There are in the New Testament two instances of the formal enumeration of laborers and gifts in connection with the Church. The first is,[1] — "God hath set some in the Church, first, Apostles; secondarily, prophets; thirdly, teachers; after that miracles; then gifts of healings, helps, governments,[2] diversities of tongues." The other is,[3] — "Wherefore he saith, when he ascended up on high, he led captivity captive, and gave gifts unto men. And he gave some, Apostles; and some, prophets; and some, evangelists; and some, pastors and teachers."

Here are, in addition to those we have already considered, and in addition to those which we reserve for consideration under the next head, these five specifications; namely: 'miracles,' 'gifts of healings,' 'helps,' 'governments,' and 'diversities of tongues.' The connection in which the words are used, evidently implies that there were in the primitive churches, either distinct classes of laborers, or distinct conditions of laboring, intended to be characterized by the different terms of this enumeration. It is obvious, moreover, from the tenor of a large portion of these catalogues, that they were rather designed to chronicle those facts which existed in the semi-miraculous age of the Church, than to lay down rules and prescribe officers for its future.[4] Still, since the normal platform on which Christ intended his Church permanently to rest, may be presumed to underlie, or interlie, whatever was miraculous and adapted specially for its initial necessities, we may hope to gain light as to the Divine plan for it in all ages, by studying these unusual provisions for its exigencies in the beginning; remembering, all the while, that the mere mention of a name here,

---

[1] 1 Cor. xii: 28.

[2] The authorized (King James') version (A. D. 1611) translates these two "helpes in governments;" running the two together. So far as we know, this was the first instance of such a rendering. The Rheims version (A. D. 1582) has it "helpes, gouernements," etc. That of Geneva (A. D. 1557) renders it "helpers, gouernors;" as does Cranmer. (A. D. 1539.) Tyndale (A. D. 1534) gives it like the Genevan rendering; while Wiclif (A. D. 1380) says "helpyngis, gouernaills."

[3] Eph. iv: 8, 11.

[4] "In the catalogue of the spiritual men given here, there is no mention made of *Bishops, Elders, and Deacons*, the standing ministers in the Church. The reason is, the Apostle mentions only those to whose offices the [miraculous] spiritual gifts were necessary, and who were to be laid aside when the spiritual gifts were withdrawn. Now Bishops, Elders, and Deacons were not of that kind." — *Macknight on the Epistles*, p. 189.

provided it occur no where else in the Bible, and particularly if it have no recognition in those portions of the New Testament which specially set forth the nature and duties of those offices which confessedly were meant to be permanent, can hardly warrant the conclusion that it describes a functionary vital to Christ's idea of the working of his Church in every age. A very probable theory, indeed, is that urged by Doddridge, and others,[1] that the reference here is not at all to distinct offices or officers, but rather to different methods of labor in which the skill and usefulness of the same persons found expression, at different times, and under different circumstances; making these, catalogues rather of ways of usefulness, than of separate helpers.

Still another explanation deserving mention is that of Dr. Owen,[2] that the reference here is to persons endowed (for the special needs of the Church in its beginning), with extraordinary gifts "which did not of themselves constitute them officers," but which "belong to the second head of gifts which concern duties only." So that, in his judgment, if these texts describe different workers, they do not necessarily describe so many different officers for the Church.

A careful examination, however, of the terms employed must be our best guide to their meaning.

Miracles (δυνάμεις — *dunameis*)[3] is obviously an abstract noun put

---

[1] "I have met with no remark here, which seems more pertinent than that of Mons. Amyraut; who thinks that the same persons might possess *many* of these gifts, and sustain *several* of these characters, which were not stated distinct offices; and might be called *helpers* in reference to their great dexterity and readiness to help those in distress; and *governments* in regard to that genius for business, sagacity in judging the circumstances of affairs, and natural authority in the councils and resolutions of societies, which rendered them fit to preside on such occasions."— *Doddridge.* "*Family Expositor,*" *in loco. Works.* (Leeds, 1805.) Vol. ix. p. 67.

"It may indeed have happened, that one individual was endowed with many gifts, and sustained two of the offices here enumerated; nor was there in this any inconsistency."— *Calvin. Comment. in loco.*

"It is a matter of course that one individual might enjoy at the same time several gifts, and that the principal Apostles especially possessed many Charismata." — *Olshausen. Comment.* 1 Cor. xii: 7–11. (Kendrick's Ed.) Vol. iv. p. 845.

"He here passes to the *abstract* nouns from the *concrete;* perhaps because no definite class of persons was endowed with each of the following, but they were promiscuously granted to all orders in the Church."—*Alford. Comment. in loco.* Vol. ii. p. 552.

[2] *Works.* (Ed. 1852.) Vol. iv. p. 439.

[3] The Tigurine version of the New Testament by Petrus Cholinus, and Rodolphus Gualtherus — on the basis of that of Erasmus — (A. D. 1543) translates the verse thus: — "Et alios quidem posuit Deus in Ecclesia, primum Apostolos, deinde prophetas, tertio doctores, deinde *potestates* [the Vulgate says here — '*virtutes*'] deinde dona sanatiorum, subsidia, guberna-

here to a concrete use,[1] standing for *workers of miracles;* thus, by its necessary significance, excluding itself from any application to the Church in its permanent existence, after the day of miracles should cease.

Gifts of Healings (χαρίσματα ἰαμάτων — *charismata iamatōn*) has, as obviously, reference to those miraculous endowments for the cure of disease, which were conferred by the Holy Spirit upon early Christian teachers;[2] and by the same necessity is in like manner excluded from our consideration as a permanent element in the agencies of the Church.

Helps (ἀντιλήψεις — *antilēpseis*) primarily means *laying hold of,* whence it gets a secondary meaning of *laying hold of for the purpose of aiding and supporting,* whence it derives the sense, in which it seems to be employed here (its only use in the New Testament,) of *those who help, or support.* The most natural reference of it is to the deacons of the Church, whose office it exactly describes.[3]

Governments (κυβερνήσεις — *kubernēseis*) is a word found no where else in the Bible. Its primary significance is sufficiently plain from

---

tiones, genera linguarum." And Gualtherus, in his "*Homiliæ in Priorem D. Pauli Epistolam ad Corinthios,*" comments on this translation thus: — "Quarto loco *Potestates* numerantur, pro iis, qui potestatem in Ecclesia legitimam exercent. Erant hi seniores, qui disciplinæ præfecti eos corrigebant, qui aliquid contra hominis Christiani officium fecissent: impios vero et contumaces majori spiritus virtute cohercebant." — (Ed. 1572.) p. 196.

[1] " More Hebræo abstractum pro concreto, ut in sequentibus."— *Grotius. Comment. in loco.*
" Abstractum pro concreto, etiam in sequentibus."—*Bengel. "Gnomon," in loco.*
" After that, such as have the gift of miracles."—*Heylyn. "Lectures."* (Ed. 1671.) Vol. ii. p. 116.
" Here, and in what follows, abstract terms are used for concrete — *miracles* mean men endowed with the power of working miracles."—*Hodge. Comment. in loco.* p. 262.

[2] " Eos qui morbos sanandi potestatem accepere."—*Grotius. Comment. in loco.*

[3] " Hoc est, sustentare infirmos."—*Athanasius, in loco.* (Ed. Erasmi, 1522.)
"Nimirum qui egentibus opem ferunt, sive illi Ecclesiæ domestici, sive peregrini fuerint." — *Gualtherus, in loco.*
" Pro auxiliatoribus vel adjutoribus eorum quos supra memoravit supremos ecclesiæ doctores, in spiritualibus ministeriis."—*Brennius. "Notæ," etc. in loco.* (Ed. 1664.) p. 84.
" Qui aliis opitulantur per opera misericordiæ, seu spiritualia, seu corporalia, circa ægros, pauperes, miseros, peregrinos, nempe Diaconos."—*Menochius and Tirinus, in loco. in "Synopsis Criticorum."* (Ed. Lond. 1676.) Vol. iv. p. 493.
" Whether he meaneth Deacons, or Widows [deaconesses] elsewhere mentioned as helpful in the case of the poor, or some that assisted the pastors in the government of the Church, or some that were extraordinary helps to the Apostles in the first plantation of the Church, is very hard to determine."— *Poole's "Annotations," in loco.*
" Persons qualified and appointed to help the other officers of the Church, probably in the care of the poor and the sick. These, according to the common understanding from Chrysostom to the present day, were deacons and deaconesses."—*Hodge. Comment. in loco.* p. 262.

its relationship to the verb which means *to steer*, thence *to pilot*, and thence to *direct* or *govern a state*. But what specific persons, if any, it means here to describe in the primitive Church as being its *pilots*, or *directors*, it is difficult to determine.[1] Our Presbyterian friends, of course, take it as referring to those ruling elders which make an essential part of their system; and if there had been any ruling elders — in their sense — in the primitive Church, or if there were any allusion to such officers elsewhere in the New Testament, this might be a good proof-text for them. But — if we mistake not — we shall see, by and by, that there is no good ground for such reference.[2] The most probable sense of the word appears to be that which refers it to the pastors who presided over the administration of government in the Church;[3] though Lightfoot, Horsley, Mosheim, and Macknight may be right in their opinion that the term was intended to designate persons of special discretion and prudence to whom the spirit of wise counsel was imparted in miraculous measure by the Holy Ghost.

---

[1] Gualtherus supposes here a reference to a class of officers in the Church to meet the want arising from Paul's prohibition to "go to law before the unjust, and not before the saints." (1 Cor. vi: 1.) He says: — Quibus comprehenduntur viri politici, qui in rebus hujus seculi quosuis juvabant, et causas cognoscebant, si quæ inter Christianos orirentur. Nam ut Capite sexto dictum est, nolebant Apostoli, ut qui Christum profitebantur apud Ethnicorum tribunalia de fortunis suis aliisque rebus ad hanc vitam pertinentibus litigarent. Præficiebantur ergo ejusmodi causis viri prudentes et rerum usu exercitati, quorum authoritate et consilio lites dirimerentur."—*Hom.* p. 196.

[2] See page 00.

[3] "Alii hosce Presbyteros regentes designari putant, 1 Cor. xii: 28, ubi inter munera nominantur gubernationes, sed locum inspicienti manifestum est, loqui illic Apostolum de muneribus extraordinariis: tum, incertum est, quale donum hoc fuerit; et ex nuda voce argumentum velle petere, admodum frivolum est."—*Limborch.* "*Theolog. Christ.*" Lib. vii. Cap. iv. p. 751.

"Ili sunt qui ex Syriaco *pastores* (Eph. iv: 1) *qui præsunt* (Rom. xii: 8) alibi *seniores*, qui singulas regebant ecclesias."—*Grotius. Comment. in loco.*

"Qui antea *doctores*, a docendo dicti, iidemque hic *gubernationes*, a regimine illis commisso." Hammond. *Comment. in loco.*

Neander teaches that the persons here referred to were those elsewhere styled 'elders' and 'overseers.'—"*Planting and Training.*" Book iii. chap. v.

"Who these persons ['governments'] were, it is difficult to determine with certainty; but it is most probable that elders or bishops are principally meant."—*Davidson.* "*Ecclesiastical Polity of the New Testament.*" p 193.

"When these 'helps' and the extraordinary functionaries are left out of the Apostolic catalogues, it is rather singular that, in the passage addressed to the Ephesians, we have nothing remaining but 'Pastors and Teachers,' and in that to the Corinthians, nothing but 'Teachers' and 'governments.' There are good grounds for believing that these two residuary elements are identical — the 'Pastors' mentioned before the Teachers in one text, being equivalent to the 'governments' mentioned after them in the other. Nor is it strange that those

The phrase *Diversities of tongues* (γένη γλωσσῶν — *genē glōssōn*) so evidently refers to that miraculous gift 'of tongues,' which, whether it enabled its recipients to speak in languages unknown to them before, or only to interpret such languages from the lips of others (see Barnes on 1 Cor. xii: 10), was an unusual bestowment upon the Church during the exigencies of its earliest years, ceasing afterward, as to make any delay upon its exact significance foreign to the necessities of the inquiry which we have now in hand.

We infer then that of these five, whatever was included in the terms 'miracles,' 'gifts of healings,' and 'diversities of tongues,' belonged to the age of miracles, and had no perpetual relation to the Church, and describes no permanent office in it; while 'helps' and 'governments' refer to those officers usually spoken of as Pastors and Deacons. So that all the names which the New Testament uses to describe the permanent officers of a Christian Church, reduce themselves to these, and their synonymes, namely: Pastors, Teachers, Elders, Bishops or Overseers, and Deacons. If now it be true that Pastors, Teachers, Elders, and Bishops or Overseers, are all different names for one and the same laborer, it will follow that this office, and that of the Deacon, constitute the only two permanent offices which Christ has designated for his churches. To the proof of that proposition we now advance.

2. *The first class of permanent officers which Christ designated for his Churches — to take oversight of their spiritual concerns — is indiscriminately spoken of in the New Testament under the names of Pastor, Teacher, Presbyter or Elder, and Bishop or Overseer.* The truth of this proposition we propose to establish by reference to three sources of evidence, namely: the opinion of men of learning and candor who have investigated the facts; the declarations of ecclesiastical history, and of the early writers of the Church; and the testimony of Scripture itself. In order to facilitate as much as

---

entrusted with the ecclesiastical government should be styled Pastors or Shepherds; for they are the guardians and rulers of the 'flock of God.'"—*Killen's "Ancient Church."* p. 231.

"The conception of *offices* is subordinated to that of *gifts*. Thus there was in the Church no separate prophetic office, but the Apostles were at the same time prophets, although every prophet was not necessarily an Apostle; so also the so-called 'Evangelists,' *i. e.* travelling teachers, who preached where as yet no Church had arisen. The teachers, however, were alike teachers proper and rulers (κυβερνῶντες); their official appellation was πρεσβύτεροι or ἐπίσκοποι."—*Olshausen. Comment. in loco.* (Kendrick's Ed.) p. 348.

possible the compression of this argument, it may be premised here that all writers who limit the number of the officers of the primitive Church to *two* — one of which is that of Deacon — do for substance, of course, affirm the identity of Pastors, Teachers, Elders, Bishops, and Overseers, as constituting, under whichever name, the other class ; and that the main question always must be whether Bishops are identical with Pastors, Teachers, and Elders, or officially superior to them.

(1.) *We adduce the opinion of eminent and candid scholars who have investigated the facts.* WICKLIFFE — who struck the first spark of the Reformation — (A. D. 1324–1384) spake, in the face of the overbearing hierarchy of his time, as follows: — " By the ordinance of Christ, Priests and Bishops were all one.... I boldly assert one thing, namely, that in the primitive Church, or in the time of Paul, two orders of the clergy were sufficient ; that is, a priest [presbyter] and a deacon. In like manner I maintain that, in the time of Paul, presbyter and Bishop were names of the same office. All other degrees and orders have their origin in the pride of Cæsar. If indeed they were necessary to the Church, Christ would not have been silent respecting them."[1] JOHN of Goch (A. D. 1400–1475), also a ' Reformer before the Reformation,' has left on record his judgment of the equality of the priest, or presbyter, with the bishop; stoutly maintaining that the position of a priest is the highest position in the Church.[2] LUTHER, in his Essay " concerning the power of the Pope," concludes, from his examination of various passages of the New Testament, that " it is proved that Bishop and Presbyter are the same ;"[3] and he sums up the whole essay by saying, " therefore, by Divine Law, the Pope is neither superior to the Bishops, nor the Bishops superior to the Presbyters,"[4] etc. CALVIN, in his exposition of the teachers and ministers of the Church, says : " In giving the name of Bishops, Presbyters, and Pastors indiscriminately to those who govern churches, I have

---

[1] As quoted in *Conant's "English Bible."* (New York, 1856.) p. 69.
[2] " Ordo sacerdotalis est summus in ecclesia militante.... Ipse ordo est superior aliis et consummativus aliorum omnium ordinum," etc. — "*Dialogus de quatuor Erroribus,*" etc., in *Walch's "Monimenta Med. Ævi."* (Goettingen, 1760.) Vol. 1. fasc. iv. p. 105.
[3] "In quo manifestissime comprobatur, eundem esse Episcopum atque Presbyterum." — "*De Potestate Papæ.*" *Lutheri Opera.* (Ed. Jenæ, 1612.) Vol. i. p. 279.
[4] " Ergo nec Papa est Episcopis, nec Episcopus est superior Presbyteris jure divino," etc. — *Ibid.* p. 283.

done it on the authority of Scripture, which uses the words as synonymous."¹ So, in commenting on 1 Tim. iii: 1, he says: "it is necessary to observe what it is that Paul calls 'the office of a Bishop;' and so much the more, because the ancients were led away, by the custom of their times, from the true meaning; for, while Paul includes generally all pastors, they understand a Bishop to be one who was elected out of each college to preside over his brethren. Let us remember, therefore, that this word is of the same import as if he had called them ministers, or pastors, or presbyters."² He reiterates the same sentiment in his comments on Acts xx: 28, Philip. i: 1, and 1 Pet. v: 2, and in his treatise on "the necessity of reforming the Church."³ CRANMER says, Bishops and Priests [presbyters] "were not two things, but both one office in the beginning of Christ's religion."⁴ MELANCTHON, in his "Outlines of Theology," uses the terms Bishop and Presbyter, or Elders, as synonymes.⁵ MYLES COVERDALE (A. D. 1488–1569) — though himself Bishop of Exeter — says, the Apostles "gave unto every Church their peculiar bishop, to keep the Lord's flock, whom they also called *priest, or elder;* giving them a title of reputation, either because of their age, or by reason of their excellent gravity and virtuous conversation. . . . As for high Bishop, under Christ, they knew none. They had all like authority,"⁶ etc. POLANUS argues that Presbyters and Bishops are the same by divine enactment, "that is, they administer the same office, in the same way, and by the same authority."⁷ LIMBORCH declares it to be the "common opinion of Protestants, that the Scriptures recognize no difference between the Bishops and Presbyters, or Elders, so that the two terms are interchanged as equivalents."⁸

---

1 "*Institutes.*" (*Calvin Trans. Soc. translation.*) Vol. iii. p. 64.
2 *Comment. in loco.* (*Calvin Trans. Soc. translation.*) p. 75.
3 *Calvin's Tracts.* (*Calvin Trans. Soc. translation.*) Vol. i. p. 155, 156.
4 "*Questions and Answers concerning the Sacraments.*" *Miscellaneous Writings, and Letters of Thomas Cranmer.* (Parker Society's Ed. 1846.) p. 117.
5 "Episcopi seu Presbyteri dicebantur, qui docebant, lavabant, et benedicebant Mensæ. Diaconi, qui eleemosynas partiebantur inter inopes." — "*Hyp. Theol.*" *De Par. Men. Dom.* (Ed. Lipsiæ, 1821.) p. 157.
6 "*Remains of Bishop Coverdale.*" (Parker Society's Ed.) p. 464.
7 "Iidem Episcopi vocantur etiam Presbyteri. . . . Proinde etiam Presbyteri et Episcopi sunt jure divino pares; id est, administrant idem officium, eodem modo et eadem autoritate," etc.— "*Syntagma Theologiæ.*" (Ed. Genevæ, 1617.) p. 538.
8 "Communis Protestantium sententia est, nullum inter Episcopos et Presbyteros Scripturam agnoscere discrimen; eo quod voces illæ, tanquam æquipollentes, inter se permutentur."—"*Theologiæ Christianæ.*" Lib. vii. Cap. iv. sec. 5. p. 749.

EPISCOPIUS, in remarking upon 1 Tim. v: 19, says, "by 'Elder' here we may understand *Bishop*, as the terms are used in the Scriptures as one and the same."[1] ARMINIUS argues that, after the days of miracles, the offices of the Church were imposed "mediately on those who were called pastors or teachers, and bishops or priests, [presbyters] who were placed over certain churches. . . . These are so ordered that one person can discharge them all at the same time."[2] WOLLEBIUS teaches, that " the name of Bishop rightfully belongs to all Pastors." [3] AMES says, that the " Elders of one congregation, in the same sense, are also called Bishops in the Scriptures."[4] JOHN ROBINSON habitually uses these terms as synonymous, as where he says, " whensoever the Scriptures do mention elders, or bishops, either in respect of their calling or ministration, they still speak of them, as in or of, such and such particular churches, and none otherwise." [5] LORD PETER KING says, as the Apostles "came to any city, town, or village, they published to the inhabitants thereof the blessed news of life and immortality through Jesus Christ, constituting the first converts of every place through which they passed *Bishops* and *Deacons* of those churches which they there gathered." [6] SCLATER, in his reply to Lord King's volume, confesses that " the names of Presbyter and Bishop were indifferently used at first," [7] and then attempts to show that there was no "danger of misunderstanding about it," in that Apostolic age. TURRETIN argues, that the terms Bishop and Presbyter were originally identical in use, and that the Episcopal distinction between them is a subsequent and arbitrary one, growing out of the custom of the Church, and human wisdom, rather than from the will of God.[8] STAPFER refers to the same identity,

---

[1] " Per *Presbyterum* enim hoc loco intelligi potest *Episcopus*, prout in Scripturis pro uno et eodem accipiuntur."—"*Lectiones Sacræ in Cap.* ii. & iii. *Apoc.*" *Works.* (Ed. Rotterdam, 1665.) Vol. ii. p. 552.

[2] "*Private Disputations.*" *Writings.* (Nichol's Ed.) Vol. ii. p. 150.

[3] " Pastoribus omnibus nomen Episcopi competit." — "*Christianæ Theologiæ.*" Lib. i. Cap. 26, p. 128.

[4] "*Marrow of Sacred Divinity.*" Lib. i. Cap. 39, sec. 28.

[5] *Works.* (London Ed. 1851.) Vol. ii. p. 416.

[6] "*Enquiry into Constitution, etc. of the Primitive Church.*" (Ed. 1712.) p. 10.

[7] "*Original Draught of the Primitive Church.*" (Ed. 1833.) p. 181.

[8] " *Episcopale Regimen* aliud est *primitivum* et *Apostolicum*, quod idem est cum Presbyterali, quod ab Apostolis ex Christi voluntate et præcepto institutum est: aliud *secundarium* et *Ecclesiasticum* a Presbyteriali distinctum, Ecclesiæ consuetudine, et humano consilio, potius quam dispositionis Dominicæ veritate introductum."—*Opera.* (Ed. Edinburgh.) Vol. iii. p. 176.

and considers Paul and Peter both, (Tit. i., Acts xx: 17, 28, 1 Pet. v: 1, 2) as rendering it certain.[1] RICHARD HOOKER concedes that the same officers of the Church, "in their writings they [the Apostles] term sometimes presbyters, sometimes bishops."[2]

MILTON devotes his whole treatise on "Prelatical Episcopacy" to the proof of the position for which we are now arguing, in which, after a thorough review of those arguments from 'the Fathers' accustomed to be alleged in proof of the superiority of Bishops over Presbyters, he sums up his argument by saying: — "I do not know, it being undeniable that there are but two ecclesiastical orders, bishops, and deacons, mentioned in the Gospel, how it can be less than impiety to make a demur at that, which is there so perspicuous, confronting and paralleling the sacred verity of St. Paul with the offals and sweepings of antiquity, etc. . . . Certainly if Christ's Apostle have set down but two, then, according to his own words, though he himself should unsay it, and not only the Angel of Smyrna, but an angel from heaven should bear us down that there be three, St. Paul has doomed him twice: 'Let him be accursed;' for Christ has pronounced that no tittle of his word shall fall to the ground; and if one jot be alterable, it is possible that all should perish; and this shall be our righteousness, our ample warrant, and strong assurance, both now and at the last day, never to be ashamed of, against all the heaped names of angels and martyrs, councils and fathers, urged upon us, if we have given ourselves up to be taught by the purest living precept of God's word only; which, without more additions, nay, with a forbidding of them, hath within itself the promise of eternal life, the end of all our wearisome labors, and all our sustaining hopes. But if any shall strive to set up his ephod and teraphim of antiquity against the brightness and perfection of the Gospel, let him fear lest he and his Baal be turned into Bosheth. And thus much may suffice to shew, that the pretended Episcopacy cannot be deduced from the Apostolical times."[3] LARDNER says, "there were at the very time

---

[1] "Non magna tamen, aut temporibus Apostolicis plane nulla, inter Episcopum et Presbyterum fuit differentia, cum nomina hæc inter se commutentur. Ita Apostolus Paulus jussit Titum Presbyteros constituere, requisita autem illorum indicans Episcopum describit iisdem nomen Presbyterorum et Episcoporum datur. Similiter Apostolus Petrus id facit." — "*Institutiones Theologiæ*." (Ed. Tiguri, 1743.) Vol. 1. p. 431.

[2] "*Ecclesiastical Polity*." Book vii. ch. 5, sec. 1.

[3] *Milton's Prose Works*, (Bohn's Edition.) Vol. ii. p. 436. See also pp. 457-459, and Vol. 1. pp. 436-440.

of forming such societies, [the early churches] or soon after, appointed in them officers and ministers, called bishops, or elders, or pastors, or teachers; and deacons: men who had been before approved, as persons of integrity and capacity for the work to which they were appointed. (1 Tim. iii: 10.) The peculiar work of the former of whom was to preach the word and feed the flock of which they were overseers, with wholesome and sound doctrine and instruction, 'to reprove, rebuke, exhort with all long-suffering and doctrine;' of the latter — the 'serving of tables,'" etc.[1] GIBBON says of the early Christian churches: — " the public functions of religion were solely intrusted to the established ministers of the Church, the *bishops* and the *presbyters;* two appellations which, in their first origin, appear to have distinguished the same office, and the same order of persons. The name of Presbyter was expressive of their age, or rather of their gravity and wisdom. The title of Bishop denoted their inspection over the faith and manners of the Christians who were committed to their pastoral care."[2] BAXTER says, " what is meant by Ἐπισκόπους *(episkopous) bishops* or *overseers,* here [Acts xx: 28] is thus far agreed on: that they were officers appointed to teach and guide those churches in the way to salvation; and that they are the same persons that are called elders of the Church of Ephesus before, and bishops here. . . . By a pastor or bishop here is meant an officer appointed by Christ for the ordinary teaching and guiding a particular Church and all its members, in order to their salvation, and the pleasing of God."[3] DODDRIDGE says, the first class of officers in the Church "are frequently called *Elders* and *Presbyters,* as the Jews used to call those who presided in their ecclesiastical or civil assemblies; and from their office of *overseeing* the people, the name of ἐπίσκοποι or *Bishops,* was also given them, and whatever alteration might afterwards be made in the sense of that word, and whatever distinction might early be introduced between bishops and presbyters as signifying two different ranks of ministers, it is certain that in the New Testament the words are used promiscuously. Bishop Hoadley and Dr. Hammond do both of them allow this; and it is Dr. Hammond's opinion that there were only presbyters or bishops, and deacons, in each Church,

---

[1] *Works.* (Ed. London, 1838.) Vol. ii. p. 14.
[2] "*Decline and Fall.*" (Smith's Milman's Ed. 1854.) Vol. ii. p. 191
[3] "*Gildas Salvianus.*" (Carter's Ed. 1860.) pp. 61, 69.

at first."[1] OWEN says, "in the whole New Testament, bishops and presbyters, or elders, are everyway the same persons, in the same office, have the same function, without distinction in order or degree — which also, as unto the Scripture, the most learned advocates of Prelacy begin to grant."[2] JOHN COTTON says, "it is apparently contradictory to the institutions given by Paul in the Epistles to Timothy and Titus, to set up any eminent or transcendent Bishop in the Church in respect of rule, or exercise of office of more honour and power than pertaineth to *all* the ministers of the Word."[3] JOHN DAVENPORT says, "we read of Bishops in the New Testament, but what? not one Bishop over many churches, but many Bishops over one Church; not Diocesan, but Congregational Bishops — the Bishops which the Apostles acknowledge to be Christ's ordinance, to continue in the Christian Church, are Congregational Elders," etc.[4] THOMAS HOOKER says, "though the nakedness of the assertion, that would difference *Episcopus* and *Presbyter* by Divine right, hath been of former, and much moré of latter times laid open to the view of the world, so that there needs nothing to be added here; yet to leave it upon record, that we concur with these worthies in the defence of the same truth, we shall, in short, set down our witness against them;" and then devotes several pages to the proof that Bishops "have no distinct operations from Presbyters."[5] COTTON-MATHER says, "the churches of New England think that the Apostles knew of no Bishops, but only those pastors, whereof there may be several in a parity, feeding one small congregation;" and quotes many Fathers and learned men to the effect that it is "as plain as the noonday sun could make any thing in the world," that "Bishops and Presbyters were of old the very same."[6] Dr. CHARLES CHAUNCY published a volume in Boston, in 1771, devoted to the refutation of the Episcopal theory of the inequality of Bishops and Presbyters, which he sums up by declaring that that theory has "no support, either in point of *right*, or *practice*, from any thing met with in the writers within the two first ages of the Christian Church."[7] EDWARD

---

[1] "*Lectures on Divinity.*" Works. Vol. v. p. 299.
[2] "*True Nature of a Gospel Church.*" Works. Vol. xvi. p. 44.
[3] "*Way of the Churches.*" p. 48.
[4] "*Power of Congregational Churches,*" etc. p. 79.
[5] "*Survey of the Summe of Church Discipline.*" Part ii. p. 22.
[6] "*Ratio Disciplinæ.*" (Boston, 1726.) pp. 196-205.
[7] "*Compleat View of Episcopacy.*" p. 474.

WIGGLESWORTH says — after an examination of the New Testament, covering one hundred and nineteen pages — "we plainly find but one order of officers, the eleven Apostles, left in the Church by Christ himself at his ascension into heaven; and one order more, the seven Deacons, instituted afterwards by the Apostles under the conduct of the Spirit of God. These two orders are unquestionably of Divine Institution; but more we cannot find to be so. We desire to preserve to each of these all the ordinary powers they were entrusted with by divine appointment, and not to thrust either of them into employments which the wisdom of God never allotted to them. We are far from saying that either of these offices was temporary. We only affirm that the former of them had some powers at the beginning which were extraordinary and temporary, and expired with the persons they were committed to; but that, as to their ordinary powers, they have been, and shall be succeeded to the end of the world, by Presbyters or Bishops, whom we everywhere find in Scripture to be one and the same order."[1] THOMAS FOXCROFT says, "we know of no ministers in Scripture that were Presbyters in the modern (Church of England) sense of the word. We deny any such officer in the Church as a *mere* Presbyter; that is, a minister of the word destitute of Episcopal power over the flock. The Elders, or Presbyters, we read of in 1 Peter v: 1, were Bishops. *Such* Bishops we are for, and *such* Elders; but we know of no institution for Elders that do not rule over the flock, or for Bishops that rule over Elders. We are for *Congregational Bishops*, and such, we conclude, were the Presbyters that ordained Timothy."[2] JONATHAN DICKINSON argues that the New Testament ascribes to Bishops and Presbyters a community of names of office and of order; that there are no Gospel ministers in a regularly constituted Church, but Bishops, and that Presbyters are the only ordinary ministers of the Gospel; that Presbyters have power of ordination, and that the Apostles were Presbyters, while there is no mention of Bishops superior to Presbyters — from all which he infers that by the Scriptures the two offices are coördinate, and says "there is a community of order and office, as well as of name, between *Bishop* and *Presbyter*."[3] THOMAS WALTER says,

---

[1] "*Sober Remarks on the 'Modest Proof.'*" (Boston, 1724.) p. 120.
[2] "*Ruling and Ordaining Power of Cong. Bishops defended,*" etc. (Boston, 1724.) p. 8.
[3] "*Defence of Presbyterian Ordination.*" (Boston, 1724.) pp. 40-43.

"not only is a Presbyter called a Bishop, but a Bishop is called a Presbyter. Which is of more force than if either a Presbyter were called a Bishop, and a Bishop called nothing else but Bishop, or a Bishop were called Presbyter, and Presbyter called only Presbyter;" whence he argues the complete identity of the two.[1] THOMAS SHEPARD says, "we read in Scripture of many Elders and Bishops in the same Church (Acts xx: 28), but never of any one ordinary minister, or officer over many churches, either to govern or to baptize."[2] WILLIAM JAMESON says, "under the Gospel the Apostles retaining the name, and the manner of ordination, but not conferring that judiciary power by it, which was in use among the Jews; to shew the difference between the Law and the Gospel, it was requisite some other name should be given to the Governors of the Church, which should qualify the importance of the word *Presbyters* to a sense proper to a Gospel state; which was the original of giving the name ἐπισκόποι (*Bishops*) to the Governors of the Church under the Gospel; — a name importing duty more than honor, and not a title above Presbyter, but rather used by way of diminution and qualification of the power implied in the name of Presbyter."[3] JOHN WISE says, "though there were some distinctions in point of a titular dignity and degree between a Bishop and a Presbyter; yet they were really equal in order, and in the nature of their trust. For that in an Ecclesiastical sense, Bishops and Presbyters are synonymous terms, setting forth the same office; and signify no more but an elder, a pastor, ruler or overseer of a Church."[4] DR. SAMUEL HOPKINS says of the two offices appointed by Christ for his churches, "of these, Pastors, Elders, Presbyters or Bishops are the first and most important. By these names, not different orders, higher and lower, or different offices are meant; but one and the same person, in one and the same office, is called by all these names, and, therefore, they denote the same office."[5] DR. EMMONS says, "in a Christian Church there are only two distinct officers, Bishops and Deacons. The Bishop, in the Apostolic times, was a mere pastor, teacher, or watchman, without any

---

[1] "*Essay upon that Paradox, 'Infallibility may sometimes mistake,'*" (Boston, 1724.) p. 100.
[2] "*Wholesome Caveat for a time of Liberty.*" *Works.* (Ed. 1853.) Vol. iii. p. 333.
[3] "*Fundamentals of the Hierarchy examined and disproved.*" (Glasgow, 1697.) p. 208.
[4] "*Vindication of the Government of New England Churches.*" (Ed. 1772.) p. 9.
[5] *Works.* (Ed. 1852.) Vol. ii. p. 75.

superiority or power over any of his fellow pastors. He had only the watch, and care, and instruction of the particular Church in which he was placed."[1] DR. DWIGHT devotes two sermons to the proof "that there are but two classes of permanent officers in the Christian Church, designated in the Scriptures," the first of which "is spoken of under the names Elders, Pastors, Bishops, Teachers," and the second "under that of Deacons."[2] Dr. J. M. MASON says, "that the terms *Bishop* and *Presbyter* in their application to the first class of officers [of the church] are perfectly convertible, the one pointing out the very same class of rulers with the other, is as evident as the 'sun shining in his strength.'"[3] DR. WOODS says, "the *Presbyters* were *Bishops*. The two words were used interchangeably. They were applied to the same men, and denoted the same office."[4] GUIZOT's exposition of these officers of the early Church is: — "in the various Christian congregations, there were men who preached, who taught, who morally governed the congregation," — making all as, at first, one order.[5] COLERIDGE says, "in the primitive times, and as long as the churches retained the form given them by the Apostles and Apostolic men, every community, or in the words of a Father of the second century (for the pernicious fashion · of assimilating the Christian to the Jewish, as afterward to the Pagan, ritual by false analogies, was almost coeval with the Church itself), every altar had its own bishop, every flock its own pastor, who derived his authority immediately from Christ, the universal Shepherd, and acknowledged no other superior than the same Christ, speaking by his Spirit in the unanimous decision of any number of bishops or elders, according to his promise, 'where two or three are gathered together in my name, there am I in the midst of them.'"[6] DR. SMYTH says, "throughout the whole New Testament the words *Presbyter* and *Bishop*, with their cognate terms, both as they refer to the office and its incumbent, are used interchangeably, and as perfectly synonymous."[7] DR. BENNETT says, "of the ordination of a Pres-

---

[1] *Works.* (Ed. 1860.) Vol. iii. p. 580.
[2] *Sermons*, CL. CLI. *Works.* (Ed. 1819.) Vol. v. pp. 167–200.
[3] "*Essays on Episcopacy.*" *Works.* Vol. ii. p. 41.
[4] "*Church Government.*" *Works.* Vol. iii. p. 517.
[5] "*History of Civilization.*" (Hazlitt's Trans.) Vol. i. p. 50.
[6] "*Idea of the Christian Church.*" *Works.* (Shedd's Ed.) Vol. vi. p. 100.
[7] "*Presbytery and not Prelacy the Scriptural and Primitive Polity.*" (Ed. Glasgow.) p. 82.

byter that was not a Bishop, the Scriptures say nothing; for their Presbyters are Bishops, and their Bishops Presbyters," etc.[1] DR. COLEMAN devotes one hundred and twenty-one pages of his very learned work, entitled, "The Apostolical and Primitive Church" to the proof of the original equality of Bishops and Presbyters, shewing that they had the same names, titles, and functions, and that the fact of their original equality continued to be acknowledged even down to the time of the Reformation.[2] DR. SCHMUCKER says, "the different names applied to ministers, such as bishops, presbyters or elders, etc., are used as convertible terms, and therefore must imply equality of rank."[3] DR. N. W. TAYLOR said, "there are but two classes of officers known in the Church, Bishops — or Elders, or Presbyters, or Pastors, or Teachers — and Deacons; and but one order of ministers. All of these except Deacons are the same, and have the same powers, duties, and qualifications."[4] SAWYER says, "Bishops are in the New Testament called Presbyters; and their titles are used interchangeably to denote the same officers."[5] DR. BRECKENRIDGE says, God gives to each Church "a Pastor or Bishop — or two, or three, or more, if need require. And all these Pastors, Bishops, and Elders, are alike Presbyters; and all jointly rule, and the Pastors or Bishops besides this, labor in word and doctrine."[6] DR. POND states it, "with entire confidence" as "the doctrine of the New Testament, that there are but two distinct *orders* or *classes* of officers in the Church of Christ; the one having charge of the *spiritual* concerns of the Church, the other of its *temporal* concerns; the one commonly denominated bishops or presbyters, the other deacons."[7] DR. DAVIDSON says, "there were no gradations of office among *elder, bishop, pastor,* and *teacher* in the Apostolic age. Character and talents were the only ground of distinction. There was then a simplicity in the arrangements of God's house, unlike the cumbrousness introduced in later times of degeneracy."[8] PUNCHARD says, "the case is so plain that no one need doubt that the same order of men are called either Elders, Bishops, or Overseers, interchangeably."[9] UPHAM says, "it

---

[1] "*Theology of the Early Church.*" p. 159.
[2] "*Elements of Popular Theology.*" (Ed. 1860.) p. 221.
[3] (Ed. 1853.) pp. 124-245.
[4] *MSS. report of Lectures.* "*The Church.*"
[5] "*Organic Christianity.*" p. 54.
[6] "*Knowledge of God subjectively considered.*" p. 635.
[7] "*The Church.*" p. 71.
[8] "*Ecclesiastical Polity of the New Testament.*" p. 157.
[9] "*View of Congregationalism.*" (Ed. 1860.) p. 94.

WHENCE CONGREGATIONALISM IS.

would seem that Elders and Bishops, or Overseers, whatever might be their appropriate duties, and whatever relation they might sustain to the subordinate office of Deacons, were one and the same grade, or species, of Church officer."¹ GARRATT says, "at first this threefold distinction of Bishops, Elders, and Deacons does not appear to have prevailed, at least universally; the words Bishop and Elder being used interchangeably in St. Paul's Epistles, and in the Acts of the Apostles."² DR. VAUGHAN says, "the word Bishop, which, beyond controversy, is synonymous with the word Elder or Presbyter, occurs in such a manner in the introduction of the Epistle to the Philippians, as to show that more than one person in that Church sustained this office; and that among the persons sustaining it, there was no official precedence."³ DR. HILL says, the same persons whom the writers of the New Testament, in speaking of other churches, call Presbyters, in the Epistle to the Philippians, are termed Bishops, and adds, "as Presbyters are thus called Bishops, so the Apostles, the highest officebearers in the Church, did not think it beneath them to take the name of Presbyters."⁴ JACOBSON says, "in the Bible the two words [Presbyter and Bishop] are synonymous, so that the offices of Overseer and of Elder are the same.... There is not the least trace of difference between ἐπίσκοπος and πρεσβύτερος."⁵ F. W. NEWMAN says, these officers of the Church "were ordinarily called *Elders* from their age, sometimes *Bishops* from their office.... That during St. Paul's lifetime no difference between Elders and Bishops yet existed in the consciousness of the Church, is manifest," etc.⁶ PROF. PLUMPTRE says, "that the two titles were originally equivalent, is clear," etc.⁷ CONYBEARE AND HOWSON say, "of the offices concerned with Church government, the next in rank to that of the Apostles was the office of Overseers or Elders, more usually known (by their Greek designations) as Bishops or Presbyters. These terms are used in the New Testament as equivalent, the former (ἐπίσκοπος) denoting (as its meaning of *overseer* implies) the duties, the latter (πρεσβύτερος)

---

1 "*Ratio Disciplinæ*." (Ed. 1844.) p. 80.
2 "*Scriptural View of the Constitution of a Christian Church*." (London, 1846.) p. 155.
3 "*Causes of the Corruption of Christianity*." p. 416.
4 "*Lectures in Divinity*." (Carter's Ed) p. 723.
5 *Bomberger's Herzog's* "*Real Encyclopedia*." Art. "*Bishop*." Part iv. p. 435.
6 *Kitto's* "*Cyclopedia*." Art. "*Bishop*." Vol. i. p. 333.
7 *Smith's* "*Dictionary of the Bible*." Art. "*Bishop*." Vol. 1. p. 217.

the rank, of the office."¹ ULLMAN says, "the Apostolical age, at least in its first stadium, knew no difference between Presbyter and Bishop."² DR. HALL says, "the two Apostles, Peter and Paul, entirely agree in making the Bishop, the Presbyter, the Pastor, one and the same office in one and the same person. . . . The Bible Bishop is uniformly the Pastor, or one of the Pastors of a congregation; never is the name Bishop given to a Diocesan, or an Apostle, either by the Apostles, or in the Apostolic age. It is absolutely certain, that for a hundred years after Christ, the name Bishop, whether used by Apostles or Fathers, signified the Pastor of a Church; never a person holding a degree above that office."³ DR. BACON says, "it is admitted on all sides, that in the New Testament, the words translated respectively 'Bishop' and 'Elder' are used interchangeably."⁴ MR. WELLMAN says, "those who held this office [that of the Pastorship] in the time of the Apostles were called Elders, Bishops, Overseers, Presbyters, Teachers, Guides; all these terms being used to designate one office — just as we now use the terms Minister and Pastor to designate, not two distinct orders in office, but the same order."⁵

To these witnesses from the ranks of the learned in all ages, since the dark ages, and of all schools of faith, might be added as many from the professed commentators on the Bible. We append only a few of the more striking of their testimonies. ATHANASIUS, explaining Phil. i: 1, and Tit. 1: 5, fully recognizes the identity of Bishops with Elders.⁶ CARDINAL CAJETAN distinctly affirms the same original identity, in his comment on Acts xx: 28.⁷ GUALTHERUS emphatically bears the same testimony; in his homily on 1 Cor. xii: 28, denouncing the assumptions of the Romish hierarchy, and asserting that all the officers which the Church of Christ needs

---

1 "*Life and Epistles of St. Paul.*" (London. 4to Ed. 1853.) Vol. l. p. 465.
2 "*Reformers before the Reformation.*" (Clark's Ed.) Vol. l. p. 124.
3 "*Puritans and their Principles.*" (Ed. 1847.) p. 310.
4 *Review of Chapin's "Primitive Church."* *New Englander.* (1843.) Vol. l. p. 405.
5 "*Church Polity of the Pilgrims.*" p. 34.
6 "Cum impositionem manus Presbyterii, hoc est, episcoporum. . . . Presbyteri Episcopi nomen sortiebantur, ut qui curæ populi invigilarent, purgarentque, et illuminarent quos foret necesse."—*Comment.* Phil. l: 1. (Ed. Argent. 1522.) folio 133.
"Presbyteros hoc loco Episcopos dicit, sicuti et in epistola ad Timotheum prædixerat." —*Ibid.* *Tit.* 1: 5. folio 194.
7 "Illinc apparet quod eosdem appellat hic Episcopos quos prius appellavit Lucas presbyteros, officii siquidem nomen est Episcopus."—*Comment.* Acts xx: 28. (Ed. Venice, 1530.) p. 231.

for its spiritual direction, are Pastors and Teachers.[1] ZANCHIUS says, in his remarks on Phil. i: 1, that Paul, by Bishops, here means the Elders in the city of Philippi, and its suburbs.[2] GOMARUS, in commenting on the same passage says, that "by Bishops, Paul here intends the Elders or Pastors of a Church."[3] GROTIUS, in expounding Acts xx: 17, says that "the Elders of the churches are called Bishops, because they were the *overseers* of the flock;" and in his comment on verse 28 of the same chapter, he adds, they "were called Pastors, because Pastors (*Shepherds*) are [ἐπίσκοποι ποίμνιου — *episkopoi poimniou*] Bishops [overseers] of their flocks."[4] BRENNIUS, in commenting on 1 Pet. v: 1, uses the terms Elder, Bishop, and Pastor, as synonymous.[5] POOLE'S ANNOTATIONS set down "Bishops," as used by Paul in Phil. i: 1, as meaning, with the deacons, the "two orders of ordinary standing officers which are appointed for the Church."[6] HENRY, in remarking upon Phil. i: 1, says it refers to "the Bishops or Elders," and "the Deacons," adding — "these were all the offices then known in the Church, and of Divine appointment."[7] BENGEL, on Acts xx: 28, says, that at that time the title of Bishop pertained to all Presbyters.[8] MACKNIGHT, in his exegesis of Phil. i. 1, refers to the fact that the Elders whom the Apostles set over the churches were called Bishops.[9] ADAM CLARK bears similar testimony in his exposition of Phil. i: 1, and 1 Pet. v: 2.[10]

---

[1] "Omnes enim illi antichristi creaturæ sunt, nec digni, qui in Ecclesia locum aliquem habeant. Nobis sufficiat, si in Ecclesia fidi et idonei Pastores atque Doctores sint," etc.—*Hom. in* 1 *Epis. ad Cor.* (Ed. 1572.) p. 197.

[2] "Intelligit *parochos* omnes in urbe et pagis ejus, ut sit synecdoche in voce *Philippis*."—*In loco*. Poole's *Syn. Crit.* Vol. iv. p. 831.

[3] "Per Episcopos hic intelligit Presbyteros, sive pastores Ecclesiæ."—*In loco*. Poole's *Syn. Crit. Ibid.*

[4] "Vocantur iidem et *Episcopi*, nempe quia inspectores erant gregis. . . . Explicat nomen muneris, quod erat *pastores*, nam pastores sunt *inspectores gregis*."—*In loco. Opera.* (Ed. 1679.) Vol. ii. p. 642.

[5] "Presbyteris, quorum proprium munus est pascere gregem Dei, et episcoporum ac pastorum instar curam ejus gerere, se tanquam compresbyterum conjungit tantus Apostolus, ut eos propositio sui ipsius exemplo ad officium faciendum exsuscitet."—*Com.* 1 *Pet.* v: 1. *"Notæ in Secundum Partem, New Test."* p. 127.

[6] Vol. ii. (Ed. 1700.) *In loco*.

[7] *In loco. "Comprehensive Commentary."* Vol. v. p. 407.

[8] "Hoc tempore appellatio episcoporum nondum erat solennis et propria, sed competit in omnes *Presbyteros*," etc.—*Com. in loco.* (Ed. Tubingæ, 1855.) p. 501.

[9] "That the Apostles ordained Bishops and Deacons in all the churches which he planted, I think evident from Acts xiv: 23, where they are called by the general name of Elders," etc. —*"Epistles."* (Ed. 1841.) p. 356.

[10] "*Episcopois* — the *overseers* of the Church of God and [deacons] those who ministered to

WHITBY says, the "names were then common to both orders, the Bishops being called Presbyters, and the Presbyters, Bishops."[1] SCOTT, in remarking upon Acts xx: 17, says, "the same persons are in this chapter called elders or presbyters, and overseers or bishops; it must therefore be allowed that these were not distinct orders of ministers in the Church at that time," etc.[2] The "ASSEMBLY'S ANNOTATIONS" say, upon the word 'overseer' (Acts xx: 28), "this name of Bishop here, as elsewhere, is put for a *Pastor of the Church*, or minister of the word."[3] BLOOMFIELD says, on Acts xx: 17, "the best commentators, ancient and modern, have, with reason, inferred that the terms [elder and bishop] as yet denoted the same thing."[4] BAUMGARTEN affirms the same identity in his exposition of Acts xx: 28.[5] EADIE says, on Phil. i: 1, "the official term ἐπίσκοπος, (*Bishop*), of Greek origin, is in the diction of the New Testament the same as πρεσβύτερος (*Elder*) of Jewish usage — the name expressive of gravity and honor."[6] HODGE says, on Eph. iv: 12, "the Apostle intended to designate the same persons as, at once, pastor sand teachers. The former term designates them as ἐπίσκοποι (*Bishops — overseers*), the latter as instructors. Every Pastor or Bishop was required to be apt to teach."[7] BARNES says, on Acts xx: 28, "this passage proves that the name was applicable to Elders, and that in the time of the Apostles, the name bishop and presbyter, or elder, was given to the same class of officers, and of course that there was no distinction between them."[8] ALEXANDER sums up his remarks on the same passage by saying, "there is no tenable ground, therefore, but the obvious and simple one, now commonly adopted even by Episcopalians, that bishops and presbyters, when Paul

---

the poor, and preached occasionally. There has been a great deal of paper wasted on the inquiry, 'who is meant by *bishops* here, as no place could have more than one Bishop!' To which it has been answered: 'Philippi was a metropolitan see, and might have several Bishops!' This is the extravagance of trifling. I believe no such officer is meant as we now term *Bishop*."—*Commentary*. Vol. vi. p. 490.

"This is another proof that Bishop and Presbyter were the same order in the Apostolic times," etc.—*Ibid*. p. 868.

[1] *Cited in* "*Comprehensive Com.*" Vol. v. p. 407.   [2] *Commentary*. (Ed. 1812.) Vol. v.
[3] *In loco*. (Ed. London. 1657.)   [4] *Comment. in loco.*
[5] "He speaks of the Elders of Ephesus as the Bishops and Pastors whom the Holy Spirit had appointed."—*Apol. Hist*. Sec. xxx.
[6] "*Commentary on the Greek Text of the Epistle to the Philippians.*" p. 4.
[7] "*Commentary on Epis. to the Ephesians.*" p. 226.
[8] *Commentary on Acts*. p. 280.

spoke, and when Luke wrote, were the same thing; a fact affirmed also by Theodoret and Jerome."[1] HACKETT reaches the same conclusion.[2] MACK even — a modern Roman Catholic expositor — concedes the full identity of the New Testament Presbyters and Bishops;[3] and ALFORD — himself a Church of England man — speaks very strongly in the same vein. He says, on Acts xx: 17, "the English version has hardly dealt fairly in this case with the sacred text, in rendering ἐπισκόπους, (v. 28,) '*overseers;*' whereas it ought there, as in all other places, to have been '*bishops,*' that the fact of *elders and bishops having been originally and Apostolically synonymous,* might be apparent to the ordinary English reader, which now it is not."[4] So, on 1 Tim. iii : 1, he says, " it is merely laying a trap for misunderstanding to render the word, at this time of the Church's history, 'the office of a Bishop.' The ἐπίσκοποι [Bishops] of the New Testament have officially nothing in common with our Bishops. . . . The identity of the Bishop and Elder in Apostolic times is evident from Tit. i : 5–7."[5]

It is worthy of notice in this connection that the Peshito-Syriac version of the New Testament — supposed to have been made within less than one hundred years after Christ — renders Phil. i : 1, thus : " Paul and Timothy, servants of Jesus the Messiah, to all the saints that are in Jesus the Messiah at Philippi, with *the elders* and deacons."[6] MICHAELIS uses this fact as an argument in proof of the venerable antiquity of this version — that it was evidently made when no difference between Bishops and Presbyters was as yet known.[7]

---

[1] *Commentary on Acts.* Vol. ii. p. 250.
[2] " The Elders, or Presbyters, in the official sense of the term, were those appointed in the first churches to watch over their general discipline and welfare. With reference to that duty, they were called also ἐπίσκοποι, *i. e.* superintendents or bishops. The first was their Jewish appellation, transferred to them perhaps from the similar class of officers in the synagogues; the second was their foreign appellation, since the Greeks employed it to designate such relations among themselves. In accordance with this distinction, we find the general rule to be this: those who are called Elders in speaking of Jewish communities, are called Bishops in speaking of Gentile communities. Hence the latter term is the prevailing one in Paul's Epistles. That the names, with this difference, were entirely synonymous, appears from their interchange in such passages as Acts xx: 17, 28, and Tit. l: 5–7."—*Comment on Acts.* (Ed. 1858.) p. 236.
[3] "*Commentar über die Pastoralbriefe des Ap. Paulus.*"—(Tübingen, 1836.) p. 60.
[4] *Greek Testament.* (London Ed.) Vol. ii. p. 2)9.
[5] *Ibid.* Vol. iii. p. 305.
[6] *Murdock's Translation* (Ed. 1851.) p. 359.
[7] "*Der Einleitung,*" etc. T. 1. p. m. '65, *sq.*

Having glanced, thus, at the vast amount of evidence furnished by the opinion of the learned, in proof of the proposition before us, we are prepared to advance to the consideration of the evidence in the same direction, which is found: —

(2.) *In the declarations of Ecclesiastical History, and of the early writers of the Church.* As the latter must largely furnish the basis for the judgments arrived at by the former, we will take them first in order.

CLEMENT OF ROME (who wrote about A. D. 96) knew only two orders of Church officers; the first of which he speaks of indifferently as Presbyters, or Bishops. In his first *Epistle to the Corinthians*, he says, "the Apostles preaching in countries and in cities, appointed the first fruits of their labors *bishops and deacons*, having proved them by the Spirit."[1] And he adds, in another place, " it would be a great sin to reject those who have faithfully performed the duties of the office of a *Bishop*. Blessed are those *Elders* who have finished their course and gone to their reward,"[2]—evidently referring, in both sentences, to the same men under different names. It is particularly noticeable that when speaking of those officers whose authority will suitably regulate the Church, he especially says, "the flock of Christ can abide in peace only when *Elders* have been set over it."[3] POLYCARP, (who wrote about A. D. 140, and was a pupil of the Apostle John), in his *Epistle to the Philippians*, evidently was unacquainted with any Bishops in the churches, inasmuch as he never mentions the name of such an officer. He opens his Epistle by saying, "Polycarp, and the *Elders* that are with him, to the Church at Philippi," etc.[4] He next exhorts that Church to "*be subject to the elders and deacons*,"[5] and then goes on to enlarge upon the qualifications necessary for the right discharge of the offices of both elder[6]

---

[1] " Κατὰ χώρας οὖν καὶ πόλεις κηρύσσοντες καθίστανον τὰς ἀπαρχὰς αὐτῶν, δοκιμάσαντες τῷ πνεύματι, εἰς ἐπισκόπους καὶ διακόνους τῶν μελλόντων πιστεύειν."—1. *Epist. ad Cor.* Sec. xlii. (Ed. Tubingæ, 1839.) p. 57.

[2] "'Αμαρτία γὰρ οὐ μικρὰ ἡμῖν ἔσται, ἐὰν τοὺς ἀμέμπτως καὶ ὁσίως προσενέγκοντας τὰ δῶρα τῆς ἐπισκοπῆς ἀποβάλωμεν. Μακάριοι οἱ προοδοιπορήσαντες πρεσβύτεροι, οἵτινες ἔγκαρπον καὶ τελείαν ἔσχον τὴν ἀνάλυσιν."—*Ibid.* Sec. xliv. p. 58.

[3] " Μόνον τὸ ποίμνιον τοῦ χριστοῦ εἰρηνευέτω, μετὰ τῶν καθεςταμένων πρεσβυτέρων."— *Ibid.* Sec. liv. p. 64.

[4] " Πολύκαρπος καὶ οἱ σὺν αὐτῷ πρεσβύτεροι τῇ ἐκκλησίᾳ," etc.—*Epis. ad Phil.* (Ed. Tubingæ, 1839.) p. 117.

[5] "Διὸ δέον ἀπέχεσθαι ἀπὸ πάντων τούτων, ὑποτασσομένους τοῖς πρεσβυτέροις καὶ διακόνοις, ὡς θεῷ καὶ χριστῷ."—*Ibid.*—Sec. v. p. 120.

[6] *Ibid.* Sec. vi. p. 120.

and deacon,[1] but makes no allusion to any such office as that of a Bishop in the sense in which the word is now used, or in any sense different from that which makes it entirely synonymous with 'elder' or 'presbyter.' JUSTIN MARTYR, (died A. D. 165), refers to only one office in the Church in his time, besides that of the deacon. In describing the order of worship then practised, he says, "there is brought to him *who presides over the brethren*, bread and a cup of water and wine, etc. And *he who presides* having given thanks, and the whole assembly having expressed their assent, they whom we call *deacons* distribute the bread," etc.[2] He in another place, also, describes their worship, specifying the same officers, and never alluding to others.[3] Whence we gather the fair inference that there were no Bishops — in the modern sense, in his time, but that the only officer beside the deacon, was this *president*, or Elder. IRENÆUS, (died A. D. 202,) — a disciple of Polycarp, and so a spiritual grandson of John — often uses the terms Elder and Bishop with reference to the same persons, and in a sense entirely synonymous. In his "Treatise against Heresies," he says of Marcion and certain others, " when we appeal to that Apostolic tradition, which by the succession of *Elders* remains in the churches, they resist the tradition, assuming to be more wise, not only than the *Elders*, but than the very Apostles, and to have found out the exact truth."[4] He then immediately, in the next section, refers to these same Elders as " *Bishops*, instituted by the Apostles in the churches."[5] So, in another place, he says, " we ought to obey those *Elders* in the Church, who—as we have shown—have succession from the Apostles, who, *with the office of a Bishop*, received also the charism of truth," etc.[6] Again, on the next page, he says, after having alluded to the kind of teachers who fairly

---

[1] *Ibid.* Sec. v. p. 120.

[2] "Επειτα προσφέρεται τῷ προεστῶτι τῶν ἀδελφῶν ἄρτος καὶ ποτήριον ὕδατος, etc. Εὐχαριστήσαντος δὲ τοῦ προεστῶτος, καὶ ἐπευφημήσαντος παντὸς τοῦ λαοῦ, οἱ καλούμενοι παῤ ἡμῖν διάκονοι, διδόασιν ἑκάστῳ τῶν παρόντων μεταλαβεῖν."—*Apol.* I. c. lxv. p. 82.

[3] *Ibid.* I. c. lxvii. p. 83.

[4] " Quum autem ad eam iterum traditionem, quæ est ab Apostolis, quæ per successiones *Presbyterorum* in Ecclesiis custoditur, provocamus eos; adversantur traditioni, dicentes se non solum *Presbyteris*, sed etiam Apostolis exsistentes sapientiores, sinceram invenisse veritatem." —"*Contra Hær.*" Lib. iii. Cap. 2 *Opera.* (Massuet's Ed. Venice, 1734.) Vol. i. p. 175.

[5] " Eos qui ab Apostolis instituti sunt *Episcopi* in Ecclesiis," etc.—*Ibid.* Cap. 3. Vol. i. p. 175.

[6] " Quapropter eis qui in Ecclesia sunt, *Presbyteris* obaudire opertet, his qui successionem habent ab Apostolis, sicut ostendimus; qui *cum Episcopatus* successione charisma veritatis certum, secundum placitum Patris acceperunt."—*Ibid.* Lib. iv. c. 26. Vol. i. p. 262.

represent the Apostles, "*such* elders the church cherishes; concerning whom, also, the Prophet says: 'I will give your princes in peace, and your *bishops* in uprightness,'"—which last is the Septuagint rendering of Isaiah lx: 17.[1] So again, further on in the same treatise, he speaks of "the *Bishops* to whose care the Apostles left the churches,"[2] and then says, "they who give up preaching to the Church, prove their ignorance of the duty of the consecrated *Elders*," etc.[3] So he calls Polycarp, whom he had elsewhere called a *bishop*, a "blessed and Apostolic *elder*;"[4] leaving no doubt that in his time, and in his opinion, the two words were synonymous. CLEMENT OF ALEXANDRIA, (died A. D. 220,) also uses interchangeably the words 'elder,' and 'bishop,' and though he sometimes speaks of "bishops, presbyters, and deacons," when he seems to mean by 'bishop,' the presiding presbyter, who acted as moderator in meetings of the elders of the churches, he yet distinctly recognizes only two offices in the Church, for he says—after having observed that in most other things there are two orders of service, one of which is more dignified than the other—"it is the same in the Church, where the *elders* are entrusted with the dignified, the *deacons* with the subordinate ministry."[5] HILARY (A. D. 384) says, "the Apostle calls Timothy—whom he had made an *Elder*—a *Bishop*, (for the first Elders were called Bishops,) that when he departed, the one who came next might succeed him," etc.[6] But JEROME (died A. D. 420) gives us perhaps the most important testimony of any of the Fathers, inasmuch as he recognizes the original equality of the offices of elder and bishop, and states the reason of the change which afterward took place, in the elevation of the latter above the former; and as he was the most learned man of his time, and perhaps of the early ages, his witness should

---

[1] "Τοιούτους πρεσβυτέρους ἀνατρέφει ἡ ἐκκλησία, περὶ ὧν καὶ προφήτης φησιν, δώσω τοὺς ἄρχοντάς σου ἐν εἰρήνη, καὶ τοὺς ἐπισκόπους σου ἐν δικαιοσύνῃ."—*Ibid.* Lib. iv. c. 26. p. 263.

[2] "Episcopi, quibus Apostoli tradiderunt Ecclesias."—*Ibid.* Lib. v. c 20. p. 317.

[3] "Qui ergo relinquunt præconium Ecclesiæ, imperitiam *sanctorum Presbyterorum* arguunt," etc.—*Ibid.* p. 317.

[4] "'Εκεῖνος ὁ μακάριος καὶ ἀποστολικὸς πρεσβύτερος."—"*Fragmentum Epistolæ ad Florinum.*" *Ibid.* Vol. l. p. 340.

[5] "'Ομοίως δὲ καὶ κατα τὴν ἐκκλησίαν, τὴν μὲν βελτιοτικὴν οἱ πρεσβύτεροι σώζουσιν, εἰκόνα τὴν ὑπερτικὴν οἱ διάκονοι."—"*Stromata.*" Lib. vii. p. 700.

[6] "Timotheum, *presbyterum* a se creatum, *Episcopum* vocat, quia primi presbyteri episcopi appellabantur, ut recedente uno sequens ei succederet," etc.—"*Com. on Eph.* iv. 11, 12." *Opera Ambros.* (Ed. Ben.) Vol. ii p. 241.

be conclusive upon the point before us. He says, in a letter to *Oceanus*, "with the ancients, bishops and elders were the same, the one being a name of age, the other of office."[1] So in his *Epistle to Evangelus*, after asserting the identity of elders and bishops, he goes on to prove his point from Phil. i: 1, Acts xx: 17, 28, Tit. i: 5, 1 Tim. iv: 14, and 1 Pet. v: 1; and then says, "does the testimony of these men seem of small account to you? Listen then to the clang of that gospel trumpet—that son of thunder, whom Jesus loved, who drank at the fountain of truth from the Saviour's breast, 'the ELDER to the elect lady and her children,' (2 John i: 1); and in another epistle, 'the ELDER to the well beloved Gaius,' (3 John i: 1). As to the fact that *afterward* one was elected who should preside over the rest, it was done as a remedy against schisms, lest every one drawing his disciples after himself should rend the Church of Christ," etc.[2] So, most emphatically, he says again, (in commenting on Tit. i: 5,) "*an elder is the same as a bishop*, and before there were, by the instigation of the devil, parties in religion, and it was said among different people, 'I am of Paul,' and 'I of Apollos,' and 'I of Cephas,' the churches were governed by the joint counsel of the elders. But afterwards, when every one accounted those whom he baptized as belonging to himself, and not to Christ, it was decreed throughout the whole world, that one chosen from the elders should be called to preside over the rest, and the whole care of the Church be committed to him, that the seeds of schism might be taken away. Should any think that this is merely my private opinion, and not the doctrine of the Scriptures, let him read the words of the Apostle in his epistle to the Philippians: 'Paul and Timothy, servants of Jesus Christ, to all the saints in Christ Jesus, which are at Philippi, with the bishops and deacons.' Now Philippi is a *single* city of Macedonia, and certainly in one city there could not be *several* modern bishops; but as they then called the very same persons bishops whom they called elders, the

---

[1] "Apud veteres idem *episcopi* et *presbyteri* fuerint; quia illud nomen dignitatis est; hoc, ætatis."—"*Ep. ad Oceanum.*" *Opera.* (Ed. Erasmi. Basle, 1537.) Vol. ii. p. 320.

[2] "Parva tibi videntur tantorum virorum testimonia? clangat tuba evangelica, filius tonitrui, quem Jesus amavit plurimum; qui de pectore salvatoris doctrinarum fluenta potavit: 'Presbyter electæ dominæ et filiis ejus, quos ego diligo in veritate.' Et in alia epistola: 'Presbyter Caio carissimo, quem ego diligo in veritate.' Quod autem postea unus electus est, qui ceteris præponeretur, in schismatis remedium factum est, ne unusquisque ad se trahens Christi ecclesiam rumperet."—"*Ep. ad Evang*," or "*Evagr.*" *Ibid.* Vol. ii. p. 329.

Apostle has spoken without distinction of bishops as elders."[1] And a little further on, he says again, "I say these things that I may show that *among the ancients, elders and bishops were the very same;* but that little by little, that the plants of dissension might be plucked up, the whole oversight was devolved upon one. As the elders therefore know that they are inferior, by the custom of the Church, to him who is set over them, so let the bishops know that they rank above elders, *more by custom than by any desire of Christ.*"[2]

Equally distinct proof of the point before us might be added from CHRYSOSTOM[3] (A. D. 407), and from THEODORET[4] (died A. D. 457); but space enough has already been devoted to this branch of the argument,[5] and we only reserve room for a remarkable concession of Pope Urban II (A. D. 1091), before proceeding to cite the opinion of the professed historians of the Church. He says, "we consider the

---

[1] "*Idem est ergo presbyter, qui et episcopus,* et antequam diaboli instinctu, studia in religione fierent, et diceretur in populis: 'Ego sum Pauli,' 'ego Apollo,' 'ego autem Cephæ,' communi presbyterorum consilio ecclesiæ gubernabantur. Postquam vero unusquisque eos, quos, baptizaverat, suos putabat esse, non Christi; in toto orbe decretum est, ut unus de presbyteris electus superponeretur cæteris ad quem omnis ecclesiæ cura pertineret, et schismatum semina tollerentur. Putat aliquis non Scripturarum, sed nostram, esse sententiam episcopum et presbyterum unum esse; et aliud ætatis, aliud esse nomen officii; relegat Apostoli ad Philippenses verba dicentis; 'Paulus et Timotheus servi Jesu Christi omnibus sanctis in Christo Jesu qui sunt Philippis cum episcopis et diaconis, gratia vobis et pax, et reliqua.' Philippi una est urbs Macedoniæ, et certe in una civitate plures ut nuncupantur Episcopi esse non poterant. Sed quia eosdem Episcopos illo tempore quos et presbyteros apellabant, propterea indifferenter de Episcopis quasi de Presbyteris est locutus."—*Com. in Tit.* 1:5. *Ibid.* Vol. ix. p. 245.

[2] "Hæc propterea, ut ostenderemus apud veteres eosdem fuisse presbyteros et episcopos; paulatim vero, ut dissentionum plantaria evellerentur, ad unum omnem solicitudinem esse delatam. Sicut ergo presbyteri sciunt se ex ecclesiæ consuetudine ei, qui sibi propositus fuerit esse subjectos, ita episcopi noverint se magis consuetudine quam dispositionis dominicæ veritate, presbyteris esse majores."—*Ibid.* Vol. ix. p. 245.

[3] See Chrysostom's *Epis. ad Phil.* and *Epis. ad Tim. Opera.*—Vol. xi. p. 194, and p. 604.

[4] See Theodoret's *Epis. ad Phil.* and *Epis. ad Tim. Opera.*—Vol. iii. p. 445, and p. 459.

[5] To these might be added many less clear and forcible testimonies, which are yet interesting to the student and essential to a complete view of the evidence on the question. Among these may be mentioned that of ISODORE, of Seville (A. D. 636) (*Etymol.* vii. c. 12); of BERNALDUS CONSTANTIENSIS (A. D. 1088) (*De Pres. offic. Tract —in Monumentorum res Allemannorum. S. Bias.* 1792. 4to. Vol. ii. p. 384); of TUDESCHUS (A. D. 1428) (*Super prima parte Primi.* cap. v. Ed. Lugdun. 1547. fol. 112, b); and of NICOLAUS CUSANUS (A. D. 1435) (*De concordantia cath.* lib. iii. c. 2.—*in Schardii Syntagma tractatuum,* p. 358.) And even JO. PAUL LAUNCELOT (A. D 1563), the Papal Canonist, quotes Jerome's strong and clear assertion of the identity of Elders and Bishops, without any attempt at confutation. (*Institut. Juris Canon* lib. 1. tit. 21. Sec. 3.) AUGUSTINE mentions it as a heresy of ÆRIUS and his followers, that they were able to discern no difference between an Elder and a Bishop. ("Dicebat etiam presbyterum ab episcopo nulla differentia debere discerni."—"*Liber de Hæresibus.*" Sec. liii. *Opera.* Ed. Antwerpiæ, 1700. Vol. viii. p. 14).

eldership and the deaconship as the sacred orders. These indeed are all which the primitive Church is said to have had. For them alone have we Apostolic authority."[1]

Of the best Ecclesiastical Historians the judgment is one and the same in this matter. MOSHEIM says, "the rulers of the Church were denominated, sometimes *presbyters* or *elders*,— a designation borrowed from the Jews, and indicative rather of the wisdom than the age of the persons; and sometimes, also, *bishops;* for it is most manifest, that *both terms* are promiscuously used in the New Testament, of one and the same class of persons."[2] WADDINGTON — an Episcopal historian — concedes, "it is even certain, that the terms bishop and elder, or presbyter, were, in the first instance, and for a short period, sometimes used synonymously, and indiscriminately applied to the same order in the ministry."[3] MILNER — also a Churchman — says, "at first, indeed, or for some time, Church governors were of only two ranks, presbyters, and deacons," etc.[4] CAMPBELL sums up an elaborate discussion of the question, covering near fifty pages, thus — "the bishops or presbyters (for these terms, as we have seen, were then used synonymously) appear to have been all perfectly coördinate in ministerial powers."[5] GIESELER says, "their [the early churches'] presidents were the *elders* ($\pi\varrho\varepsilon\sigma\beta\acute{v}\tau\varepsilon\varrho\sigma\iota$, $\dot{\varepsilon}\pi\acute{\iota}\sigma\varkappa\sigma\pi\sigma\iota$), officially of equal rank;"[6] — a proposition which he establishes in a long note, filled with citations from the Scriptures and the Fathers. GUERICKE says, "that both names [elder and bishop,] originally denoted the same office — as is conceded even in the fourth century by Jerome; by Ambrosiaster, or Hilary of Rome; also, to some extent, by the *Constitutiones Apostolicæ;* for substance, by Chrysostom also, and Theodoret—is plain from the New Testament passages in which the names are used interchangeably; and in which bishops and deacons, without the mention of presbyters intermediate, are mentioned as the only ecclesiastical officers in the single churches. The original

---

[1] "Sacros autem ordines dicimus diaconatum et presbyteratum. Hos siquidem solos primitiva legitur ecclesia habuisse; super his solum præceptum habemus Apostoli."— *Conc. Benevent.* (A. D. 1091.) *Canon* 1.
[2] *Murdock's translation.* Vol. 1. p. 69.
[3] "*History of the Church,*" ch. ii. sec. 2.
[4] "*History of the Church of Christ.*" (Philadelphia Ed. 1835.) Vol. 1. p. 92.
[5] "*Lectures on Eccl. Hist.*" (Ed. London. 1840) p. 99.
[6] "*Compendium of Eccl. Hist.*" (Davidson's trans. Harper's Ed. 1849.) Vol. 1. p. 90.

identity of elders and bishops is also proved by those passages in the New Testament in which, the office of bishop being passed over, that of elder is spoken of as next to that of the Apostles; in which the term elder denotes the one only office of ruling and pastoral care; and in which the Apostles denominate themselves co-elders."[1] SCHAFF says, "the two appellations belong to one and the same office; so that the bishops of the New Testament are to be regarded not as diocesan bishops, like those of a later period, but simply as Congregational officers. This is placed beyond question by every passage in which we meet with this title."[2] KURTZ says, "that originally the πρεσβύτεροι (elders) were the same as the ἐπίσκοποι (bishops), we gather with absolute certainty from the statements of the New Testament, and of Clement of Rome, a disciple of the Apostles," and then, after reference to three points of that witness which they furnish, he adds, "in the face of such indubitable evidence, it is difficult to account for the pertinacity with which Romish and Angelican theologians insist that these two offices had from the first been different in name and functions; while the allegation of some, that although, originally, the two designations had been identical, the offices themselves were distinct, seems little better than arbitrary and absurd. Even Jerome, Augustin, Urban II., and Petrus Lombardus admit that originally the two had been identical. It was reserved for the Council of Trent to convert this truth into a heresy."[3] KILLEN says, "the elders or bishops were the same as the pastors and teachers; for they had the charge of the instruction and government of the Church."[4] And NEANDER — prince of all who have devoted their labors to the exposition of the affairs of the early Church — says; "that the name ἐπίσκοποι or bishops, was altogether synonymous with that of Presbyters, is clearly evident from those passages of Scripture, where both appellations are used interchangeably."[5]

---

[1] "*Manual of Church History.*" (Shedd's trans. 1857.) p. 107.
[2] "*History of the Apostolic Church.*" (Yeoman's trans. 1858.) p. 523. See also "*History of the Christian Church,*" by the same author. p. 134.
[3] "*Text Book of Church History.*" (1860.) Vol. 1. p. 67. See also "*History of the Christian Church,*" by the same author. (Clark's Ed.) Vol. i. p. 68.
[4] "*The Ancient Church.*" (1859.) p. 232.
[5] "*General History of the Christian Religion and Church.*" (Torrey's trans.) Vol. 1. p. 184. So also, in his "*Planting and Training of the Chr. Church.*" (Ryland's trans.) (p. 92.). he enlarges on the same point, and concludes; "originally both names related entirely to the same office, and hence both names are frequently interchanged as perfectly synonymous." And in

Having thus observed with what singular unanimity and force,[1] the current of learning and the judgment of antiquity sets toward that

---

his Introduction to Dr. Coleman's "*Apostolical and Prim. Church,*" (p. 20), he says, "the name of *presbyters* denoted the dignity of their office. That of *bishops*, on the other hand, was expressive rather of the nature of their office, *to take the oversight of the Church.* Most certainly no other distinction originally existed between them."

[1] The question may here naturally arise in the reader's mind, how, if the voice of the past is so clear and strong as would appear from the foregoing testimonies, the advocates of Papal and Episcopal power can attempt to maintain their theory also from antiquity? They do it mainly on the testimony of certain documents which are claimed to be Epistles of Ignatius (who died A. D. 107, or 116), which contain frequent and decided reference to bishops, as a rank above presbyters, and bearing authority. These Epistles are fifteen in number, namely: (1) *Ad Ephesios*, (2) *Ad Magnesianos*, (3) *Ad Trallianos*, (4) *Ad Romanos*, (5) *Ad Philadelphenos*, (6) *Ad Smyrneos*, (7) *Ad Polycarpum*, (8) *Ad Mariam*, (9) *Ad Tarsenses*, (10) *Ad Antiochenos*, (11) *Ad Heronem*, (12) *Ad Philippenses*, (13) *Ad Joanni Evan.*, (14) *Ad Eundem*, (15) *Beatæ Virgini*. They were brought to the attention of the learned world at different times, and, after all were printed, they seem to have been received without question until about the middle of the sixteenth century. Then, when scholarship began to be more critical, and the Reformation turned special attention to some portion of their contents, doubts began to be expressed in regard to them. They contain such precepts as these: "all should follow the Bishop, as Jesus Christ, the Father," (*Ad Smyrnæos*, Sec. viii.); "It is not allowable, without the Bishop, either to baptize or to administer the eucharist," (*Ibid*) ; "Whoso honors the Bishop, shall be honored of God." (*Ibid.* Sec. ix.) So, they intimate that the Bishop ought to be reverenced as Christ himself, (*Ad Ephesios*, Sec. vi.) ; that he presides in the place of God, (*Ad Magnesianos*, Sec. vii.) etc. It was not strange that such passages — so wholly unlike the ordinary tenor of the speech of that age — together with others concerning Lent, and many corruptions which had crept into the Church, should lead, first to doubts, next to a rigid examination, and then to a rejection of large portions, if not the whole, as being the work of a later date — seeking, by forgery, to gain the reverence natural to the letters of such a man. The authors of the *Centuriæ Magdeburgenses* led off in this work. Calvin soon expressed his opinion, saying : "nothing can be more nauseating than the absurdities which have been published under the name of Ignatius; and therefore, the conduct of those who provide themselves with such masks for deception is the less entitled to toleration." (*Institutes*, Book i. chap. xiii. sec. 29.) The fight waxed warm ; Churchmen generally contending on the one side, and Reformers on the other. The three Epistles last enumerated — which were extant only in Latin versions — were soon given up as spurious. In 1623, Vedelius arranged the first seven of the remaining twelve, apart from the 8th, 9th, 10th, 11th, and 12th, pronouncing those seven to be, for substance, genuine — with interpolations, which he endeavored to indicate — and the others to be forgeries. The controversy went on for several years, until, in 1666, Daillé, one of the most eminent of the French Protestants, vigorously attempted to establish the fraudulent origin and character of the entire list. To him Bishop Pearson replied, in 1672, saying all that could well be said in defence of the genuineness of a portion of the list. The result of the contest thus far, was the general conviction on the part of Churchmen that the first seven — at least in their shortened form, after the interpolations should be thrown out — were reliable ; and a concession on the part of their antagonists that this *might* be so.

A recent discovery has re-opened the discussion. In the library of the Syrian Convent at Nitria, in Egypt, was found, a few years since, a Syriac version of the 1st, 4th, and 7th Epistles, (*Ad Ephesios, Ad Romanos*, and *Ad Polycarpum*,) which was purchased for the British Museum. This version has been translated and published by the Rev. W. Cureton (London, 1845). It now turns out that this old Syriac MSS. omits *two-thirds* of the Epistle to the Ephesians, and large portions of the other two — *as compared with those Epistles after they had been previously reduced by throwing out all which seemed to be interpolated;* thus prompting the inference that a still farther important excision is necessary before the letters of Ignatius, *as he*

view of the parity — under whatever name — of the first officers of the early Christian Church, which our Congregational Fathers held; we are prepared to advance to the direct examination, in the last place: —

(3.) *Of the testimony of the Scriptures themselves.* Those passages which bear upon this subject are few and unambiguous. It will be borne in mind that the exact question before us, concerning which they are to be examined is, whether the four terms, 'Pastor,' 'Teacher,' 'Presbyter' (or elder), and 'Bishop' (or overseer), are intended to designate one and the same office, or two or more offices, of different rank.

(a.) *The first proof that they designate one office only, is afforded by an examination of the words themselves.* The term *Pastor* ($\pi o\iota\mu\dot\eta\nu$ — *poimēn*) is the word which is usually translated 'Shepherd.' It occurs *eighteen* times in the New Testament. In thirteen of these it is applied, either in the way of narrative or of parable, to the ordinary relation of a shepherd to his flock. In four instances it is applied metaphorically to Christ; as the 'good Shepherd,' the 'great Shepherd,' etc. In the remaining instance (Eph. iv: 11), it is used to designate those persons whom Christ gave to his Church, in connection with Apostles,

---

wrote them, shall be in our possession. It is remarkable also that the portions thus thrown into discredit as being fraudulent additions of a later date than the genuine Epistles, bear directly upon the Episcopal and Arian controversies; rendering it almost certain that these additions were the work of some party interested in those controversies, and desiring shelter under the name of Ignatius. It may be noted here, also, that the translator of *Guericke* suggests that these passages, if genuine, exhibit merely "the high Church tendency of a locality (Asia Minor), and not the theory of polity universally established and prevalent at the time." —(*Shedd's "Guericke."* Vol. i. p. 113, note.)

Such being the facts in regard to these Epistles — it being wholly uncertain whether those passages which Episcopalians quote from them in proof of the early existence and authority of Bishops as an order superior to Elders, were ever written by Ignatius, or even within two hundred years of his time; and it being entirely certain that the general testimony of the Fathers before and after him, is against any such Bishops — as we have seen; we feel that sound reasoning and the decision of common sense will rule Ignatius out of court as a witness against the great array on the other side.

Those who desire to review this controversy, can consult *Vedelius*, (4to Geneva, 1623); *Archbishop Usher*, (4to, Oxford, 1644); *Daille's "De Scriptis quæ sub Dionys. Areop. et Ignatii Antioch. circumferentur, Libri duo."* (4to, Geneva, 1666); *Pearson's "Vindiciæ Ignatianæ,"* (4to, Cambridge, 1672); *Cureton's "Ancient Syriac version of Epis. of Ignat."* (8vo, London, 1845); *Bunsen's "Ignatius von Antiochien, und seine Zeit."* (Hamburg, 1847). *Cave's "Hist. Litt."* (Oxford, 1740), Vol. i. p. 41.; *Oudin "de Scrip. Eccl."* Vol. i. cod. 71.; and *Ceillier's "Auteurs Sacrés."* Vol. i. p. 620. See also *Neander*, (Torrey's trans.) Vol. i. p. 661. See also Articles in *Princeton Review*, Vol. xxi. p. 378; *New Englander*, Vol. vii. p. 501; *Edinburgh Review*, Vol. xc. p. 82; *Monthly Christian Spectator*, Vol. v. p. 393; *Church Review*, Vol. i. p. 566, and Vol. ii. p. 194; *London Quarterly*, Vol. lxxxviii. p. 36; and *Kitto's Journal*, Vol. v. p. 399.

prophets and evangelists, for 'the perfecting of the saints,' and 'the work of the ministry,' etc. Here it is expressly said that these persons are 'pastors *and* teachers;' the grammatical construction of the sentence being such as to render it certain that, in this only case where 'Pastors' are spoken of, they are the same persons as 'Teachers.'[1]

The term *Teacher* (διδάσκαλος — *didaskalos*) is the word usually translated 'master.' It is found *fifty-eight* times in the New Testament. In forty-seven of these cases it is rendered 'master;' in one instance 'doctors,' and in the remaining ten, 'teacher,' or 'teachers.' In four of these ten, (John iii: 2, Rom. ii: 20, 2 Tim. iv: 3, Heb. v: 12), the application is to the ordinary function of imparting knowledge. In two, (1 Tim. ii: 7, 2 Tim. i: 11), of the remaining six, Paul applies it to himself, describing himself as 'a preacher and an Apostle, and a teacher of the Gentiles.' In the remaining four cases (Acts xiii: 1, 1 Cor. xii: 28, 29, Eph. iv: 11), it is used to describe those officers of the churches who taught the people; and in no case in such a connection as to destroy that identity between them and the Pastors, which is affirmed in Eph. iv: 11, and intimated in the way in which Paul — as we have just seen — takes the word as a synonyme for his own office as a preacher.

The term *Presbyter*, or Elder, (πρεσβύτερος — *presbuteros*) occurs in *sixty-seven* places in the New Testament. In thirty-one instances it is employed to designate the Elders of the Jewish Sanhedrim — officers so often mentioned in connection with the Chief Priests, and not wholly unlike the Aldermen of our own time; both terms in their structure recalling the unquestionable fact that age originally was a

---

[1] "Non dicit *alios pastores, alios doctores*, sed *alios pastores et doctores*, quia pastores omnes debent esse et doctores."—*Estius and Erasmus, in loco. Poole, Syn. Crit.* Vol. iv. p. 789.

"The union of the two, [pastors and teachers] in general as one class, to which either designation might in some degree apply, seems to be intimated by the construction of the Greek, which places before each of the preceding nouns, the same article which qualifies these two."— *Turner's "Ephesians,"* p. 125.

"The absence of the article before διδασκάλους proves that the Apostle intended to designate the same persons as at once pastors and teachers. . . . This interpretation is given by Augustine and Jerome; the latter of whom says, 'non enim ait: alios autem pastores et alios magistros, sed alios pastores *et* magistros, ut qui pastor est, esse debeat et magister.' In this interpretation, the modern commentators, almost without exception, concur."—*Hodge's "Ephesians,"* p. 226.

"From these latter teachers not being distinguished from the pastors by the τούς δέ, it would seem that the two offices were held by the same persons."—*Alford. in loco.* Vol. iii. p. 113.

prominent qualification for such a dignity. In twelve instances it is applied to the 'four and twenty elders' of the Apocalypse. Once (Heb. xi: 2), it is used of the Ancient Hebrews. In six cases it is simply the adjective of age — 'elder,' 'eldest,' etc. In the remaining seventeen instances — *ten* being in the Acts — it refers to those officers of the Christian churches who were called *Elders*, and who, in fifteen of the seventeen cases, were, so far as record is made,[1] the *only* officers, except the deacons, which the churches had; leaving the necessary inference that they must have been the same persons who are elsewhere styled 'pastors' and 'teachers.'

The term *Bishop* or Overseer (ἐπίσκοπος — *episkopos*) occurs only five times in the New Testament. Once (1 Pet. ii: 25), it is applied to Christ as 'the Shepherd and Bishop' of souls; where it is coupled with the word usually translated 'Pastor,' as already mentioned.[2] Three times it is used in such connection as to make it obviously the title of the one office of the Church beside that of deacon; viz: (1 Tim. iii: 2), where Paul, after describing the qualifications needful for a Bishop, passes at once to say, "likewise must the *deacons* be grave," etc.; and (Tit. i: 7), where he speaks of Timothy's "ordaining *elders* in every city," and proceeds to say that they [the elders] must " be blameless," etc., "*for* a *Bishop* ought to be blameless, as the steward of God," — there being no possibility of any sound logical or grammatical construction which shall avoid the identity of the Bishop with the Elders just spoken of;[3] and (Phil. i: 1,) where Paul addresses the saints at Philippi " with the Bishops and deacons " — no mention

---

[1] Acts xi: 30; xiv: 23; xv: 2, 4, 6, 22, 23; xvi: 4; xx: 17; xxi: 18; 1 Tim. v: 17, 19; Tit. i: 5; James v: 14; 1 Pet. v: 1.

[2] See page 100.

[3] " This passage plainly shows that there is no distinction between a presbyter and a bishop; for he [Paul] now calls indiscriminately by the latter name, those whom he formerly called presbyters; and farther in conducting this very argument, he employs both names in the same sense, without any distinction; as Jerome has remarked, both in his commentary on this passage, and in his Epistle to Evagrius."—*Calvin. Comment. in loco.* p. 294.

" That the expression *elders* (v. 5) designates the same office as *Bishop* in v. 7, is acknowledged by all who *can* acknowledge it."—*Olshausen.* (Kendrick's Ed.) Vol. v. p. 566.

" We see here a proof of the early date of this Epistle, in the synonymous use of 'ἐπίσκοπος and πρεσβύτερος; the latter word designating the *rank*, the former, the duties of the presbyter."—*Conybeare and Howson.* Vol. ii. p. 477.

"'*For it behooves an*' (τόν, as so often, generic, *the*, i. e., every: our English idiom requires the indefinite article) ' *overseer* ' — (here most plainly identified with the *presbyter* spoken of before) ' *to be blameless,*' " etc.—*Alford. Com. Tit.* i: 7. Vol. iii. p. 391.

being made of any other office as being known to him, or them, in connection with the Church. The only other instance of the use of the word is (Acts xx: 28,) where, at Miletus, Paul expressly tells the *elders* of the Church at Ephesus, that the Holy Ghost has made them ἐπισκόπους (*episkopous*) *Bishops*, or overseers, over that 'flock,' to 'feed the Church of God which he hath purchased with his own blood.'

So far as the usage and signification of the words themselves are concerned, then, it is obvious that they are irreconcilable with any other theory than that which applies them to one office only. There are also two instances of the use, by Paul, of kindred words, in such a way as to prove the same point. One is (1 Pet. v: 2, 3) where he, as a 'fellow-elder,' exhorts "the *elders* which are among you," to "feed the flock of God which is among you, ἐπισκοποῦντες (*episkopountes*), [the *verb* which signifies the activity of the noun 'Bishop,'] *acting the Bishop* over them, not by constraint, but willingly," etc. But if Paul exhorted Elders to act as Bishops, it could only be because he understood them to *be* Bishops! The other is (1 Tim. iii: 1), where the same Apostle says, "if a man desire ἐπισκοπῆς (*episkopēs*) [the *noun* denoting the activity of the noun 'Bishop'] *the office of a Bishop*, he desireth a good work," etc., going on immediately to discourse of the qualifications of bishops and deacons, as if they were the only Church officers concerning whom he had any knowledge, or any counsel to give; a thing simply incredible on the Episcopal theory. It is noticeable in this connection, also, that the name 'Apostle' is never, in a single instance, used interchangeably for that of Bishop or Deacon; while the Apostles did sometimes style themselves 'Elders;'[1] which would argue that (if either are) *Elders* rather than Bishops must be "successors of the Apostles," in an official sense.

(*b.*) *The second proof from the Bible that the terms Pastor, Teacher, Elder, and Bishop, designate one and the same office, is found in the fact that the same qualifications are demanded of all.* We have seen that the terms 'Pastor' and 'Teacher' are never used to distinguish offices different from the Elders and Bishops. So that the real question is whether the Scriptural qualifications of Elders and Bishops are the same, or not? Paul has given, at some length, the requisites

---

[1] 2 John 1: 1; 3 John 1: 1; 1 Pet. v: 1.

for the faithful performance of both offices, and when arranged in parallel columns, it will be easy to see how far they agree, and whether, anywhere, they differ.

For an Elder.	For a Bishop.
Tit. 1: 6-10.	1 Tim. iii: 2-7.
If any be blameless, the husband of one wife, having faithful children — not accused of riot, or unruly.	A bishop must be blameless, the husband of one wife, one that ruleth well his own house, having his children in subjection with all gravity. For if a man know not how to rule his own house, how shall he take care of the Church of God?
A lover of hospitality, a lover of good men, sober, just, holy, temperate, holding fast the faithful word as he hath been taught, that he may be able by sound doctrine both to exhort, and to convince the gainsayers. Blameless, as the steward of God, not self-willed, not soon angry, not given to wine, no striker, not given to filthy lucre.	Vigilant, sober, of good behavior, given to hospitality, apt to teach.
	Not given to wine, no striker, not greedy of filthy lucre, but patient, not a brawler, not covetous. Not a novice, lest being lifted up with pride, he fall into the condemnation of the devil. Moreover he must have a good report of them which are without, lest he fall into reproach, and the snare of the devil.

These qualifications are identical. Elders and Bishops must *both* be blameless, the husband of one wife, faithful parents, circumspect, sober, hospitable, temperate, patient, humble, quiet, long-suffering, and able to teach others. If, in these catalogues of necessary graces, either has the advantage of the other, the Elder has it in the fact that Paul mentions it as of importance for him to possess and use "sound doctrine" for exhortation and conviction, a thing which he leaves to inference in the case of the Bishop. How inevitable the conclusion that, in Paul's mind, the two offices were the same!

(*c.*) *The third proof, from the Bible, that the terms Pastor, Teacher, Elder, and Bishop designate one and the same office, is found in the fact that the same duties are assigned to all.* These duties are to guide; to instruct; to administer the ordinances; and perhaps to ordain. We shall see that they are made the duties of Elders and Bishops alike, or, at least, that the Bishops have no preëminence in regard to them.

(*aa.*) *It is their duty to guide the Church by counsel and authority.* All will, of course, concede that if there were any such Bishops in the days of the Apostles as are now known by that name, this must have been, by emphasis, *their* duty. But the New Testament makes it clear that the *Elders* were charged with it as a part of their function, for Paul says (1 Tim. v: 17), "let the *Elders* that *rule well*, (οἱ καλῶς προεστῶτες πρεσβύτεροι — *hoi kalōs proestōtes presbuteroi*), be counted worthy of double honor." So Paul tells the *Elders* of the Church at Ephesus who assembled at Miletus to meet him (Acts xx: 28), to 'take heed unto themselves, and to all the flock, over which the Holy Ghost had made them Bishops, that they (ποιμαίνειν — *poimainein*) *feed* the Church of God which he hath purchased with his own blood.' In the classic Greek this verb here rendered 'feed,' had the meaning 'to take care of, to guide, to govern,'[1] and in four of the eleven instances of its use in the New Testament, the common version renders it '*rule.*'[2] Its natural sense seems to be, however, that of *acting the shepherd* to a flock, which includes prominently the idea of leading and guiding — driving, if need be — them to such fields and streams as are best fitted for their nourishment and repose. And it is quite worthy of notice that this same word which is applied (Matt. ii: 6) to the rule of Christ over his Church, is here used as descriptive of the relation of the *Elders* to the churches. It may be remembered here, also, that in all the record of the council at Jerusalem (Acts xv: 1–31), the Elders are the only officers of the churches who are mentioned as taking part in the debate or the decision, with 'the Apostles' and 'the whole Church.'

(*bb.*) *It is the duty of Bishops and Elders alike to instruct the Church.* This is clear indirectly from the tenor of many passages, but directly from the demands before quoted,[3] that the Bishop be 'apt to teach,' and the Elder 'be able by sound doctrine, both to exhort and to convince the gainsayers.'

(*cc.*) *It was the duty of Bishops and Elders alike to administer the ordinances of the Gospel.* We are left indeed without the direct tes-

---

[1] See "Liddell and Scott." [2] Matt. ii: 6; Rev. ii: 27; xii: 5; xix: 15. [3] See page 104.

timony of any Biblical record, or command, to settle this, but the circumstantial evidence in proof of the position is very strong. It is clear that *somebody* must have administered the ordinances of Baptism and the Lord's Supper, and that such administration was a thing of standing necessity, not only for the introduction of all believers into the Church, but for their edification afterwards — since it is in evidence that the Lord's Supper was first administered daily;[1] and subsequently every week.[2] These ordinances — being thus a part of the ordinary demand of the churches for their regular service, their administration must be presumed to have formed a part of the regular duty of those who had the oversight of the churches, and performed the ordinary functions of the pastoral office, *unless some special reservation is made of this duty for some one class of laborers.* No such reservation in favor of Bishops is found on the record of the New Testament; while it is noticeable that the Apostles seem to have thrown off the administration of the rite of Baptism upon the ordinary teachers of the Church. Paul thanked God that he baptized none of the Corinthians but Crispus and Gaius, and the household of Stephanas, saying that Christ 'sent him not to baptize, but to preach the Gospel.' Peter did not baptize Cornelius.[3] The inference is an easy one that God's design was that the administration of the ordinances of Baptism and the Lord's Supper should devolve upon the ordinary ministers of the Church; whether named Pastors, or Teachers, or Elders, or Bishops.

(*dd.*) *If it was the duty of Bishops, it was also of the Elders to ordain.* It would be claimed by the advocates of the modern theory of the Episcopal office, that, if there were any Bishops in the Apostolic Church, it must have been a part of their business to induct their fellow laborers into office, by ordination. But the New Testament — while it says not a word about ordination by Bishops — does speak of what may have been the ordination of Timothy by the laying on

---

[1] Acts ii: 42-46; 1 Cor. x: 21.

[2] See "Pliny's letter to Trajan," and Coleman's "Ancient Christianity," p. 425.

[3] Tertullian argues that even laymen have the right to baptize and to administer the sacrament. He says: — "Vani erimus, si putaverimus, quod sacerdotibus non liceat, laicis licere. Nonne et laici sacerdotes sumus? Scriptum est: Regnum quoque nos et sacerdotes, Deo et Patri suo fecit. Differentiam inter ordinem et plebem constituit ecclesiae auctoritas, et honor per ordinis consessum sanctificatus. Adeo ubi ecclesiastici ordinis non est consessus, *et offers, et tinguis* et sacerdos es tibi solus."—*De Exhorta. Cast.* c. 7. (Ed. Lipsiae.) Vol. ii. p. 105.

See Grotius' comment upon this, and on the general subject, in his tract "*De cœna administratione, ubi pastores non sunt.*"—*Works.* (Ed. 1679.) Vol. iv. pp. 507-509.

of the hands *of the Presbytery;* that is, of the company of Presbyters, or Elders.¹ While, therefore, there is neither precept, nor very clear example of what we call ordination, as a custom of the primitive Church recognized as imperative and perpetual by the Scriptures, it is at least true that, so far as there is any hint in that direction, it is in favor of Elders rather than of Bishops, as those by whose hands it should be given.

(*d.*) *The fourth proof that the Scriptures recognize Pastors, Teachers, Elders, and Bishops as names for one office only, is found in the fact that those texts which have been claimed as indirectly implying that Bishops were a superior order, fail to sustain that claim.* It has been asserted that James was Bishop of Jerusalem, Titus Bishop of Crete, and Timothy Bishop of Ephesus; though tradition, rather than Scripture, has been mainly relied on for proof.² Reference has, however, been made, by those who maintain that James was the first "Bishop of Jerusalem," to the fact that Peter told the company who were praying at the house of Mary on the night of his deliverance from prison, to "go show these things unto *James* and to the brethren;"³ to the fact that James presided when the multitude "gave audience to Barnabas and Paul,"⁴ and said, "wherefore *my sentence is* that we trouble not them," etc.; to the fact that Paul, in describing a certain matter to the Galatians, refers to the arrival of some brethren from Jerusalem, as that of certain who "came from James;"⁵ and to the record that Paul went in "*unto James,* and all the Elders were present,"⁶ on his arrival at Jerusalem from Miletus. But there is only one of these passages which would not be just as appropriate on the Congregational theory that James was Senior Pastor of the Church at Jerusalem; and that was unwarrantably modified from the original in the process of translation, by those who believed that James was Bishop of Jerusalem, and desired to harmonize the record with that belief. The "wherefore *my sentence* is," is Διὸ ἐγὼ κρίνω (*dio egō krinō*), which simply means; "*wherefore I am of*

---

¹ "'*Of the presbytery*'—*i. e.* of the body of Elders who belonged to the congregation in which he was ordained. Where this was, we know not: hardly in Lystra, where he was first converted: might it not be in Ephesus itself, for this particular office?"—*Alford. Com. on* 1 Tim. iv : 14. (Vol. iii. p. 326.)

² Bingham refers to Jerome, Epiphanius, Chrysostom, Eusebius, Hilary the Deacon, and Theodoret, in proof; but quotes no Scripture in evidence.—"*Antiquities.*" Vol. l. pp. 20, 21.

³ Acts xii : 17.   ⁴ Acts xv : 13-19.   ⁵ Gal. ii : 12.   ⁶ Acts xxi : 18.

opinion that," etc.[1] So that this amounts to nothing in the way of argument.

All the Scripture claimed as evidence that Titus was Bishop of Crete, is the record that Paul left him in Crete to "set in order the things that are wanting, and ordain Elders in every city, as I had appointed thee."[2] But this passage is much more consonant with the Congregational theory that Paul desired him to act as an Evangelist, or temporary Missionary Superintendent of these semi-heathen churches; to comfort and instruct them, and perfect their organization. That Paul did not intend for him to assume any permanent office over them, is rendered sure by his direction to him to fail not to 'come unto him at Nicopolis,'[3] before winter,[4] and the mention of his subsequent departure to Dalmatia.[5]

The Episcopal claim in the case of Timothy rests on a foundation in the New Testament so slight, that it is amazing with what cool assumption he is asserted to have been "Bishop of Ephesus." When

---

1 "There does not seem to be in the following speech, any decision *ex cathedra*, either in the ἀκούσατέ μου, or in the ἐγὼ κρίνω: /the decision lay in the weightiness, partly no doubt of the person speaking, but principally of the matter spoken by him."—*Alford. Comment. in loco.* Vol. ii. p. 151.

"'*I—for my part, without dictating to others—judge,* i. e. *decide as my opinion.*' The verb affords no proof that the speaker's authority was greater than that of the other Apostles."—*Hackett.* Acts, p. 245.

"Id est, *ita censeo.*"—*Grotius, in loco.* Vol. ii. p. 620.

"'Wherefore *I think* that we ought not to trouble,' etc. . . . We may gather out of this narrative that they made no small account of James, forasmuch as he doth with his voice and consent so confirm the words of Peter, that they are all of his mind. . . . The old writers think that this was because he was Bishop of the place; but it is not to be thought that the faithful did, at their pleasure, change the order which Christ had appointed."—*Calvin. Comment. in loco.* pp. 63-70.

"'*I judge*'— a common formula, by which the members of the Greek assemblies introduced the expression of their individual opinion, as appears from its repeated occurrence in Thucydides; with which may be compared the corresponding Latin phrase (*sic censeo*) of frequent use in Cicero's orations. That James here settles the whole question by a decision *ex cathedra*, is as groundless an opinion as that Peter had already done so by his *dictum.*"—*Alexander.* Acts. Vol. ii. p. 83.

2 Titus i: 5.   3 Titus iii: 12.

4 "At this latter date (A. D. 67) we find him [Titus] left in Crete by St. Paul, obviously for a temporary purpose, viz: to 'carry forward the correction of those things which are defective,' and among these principally, to establish presbyteries for the government of the various churches, consisting of ἐπίσκοποι. His stay there was to be very short (Ch. iii: 12) and he was, on the arrival of Tychicus or Artemas, to join the Apostle at Nicopolis. Not the slightest trace is found in the Epistle, of any intention on the part of St. Paul, to place Titus permanently over the Cretan Churches: indeed, such a view is inconsistent with the data furnished us in it."—*Alford. Introduction to Epis. to Tit.* Vol. iii. p. 107.

5 2 Tim. iv: 10.

Paul (A. D. 57 or 58), left Asia Minor for Greece, he desired Timothy to take temporary charge of the Church at Ephesus — as it is written : " I besought thee to abide still at Ephesus, when I went into Macedonia " — not to become its permanent head, but for a specified purpose — " that thou mightest charge some that they teach no other doctrine, neither give heed to fables and endless genealogies," etc.[1] With the exception of an incidental allusion to his "ministering"[2] to Paul while there, this is the *only intimation* in the New Testament that Timothy ever was at Ephesus at all! And that the purpose for which Paul commissioned him was a temporary one, is clear from the tenor of the Epistle. Paul says, "*till I come*, give attendance to reading," etc.[3] So he says, "these things write I unto thee, hoping to come unto thee shortly; but *if I tarry long*," etc.[4] Nor do we find the least hint that Timothy, or any one else, was, or was ever to be, Bishop — in the Episcopal sense — of the Church at Ephesus, either in Paul's address to its Elders when they met him at Miletus,[5] or in his Epistle to it; while the tenor of the Epistle coincides with his recorded counsel to those Elders to take care of it, as being themselves its Bishops — in the Congregational sense.[6] Moreover, long after the date when Paul is claimed to have set Timothy over the Ephesian Church as Bishop, he writes to him to "do the work of — an Evangelist."[7] We dismiss, then, these assumptions on behalf of the Episcopal dignity of Timothy, and Titus, and James, with the irresistible conclusion that, but for the reactionary influence of a corrupt subsequent condition of the churches, leading early writers and later historians to seek to manufacture precedents in the very time of the Apostles, no man in his senses would ever have dreamed of attempting to draw such inferences from such premises.[8] And we conclude also — since these texts, claimed to establish the New Testament origin of Bishops as an order superior to Elders, fail thus to justify that claim; and since the duties and qualifications recorded

---

[1] 1 Tim. 1: 3. [2] Acts xix : 22. [3] 1 Tim. iv : 13. [4] 1 Tim. iii : 14, 15.
[5] Acts xx : 17–38. [6] Acts xx : 28. [7] 2 Tim. iv : 5.
[8] "How little does all this look as if Timothy were the permanent Bishop of Ephesus ! A man who is never mentioned as being there but for a temporary purpose; who received no charge, even in a letter addressed to him there, but such as might be given to any minister of the Gospel ; who is repeatedly mentioned as being elsewhere united with Paul in his toils and trials ; and of whom there is no intimation that he ever did return, or ever would return, for any purpose whatever ! Such is the *strong case* on which so much reliance is placed in sustaining the enormous fabric of Episcopacy in the world!"—*Barnes' "Apostolic Church."* p. 100.

of Bishops and Elders are identical; and since there is nothing in the sense, or use, of the words themselves to warrant any other deduction — that the Scriptures teach the full identity of these offices. Whence also we further judge — since the voice of Scripture, of Ecclesiastical History, and of the early writers of the Church, and the opinion of so many eminent and candid scholars concur in the affirmation, — that the first class of permanent officers which Christ designated for his churches, is indiscriminately spoken of in the New Testament under the names of Pastor, Teacher, Elder, and Bishop.

Here, as well as anywhere, may be considered a question which must be answered somewhere, namely:

Does the New Testament teach, or authorize, any such distinct office in the Church as that of Ruling Elder? The Presbyterian "Form of Government" teaches that there is such an office.[1] The Dutch Reformed, and American Lutheran, and some other churches, are of the same opinion.[2] And it is well known that our Pilgrim Fathers originally held to a distinct office of Ruling Elder, though it soon went into disuse in New England. This — as now held — is a *lay* office, and an office of *ruling* simply, as distinguished from *teaching*; the Presbyterian 'Book' declaring that: "the ordinary and perpetual officers in the Church are Bishops or Pastors; and *the representatives of the people*, usually styled Ruling Elders and Deacons" — so that the claim of its advocates is that there are three orders of permanent officers in the Church; one of the ministry, and two of the laity. Of course, then, Ruling Elders must be radically distinguished from those Elders who are the same as "Bishops or Pastors;" and the question becomes two-fold; — whether there are any Elders whose sole business is ruling, distinct from other Elders; and, if so, whether they are laymen?

The following are the passages by which it is claimed that this office roots itself in the soil of the New Testament, namely:

---

[1] "Ruling Elders are properly the representatives of the people, chosen by them for the purpose of exercising government and discipline, in conjunction with pastors or ministers. This office has been understood, by a great part of the Protestant Reformed Churches, to be designated in the Holy Scriptures, by the title of 'governments,' and of those who 'rule well,' but do not 'labor in the word and doctrine.'"—*Form of Gov. of Pres. Church.* Book i. ch. 5.

[2] See *Formula of Government and Discip. of Evang. Luth. Church.* Chap. iii. sec. 6; and a "*Message to Ruling Elders*," etc. *Board of Pub. Ref. Prot. Dutch Church*, passim.

"Let the Elders *that rule well*, be counted worthy of double honor, especially they who labor in the word and doctrine."[1] "And God hath set some in the Church, first Apostles, secondarily prophets, thirdly teachers, after that miracles, then gifts of healings, helps, *governments*, diversities of tongues."[2] "Having then gifts, differing according to the grace that is given to us, whether prophecy, let us prophesy according to the proportion of faith ; or ministry, let us wait on our ministering; or he that teacheth, on teaching ; or he that exhorteth, on exhortation; he that giveth, let him do it with simplicity; *he that ruleth with diligence ;* he that showeth mercy, with cheerfulness."[3] " It seemed good unto us, being assembled with one accord, *to send chosen men* unto you, with our beloved Barnabas and Paul ; men that have hazarded their lives for the name of our Lord Jesus Christ."[4]

These are all the proof-texts which the Presbyterian 'Book' cites in evidence. Dr. Owen refers to two or three others, which are collateral and prove nothing unless the office be first established from these;[5] so that we may feel quite sure that if the divine right of the Ruling Lay Eldership is not here, it is not anywhere in the New Testament. But is it here? The last text quoted, clearly says nothing about Ruling Elders. Judas and Silas, we are told in a previous verse[6] (where, if they had had any official relation to the Church, such a fact must have received mention), were — not Ruling Elders, but — ἄνδρας ἡγουμένους (*andras hēgoumenous*), [literally], '*leading men* among the brethren;' who were here selected to be sent as delegates to the Church at Antioch. A little further on,[7] we read that they were 'prophets;' and the history of Silas is such as to make it to the last degree improbable that he sustained *any* permanent official relation to the Church *at Jerusalem*.[8] Unless every delegate which a Church chooses from among its 'leading men' to represent it before another Church, or a council of churches, is thereby made a Ruling Elder, this text has no bearing upon the question in

---

[1] Tim. v: 17. [2] 1 Cor. xii : 28. [3] Rom. xii: 6, 8.
[4] Acts xv: 25, 26. [5] Acts xx: 28; 1 Tim. iii: 6; Heb. xiii: 7, 17; Rev. ii, iii.
[6] Acts xv: 22. [7] Verse 32.
[8] He accompanied Paul on his second Missionary journey through Asia Minor to Macedonia, (Acts xv: 40; xvii: 4), remained behind in Berea (xvii: 10, 14), and joined Paul again in Corinth (xviii: 5; 1 Thess. i: 1; 2 Thess. i: 1), where he preached with Paul and Timotheus (2 Cor. i: 19), he being called also Silvanus. See *Alford Com.*, Acts xv: 22.

hand. The second text quoted is as good in proof of *eight* different kinds of Church officers, as of three; and — so far as its mention of 'governments' is concerned — its etymological force, as we have already seen,[1] is exhausted when it is held to refer to those persons in the Church who 'pilot' its movements. It does not assert that they are officers specially appointed for this duty and doing nothing else; nor does it intimate that, if so, they are laymen. The most which can be claimed from it is, that if any other passages can be found establishing the lay Eldership, it may refer to such lay Elders as 'governments;' otherwise not. The same remarks apply to the third passage. It will hardly be safe to infer from it that there are to be *seven* officers in every Church: — one to prophesy, another to minister, another to teach, another to exhort, another to give, another to rule, and another to show mercy, yet there is as much evidence from it of seven distinct officers, with those respective functions, as there is from it that "he that ruleth — with diligence," is a distinct officer known as a lay Ruling Elder. If any other texts settle it that there were in the Apostolic churches, and were Divinely intended to be in every Church, lay Ruling Elders, to whom belongs the administration of government and discipline, then this 'ruling, with diligence,' doubtless refers to them; otherwise not. The whole question of direct Scriptural testimony establishing the Divine origin and authority of lay Ruling Elders is then thrown upon the single text first cited above, namely: "let the Elders that rule well be counted worthy of double honor, especially they who labor in the word and doctrine." If this passage establishes the office of lay Ruling Elders, then it will explain into harmony with itself the other texts to which allusion has been made, and we shall have Scriptural warrant for such an office; if it fails, the whole theory falls to the ground. Concerning it, we suggest: —

1. These 'Elders' here spoken of, it is reasonable to infer — in the absence of any hint to the contrary, in the structure of the text — must be the same πρεσβύτεροι, (*presbuteroi*), of whom Paul has been speaking in the earlier portion of the Epistle,[2] and whom he speaks of again[3] before its close; the same persons, in fact, who are commonly referred to, under that name, in the New Testament. Unless

---

[1] See pp. 74, 75.   [2] 1 Tim. iii: 1-7; v: 1.   [3] Verse 19.

this is so, the Apostle here violates the first principles of the use of language, and could not expect to make himself rightly understood. But, if the Elders here spoken of are the same as have been everywhere else called by that name, they are the same persons who are also called 'Bishops,' and 'Pastors,' and 'Teachers;' namely: the Spiritual guides of the Church; and hence they cannot be *lay* Elders — whether 'Ruling,' or otherwise.

2. The very structure of the verse is such as grammatically to compel the inference that the Elders who 'rule well,' are of the same kind of Elders who 'labor in the word and doctrine.' This results from the necessary force of the adverb μάλιστα (*malista*), '*most of all*,' whose force is not to divide into classes, but to indicate a distinction of emphasis between individuals of the same class. It is used only twelve times in the New Testament. Of these, in three cases,[1] it simply adds energy to the assertion which is made. In every instance of the remaining eight (the passage under consideration being left out of the account), it introduces the mention of particulars on which stress is laid, which are included in the general mention of the first member of the sentence.[2] So that to read this adverb here as seclud-

---

[1] Acts xx: 38 "Sorrowing *most of all* for the words which he spake, that they should see his face no more;" Acts xxv: 26, — "*Specially* before thee, O King Agrippa," etc.; Acts xxvi: 3, — "I think myself happy, King Agrippa, etc., *especially* because I know thee to be expert," etc.

[2] Gal. vi: 10. "Let us do good unto all men, *especially* unto them, [that portion of 'all men'] who are of the household of faith."

Phil. iv: 22. "All the saints salute you, *chiefly* they, [that portion of 'all the saints'] that are of Cæsar's household"

1 Tim. iv: 10. "Who is the Saviour of all men, *specially* of those [that portion of 'all men'] that believe "

1 Tim v · 8. "But if any provide not for his own, and *specially* for those [that portion of 'his own' that are of] his own house, he hath denied the faith, and is worse than an infidel."

2 Tim. iv: 13. "The cloak that I left at Troas with Carpus, when thou comest, bring with thee, and the books, but *especially* [(all books were 'parchments' then) that portion of his 'books' which Timothy would understand by the term τὰς μεμβράνας] the parchments."

Titus i: 10 "For there are many unruly and vain talkers and deceivers, *specially* [worst among the 'many'] they of the circumcision."

Philemon *v.* 16. "A brother beloved [of all who know him] *specially* to me [of that all] but how much more unto thee," etc.

2 Peter ii: 9, 10 "The Lord knoweth how to deliver the godly out of temptations, and to reserve the unjust unto the day of judgment to be punished: but *chiefly* them [the Lord knoweth how to 'reserve' that portion of the 'unjust'] that walk after the flesh in the lust of uncleanness," etc. If, now, we read the text under consideration by this invariable usage of μάλιστα in such connection in the New Testament, it will stand thus: — "Let the Elders that rule well be counted worthy of double honor; *especially* they [that portion of ' the Elders that rule well'] who labor in the word and doctrine."

ing Elders that 'rule well,' into a class different from those who 'labor in the word and doctrine,' would be to do violence to the analogy of its use in every kindred passage in the New Testament. But if the Elders that 'rule well,' are of the same class as those who 'labor in the word and doctrine,' they cannot be *lay* Elders.

3. Further, if these 'elders that rule well,' are of such a kind that any of them also 'labor in the word and doctrine,' they cannot be distinguished into a class which shall have ruling *solely* for its function; for the ruling Elders of which this text speaks, are to be doubly honored for 'laboring in the word and doctrine;' that is,—on the Presbyterian theory—they are to be specially commended for forsaking their own function, and doing that, the not doing of which is the only ground for the separate existence of their office in the Church.

4. There is, then, not only nothing in this text which can be made, without violent perversion of its plain sense, to teach the Divine intention of lay Ruling Elders as a distinct and permanent office in the

---

The inevitable suggestion of this text is, then, that ruling belongs *to all Elders*, and laboring in the word and doctrine only to some; while those who rule best must be honored, particularly if, in addition, they also teach.

See Davidson (*Ecclesiastical Polity of the New Testament.*" p. 183, 184.)

Olshausen says: "It is evident that the Apostle here distinguishes between two kinds of *ruling presbyters* — those who labor in the word, and those who do not. Both are *ruling* presbyters, and from this it already appears that it is not *lay presbyters*, as many have thought, that are here spoken of in contradistinction to clerical presbyters; for by προεστῶτες πρεσβύτεροι can be understood only presbyters merely as they are already known to us."—"*Kendrick's Trans.*" Vol. vi. p. 135.

Alford says of the πρεσβύτεροι generally in the New Testament (including those mentioned here), "they are identical with ἐπίσκοποι."—Vol. ii. p. 118.

Even that eminent Presbyterian, Rev J P Wilson, D.D., who investigated the question most thoroughly, in his work on the "*Primitive Government of Christian Churches*," concedes in regard to this text (1 Tim. v: 17) that it "expresses a diversity in the exercise of the presbyterial office, *but not in the office itself.*" pp. 282, 283. And he consistently refused to have any Ruling Elders in his own Church. See *Princeton Review.* (1843.) Vol. xv. p. 325.

So, too, an able writer in the *Spirit of the Pilgrims* on "Church Officers," says of this text, "here the Elder is seen to be one who 'labors in the word and doctrine,' *i. e.*, who is in the ministry; and another word would not be necessary, were it not that some have thought two classes of Elders are here spoken of — one *governing* and the other *teaching* the Church. But it does not appear that the Scriptures elsewhere appoint, or even recognize, a second and subordinate class of Elders. A single passage, it is true, if it fairly taught the doctrine, were enough; and, like the oath of confirmation, should be 'the end of all strife.' But inasmuch as this text is alone, even in *seeming* to intimate such a sentiment; and inasmuch as the intimation, if it be one, is very remote, while the passage may well be interpreted differently; — in such a case to graft the sentiment in question upon the Bible, as an item of Scriptural doctrine, seems quite gratuitous. The question may well arise whether the *ruling*, spoken of in this passage, is not the prerogative of the ministry? Of this, I think, there can be no serious doubt."—*Spirit of the Pilgrims.* (1831.) Vol. iv. p. 190.

Church, or as an office in it at all,[1] but there is nothing in the least degree inharmonious with the Congregational theory that these Elders are the same as the Bishops, Pastors and Teachers elsewhere mentioned as being — with the Deacons — the only officers of the Church. We hold that there is an important sense in which every Pastor and Teacher of a Church is also its *ruler*. Ruling implies guiding and instructing, and also the carrying into execution of laws, not made by the Executive. The Governor of Massachusetts suggests to its Legislature such guidance and instruction in regard to laws that ought to be enacted by them, as his position prompts him to do; and then he puts in execution whatever laws they are pleased to enjoin. Thus he is the Chief Ruler of the Commonwealth, while, at the same time, the State, in its Legislature, retains the power to adopt, or reject, his every proposition, and to enact every law, his execution of which makes him its Chief Ruler. Similar is the relation of the Congregational Pastor to his Church. He brings to its notice such matters as seem to him to require action, and seeks to enlighten it in regard to the nature of that action, which, under the circumstances, he judges will be most grateful to Christ; and then, as its executive officer, he puts in operation such action as it may decide upon — whether in coincidence with his own suggestions or not. Thus he is, in a sense, its ruler; such a sense as, in no degree, impairs its sovereignty under Christ over all its affairs, or its responsibility to Christ for them all. In a large Church, so situated as to make this double work of ruling and teaching onerous for one Pastor, — as in some great Mission Church in a heathen land, whose members need more, both of teaching and ruling, than if they had not come out of recent paganism — two or more Pastors may be needful, and of their number, one or more, peculiarly fitted by divine grace for that department of the work, may become Elders 'that rule well,' and so 'be counted worthy of double honor;' while if they can both 'rule well,' and 'labor in the word and doctrine,' they will be 'especially' worthy of this augmented regard and reward. We have only to suppose the Church in Ephesus — where Timothy was when Paul thus wrote to him —

---

[1] "Fuerunt, qui in duas potissimum classes presbyteros primævæ ecclesiæ digererent, quarum altera *regentium* sive laicorum ; docentium altera sive clericorum esset. Quorum sententia, quum jamdudum explosa sit Vitringæ, Hugonis Grotii, Bloudelii, aliorum hae de re inquisitionibus, — decies repetita haud placebunt."—*Lücke. Com.* p. 103.

to be of this description — a supposition in itself every way a probable one — and this text describes exactly what would be natural and proper in a Congregational Church conducted on the ordinary principles of Congregationalism. But if it *can* be explained into harmony with all the other passages in the New Testament, in which Elders are mentioned always as being the same as Pastors, Teachers, and Bishops, it ought to be so explained.

Nor are we without collateral proof from other passages, that, only when so explained, do we get its true force. Paul, speaking to the Hebrews, says :[1] " Remember them *which have the rule over you*," by which he must mean 'Ruling Elders,' if there were any such in the Presbyterian sense; yet he proceeds immediately to add: "*who have spoken unto you the word of God*," etc.; proving that the Ruling Elders whom he had in mind, were not separate lay officers, but their ordinary Pastors and Teachers.[2] And in the same spirit, in the same chapter, he says again :[3] "obey them *that have the rule over you*, and submit yourselves," — (surely these must be the lay Ruling Elders, if there were any), yet he describes them as being those who " watch for your *souls* as they that must give account," etc. : — an expression that implies, if any thing emphatically can, the function of Pastors, and Teachers, and Bishops of the Church.[4] So Paul, writ-

---

[1] Heb. xiii : 7.

[2] "*Duces, præsides — leaders, guides, directors*, which here means *teachers*, as the explanatory clause that follows clearly shows."—*Stuart's* "*Hebrews*." (Robbins' Ed.) p. 494.

" Ηγουμένους is here applied to the Presbyters or Bishops of the Church."—*Conybeare and Howson*. Vol. ii. p. 547.

" *Principes*, quod nomen hic optimo jure aptatur lis qui apud Christianos, per excellentiam, tum *præsides*, tum *Episcopi* dicuntur, quorum munus est non tantum præesse presbyterio sed et laborare in verbo."—*Grotius. in loco*. Vol. iii. p. 1066.

" Ηγούμενοι (compare verses 17, 24) are their *leaders in the faith*." — *Alford. in loco*. Vol. iv. p. 263.

[3] Verse 17.

[4] "These two things ['obedience' and 'honor'] are necessarily required, so that the people might have confidence in their *pastors*, and also reverence for them."—*Calvin. in loco*. "*Hebrews*." p. 352.

"*Pastoribus* ut quibus data est potestas, et ducendi, non cogendi jus."—*Jacobus Capellus, in Poole. Syn. Crit. in loco*. Vol. v. p. 1406.

" Verbum ἀγρυπνεῖν curam et solicitudinem significant, quæ maximé in *Episcopis* requiritur."—*Gerhardus. Ibid.* p. 1407.

" Περὶ ἐπισκόπων λέγει."—*Œcumenius. Alford. in loco*. Vol. iv. p 269.

"'Αγρυπνοῦσι — *watch;* the image seems to be taken from the practice of shepherds, who watch with solicitude over their flocks in order that they may preserve them from the ravages of wild beasts."—*Stuart*. (Robbins' Ed.) *in loco*. p. 498.

ing to the Church at Thessalonica, urges them "to know them which labor among you, and *are over you* in the Lord,"[1] — (the very expression one would think it natural for him to have selected to designate their lay ruling elders, if they had any) — and yet he immediately describes the persons intended by him as being those who "*admonish* you," [*νουθετοῦντας* — *nouthetountas*], a word which here, as in several other passages,[2] seems clearly to imply the labor of the Pastor and Spiritual guide.

5. Again, the Presbyterian theory of this text conflicts with records made, and directions specially given by the New Testament in regard to the right method of ruling in the Church. That ruling must respect either the admission, dismission, or discipline of members; the choice of officers; or the transaction of current business. But we have already seen[3] that, by precept and example, the New Testament demands this action directly from the Church itself, in its entire male membership. Particularly clear is this in the matter of discipline — the gravest and most solemn subject with which the ruling of the Church can ever have to do — of which Christ himself said "tell it unto *the Church*."[4] How can this direction be complied with if a Session of Elders[5] steps in between the Church and the offender, and rules him out, (or in); with no direct action — perhaps even no knowledge — of the Church itself in the premises? And how, in the absence of any other passage claimed to teach directly any such doctrine of Ruling Elders, can it be right to interpret this passage — which will bear a natural interpretation that will harmonize with the entire record — in such a manner as to nullify all those texts which

---

[1] 1 Thess. v: 12

[2] Compare Acts xx: 31, "I ceased not to *warn* every one night and day with tears;" 1 Cor. iv: 14, "As my dear children I *warn* you;" Col. i: 28, "Whom we preach, *warning* every man, and teaching every man," etc.; where the same Greek word, translated in the text above 'admonish,' is used to describe the tenderest and solemnest function of the Pastor's office.

"The persons indicated by κοπιῶντας, προϊσταμένους, and νουθετοῦντας, are the same; viz: the πρεσβύτεροι or ἐπίσκοποι."—*Alford. Com.* 1 Thess. v: 12. Vol. iii. p. 265.

[3] See pages 9, and 40-43.

[4] Matt. xviii: 17.

[5] The assumption sometimes made by Presbyterians that Christ's command to "tell it unto the Church," means "tell it to *the Session of Ruling Elders*," (see "*Message to Ruling Elders*," p. 8, etc.) is beneath refutation, and can only amaze the mind which reflects upon it, and inquires how, with such principles of interpretation, are the Papists, and Swedenborgians, or even the Mormons, to be logically foreclosed from any conclusions their fancy may incline them to attach to any passage of the Bible!

place the responsibility and privilege of ruling, distinctly upon the Church as a body?

6. But it becomes to the last degree improbable, that this text was divinely intended to be the corner-stone of a special lay office in every Church, of a species of Elder whose sole business should be ruling, when we remember that the New Testament, in its mention of the qualifications of Elders, says of them as a class, and without exception, that they must 'hold fast the faithful word as they have been taught, that they may be able by sound doctrine, both to exhort, and to convince the gainsayers.'[1] It is strange that *all* elders should be required thus to be 'apt to teach,' if a portion of them were intended to ignore teaching altogether, and indeed to get the peculiarity of their office from so doing; while it is incredible that a separate office so easy to be confounded with that of the teaching Elder, and yet so important to be distinguished from it, could have existed in the Apostolic Church, while no reference whatever is made to it by the Holy Spirit, even when the general subject of the class, of which this is claimed to be a species, is under its consideration!

We conclude, then, that this text fails utterly to announce, to hint, or even to be in any manner, however remote, consistent with, the theory of a lay Ruling Eldership in the Church of Christ; or of *any* office of Ruling Elder distinct from the ordinary Elder, who labors 'in the word and doctrine,' and is the Pastor, or Bishop of the Church. And since this text falls, all the other texts which we have considered, and whose explanation waits to be determined by it, fall also to the ground, and leave the Presbyterian theory on this subject without the support of a single passage from the New Testament.

As to the testimony of antiquity, Vitringa,[2] Rothe,[3] and Neander,[4] have fairly shown that the few passages usually quoted by Presbyterians from the Fathers, in proof of the existence of a lay Ruling Eldership in the early Church, will not warrant the interpretation which they put upon them; and that the office originated in the mind of John Calvin.[5] The same concession has been honorably made by Rev. J. P.

---

[1] Tit. 1:9.
[2] *De Synag. Vet.* Lib. ii. Chap. 2.
[3] *Die Anfänge*, etc. 1:221.
[4] *Apos. Kirche*. 1:186.
[5] The passage of the Institutes by which Calvin first suggested the office — so say Gieseler, Davidson, and others — is the following: "Duo autem sunt quæ perpetuo manent: gubernatio, et cura pauperum. Gubernatores fuisse existimo seniores e plebe delectos, qui censuræ morum, et exercendæ disciplinæ una cum Episcopis præessent. Neque enim secus interpretari

Wilson, D D., a learned and eminent Presbyterian in this country, who published twenty-one articles in the *Monthly Christian Spectator* (A. D. 1823-1828), which were afterwards enlarged into an elaborate work, the object of which was to disprove the antiquity of the lay Eldership; to dislodge it from any imagined proofs in the patristic writings; and to show how, at Geneva, in 1541, Calvin — as the best thing which could be done to meet an exigency which had arisen then, and there,[1] — devised and brought into operation the system of lay Eldership, and afterward attempted to justify it from the Bible.[2] To the research and reasoning employed by him, nothing needs to be added, for they do the work thoroughly and forever; so that it is difficult to see how those who master the facts of his essay, can resist their force, and continue to uphold the office whose pretensions to any Divine origin, or authority, it utterly demolishes. Indeed the ablest Presbyterians are accustomed to rest the claim of the office upon expediency, rather than upon Divine enactment, or Biblical warrant; taking the ground that "having constituted the Church a distinct society, he [Christ] thereby gave it the right to govern itself,

---

queas quod dicit (*Rom.* xii : 8): 'Qui præest, id faciat in sollicitudine.' Habuit igitur ab initio unaquæque Ecclesia suum senatum, conscriptum ex viris piis, gravibus et sanctis · penes quem erat illa, de qua postea loquemur, jurisdictio in corrigendis vitiis. Porro ejusmodi ordinem non unius sæculi fuisse, experientia ipsa declarat. Est igitur et hoc gubernationis munus sæculis omnibus necessarium."—"*Institutes.*" Lib. iv. cap. iii. sec. 8. (Ed. Tholuck, 1846) p 218.

Dr. Davidson says : " The office now termed the Ruling Eldership was invented by Calvin After creating it, he naturally enough endeavored to procure Scripture proof in its favor Dr King quotes the usual passages from Cyprian, Origen, and Hilary, to show that these fathers were acquainted with this office ; but the proof will not suffice to convince an honest inquirer. Surely if he had known the thorough examination to which these quotations have been subjected by Rothe and Neander, he would have allowed them to sleep undisturbed, rather than affix interpretations to them which they refuse to bear. We repeat our assertion that Calvin created that office. Vitringa demolished it with learned and unanswerable arguments Let the advocates of it refute him if they be able."—*Ecclesiastical Polity of New Test.*" p. 193.

[1] Calvin himself says in regard to it, after its establishment. — " Nunc habemus qualecunque Presbyterorum judicium, et formam disciplinæ *qualem ferebat temperum infirmitas.*" — *Epist.* 54.

[2] Dr. Wilson sums up his argument, as follows · — " It has now fairly resulted from this investigation, that a special form of ecclesiastical government was adopted by the Genevese at the Reformation ; not because it was found, by Scriptural precept or example, to have been the original Apostolic scheme ; but because the nearest approach to the true one, which the peculiar circumstances of the Canton, and the exigencies of the times, would admit. . . . Had Calvin justified the expedient by the necessity of the case, he would have betrayed his design, and prevented others from the benefit of his example : but he gave ease to his conscience, and plausibility to his conduct, by seeking a defence from the Scriptures."—*Monthly Christian Spectator.* Vol x. (1828.) p. 64.

according to the general principles revealed in his word;" and, if it be objected against this that it opens the way for "human devices," replying that "if Christ has given his Church the power of self-government, what the Church does in the exercise of that power—if consistent with his revealed will¹—has as much his sanction as it well could have under any theory of Church government."² Upon this question of the expediency of the government of the Church by lay ruling Elders, we shall have something to say hereafter,³ only here remarking that the acceptance of such a vital change in the method of Church ruling which Christ suggested, and the Apostles arranged, and the early Churches practiced, avowedly on the ground of simple expediency, seems to us a procedure opening a very wide logical door for error in other directions, which its advocates must speedily hasten to shut, if pressed by the hypothesis of 'expediency' in regard to other doctrines and practices. This danger has, indeed, been seen by some, and has led them to throw out this claim of expediency altogether, and the more earnestly to return to the Bible in the attempt to engraft the office upon some passage there.⁴ Dr. Breckinridge and Dr. Thornwell have recently made a new effort to adjust the question, by taking the ground that the Presbyterian 'Ruling

---

1 Is a Session of Ruling Elders coming between "the Church" and duties Scripturally enjoined upon it from the lips of Christ himself, "consistent with his revealed will?"
2 *Princeton Review*, (1843.) Vol. xv. pp. 319-332.
3 See Chap. iv.
4 Well say the authors of the "*Divine Right of Church Government: wherein it is proved that the Presbyterian Government may lay the only lawful claim to a Divine Right*," etc.; "If mere prudence be counted once a sufficient foundation for a distinct kind of Church officer, we shall open a door for Church officers at pleasure; then welcome commissioners and committee men, etc, yea, then let us return to the vomit, and resume prelates, deacons, archdeacons, chancellors, officials, etc, for Church officers. And where shall we stop? Who but Christ Jesus himself can establish new officers in his Church?... Certainly if the Scriptures lay not before us grounds more than prudential for the Ruling Elder, it were better never to have mere Ruling Elders in the Church."—(Ed New York, 1844.) p. 114.
So the author of a series of articles in the *Presbyterian*, on the "*Rights of Ruling Elders*," urges, with great force, the fact that the office must rest upon the ground "either of human expediency, or divine warrant If upon the *former*, then it is a human device, etc ... If the Ruling Elder is not a Scriptural 'presbyter,' and his office a Divine institution, then of course we claim for him no part of the powers of ordination, or any other presbyterial power; it would be manifestly inconsistent to accord him any, and in this view our constitution has done what it had no right to do, viz: added to the appointments of God, as to the government of the Church." So, in speaking of Acts xiv: 23, this writer affirms: "if these [Elders ordained in every Church] were all preaching Elders, it is fatal to Presbyterianism;" and adds again—"if the Ruling Elder be not a Scriptural Presbyter, but a mere layman—an officer of human appointment—why say so, and let him be shorn of all his assumed presbyterial powers," etc.—See the *Presbyterian*, (Nos. 614-626.)

Elder' is the 'Presbyter' of the New Testament — of which generic office the Preaching Elder constitutes a species; whence they argue that Ruling Elders ought to be admitted to take part in ordination with the Preaching Elders, in the "laying on of the hands of the Presbytery,"[1] etc. This view, which certainly has the advantage of *looking* more Scriptural than that of Calvin, — yet which is radically destructive of the whole Presbyterian polity — has been earnestly assaulted by Rev. Dr. Smyth, in the *Princeton Review* for 1860, at the length of more than one hundred and thirty octavo pages.[2] It may reasonably be presumed that the end of the discussion is not yet. Meanwhile it is difficult to see how, on either theory, are to be explained the practical facts that this Elder — who is specially commissioned to *rule* in the Church, whether of the same class with the Preaching Elder, or not — in reality never does rule in the judicatories of the Church, but must always yield the claim to the mere Preaching Elder;[3] and that, when he is declared worthy of "double maintenance"[4] if he can "rule well," the Ruling Elder is never supported by the Church at all, but only the Preaching Elder!

In order to understand the position of our Pilgrim Fathers on this

---

[1] "*Knowledge of God, subjectively considered.*" pp. 629, 641, and *Southern Presbyterian Review*, (1859), p. 615. Dr. Adger ("*Inaugural Discourse on Church History,*" etc., in *Southern Pres. Rev.* (1859), p. 171, and Rev. Dr. Thompson, late of Buffalo, (*in his opening discourse before the New School General Assembly of* 1859, *as reported in the New York Observer*) are understood to take substantially the same ground with Drs. Breckinridge and Thornwell.

[2] *Princeton Review*, Vol. xxxii. pp. 185-236, 449-472, 702-758. Dr. Smyth thinks he proves that this new theory (1) destroys the argument for Presbyterianism; (2) destroys the ministry as a distinct order; (3) undermines the argument for the truth of Christianity, (4) destroys the Ruling Eldership; and (5) destroys the Deaconship.

[3] "The Pastor of the congregation shall *always* be the moderator of the session."—"*Book*," Chap ix. sec. 3. So the moderator of the Synods, and of the General Assembly must *preach*, and, of course, must be a preaching Elder.—"*Book.*" Chap xi. sec 5, and Chap. xii. sec. 7.

[4] This is the conceded force of the διπλῆς τιμῆς ἀξιούσθωσαν of 1 Tim v: 17.

"It is evident that not merely honor, but *recompense*, is here in question."—*Alford. Com.* 1 Tim v: 17. Vol. iii. p 335.

"It is honor, but an honor which finds its expression in giving, as verse 18 proves."—*Olshausen* (Kendrick's Ed.) *in loco.* Vol. vi. p. 135.

"Qui vero ita *occupati erant*, minus vacabant opificio, et rei familiari, et digni erant compensatione."—*Bengel.* "*Gnomon.*" *in loco.* p 832

"Videtur autem *duplicem honorem* dicere et alimenta, quæ et ipsa illis cum honore dantur, ut Regibus tributa."—*Grotius. in loco.* Vol iii. p 975

"Duplici, id est coploso honore, sub quo etiam comprehendit alimenta, aliaque subsidia ad vitam sustentandam, munusque quod gerunt recte administrandum, necessaria, ut qui multos hospitio excipere debeant (1 Tim. iii : 2) "—*Brennius. in loco.* Fol. 88.

subject, and to know the exact type and force of their idea of Ruling Elders, we need to consider two facts. In the first place, they were led, in the outset, by their great reverence for the very letter of the Word of God, to put too close an interpretation upon Rom. xii: 7, 8, and its kindred passages; while, in the second place, they were constrained, by their reluctance to commit themselves to that democracy which was then so dreaded in the State, to repress the breadth and fullness of their exposition of such texts as throw the whole responsibility of the affairs of the Church, under Christ, upon the entire membership. Hence they started with the theory of five officers in every Church, namely: Pastor, Teacher, Ruler, Deacon and Deaconess,[1] because they supposed that number to be required by those

---

[1] Browne, in his "*Points and Parts of all Divinity*," etc. (A. D. 1582. 4to, pp. 112), calls the five officers, "*Pastor, Teacher, Elder, Reliever*, and *Widow.*"—*Defs*. 53, 54. *Hanbury*. Vol. i. p. 21
The "*True Description, out of the Word of God, of the Visible Church*," attributed to Clyfton, or Smyth (A. D. 1589, 4to, pp. 8), says of the Church, "she enjoyeth most holy and heavenly laws, most faithful and vigilant *Pastors*, most sincere and pure *Teachers;* most careful and upright *Governors;* most diligent and trusty *Deacons;* most loving and sober *Relievers;* and a most humble, meek, obedient, faithful, and loving people," etc.—*Hanbury*. Vol. i. pp. 29–34.
So, Strype tells us that in the examination of Mr Daniel Buck, Scrivener, of the Borough of Southwark, taken before three magistrates March 9, 1592-3, he saith — (in reference to the affairs of the Congregational Church of which he was a member) that "Mr. Francis Johnson was chosen *Pastor;* and Mr. Greenwood, *Doctor* [Teacher]; and Bowman and Lee, *Deacons;* and Studley and George Kniston Apothecary, were chosen *Elders*, in the house of one Fox, in St Nicholas Lane, London [this house is now known as No. 80, King William Street], about half a year sithence, all in one day, by their congregation; or at Mr. Bilson's house in Creo Church; he remembereth not whether," etc.—"*Annals.*" Vol. iv. p 174.
John Robinson, in his "*Catechism*" annexed to Mr. Perkins' "Six Principles," has the following answer to a question asking for the "gifts and works" of the five officers of the Church. " (1) The *Pastor* (exhorter) to whom is given the gift of wisdom for exhortation. (2) The *Teacher*, to whom is given the gift of knowledge for doctrine. (3) The *Governing Elder*, who is to rule with diligence (Eph. iv: 11; 1 Cor. xii: 8; Rom. xii: 8; 1 Tim. v: 17). (4) The *Deacon* who is to administer the holy treasure with simplicity. (5) The *Widow* (or Deaconess), who is to attend the sick and impotent with compassion and cheerfulness. (Acts vi: 2-7; 1 Tim. iii: 8, 10, etc.; v: 9, 10; Rom. xvi: 1).—*Works*. Vol. iii. p. 429.
Governor Bradford, in his account of the rise of the movement in England, which culminated in New England, says: "The one side laboured to have ye right worship of God & discipline of Christ established in ye Church, according to ye simplicitie of ye Gospell, without the mixture of mens inventions, and to have & to be ruled by ye laws of God's word, dispensed in those offices, & by those officers of *Pastors, Teachers & Elders*, &c., according to ye Scripture," etc. "*Plimouth Plantation.*" (Ed. 1856.) p. 4.
Gov. Bradford also has recorded the following interesting facts in reference to the emigrant churches sojourning in Holland; He says: "At Amsterdam, before their division and breach, they were about three hundred communicants, and they had for their pastor and teacher those two eminent men before named, [Johnson and Ainsworth] and in our time four grave men for Ruling Elders, and three able and godly men for Deacons, one ancient widow for a Deaconess, etc. . . And for the Church at Leyden [Robinson's own] they were sometimes not much fewer in number, nor at all inferior in able men, though they had not so many officers as the other;

passages which bear upon the subject in the New Testament; and then — in order to assign work for the 'Ruler' which should harmonize with the functions of the 'Pastor' and 'Teacher,' on the one hand, and with the rights of the membership of the Church on the other,— they evolved a theory of Ruling Eldership which was yet not very consistent with itself, nor with the Scripture on which they rested it; while it proved to be so inconsistent with other vested rights, and with the general teaching of Providence in the course of subsequent affairs, as to compel them at last to abandon the experiment, give up the office, transfer a part of the powers they had entrusted to it to the Pastor, and a part to the membership, and boldly avow that the power of Church ruling is put by Christ upon the Church, as a body, under the guidance of its Pastor and Teacher.

The function of the Ruling Elder, according to their original conception of the office, was ten-fold; namely: (1) to take the initiative in the admission and dismission of members;[1] (2) to moderate the meetings of the Church;[2] (3) to prepare all matters of business for the action of the brotherhood;[3] (4) to exercise a general oversight over the private conduct of the members of the Church, with a view to see that none walk disorderly;[4] (5) to settle all offences between brethren privately, if possible;[5] otherwise (6) to bring offenders to the judgment of the Church, and execute its censures;[6] (7) to call the Church together and dismiss it with the benediction;[7] (8) to ordain

---

for they had but one Ruling Elder, with their Pastor, a man well approved and of great integrity; also they had three able men for Deacons."—"*Dialogue between some Young Men, etc. and sundry Ancient men*," etc., in Young's "*Chronicles of the Pilgrim Fathers*," etc. pp. 455, 456.

Lechford (A. D. 1641), writes of the churches in New England, that they have five offices, "that is to say, *Pastors* and *Teachers*, *Ruling Elders*, *Deacons* and *Deaconesses* (or widowes)." —"*Plaine Dealing*." *Mass. Hist. Coll.* Vol. iii Third Series. p. 69.

[1] See Robinson's "*Just and Necessary Apology,*" etc. *Works* Vol. iii. p. 31; John Davenport's "*Power of Congregational Churches Asserted and Vindicated.*" p. 95; John Cotton's "*Way of the Churches,*" p. 36; Hooker's "*Survey of the Summe of Church Discipline.*" Part ii. p. 18; *Cambridge Platform*, Chap. vii. sec. 2. (1.); Chap. x. sec 9.

[2] Cotton's "*Way*," etc. p. 37; *Platform*, Chap. vii. sec 2. (4); Chap x. sec. 8.

[3] Robinson's "*Apology*." *Works*. Vol. iii. p. 31; Cotton's "*Keyes*," etc. p. 52; *Platform*, Chap. vii. sec. 2. (3); Hooker's "*Survey*," Part ii. p. 16

[4] Cotton's "*Keyes*," etc. p. 59; *Platform*, Chap. vii. sec. 2. (6); Hooker's "*Summe*," Part ii. p. 18.

[5] Cotton's "*Way*," etc. p. 37; *Platform*, Chap. vii sec. 2. (7); Hooker's "*Summe*." Part ii. p 18.

[6] Cotton's "*Keyes*," etc. p. 52; "*Way*," etc. p 36; *Platform*, Chap. x. sec. 9; Robinson's "*Apology*," Vol. iii p. 43.

[7] *Platform*, Chap. x. sec. 9; Cotton's "*Keyes*," etc. p. 53.

those persons whom the membership may choose to office;[1] (9) to visit the sick;[2] (10) to teach, in the absence of the Pastor and Teacher.[3]

Such varied — and much f it delicate — work as this, must have required specially wise men to do it, or it could not be well done. Moreover, such an Eldership must everywhere have threatened the rights of the membership; and must have been hard to class, and especially difficult to fill, without breeding discord in the Body. Our Fathers were not quite sure whether it was a *lay* office or not; Robinson demanding that all Ruling Elders should be "apt to teach,"[4] and Cotton 'utterly denying' them to be 'Lay-men;'[5] while the Cambridge Platform declared that "the Ruling Elder's work is to join with the Pastor and Teacher in those acts of Spiritual rule which are *distinct from* the ministry of the Word and Sacraments,"[6] and shrank their teaching into the poor lay privilege "to feed the flock of God with a word of admonition." It was agreed, however, that the Ruling Elders must act in connection with the Teaching Elders, who — in the words of Thomas Prince — "have the power both of Overseeing, Teaching, Administring the Sacraments, and Ruling too;" and "that the *Elders of Both Sorts* form the *Presbytery* of Overseers & Rulers, which shou'd be in every particular Church; And are in Scripture called sometimes *Presbyters* or *Elders*, some times *Bishops* or *Overseers*, sometimes *Guides* & sometimes *Rulers*."[7]

---

[1] Cotton's "*Keyes*," p. 51; *Platform*, Chap. ix. sec. 3. See also Mather's *Magnalia*, (Ed. 1853.) Vol. ii. p. 241.

[2] Cotton's "*Way*," etc. p. 37; *Platform*, Chap. vii. sec. ii. (9).

[3] Robinson's "*Apology*." *Works*. Vol. iii. p. 28; also Robinson's and Brewster's "*Letter to Sir John Wolstenholme*." *Works*. Vol. 3. p. 488; Cotton's "*Way*," etc. p. 37; Cotton's "*Keyes*," etc. pp. 49-51; Prince's "*Annals*." Vol. i. p. 92.

[4] *Works*. Vol. iii. p. 28.   [5] "*Way*," etc. p. 33.

[6] Chap. vii. sec. 2.

[7] "*New England Chronology*." (Ed. 1736.) Vol. i. p. 92. The actual work done by the New England Ruling Elder is perhaps better described by Gov. Hutchinson, than anywhere else; though his account indicates that there was a discrepancy on some points between the practice of the churches, and the theory set forth above. He says:—"In matters of offence, the Ruling Elder, after the hearing, asked the Church if they were satisfied; if they were not, he left it to the Pastor or Teacher, to denounce the sentence of excommunication, suspension, or admonition, according as the Church had determined. Matters of offence, regularly, were first brought to the Ruling Elder in private, and might not otherwise be told to the Church. It was the practice for the Ruling Elders to give public notice of such persons as desired to enter into Church fellowship with them, and of the time proposed for admitting them, if no sufficient objection was offered; and when the time came, to require all persons who knew any just grounds of objection to signify them. Objections were frequently made, and until they were

It is not difficult to see that such an office contained within itself the elements of its own dissolution. It could not be practically inwrought into the working of a Congregational Church, without a friction on all sides, that must inevitably lead, sooner or later, to its abandonment. If its duties were zealously performed, they would clash in several obvious particulars; on the *one* side, with *those* of the Pastor — who was already subdivided (by a process, which, if clear in theory, never became entirely so in practice), by the erection of a Co-Pastor by his side, under the name of Teacher,[1] and on the other, with those of the Deacon — so that sensible men looking on, soon came to the practical conclusion of Gov. Hutchinson, — who argued that every thing appertaining to "the peculiar province of the Ruling

---

heard and determined, the Ruling Elder seems to have moderated in the Church, but the Church's consent to the admission was asked by the *Pastor* or *Teacher*," [Lechford says, (A. D. 1641), that the *Ruling Elder* put the question to the Church, " *Plain Dealing*," Mass. Hist. Coll., Vol. iii. Third Series, p. 71], "who also rehearsed and proposed the Church covenant, and declared them members. When a minister preached to any other than his own Church, the Ruling Elder of the Church after the psalm sung, said publicly, 'if this present brother hath any word of exhortation for the people at this time, in the name of God, let him say on.' The Ruling Elder always read the psalm. When the member of one Church desired to receive the sacrament at another, he came to the Ruling Elder, who proposed his name to the Church for their consent. At the communion they sat with the minister. I find nothing further relating to this officer in their public assemblies. They were considered, without doors, as men for advice and council in religious matters; they visited the sick, and had a general inspection and oversight of the conduct of their brethren." — " *History of the Colony of Mass. Bay*," (Ed. 1765.) Vol. i. p. 426

[1] "The Pastor — on whom chiefly devolved the care of the flock when out of the pulpit — was expected to spend his strength mostly in exhortation, persuading and rousing the Church to a wise diligence in the Christian calling. The Teacher was to indoctrinate the Church, and labor to increase the amount of religious knowledge. His workshop was the study; while the Pastor toiled in the open field...... In the estimation of our fathers, the Pastor's station was considered to have rather the priority in importance and dignity." — McClure's *Life of John Cotton*, pp. 115, 116.

The only instance in which this distinction was practically recognized in the churches of New Hampshire, is believed to have been by the Church in Hampton — the oldest in that State — which, in 1639, invited Rev. Timothy Dalton to act as Teacher, with Rev. Stephen Bachiler as Pastor; and which subsequently associated with Mr. Dalton two other ministers in succession. (See Lawrence's *New Hampshire Churches*, pp. 64, 65.) Some idea of the respective salaries of Pastor, Teacher, and Ruling Elder (when the latter had any pay,) may be got from the following entry in the Church Record of the Second Church in Boston, of date, — "21st day of y⁰ 6th mo. 1662." — "The Church of y⁰ North end of Boston met at Bro. Collicott's, and there did agree y⁰ Mr Mayo [Pastor] should have, out of what is given to y⁰ Church annually £65, Mr Mather [Increase, who was 'Teacher'] £50; and Mr Powell [Ruling Elder] £25; and this annually, provided they that have engaged perform their engagement. And of y⁰ *contribution*, Mr Mayo to have s.20 weekly, and Mr Mather s.20, and Mr Powell s.15 weekly, — provided y⁰ contribution hold out; and, if it abate, each one of the above-said to abate according to proportion; and if y⁰ contribution superabound, then y⁰ overplus to be kept, till occasion call for it, and then to be disposed of by the Church's order. And to this we are all agreed." (See Robbins' *History of the Second Church*, pp. 11, 12.)

Elder, so far as it is in itself necessary or proper, may with propriety enough be performed by the minister."[1] The main objection, however, to the office, consisted in the fact that so far as this 'Presbytery'—composed of the Teaching and Ruling Elders—really attempted to *rule* the Church, they came into conflict with the claims of the membership to rule themselves—founded on one of the great first principles of the Puritan movement, and guaranteed by the conceded force of clear Scriptural warrant; while if they only 'made believe' rule, they stultified themselves, and by practically emptying the passages on which the office was based of all real force, they, for substance, acknowledged that it was a sham and a failure. This led to inconsistencies, in both theory and practice, from which even the clear mind of John Robinson did not relieve itself.[2] Differences arose

---

[1] *History of Massachusetts Bay.* Vol. i. p. 426.

[2] When pressed towards the democratic aspect of the Church, we find him acknowledging it to the full. He says (*Works*, Vol. ii. p. 132), "This we hold and affirm, that a company *consisting though but of two or three*, separated from the world (whether unchristian or anti-christian), and gathered into the name of Christ by a covenant made to walk in all the ways of God made known unto men; is a Church, *and so hath the whole power of Christ.*" So he says (Vol. iii. p. 31), "We deny plainly that they [Church acts] are, or can be rightly and orderly done, but with the people's privity and consent." So he says (Vol ii. p 191), that "by 'two or three' having this power ['binding and loosing'] cannot be meant two or three ministers, considered severally from the body (which alone are not the Church for any public administration, but the officers of the Church), but by 'two or three' are meant the meanest communion or society of saints, whether with officers or without officers." So he sums up one part of his argument against Bernard (Vol. ii. p 448) thus: "The *people* have power to censure offenders: for they that have power to elect, appoint, and set up officers, they have also power, upon just occasion, to reject, depose, and put them down," etc.

On the other hand, when pressed with objections against the Democracy of this system, we find him retreating to the theory of the Eldership as a retort. Thus he replies to Bernard, when expressly charged by him with putting the "power of Christ" into "the body of the congregation, the multitude called the Church" (*Works*, Vol. ii. p. 7), "on the contrary we profess the bishops, or elders, to be the only ordinary governers in the Church," etc And in his "*Just and necessary Apology*," he says, (*Works*, Vol. iii. p 42, 43), "but now lest any should take occasion, either by the things here spoken by us, or elsewhere of us, to conceive, that we either exercise amongst ourselves, or would thrust upon others, *any popular or democratical Church government;* may it please the Christian reader to make estimate of both our judgment and practice in this point, according to the three declarations following." He then goes on—with other statements—to suggest what was doubtless the method in which his own mind harmonized the two conflicting positions which he held, namely: "it appertains to the people freely to vote in elections and judgments of the Church. In respect of the other, we make account it behoves the Elders to govern the people, *even in their voting.*" "Let the Elders publicly propound, and order all things in the Church, and so give their sentence on them; let them reprove them that sin, convince the gainsayers, comfort the repentant, and so administer all things according to the prescript of God's word: let the people of faith *give their assent to* their Elders' holy and lawful administration: that so the ecclesiastical elections and censures *may be ratified,* and put into solemn execution by the Elders, either in the ordination of officers after election, or excommunication of offenders after obstinacy in sin."

concerning it in the Church at Amsterdam, under the charge of Francis Johnson and Henry Ainsworth, as Pastor and Teacher. The former, with a portion of the Church, desired to restrict Church power to the Elders and officers; the latter to lodge it in the entire membership. Robinson consistently proposed, as a plan of settling the difficulty, that all the business of the Church should first be considered and resolved on by the Presbytery privately, and then submitted to the membership for confirmation only; but the proposition was not accepted, and the Church was divided into two, upon the issue.[1]

It looks very much as if Robinson and his Church, while yet in Leyden, were tacitly distrustful of the practical effect upon their fundamental principle of the power of the people under Christ, of that theory of five distinct offices which they yet nominally held to be the demand of Scripture for every Church; for Gov. Bradford tells us that, although they had sometimes near three hundred communicants, nor were "at all inferior in able men," they had "not so many officers as the other" [Church at Amsterdam], and mentions only the Pastor, one Ruling Elder, and three Deacons, as serving them in Leyden;[2] while Elder Brewster's place was never filled there, so that, for the last five years of Robinson's life, his Church was officered only by Pastor and Deacons,[3] although, by the express agreement of parting, those who staid, and those who went, were each to be "an absolute Church of themselves."[4] However this may have been, that terrible 'democracy'— which was such a bugbear in England,

---

[1] See Robinson's Works, Vol. iii. p. 464, etc.
The objection to such an arrangement — by which the Elders were to tell the people what to vote, and then the people were to vote accordingly — that it degraded the action of the body of the Church to a mere farce, and really left them in the hands of the Presbytery, as fully as Presbyterianism itself, does not appear to have occurred to Robinson; — who seems to have been mainly solicitous to reconcile his misinterpretation of 1 Tim. v: 17, etc., with those texts which deposite all power in the membership; and who, not seeing that the inevitable drift of his opinions, on the whole, was toward democracy in Church and State, was not disposed to submit them to the popular odium then associated with sentiments of that description.

[2] "*Dialogue between Young Men and Ancient Men*," etc., in Young's *Chronicles of Plymouth*, p. 456.

[3] Roger White writes to Gov. Bradford, giving the sad information of Robinson's death, and describes the condition of the bereaved Church as "wanting him and all Church governers, not having one at present that is a governing officer [*i. e.*, a Preaching, Teaching, or Ruling Elder] amongst us."— See Letter, in Young's *Chronicles of Plymouth*, p. 479.

[4] See Young's *Chronicles of Plymouth*, p. 77; also Gov. Bradford's *Plimouth Plantation*, p. 42.

and which, only after the long process of years, by its seen and felt safety and benefit, conquered the prejudices of the aristocratic 'gentlemen' of Massachusetts—was a legitimate outgrowth of the Leyden teachings, and became a practical necessity in the state in that condition of affairs in which the Plymouth Colonists vacated the Mayflower. The facts that, in the Providence of God, Robinson did not accompany his Church on its emigration, and that they failed of obtaining Mr. Crabe,[1] while, by their hope of Robinson's following, they were long kept from choosing another Pastor, and so continued under Ruling Elder Brewster, (who was practically their Pastor, although he did not administer the Sacraments[2]) enabled the Plymouth Church to try thoroughly the experiment of a more popular government than their creed would have favored; and doubtless had its influence in lightening their faith in the practical value of the democratic principle in the Church, as well as in the state. Certain it is that the tap root both of American Congregationalism, and of American Democratic Republicanism, runs its deepest and vitalest fibers back into the doctrines of Robinson, as Providentially developed and self-harmonized in the practice of the Plymouth company.[2] Their study was rather of the Acts than of the Epistles; their main endeavor, to reproduce exactly the Apostolic pattern[3]—where they found more of the democracy of the action of the whole Church, than they did of the

---

[1] See Robert Cushman's Letter, in Gov. Bradford's *Plimouth Plantation*. p. 58.

[2] "Now touching ye question propounded by you, I judg it not lawfull for you, being a Ruling Elder, as (Rom. xii: 7, 8, & 1 Tim. v: 17) opposed to the Elders that teach & exhorte and labore in ye word and doctrine, to which ye sacraments are anexed, to administer them; nor convenient if it were lawfull."—*Robinson's* "*Letter to Elder Brewster*," A. D. 1623, in *Bradford's* "*Plimouth Plantation*," p. 166.

[3] "Many philosophers have since appeared, who have, in labored treatises, endeavored to prove the doctrine, that the rights of men are unalienable, and nations have bled to defend and enforce them, yet in this dark age, the age of despotism and superstition, when no tongue dared to assert, and no pen to write this bold and novel doctrine—which was then as much at defiance with common opinion as with actual power, (of which the monarch was then held to be the sole fountain, and the theory was universal, that all popular rights were granted by the crown) —in this remote wilderness, amongst a small and unknown band of wandering outcasts, the principle that *the will of the majority of the people shall govern* was first conceived, and was first practically exemplified. The Pilgrims, from their notions of primitive Christianity, the force of circumstances, and that pure moral feeling which is the offspring of true religion, discovered a truth in the science of government which had been concealed for ages. On the bleak shore of a barren wilderness, in the midst of desolation, with the blasts of winter howling around them, and surrounded with dangers in their most awful and appalling forms, the Pilgrims of Leyden laid the foundation of American liberty."—*Baylies*' "*Old Colony*." Vol. i. p. 29.

[4] See an eloquent argument in Edward Winslow's *Brief Narration*, in Young's *Plymouth Chronicles*. pp. 396-408.

aristocracy of ruling by an Eldership. So that gradually, yet inevitably, they seem to have drifted on the stream of Providence to the conclusion that the practical remedy for all perplexity growing out of needless Church offices, was to let them quietly die out of usage.

It is well known that — through the "indefatigable and ubiquitous Dr. Fuller"[1] — the Plymouth Colony had great influence over the Church foundations which were afterwards laid in the Massachusetts Colony, nor is it matter of doubt that that influence was not of a character to weaken the effect of the democratic principle upon the general mind. It was only after many years,[2] and many struggles,[3]

---

[1] See Young's *Plymouth Chronicles*, p. 223; also Clark's *Congregational Churches of Massachusetts*, pp. 7–9.

[2] In 1636, John Cotton wrote to Lord Say and Seal, in reply to his (and Lord Brooke's) proposals of conditions on which they, and other "persons of quality" might be induced to favor New England with their presence: "Democracy, I do not conceyve that ever God did ordeyne as a fitt government eyther for Church or Commonwealth. If the people be governors, who shall be governed?" [*Hutchinson*, Vol. i. p. 497.] So we find Thomas Shepard of Cambridge, in 1652 (in his *Wholesome Caveat for a time of Liberty*), using the following language: "though the estate of the Church be democratical and popular, and hence no public administrations or ordinances are to be administered publicly, without notice and consent of the Church, yet the government of it under Christ the Mediator and Monarch of his Church, it is aristocratical, and by some chief, gifted by Christ, chosen by the people to rule them in the name of Christ, who are unable and unfit to be all rulers themselves; and to cast off these, or not to be ruled by these, is to cast off Christ," etc.—*Works*. (Ed. 1853.) Vol. iii. p. 332. And so late as 1702, we find Cotton Mather, while acknowledging that "partly through a prejudice against the office [of Ruling Elder], and partly — indeed chiefly — through a *penury* of men well qualified for the discharge of it, as it has been heretofore understood and applied, our churches are now generally destitute of such helps in government," pleading that the Elders (*i. e.*, the Presbytery of Teaching and Ruling Elders in each Church), should "have a *negative* on the votes of the brethren;" on the ground that, "to take away the negative of the Elders, or the necessity of their consent unto such acts," is to "*take away all government* whatsoever, and it is to turn the whole 'regimen of the Church' into a pure 'democracy!'"—*Magnalia*, Vol. ii. pp. 239, 249.

[3] Some of the shifts which were adopted in order to save the power of the Eldership on the one side, and of the membership on the other, seem now truly laughable; though grave matters enough at the time. In 1636-7, several Puritan clergymen in Old England, sent over thirty-two questions in regard to the facts of Church matters here, to which answer was requested. The tenor of the questions would indicate a feeling of distrust in England lest the Colonists here were getting on too fast in freedom, and one of them (Ques. 17) asks, in so many words, "whether, in voting, doe *the major part alwayes, or at any time, carry ecclesiasticall matters with you*," etc. To this it was duly replied, for substance, that if the "Elders and major part of the Church" agree, all is well. If dissent is made, the brothers dissenting are patiently heard, and if they dissent on good grounds [the "Elders and major part of the Church" of course being the judges], the "whole Church will readily yield." If not, the dissentients are "admonished," — and so "standing under censure their vote is nullified." After further detail, the answer *naively* concludes: "these courses, with God's presence and blessing (which usually accompany his ordinance), faithfully taken and followed, will prevail either to settle one unanimous consent in the thing, or, *at least, to preserve peace in the Church by the dissenters' submission to the judgment of the major part*."— See Felt's *Eccl. Hist. of New England*. Vol. i. pp. 278–282, and pp. 380–386.

however, that the fundamental tenets of the Congregational churches were harmonized with themselves, and put into a position of logical repose, by the straight-forward recognition of the Supreme power — under Christ — of the membership of each Church over its own affairs. The Elders (at least, the Teaching Elders) of the Massachusetts Colony — who had mostly left England as Nonconformists, and not as Separatists, and whose ideas of hierarchal and priestly power, were by no means yet clarified — were a long time in becoming convinced that matters Ecclesiastical could be trusted to go right without some absolute control, as well as guidance, from themselves. Synod after Synod was held for the settlement of doctrine and practice,[1] and it was long before the veto power, or, as they phrased it, 'the *negative of the Elders*,' was relinquished, and rest gained in the conviction that it is safe to trust the membership of a Church, under Christ, to manage all its affairs with nothing more than the leading and instruction of those officers which it has chosen for that purpose. John Wise — writing in 1717 — is, so far as we know, the first of the New England Theologians, who was not afraid to state, and demonstrate, the proposition that "DEMOCRACY is Christ's government, in Church and State."[2] And his vigorous "Vindication of the Government of the New England churches," not only had immense influence in removing all obstacles out of the way of a consistent holding of their own principles by Congregationalists, but also in preparing the country for the Revolutionary struggle. But even he was not yet clear on the subject of Ruling Elders.[3]

In the long run, the strongest Scriptural truths in a mixed and partially discordant creed may be relied on to work themselves clear, and control the whole; and so, in the end, it came to pass that the democratic principle strengthened its power over the Puritan doctrine until it sloughed off the excrescence of the Ruling Eldership, even in name, and placed the system upon a self-complete and simple basis, which, in subsequent working, has proved itself to be in no respect

---

[1] Gov. Winthrop gives account of three, held respectively in 1637, 1643, and 1647. Vol. i. p. 237; Vol. ii. pp. 136, 264, 269, 308, 330. Savage's *Winthrop*. Ed. 1853. Others were subsequently convened. In reference to the theory of Synods held by our fathers in Massachusetts, see the Cambridge Platform, Chap. xvi., and Mather's *Magnalia*, Vol. ii. p. 248, etc.; also, Hooker's "*Survey of the Summe*," etc. Part. iii. pp. 1–59.

[2] See Bancroft, Vol. ii. p. 429.

[3] See *Churches' Quarrel Espoused*. Pet. iv.

liable to the fears which were expressed with regard to it, by those who still fondly clung to the old encumbrance.[1]

The custom of choosing Ruling Elders hardly became, at first, a universal one in the churches of New England,[2] while, in fifty years from the settlement of the country, it had gone into comparative disuse;[3] and has long since disappeared altogether,[4] leaving a record behind it which well illustrates the acute remark made of it by one of the leading civilians of 1760, that "the multiplying unnecessary and mere nominal officers, or officers whose duties and privileges are not with certainty agreed upon and determined, seems rather to have a natural tendency to discord and contention, than to harmony and peace."[5]

In brief, then, it may be said of the Ruling Eldership of our Pilgrim Fathers, that it was an illogical and unscriptural,—and therefore

---

[1] Joshua Scottow (A. D. 1691) published a most moving appeal, under the title of "*Old Men's Tears for their own Declensions, mixed with Fears of their and their Posterities' further falling off from New England's Primitive Constitution,*" in which, after mournfully inquiring " where are the Ruling Elders, who as porters were wont to inspect our Sanctuary gates, and to take a turn upon the walls ? " etc., he adds, " it is questioned by some among us, whether such an officer be *jure divino*, or any rule for them in God's word, which occasions a Reverend Elder to take up the argument against such, and bewails the neglect of them in the churches, as a sad omen of their turning *popular or prelatical*, and if so, then to be regulated either by *Lord Brethren*, or Lord Bishops. Is not this a great derogation from Christ's authority to say, that deacons may serve the churches' turn, who may officiate to do these Elders' work ? Is it not a preference of men's politics before Christ's institutes ? Did not the practice of men's prudentials prove the ruin of the churches and rise of Antichrist ? "— See Savage's *Winthrop*, Vol. I. p 38.

[2] See Clark's *Historical Sketch of the Congregational Churches in Massachusetts*, p. 93.

[3] See *Hutchinson*, Vol. I. p. 426 ; Savage's *Winthrop*, Vol. I. p. 37.

[4] Elder Brewster was the only Ruling Elder in the Plymouth Colony (as well as Church), during the first *twenty-nine* years of its existence ; Mr. Thomas Cushman, the first chosen by them in this country, having been elected in 1649—five years after Brewster's decease. Elder Cushman served the Church until his much lamented death, in 1691. In 1699, the Church filled the vacancy by the election of Dea. Thomas Faunce, who officiated until his death, at the age of 99, in 1746; and was the last who sustained the office in Plymouth. (See Steele's "*Chief of the Pilgrims,*" p. 398, and Thacher's *History of Plymouth*, pp. 270-285.) The name of but one Ruling Elder appears upon the records of the Old South Church in Boston, though it is supposed others were chosen, without record (See Wisner's *History of the Old South Church*, p. 79.) The present meeting house (built A. D. 1730), originally contained an elevated "Elder's Seat," above the "Deacon's Seat," and below the pulpit. The last record on the books of the First Church in Boston, of the election of a Ruling Elder is believed to be of date August 3, 1701. An effort was made in the New Brick Church, in 1735, to reintroduce this "obsolete " office, but, in Nov. 1736, only one person had been found to accept the office, and the Church voted not to choose another. Mr. William Parkman (chosen Sept 1743, died 1775-6) was the last Ruling Elder of the New North Church. (Appendix. Wisner's *Old South*, p 80) It appears from Dr. Felt's *History of Salem*, that the North Church in that town, in 1826, "as the only continuation of an ancient custom," chose Jacob Ashton, Ruling Elder. Probably this may have been the last instance of such an election by any Congregational Church of New England. (Felt's *Salem*, Vol. II. p 608.)

[5] *Hutchinson*, Vol. I. p. 426.

temporary—concession, in part, to the too literal sense of two or three texts which they were in a most unfortunate position rightly to interpret, and in part to the spirit of the age; that it never, either in their theory or their practice, approximated to the Presbyterian idea of the Ruling Eldership; and that its entire disuse — throwing its old functions partly upon the Pastor, partly upon the Deacons, partly upon the "Examining Committee"[1] (where one exists), and partly upon the membership at large — is a thing which causes the denomination no regret, except that it had not earlier entered as a tranquilizing element into some of the anxieties of the Fathers.

3. *The second class of permanent officers set by Christ in his Churches — for the care of their temporal concerns — are called Deacons.* This is made sure by the record of the appointment of the "seven," in the Acts; by the records and precepts of the Epistles; and by the testimony of early history.

(1.) *Let us examine the record of the Acts of the Apostles.*[2] Reference has been already made to this.[3] The simple facts were that — in consequence of 'murmuring' from the foreign, or Greek-speaking portion of the Church, as if they had not received their equitable share of the daily distribution of food, etc., 'as every man had need'[4] — the Apostles — 'at whose feet' (*i. e.* in whose sole control) the whole matter had been previously 'laid' — called the whole

---

[1] We have been sorry to see occasional suggestions to the effect that it might be well for our denomination to revive this office, or to use the name as a designation for the "examining committee"—it being assumed that there would be a fitness in such an application. It is true that that committee usually performs a part of the service which used to be done by the Ruling Elders — in paving the way for the admission of new members to the Church, etc. But this was not that function of the Ruling Elders from which they were *named*. That was such an approach to a real control over the Church — doing its work, and then permitting it to assent to, and confirm their acts — as is totally at variance with the true principles of Congregationalism. Mr. Eddy — a late eminent lawyer of the Old Colony, of wide renown in our churches — says in the "Book" of the Church in Middleborough, to which he belonged, "we have never had any Ruling Elders in this Church. There is not much in a *name*." [*Book*, p. 29.] But there *is* a good deal in a 'name,' if it will mislead Presbyterians into the idea — as it often has, in reference to our early history — that we are either aping their system, or approaching it. There is no possible resemblance between our "examining committees," (renewed every year, and simply preparing business for the Church's vote — often without even recommending action, yea or nay, upon the propositions which they make), and a Presbyterian Session chosen for life, and ultimating the business of the Church — without its presence, and, likely enough, without its knowledge or consent. We go for calling things by their right names, and for leaving the old yoke which our fathers were not able to bear, to rot where they left it, afield.

[2] Acts vi: 1-6.   [3] See page 15.   [4] Chaps. ii: 45; iv: 35.

Church together, and declaring it was 'not reason' that the sole care of both the temporal and spiritual exigencies of the multitude of believers should longer remain upon them, desired the Church to choose seven 'men of honest report,' to whom 'this business' might be entrusted. 'The saying pleased the whole multitude,' and they chose Stephen, Philip, Prochorus, Nicanor, Timon, Parmenas, and Nicolas, a proselyte of Antioch;[1] whom the Apostles then publicly and solemnly 'appointed' to 'serve tables.'

Four things seem to be self-evident in this narrative, namely: that these seven were appointed to take the charge of the temporalities of the Church, and particularly of the distribution of its charities to its poor members; that they were chosen by the free suffrage of the brotherhood, that they were set apart to their work by prayer and the laying on of the hands of the Apostles; and — since every Christian Church has 'temporalities' which require somebody's care and thought — that here was intended to be given a hint and pattern for the copying of every such organization to the world's end.[2] It is true that these seven are never called 'Deacons' in the Acts, but only 'the seven,'[3] but it is likely that this grew out of the fact that the office was so familiarly known as not to need special naming,[4] as the Apostles were familiarly called 'the twelve.'[5] Moreover, they are, for substance, named 'Deacons,' in the very Greek words which record the work to which they were chosen (v. 2), which are διακονεῖν τραπέζαις — *diakonein trapezais*; which literally mean to *deacon*

---

[1] "These names are *all Greek*, but we cannot thence infer that the seven were all Hellenists; the Apostles Philip and Andrew bore Greek names, but were certainly not Hellenists. ... The title of 'deacons' is nowhere applied to these seven in Scripture, nor does the word occur in the Acts at all. In 1 Tim. iii: 8, etc., there is no absolute identification of the duties of deacons with those allotted to these seven, but, at the same time, nothing to imply that they were different And ἀνέγκλητοι, verse 10, seems to refer to our μαρτυρουμένους, verse 3. . . . The only one of these seven mentioned in the subsequent history (ch. xxi: 8) is called Φίλιππος ὁ εὐαγγελιστής, probably from the success granted him as recorded in ch. viii: 12. In these early days titles sprung out of realities, and were not yet mere hierarchical classifications."— Alford. *Com.* Acts vi: 5. Vol. ii. p. 57.

[2] "Manente ratione, manet ipsa lex." [3] Chap. xxi. 8.

[4] "Nor is it any objection, that in Acts xxi: 8, they are merely called '*the seven*,' for as the name of Deacon was then the usual appellation of a certain class of officers in the Church, Luke uses this expression to distinguish them from others of the same name, just as '*the twelve*' denoted the Apostles."—Neander. *Planting and Training*, etc. p 34, note.

[5] See Matt. xxvi· 14, 20, 47; Mark iv: 10, vi: 7; ix: 35; x: 32; xi: 11; xiv: 10, 17, 20, 43; Luke viii: 1; ix: 12; xviii: 31, xxii: 3, 47; John vi: 67, 71; xx: 24; Acts vi: 2; 1 Cor. xv: 5

[*i. e.* to officiate as deacons at] *tables* ' — διακονεῖν being the verb expressing the activity of the noun διάκονος — *diakonos* — 'deacon.'

It has been urged that this office existed before this date. Mosheim, Kuinœl, Olshausen and even Whately have supposed that the 'young men,'[1] who carried out the bodies of Ananias and Sapphira, were the deacons of the Church at Jerusalem. But the weight of authority is against this theory, and common sense condemns it.

(2.) *The records and precepts in the Epistles, afford further evidence of the fact that the deaconship is the second, and temporal, office in the Church.* Paul, in writing to the Philippians, addresses "the saints in Christ Jesus, which are at Philippi, with the Bishops and *Deacons*,"[2] showing that, so far as this Church was concerned, this office had existence then — A. D. 63,— probably thirty years after the choice of Stephen and his fellows at Jerusalem.

And, in addressing Timothy,[3] the same Apostle, after having given at length the qualifications to be regarded by the Churches in their choice of Pastors, proceeds to say, "likewise must the *Deacons* be grave, not double-tongued, not given to much wine, not greedy of filthy lucre; holding the mystery of the faith in a pure conscience. And let these also first be proved; then let them use the office of a Deacon, being found blameless," etc. These directions clearly imply Paul's judgment that the office of a Deacon was the second, and — since he names no other besides the Pastor — the only office in the Church remaining to be referred to, while the nature of his counsel would indicate his care to secure the selection of such men as would be eminently suitable to its peculiar functions. It is true that the specific duties connected with this office in the 6th of Acts, are not here recounted, but, evidently, because they were so well understood that there was no need of it; so that Paul — assuming that every Christian knew then, as now, what are the duties of a Deacon — proceeded to speak of the *qualifications* which he needs to possess, to secure the due discharge of those duties.

(3.) *The history of the early days establishes the fact that the of-*

---

[1] See Davidson's *Eccles. Pol. of New Test.* (pp. 167-170), for a thorough examination and refutation of this theory. See also Mosheim (*Comm. de reb. Chr.* etc. p. 114, etc.) Mack (*Commentar uber die Pastoral-briefe*, p 209), and Kuinœl, Meyer, and Olshausen (on Acts v: 6, and vi: 1); also Conybeare and Howson (*St. Paul*, i. p. 466.)
[2] Phil. 1: 1.   [3] 1 Tim. 3: 1-15.

fice of Deacon was, in primitive times, the second and only office in the Church, and had the care of its temporal affairs. NEANDER says, "besides these [the Presbyter-Bishops], we find only one other Church office in the Apostolic age; that of Deacons. The duties of this office were, from the beginning, simply external, as it was instituted in the first place, according to Acts vi., to assist in the distribution of alms. The care of providing for the poor and sick of the communities, to which many other external duties were afterward added, devolved particularly on this office."[1] GUERICKE says, "the second Ecclesiastical office in the single Church, was that of Deacon (*Διάκονοι—diakonoi*, Phil i: 1; 1 Tim iii: 8, 12), of whom originally there were seven. This office was at first established for the collection and distribution of alms, and for the care of the poor and the sick," etc.[2] SCHAFF says, "Deacons, or helpers, appear first in the Church of Jerusalem, seven in number, appointed in consequence of a complaint of the Hellenistic Christians that their widows were neglected in favor of the Hebrew Christians. The example of that Church was followed in all the other congregations, though without particular regard to the number seven. The office of these deacons, according to the narrative in Acts, was, to attend to the wants of the poor and the sick. To this work, a kind of pastoral care of souls very naturally attached itself; since poverty and sickness afford the best occasions and the most urgent demand for edifying instruction and consolation. Hence living faith and exemplary conduct were necessary qualifications for the office of Deacon."[3] KURTZ says, "Conjoined with, but subordinate to, the office of Presbyter or Bishop, of which the Apostles themselves for so considerable time discharged the duties at Jerusalem, was the office of Deacon. It was first instituted by the Apostles, with consent of the people, for the purpose of caring for the poor and the sick at Jerusalem. Thence it spread to most other Christian communities," etc.[4] COLEMAN says, "Besides the Elders, there was, in the Apostolical and Primitive ages of the Church, only one other office — that of Deacon. The specific duty to which the Deacons were originally appointed, was to assist in the distribution of alms. The care of providing for the poor, the sick,

---

[1] "*General History of Christian Religion and Church,*" etc Vol. 1. p. 188. (Torrey's Trans.)
[2] Shedd's *Guericke*. Vol. 1. p. 109.   [3] *History of the Christian Church,* p. 134.
[4] *Text Book of Church History,* p. 68.

and of bestowing other needful attentions upon the members of the community, for the relief of those who were occupied with the duties of the ministry, devolved upon them."[1]

This office did not escape perversion in the general corruption which soon came upon the churches. When Bishops were elevated above pastors, deacons were raised out of the ranks of the laity, and made a third order in the ministry. As early as the time when Ignatius is claimed to have written the epistles called by his name, there are symptoms of this change,[2] and in the third century it became still clearer.[3] The Puritans re-discovered and re-introduced the office as it was known to the Apostles and the Primitive Church, but to this day, the Hierarchal churches pervert it as the third order of the clergy.[4]

4. *Both Pastors (or Bishops, or Elders, or Teachers), and Deacons, are to be chosen and set apart by the Church, from its own membership.* Here are three points, namely: that the Church is to elect; to ordain — or otherwise set apart to office, its Pastor and Deacons; and that that election should be from among its own membership.

(1.) *Every Church is to elect its Pastor or Pastors, and Deacons.* That is, the right and duty of such election is resident in the Church, and not in any other power or body whatsoever. This has been already sufficiently dwelt upon.[5]

(2.) *Every Church is to ordain — or otherwise set apart to office — its Pastor, or Pastors, and Deacons.* To many minor offices — such as Clerk, Treasurer, Committees, and the like — election, with notification, is a sufficient 'setting apart;' and this, the nature of the transaction necessarily implies, must be done by the Church. The only question is whether, when the Church has chosen its Deacons, or its Pastor, and notified them, any further and special action is requisite on the part of the Church, or of any other party, in order so

---

[1] *Ancient Christianity*, p. 96.
[2] "Οὐ γὰρ βρωμάτων καὶ ποτῶν εἰσιν διάκονοι, ἀλλὰ ἐκκλησίας θεοῦ ὑπηρέται."—*Epist. ad Trall.* Sec. ii. p. 93.
[3] See *Apostolic Constitutions*, iii. c. 19; ii. c. 57; also Justin Martyr, Apol. i. c. 67; also Isodore, in c. 1. sec. 13, Diss. xxi; Also Conc. Trident. s. xxiii. c. 17.
[4] See *Congregational Quarterly*, Vol. i. (1859.) pp. 66–70.   [5] See pp. 40–42.

to 'set' them 'over' the Body, that all the functions of their offices may be rightly administered? This question may be answered from the proprieties of the case, from the Scripture record, and from the usage of the past.

(*a.*) The proprieties of the case suggest that induction into, and entrance upon the duties of, offices of so much weight and solemnity, may suitably be connected with some service of special consecration of the new incumbent to those duties, and of special supplication to God, — that he may have grace to discharge them wisely and well. Such service — aside from its probable relation to God's pleasure in the matter — may be regarded as naturally tending, on the one hand, to highten the beginner's conception of the importance of the work which he undertakes, and so to increase his humility, prayerfulness, and self-consecration ; and, on the other, to deepen those convictions in the minds of the Church which may lead them to all due submission, respect, and coöperation. So that a merely reasonable view of the matter would prompt some ceremony of induction into these high offices; and suggest that since the Church, under Christ, is supreme in the matter, she should assume the sole responsibility of that ceremony. So far as the office of Deacon is concerned, there is no contact between the appointing Church and the sisterhood, so that that comity and coöperation which create the difference between Congregationalism and Independency, make no claim that, with regard to the incumbency of this office, conference should be had with other churches. In the case of the Pastor, however, the fact is different. He sustains a *quasi* relation to all Congregational churches, as well as to that Church which has chosen him. He is to be recognized by other churches, as the Pastor of his own Church; and, in exchange with their Pastors, and in the varied courtesies and activities of the Pastoral life, all neighboring Congregational churches have an interest in his personal ability, discretion, and soundness in the faith. It is, therefore, a prompting of the coöperative and Congregational spirit, that, when a Church has made choice of its Pastor, it invite its sister churches to assemble, by their Pastors and appointed lay delegates, to review their action, and examine the candidate for their Pastorship, that so — being satisfied of the suitableness of both — they may pronounce the benediction of the fraternity of the churches upon the union, and extend the right hand of cordial fellowship from that fraternity to the new comer. And, in token of its honesty in the transaction, and by way of concentrating upon the act which sets its Pastor in his place, all the weight of character and piety in Council assembled, it is every way suitable and fraternal for the Church to confide to these gathered representatives of the fraternity, its power of setting its Pastor in office over itself. And this is called ordination — which is the mere formal consummation of the act of election, and consecration of the elected officer to his new duties. The power which sets the new Pastor over his Church, is Christ, the Great Head, speaking through the Church. Therefore, the power which should formally call the new officer to his work, should be the Church speaking for Christ its Great Head.

(*b*.) The New Testament view of ordination is very simple, and would never have been misunderstood, but for the muddling of its clear stream by hierarchal influence. The word 'ordain' — in the apparent sense of a solemn setting apart to the functions of office — is found only twice.[1] The first instance is in the 14th of Acts, (v. 23), where it is said of Paul and Barnabas, that when they had "ordained them Elders in every Church," etc., they commended them [the converts of Lystra, and Iconium, and Antioch] to the Lord, and passed on to Pisidia and Pamphilia. The second, is where Paul declares that he left Titus (Tit. i: 5) in Crete, "to ordain Elders" in every city, etc. Careful examination, however, reveals the fact that the first of these passages simply teaches us that the Apostles *prompted, and secured, the choice and service of Elders in every Church* — without any implication of any ceremony whatever of the induction of these Elders to office;[2] and that the second, merely re-

---

[1] Other apparent instances are only *apparent*. For example, our translation makes Paul say (1 Tim. ii: 7), "I am *ordained* a preacher, and an Apostle," etc. But the Greek is ἐτέθην ἐγὼ κῆρυξ καὶ ἀπόστολος, which simply means (see Alford, *in loco*), "I was *placed as* a herald and Apostle," etc.; which carries no such sense as is conveyed by the word "ordination." So our translation says (Mark iii: 14) that Christ "*ordained* twelve, that they should be with him," etc. But the Greek here is καὶ ἐποίησεν δώδεκα, which suggests nothing more than that he *selected out* and *appointed* twelve to be Apostles, etc. (See Alford, Alexander, and Owen, *in loco*.) So, again, our translation says that Peter (Acts i: 22) told the disciples that one "must be *ordained*" to be a witness, with the eleven, of the resurrection of Christ. But here the Greek is μάρτυρα τῆς ἀναστάσεως αὐτοῦ σὺν ἡμῖν γενέσθαι, etc., which means no more than that "one must be *made* (i. e. *chosen*) to be a witness," etc.

[2] "The word 'ordain' we now use in an Ecclesiastical sense, to denote a setting apart to an office by the imposition of hands. But it is evident that the word here is not employed in that sense. . . . The word here refers simply to an election or appointment of the Elders."— *Barnes. Comment.* Acts xiv: 23.

peats the sense of the first, implying action on the part of Titus, resembling that of Paul and Barnabas[1]—there being no hint, in either case, of any thing of a character like what is commonly called 'ordination' in our time. Naturally enough—being themselves Bishops and ordained clergy, in the High Church sense—King James' translators took it for granted that Paul and Barnabas and Titus must have made what they [the translators] understood by ordination, a part of the business of organizing the work of the Eldership with the churches, and that view colored their rendering; but, as every scholar can see, there is no hint of such 'ordination' in the Greek. Fairly translated, and unmodified by any coloring from subsequent unscriptural Ecclesiastical usage, these texts would never have suggested any such act as that which is called 'ordination,' by the common speech of men.

The true Scriptural ground of ordination is found in other passages—like that which informs us[2] that after the Holy Ghost had desired the 'separation' of Barnabas and Saul to the ministry unto the Gentiles, the Church at Antioch, after fasting and prayer, "laid their hands on them," and sent them to their work; and those where Paul directs Timothy to 'neglect not the gift that is in him, which was given him by prophecy, with the laying on of the hands of the presbytery;'[3] and also commands *him* 'to lay hands suddenly on no man.'[4] These texts, taken in connection with the general tenor of the Bible, warrant the inference that it was the way of the Apostolic days, to set apart Gospel laborers to a new work,[5] by prayer and the

---

See, also, Hackett, Calvin, Alexander, Erasmus, Grotius, and Alford, *in loco*. Alford says, "the word will not bear Jerome's sense of 'laying on of hands,' adopted by Roman Catholic expositors. (Vol. ii. p. 147.) See, also, pp. 15–17 of this boo

[1] Barnes says again, on this text, —"the word 'ordain' has now acquired a technical signification which it cannot be shown that it has in the New Testament. . . . But the word used here does not necessarily convey this meaning, or imply that Titus was to go through what would now be called 'an ordination service,'" etc. (*Comment. on Titus* i: 5.) Calvin says on this text; "He [Paul] does not give permission to Titus, that he alone may do every thing in this matter, and may place over the churches those whom he thinks fit to appoint to be bishops; but only bids him preside, as moderator, at the elections, which is quite necessary. This mode of expression is very common. In the same manner, a consul, or regent, or dictator is said to have 'created consuls,' on account of having presided over the public assembly in electing them. Thus also Luke relates that Paul and Barnabas 'ordained Elders in every Church," etc. (*Comment on Tit.* i: 5. *Calvin Translation Society's translation*, p. 290.) *Conybeare and Howson* render the verse "Appoint Presbyters in every city." (Vol. i: p. 477), and Alford translates it — "Mightest *appoint*, city by city, Elders," etc. (Vol. iii. p. 391.)

[2] Acts xiii . 2, 3.   [3] 1 Tim. iv: 14.   [4] Chap. v: 22.

[5] We say to a *new work*. This transaction which took place at Antioch, was not the ordina-

laying on of the hands of the Elders. It had been, from the early ages, the practice to lay hands on the head of one on whom special blessing was invoked, and for whom specially solemn prayer was offered; as Jacob did upon the sons of Joseph,[1] as Christ did upon the little children whom he blessed,[2] as Peter and John did on the believers in Samaria,[3] as the Apostles did upon the seven deacons,[4] as Paul did upon John's disciples at Ephesus,[5] as Ananias did upon Paul, at Damascus.[6] This was a well-settled Jewish custom, and being pertinent and every way pleasing and appropriate, it was naturally adopted by the disciples. But it had no *official* intent. It conveyed no official grace — although it was sometimes connected with the bestowment of those *charismata* which distinguished its miraculous, from every succeeding age, of the Church. It was not even necessarily the symbol of the consecration of the subject of it to any distinctively *spiritual* work at all, inasmuch as we find one of its clearest records in connection with the setting apart of the seven deacons to the discharge of a purely *temporal* function.[7] As Dr. Tracy has well said, "it was merely a customary gesture, performed by any one, on any occasion, in praying for another."[8] And so far as the sacred record informs us, it was always done — when done at all in connection with the setting apart of a Church officer to his work — by "the Presbytery," that is, the assembled Elders of the churches.[9] It would seem also that, in this ceremony, they acted for the Church. If ordination is the mere solemn installation of a functionary previously appointed, in the place to which he has been chosen; since the putting in place is a lesser act than the electing to the place, and since the Church have done the greater, it must follow that the power rests with it to do the less. So that if a Church may elect its Pastor, it may ordain

---

tion of Paul and Barnabas to the Apostleship, nor to the office of the ministry; for Barnabas never was an Apostle, and Saul received his commission directly from Christ (Acts ix: 20; Gal. i: 11-17), and both had been preachers of the Gospel before (Acts ix: 27; xi: 22, 23). It was the solemn setting apart of these men to a new and special work, viz: to be missionaries to the Gentiles.

[1] Gen. xlviii: 14.   [2] Matt. xix: 13-15.   [3] Acts viii: 17.
[4] Acts vi: 6.   [5] Acts xix: 6.   [6] Acts ix: 17.
[7] Acts vi: 1-6.
[8] "Report on the Induction of Deacons," etc., in Appendix to Punchard's "*View.*" (Ed. 1860.) p. 343.
[9] Barnes says, "there is not a single instance of ordination to an office mentioned in the New Testament, which was performed *by one man alone.*"—*Comment.* 1 Tim. iv: 14.

him — which is but carrying out that election to its full completion and result. And as there is nothing in Scripture to forbid or modify this view, so there is clear inference for its support.

There is no command that this practice be continued in the churches, but there is a pleasant fitness in it which will secure its continuance to the world's end. And — on the whole — Milton has well rendered the sense of the Bible concerning it, where he says, "as for ordination, what is it, but the laying on of hands, an outward sign or symbol of admission? It creates nothing, it confers nothing; it is the inward calling of God that makes a minister, and his own painful study and diligence that manures and improves his ministerial gifts."[1]

(c.) The opinions and usages of the past speak to the same purpose. Our Fathers were clear that ordination should be the act of the Church. JOHN ROBINSON says: "I was ordained publicly, upon the solemn calling of the Church in which I serve, both in respect of the ordainers and ordained,"[2] and maintains that "if the Church without officers, may elect, it may also ordain officers; if it have the power and commission of Christ for the one, and that the greater, it hath also for the other, which is the less."[3] JOHN COTTON held not only that "the warrant by which each particular Church doth depute some of their own body (though not Presbyters), to lay their hands upon those whom they have chosen to be their Presbyters, is grounded upon the Power of the keys which the Lord Jesus Christ (who received all fullness of Power from the Father) hath given to the Church,"[4] but that a Church which has no officers of its own, "wants a warrant to repair to the Presbytery of another Church to impose hands upon their elect Elders."[5] JOHN DAVENPORT says: "their ordination of officers, by deputing some chosen out of their own body thereunto (in the want of officers), is an act of the power of the keys residing in them. For, though the offices of Elders in general, and the authority of their office, as they are Rulers, is from Christ immediately; yet the investing of this or that elect person with this Office and authority, in relation to this or that Church, by application of it to him in particular, rather than to another — this is

---

[1] *Animadversions*, etc Prose Works. (Bohn's Ed.) Vol. iii. p 78.
[2] *Defence of Synod of Dort*, etc. Works. Vol. i. p. 463.
[3] *Bernard's Reason's discussed*," etc. Works. Vol. ii. p. 445.
[4] *Way of the Churches*. p. 43. [5] *Ibid*. p. 50.

by the Church."[1] THOMAS HOOKER says: "it is plain that ordination presupposing an officer constituted, does not constitute; therefore it is not an act of *Power*, but of *Order;* therefore those who have not the power of office may put it forth; therefore, though it be most comely that those of the same congregation should exercise it, yet the Elders also of other congregations may be invited hereunto, and interested in the exercise of it in another Church, where they have no power, and upon a person who hath more power in the place than themselves."[2] So he says, again, "though the *act* of Ordination belong to the Presbytery, yet the *jus et potestas ordinandi*,[3] is conferred *firstly* upon the *Church* by Christ, and resides in her. It is in them *Instrumentaliter*;[4] in her *Originaliter*.[5] They dispense it immediately; she by them mediately."[6] SAMUEL MATHER says: "Elders meeting in a Council or Synod, with Brethren, may at the desire of a particular Church, ordain its officers. But then, as it has been the judgment of these [the New England] churches in times past, there is yet no good reason why these churches should change their judgment, that the Elders so convened in Council or Synod, with their Brethren for this service, have no power or jurisdiction of their own, but act by virtue of the power derived from the particular churches which sent for them; so that, in short, particular churches are the first subjects of this power of ordaining; as it is for particular churches that Councils or Synods convene, when they meet in order to ordain officers for them."[7] The CAMBRIDGE PLATFORM says: "Ordination we account nothing else, but the solemn putting of a man into his place and office in the Church, whereunto he had right before, by election; being like the installing of a magistrate in the Commonwealth;"[8] and further, "in such churches where there are no Elders, imposition of hands may be performed by some of the brethren orderly chosen by the Church thereunto. For if the people may elect officers, which is the greater, and wherein the substance of the office consists, they may much more (occasion and need so requiring) impose hands in ordination, which is less, and but the accomplishment

---

[1] *Power of Congregational Churches*, etc. p. 104. [2] *Survey*, etc. Part ii. p. 59.
[3] The Right and Power of Ordination. [4] Instrumentally.
[5] Originally. [6] *Survey*, etc. Part ii. p. 76.
[7] "*Apology for the Liberties of the Churches in New England*," etc. (Ed. 1733.) p. 60.
[8] Chap. ix. secs. 2, 4.

of the other." COTTON MATHER says, that "our Fathers reckoned not ordination to be essential unto the vocation of a minister, any more than *coronation* to the being of a king; but that it is only a consequent and convenient adjunct of his vocation; and a solemn acknowledgement of it, with an useful and proper benediction of *him* in it;" yet he adds "setting aside a few 'plebeian ordinations' in the beginning of the world here among us, there have been rarely any ordinations managed in our churches but by the hands of Presbyters: yea, any ordinations but such, would be but matters of discourse and wonder."[1] INCREASE MATHER says, "the old doctrine of New England was, that if the Church where ordination is to be performed has not Elders of its own, they should desire neighbor Elders to assist in the ordination of their Pastor, and that with imposition of hands as well as with fasting and prayer."[2]

These citations, we think, fairly represent the opinions and feelings of our New England Fathers, while their practice is well set forth by COTTON MATHER.[3] In the beginning, there were a few of what he

---

[1] *Magnalia.* (Ed. 1853.) Vol. ii. pp. 242, 243.   [2] *Order of the Gospel.* (A. D. 1700.) p. 100.
[3] Is ordination for life? Yes; in the sense that no other result is contemplated by it than that the newly elected Pastor will remain Pastor — he desiring to do so, and the Church desiring him to do so — until the relation be terminated by death. No, in the sense that when, for any reason, the good of the Church, or the welfare of the Pastor, require a separation, it can, and should, take place. Such was the way of our Fathers. They acted like men of piety and common sense, who were not afraid to trust both churches and Pastors to act manfully, and honestly, and in a kind and Christian spirit, in whatever exigencies might unexpectedly arise. The early Pastors were set over their churches in the hope and expectation that they would live and die with them; yet changes were always made when there was need of them. "Master Hooke" remained first Pastor of the Church in Taunton only seven years, when at the earnest request of the Church in New Haven, he became associated with John Davenport, as Teacher of that Church, in 1644-5; and Nicholas Street, his colleague and successor at Taunton, became also his successor at New Haven. John Norton left the Teachership at Ipswich, to become John Cotton's successor at Boston. Thomas Cobbet left the Church at Lynn, to become Roger's successor at Ipswich. John Wheelwright was minister to the churches in Braintree, Mass.; Exeter, N. H.; Wells, Me.; Hampton, N. H.; and Salisbury, N. H. John Higginson was Pastor at Guilford, Conn., and Salem, Mass. John Davenport left New Haven, to become Pastor (in his seventieth year) of the 1st Church in Boston. Charles Chauncy left the Pastorship of the Church in Scituate, Mass.; among other reasons, because they did not support him, and was on his way to England, when he was chosen second President of Harvard College. Samuel Newman was Pastor at Weymouth and Rehoboth. John Woodbridge left Rowley for England, and England again for Newbury, where he ceased to be pastor before his death. Joshua Moody left Portsmouth for Boston, and Boston again for Portsmouth. Scores of such instances might be enumerated, showing that the practice of the first century of the churches in New England did not differ in this regard, in point of principle, from that which is now common; though less change took place as a matter of practice. [For a statement of the principles which governed our Fathers in this matter, see *Mather's Magnalia*, (Ed. 1853.) Vol. ii. pp. 250, 251.]

calls 'plebeian' ordinations,[1] but afterward the churches generally ordained, as now, their Pastors, through delegation of their power to

---

It is deeply to be regretted that it has become common among the churches in some sections of the country, to introduce into the terms of settlement, a clause that either party may terminate the relation by giving three or six months 'notice' in writing. We most earnestly object to this practice; among other reasons, for the following:—

1. *It is unscriptural.* The tone of Scripture implies that the term of the Pastoral office is for life, or 'for good behavior.' And there is no hint of any opposite principle, or practice.

2. *It is uncongregational.* No man familiar with the records of the denomination, will contend that it is not a novelty in point of practice, and we do not see how any one who understands the principles of our system, can fail to see that it is radically inconsistent with them. It is one of the most important principles of our system that *the Church* and not the Parish, is the body which ought to choose or refuse its Pastor, and yet this clause puts it in the power of a bare majority of another body — not one of whom is necessarily a Church member — practically to terminate the relation between the Church and its Pastor. Permanence, coetaneous with faithfulness, is the fundamental idea on which Congregationalism rests its difference of practice from those systems which favor an itinerant ministry, and this 'six months' novelty is an important step down from the vantage ground of Apostolic and Puritan principles towards those of Wesley.

3. *It is unnecessary.* No Parish of common sense would wish to retain its Pastor when his sense of duty constrained him to go; no Pastor of common sense would wish to impose himself upon his Parish, when their sense of duty clearly indicated that he ought not to stay. But Parishes and Pastors are — and must be — presumed to have both common sense and some degree of Christian principle; so that no extraordinary provision is needed by either party for release, if Providence does not smile on the union. And if either party should prove to be lacking, there are ways and means enough which may legally and properly be used to force a criminally unwilling partner to the dissolution of the copartnership, without *welding a flaw into the very joint which unites them*.

4. *It is inexpedient.* It enables the relation to be sundered without the calling of a Council, and so may deprive the departing minister of any such 'papers' of dismission, as will justify him to be settled elsewhere. It holds out constant invitation to sunder the relation for every little breeze of dissatisfaction, which otherwise would at once blow harmless over; thus affecting the pastoral relation much as the marriage relation would be affected by a similar 'six months clause' in the marriage contract. It may also very easily precipitate a parish upon legal rocks, which may involve them in years of difficulty, if their action does not happen to square with the decisions of the courts.

5. *It is disgraceful to both parties entering into it.* It concedes that neither has confidence that the other can be trusted to do right, without extraordinary precautions — which is a method of doing business well enough between knaves, but out of place between Christian gentlemen.

6. *It sends both parties to the wrong resort in case real difficulties arise.* Christian principle, humiliation before God, and subjection to his wisdom, are the means of extrication from difficulty, which Christ approves for his Church; not the going down into the Egypt of some shrewd device in the ordination bargain, for help. Churches and Pastors ought to trust in the Lord and do good; so shall they dwell in the land, and verily they shall be fed!

[1] "In general, the ordination of ministers was by imposition of the hands of their brethren in the ministry, but some churches, perhaps to preserve a more perfect independency, called for the aid of no ministers of any other churches, but ordained their ministers by the imposition of the hands of some of their own brethren. The ordination at Salem, Aug. 29, 1660, was performed in this manner, as I find minuted by a gentleman just arrived from England, who was present."—Hutchinson. *Massachusetts Bay.* Vol. i. p. 424.

Lechford says that "Master Hooke" received ordination at Taunton (A.D. 1637-8) "from the hands of one Master Bishop, a schoolmaster, and one Parker, an husbandman, and then Master Hooke joyned [with Bishop and Parker] in ordaining Master Streate" [the Teacher of the Church.]—*Plain Dealing*, etc. p. 96. (*Mass. Hist. Coll.* Vol. iii. Third Series.)

the Elders of neighboring churches assembled in Council for that purpose.[1]

A word of allusion to the hierarchal theory of Ordination, may be pertinent here. That theory is that the Apostles, in virtue of their Apostleship, ordained the first Bishops of the churches, and committed to them the official duty and right of ordaining those who should come after them, and so on in endless succession to the world's end — none but Bishops ordained by Bishops having that power. This is sought to be established by the assertion that the Apostles 'ordained' the seven deacons, and consecrated James Bishop of Jerusalem, Timothy Bishop of Ephesus, and Titus Bishop of Crete. But we have seen that the case of the seven Deacons involves no such inference,[2] and that there is no evidence that either James, Timothy, or Titus, was ever a 'Bishop' in any such sense as this.[3] It is further urged that the writings of the Fathers establish the fact that "for 1600 years, all Christian churches were governed by Bishops,"[4] who ordained all clergy. But we have already seen that for the first two centuries this claim is false, and that it was not until those corruptions which overspread the Church — and which begin to show their influence in the pretended Epistles of Ignatius — had swept away the primitive purity and simplicity of the faith, that this claim for the power of the Bishops, becomes true.[5] Furthermore, on the Episcopal theory, the world is now destitute of a regularly ordained ministry, for it is impossible anywhere to establish a perfect succession — link touching link — from the hands of the Apostles. Even Archbishop Whately says, "*there is no Christian Minister now existing*, that can trace up, with complete certainty, his own ordination, through perfectly regular steps, to the times of the Apostles."[6] And when one

---

Messrs. Higginson and Skelton were ordained at Salem (A. D. 1629), by " three or four of the gravest members of the Church ;" John Wilson was so ordained at Charlestown (A. D. 1630), and Mr. Carter, at Woburn (1642). John Cotton, at Boston (A. D. 1633), and Mr. Hooker at Newtown, were ordained by the Church in presence of "neighbor ministers," who gave the right hand of fellowship, — which Hubbard says was "according to the subsequent practice in New England." — See *Gov. Bradford's Letter Book* in *Mass. Hist. Coll.*, Vol. III. p. 67 ; Appendix to Morton's *Memorial*, (Ed. 1855), p. 419 ; Eliot's History, in *Mass. Hist. Coll.*, 1st Series, Vol. ix. p. 89. Hubbard's *History of New England*, in *Mass. Hist. Coll.*, 2d Series, Vol. v. p. 189.

[1] See Cotton Mather's *Ratio Disciplinæ*, pp. 14–42 ; Increase Mather's *Disquisition concerning Ecclesiastical Councils*, p. ix. ; and Palfrey's *History of New England*, Vol. ii. p. 39.
[2] See p. 140.   [3] See pp. 107–109.   [4] Hook's *Church Dictionary*, pp. 410, 411.
[5] See pp. 77–110.   [6] *Corruptions of Christianity*, (Gowan's Ed. 1860), p. 170.

thinks of the filthy lives of some of the Popes, it seems amazing that any Church, or portion of a Church, or any holy man, should desire to establish, much less to rest his claims to ministerial character upon, it. Yet Bishop Brownwell, of Connecticut, in a charge given some years since, to his clergy, said, "if a regular ministerial succession in the order of Bishops, be not conformable to Scripture and Apostolic usage, *Episcopacy is an unjustifiable usurpation.*" [1]

(3.) *The Church must select and set apart its officers from among its own number.* In a government of the people, the essential idea of an officer is of one elected by the people from themselves, to do for them the work which is the function of that office. Monarchies and aristocracies put officers authoritatively over the people, by the action of a power without; but republicanism knows no such procedure, and since a Congregational Church is the simplest and purest form of a republic, it can consistently know no officer whom it does not raise out of its own ranks, and itself — under Christ — invest with his official dignity and power.

This is so simple, and follows so inevitably from the first principles of the Congregational Church Polity, that it could hardly have been questioned, for a moment, if Presbyterian theories and practices had not stolen in insensibly to modify their working. We never heard of any Church which doubted that its Deacons should be chosen from its own membership, but an idea obtains, to some extent, that *a Pastor* need not necessarily be a member of his own Church; nay, that it is expedient that he should not be! But any theory which would make it right for a Church to choose its Pastor from the membership of another Church, would make it right, as well, for it to choose its

---

[1] See on this general subject, an earnest discussion in Hall's *Puritans and their Principles*, (pp. 310-409); Davidson's *Ecclesiastical Polity of the New Testament*, (pp. 218-262); Dr. Owen, *Works*, (Vol. xiii. p. 219); Chauncy's *View of Episcopacy*, passim; Barnes' *Inquiry into the Organization and Government of the Apostolic Church*, etc., (pp. 89-138); Coleman's *Primitive Church*, (pp. 297-300), etc.

Also consult articles on *Apostolical Succession*, in *Princeton Review*, Vol. xix. (1847), pp. 539-564, and *Eclectic Review*, 4th Series, Vol. iv. p. 547; on *The Validity of Congregational Ordination*, by Dr. Lamson, in the *Christian Examiner*, Vol. xvii. (1834), pp. 177-202; on *Ordination*, by Dr. J. P. Wilson, in the *Monthly Christian Spectator*, Vol. i., New Series, (1827), pp. 505-512; on *Episcopacy*, by Dr. Bacon, in the *New Englander*, Vol. i. (1843), pp. 300, 545, 586, and Vol. ii. (1844), pp. 309, 440; by Dr. Bushnell, Vol. ii. p. 143-175; by Dr. J. P. Thompson, Vol. iii. (1845), pp. 140-149; by Albert Barnes, Vol. iii. (1845), pp. 333-378; in *American Biblical Repository*, 3d Series, Vol. i. (1845), by A. D. Eddy, pp. 315-359; and on the *Primitive Episcopate*, in the *Eclectic Review*, 4th Series, Vol. xxii. p. 47.

Deacons, or its clerk, or treasurer, from another Church. No logical difference can be shown between these offices in this particular. Any attempt to make such a distinction in favor of a Pastor, must ground itself upon some theory of the nature and tenure of his office, which is uncongregational, and unscriptural. If he is their guide and teacher, sent by Christ through their calling and election and consecration of him, he must be one of themselves, or they have no such control over him as makes it fit for them to order that he assume — under Christ — pastoral leadership over them. Of course they will not invite a non-Church member to be their spiritual guide; but if he must belong to *some* Church, why not to that Church? If, when attention be first turned toward him as a candidate for the pastoral office in one Church, he be a member of another, why should he not, when invited to become Pastor, on acceptance of that invitation, remove his Church connection, as well as his personal presence, to the inviting Church? If he were simply a private Church member, it would be his duty to do so, for no principle is better settled than the duty of Church members removing from one place to another, within a reasonable time, to remove their Church relation also; but his private Church membership always underlies his official character and relation. Is he afraid to trust the Church over which he is to be settled, with the custody of his Christian character? Does he intend to commit acts worthy of discipline, and does he aim to embarrass discipline by distance? Does he love his old Church better than that to which he now promises to give his best affections and all his strength? Has he some vague notion that if it should ever be his misfortune to be brought to trial on any charge, he ought to have such trial by his 'peers;' and so he will say 'hands off,' to his own Church, without remembering that they are quite as really his 'peers,' as the membership of any other Church can be; and without reflecting that in his permanent and fundamental character of a private Church member, he *will* be tried by his 'peers,' if tried by them? Does he conceive that because the Holy Ghost has made him "overseer" of his Church, he is therefore raised above accountability to it; when even the Governor of a Commonwealth, if he were to commit a crime, must be tried by the common Courts of that Commonwealth, like any other criminal, and not by a jury of Governors? Does he esteem it the course likeliest to ensure that mutual confidence and entire trust and love, which are 'the bond of perfectness' between a successful Pastor and his Church, by standing off from them in the beginning, as if he distrusted, and expected always to distrust, them so far that he will never become one with them to that degree that they will have his honor and his usefulness in their fraternal keeping?

So far as the Scripture bears upon this question, it intimates that 'Elders' are to be ordained '*in* every Church,' not *over* it; and the voice of our Congregational Fathers is one and earnest to the same effect;[1] while it is believed that the churches are growing in-

---

[1] John Robinson in his Appendix to Mr. Perkins *Six Principles*, says, in an answer to the question by whom Church officers are to have their "outward calling?" "By the Church, *whereof they are members for the present*, and to which they are to administer," and he adds that if such an officer be found "unfaithful in his place," he "is by the Church to be warned to take heed to his ministry he hath received, to fulfil it; which, if he neglect to do, by the same power which set him up, he is to be put down and deposed, *being dealt with as a brother*." — *Works*, Vol. iii. pp. 430, 431.

Thomas Welde ("Pastor of the Church of Roxborough, in New England,") says in his *Answer to W. R. etc.* (London, A. D. 1644) "it is our usual and constant course, as hath been said, not to gather any Church until they have one *amongst themselves* fit for a minister, whom with all speed they call into office, and account themselves a lame and imperfect body till that be effected." And to this he adds: "Is it not a thing most natural for a body to employ its own members? Is not the mutual interest, in each other, the stronger tie? Do not all bodies and societies in the world, the very same? Was ever any man of another corporation elected sheriff or mayor, or unto any special office in London, unless he were first seasoned with this same salt, of membership of the same body?"—*Hanbury*, Vol. ii. p. 329.

John Cotton says (*Way of the Churches*, etc.) "They look out *from amongst themselves* such persons as are in some measure qualified, etc." But if they "find out none such in their own body, they send to any other Church for fit supply." That these members of another Church, must transfer their membership on receiving office, is made clear, however, by Cotton's own example, who became a member of the Church in Boston, a month before he became its Teacher.— See *Way*, p. 39, and M'Clure's *Life of Cotton*, pp. 107-110.

John Davenport says, that a Church when formed, "must look out *from among themselves* for such officers as Christ hath given to his Church; these they must chuse and ordain, professing their voluntary submission to their office rule, and authority, in the Lord."—*Power of Congregational Churches*, etc. p. 94.

Thomas Hooker says that an officer "is a brother as well as any of the rest, and therefore the processe of our Saviour lieth as fair against him, as against another."—*Survey*, etc. Part i. p 62; also pp. 155, 192, and Part ii. p. 68.

Cotton Mather says, (*Ratio Disciplinæ*, A. D. 1726), "in these proceedings [settling a minister], there is a seasonable care taken, that if he were a member of some other Church, he have his dismission (his relation declared to be transferred) unto that which now have their eye upon him, to be their pastor; that as near as may be, according to the primitive direction, they may *chuse from among themselves*."—Ratio Disciplinæ, p. 22.

Isaac Chauncy says, (*Divine Institution of Congregational Churches*, A. D. 1697,) "none can be an officer of a corporation, but he that is incorporate first as a member."—*Div. Instit.* etc. p. 104.

Cambridge Platform says, "in case an Elder offend incorrigibly, the matter so requiring, as the Church had power to call him to office, so they have power according to order (the council of other Churches, where it may be had, directing thereto), to remove him from his office; *and*

creasingly to feel the importance of fidelity to the first principles of their Polity, and the dictates of common sense, in this particular, and many have made it one of their 'standing rules' that their Pastor shall be a member of their own body — an example which we think it would be well for every Congregational Church to follow.

A word may pertinently be added here in reference to what have, of late, been commonly called STATED SUPPLIES; that is, ministers acting as pastors for churches, without assuming the official relation of Pastor to them. It will be an obvious inference from the principles before laid down, that Congregationalism recognizes no such Church officers as a part of the regular force of her laborers. A 'Stated Supply' is not a Deacon; equally he is not a Pastor — because the Church has neither chosen nor ordained him to that post — and since Congregational churches have no other officers than Pastors and Deacons, he is not an officer of the Church; and as a mere private member of *some* Church (usually another than that with which he labors) he has no authority to perform the work of the ministry, except *ex necessitate* — in the absence of a qualified person, or while he is regularly on his way to the Pastorship.

Congregationalism indeed recognizes the right of any person whom God seems to have called to the ministry — by gifts, graces, and opportunities — and whom any Church of Christ may elect as its Teacher, to preach and teach; though — to avoid frequent mistakes, and imposition, and the precipitant running of over-fast men whom

---

being now but a member [of course, then, it is implied that in every case a Pastor will have become a member of his own Church] in case he add contumacy to his sin, the Church that had power to receive him into their fellowship, hath also the same power to cast him out, that they have concerning any other member."—*Platform*, Chap. x. sec. 6.

Prof. Upham (in his *Ratio Disciplinæ*), argues this point, (1.) because private Church members ought to remove their relation to that Church with which they worship, and so, for example's sake, should the Pastor; (2.) because he meets and acts with the Church, which ought not to be done, merely as *ex officio*; (3.) because his refusal to become a member of his own Church will tend to generate feelings of distrust and alienation; and (4.) because ministers, as well as private Christians, need the benefit of Church watch and discipline.—Upham's *Rat. Dis.* pp. 127-130; also p. 170.

Dr. Dwight held that " a minister is a member of the Church of Christ at large, but is never, in the proper sense, a member of a particular Church," (Sermon clvii.) but his head was befogged with Consociationism, and he seems to have regretted that we were not all Presbyterians, at least in our Church Judicatories. (See Sermon clxii.) The same remarks will measurably apply to Dr. Woods. (See his *Works*, Vol. iii. pp. 572-583.)

the Lord has not sent, and to insure the needful preparatory training — the system favors a regular 'licensure' of candidates for the ministry, after thorough examination by some competent persons (either a Church or an Association of Ministers), the possession of which 'licensure' shall be recognized as *prima facie* evidence that its possessor *is* 'called of God as was Aaron,' and is therefore, a suitable person to be employed to preach the Gospel, and to be thought of by a Church as its Pastor. But all this is preliminary. Such a preacher, clearly, remains a lay exhorter, until some Church has elected and ordained him to be its Pastor. Then first he ceases to be a mere private Church member (more gifted than his brethren), and becomes a 'minister of reconciliation,' fully empowered to perform all the labors and discharge all the responsibilities of the Pastoral office.

Strictly speaking, and as a matter of pure logical deduction from the principles of the case, it follows that when such a Pastor ceases to hold his official relation to the Church from which he received his elevation to the ministry, he descends into the ranks of the laity again, and is no more a minister, until some other Church shall have elected and ordained (or installed — as all ordinations of a man after his first, are usually called) him as its Pastor; when he resumes the official rank which he had demitted, rising again out of the ranks of the laity, to the function of the ministry. He has the same right to preach in this interim that he had after his licensure before his first ordination, namely: a temporary right of courtesy and general consent, until — finding that the Great Head does not call him to any pastorship — he shall subside into a mere layman; or until he shall be chosen and ordained by some other Church as its Pastor, and become a minister again. This, we say, is the necessary verdict of the principles of Congregationalism in regard to this matter; as it was the practice of the Fathers.[1] But — partly through forgetfulness of

---

[1] "They did not allow the Priesthood to be a distinct order, or to give a man an indelible character; but, as the vote of the brotherhood made him an officer, and gave him authority to preach and administer the sacraments among them, so the same power could discharge him from office, and *reduce him to the state of a private member.*"—*Account of the Brownists. Neal.* Vol. 1. p. 150.

John Robinson held that a minister's relation to his own Church was such that he had no official character away from it, even in another Church. He says: "It is not lawful for thee, reverend brother, to do the work of a Pastor where thou art no Pastor, lest thou arrogate to thyself that honor which appertains not unto thee. Thou art called, that is elected, and ordained a pastor of some particular Church, and not of all churches. . . . We will illustrate this

these principles; partly through the subtle influence of surrounding hierarchal notions, as if the ministry were a 'standing order' of men

---

by a similitude. Any citizen of Leyden may enjoy certain privileges in the city of Delft, by virtue of the politic combination of the United Provinces, and cities, under the Supreme heads thereof, the States-general; which he is bound also to help and assist with all his power, if necessity require; but that the ordinary magistrate of Leyden should presume to execute his public office in the city of Delft, were an insolent violence and unheard of usurpation. The very same, and not otherwise, is to be said of pastors, and particular churches, in respect of that spiritual combination mutual under their Chief and sole Lord, Jesus Christ." — *Works*, Vol. iii. p. 17.

The New England Elders say, in their answer to the questions sent over from England, (A. D. 1637), " we have no such indelible character imprinted on a minister, that he must needs be so for ever, because he once was so. His ministry ceasing, the minister ceaseth also."— *Answer 77.*

Allin and Shepard (A. D. 1648) say, " If a minister be [even] unjustly deposed, or forsaken, by his particular Church, and he also withal renounce and forsake them, so far as all office and relation between them cease; then he is no longer an officer or pastor in any Church of God, whatsoever you will call it; and the reason is, because a minister's office in the Church is no 'indelible character,' but consists in his relation to the flock. And if a minister once ordained, his relation ceasing, his office of a minister, 'steward of the mysteries of God' shall still remain; why should not a ruling Elder or deacon, remain an Elder or deacon in the Church as well? All are officers ordained of Christ, alike given to his Church; officers chosen and ordained by laying on of hands alike; but we suppose you will not say a deacon, in such a case, should remain a deacon in the 'Catholic' Church; therefore not a minister." — *Defence of the Answer,* etc., by John Allin, Pastor of Dedham, and Thomas Shepard, Pastor of Cambridge, in New England. London. 1648, 4to, in *Hanbury*, Vol. iii. p. 42.

Cambridge Platform says, " Church officers are officers to one Church, even that particular Church over which the Holy Ghost hath made them overseers. Insomuch as Elders are commanded to feed, not all flocks, but that flock which is committed to their faith and trust, and dependeth upon them..... He that is clearly loosed from his office relation unto that Church whereof he was a minister, *cannot be looked at as an officer, nor perform any act of office in any other Church, unless he be again orderly called unto office;* which, when it shall be, we know nothing to hinder, but imposition of hands also in his ordination ought to be used towards him again. For so Paul the Apostle received imposition of hands twice, at least, from Ananias."— Chap. ix. Sec's. 6, 7.

This Platform was agreed upon in 1648. In 1679, a Synod held at Boston 'considered' it, and voted that they " do unanimously approve of the said Platform, *for the substance of it.*" Cotton Mather explains (*Magnalia,* Vol. ii. pp. 237-247) what they meant by the use of this language, and says that, at that time, it was the general opinion that " the pastor of a *neighboring* Church may, upon the request of a *destitute* Church, occasionally administer the sacraments unto them;" and adds, "I suppose there are now few ministers in the country but what consent unto the words of Dr. Owen, 'Although we have no concernment in the figment of an *indelible character* accompanying sacred orders, yet we do not think the pastoral office is such a thing as a man must leave behind him every time he goes from home.' "

John Cotton did not baptize his child 'Seaborn,' on the voyage hither, because he held that "a minister hath no power to give the seals but in his own congregation." — *Savage's Winthrop,* Vol. i. p. 131.

Winthrop says of Mr. Ward's (of Ipswich) being chosen by some of the freemen to preach the Election Sermon, "they had no great reason to choose him, though otherwise very able, seeing he had cast off his Pastor's place at Ipswich, *and was now no minister, by the received determination of our churches.*"—*Savage's Winthrop,* Vol. ii. p. 42.

" A Church officer, of whatever degree, was an officer only in his own congregation. The primitive doctrine of New England was, that no man was a clergyman in any sense, either before his election by a particular Church, or after his relinquishment of the special trust so con-

invested, by ordination, with an official dignity of which nothing short of deposition can divest them; and partly through that natural and praiseworthy kindness of heart which leads men to refrain from reminding a man of any change in his position from a higher to a lower — the practice of the denomination has, of late years, been to consider a man who is once a minister as always a minister, unless he be deposed; even when he has left the work of the ministry and become permanently engaged in secular pursuits for his daily bread. This has led the churches so far to forget the only real ground on which a man's right to the ministry rests, that they seem largely to have come to suppose that right to be lodged in the 'licensure' of some Association of Ministers, or the action of an Ordaining Council, rather than in their own choice and consecration. And, being, perhaps, feeble and doubtful how long they may be able to maintain the ministry of the word among them; being, it may be, uncertain how great will be the success of that preacher whom they, on the whole, desire to undertake the work; and being, not unlikely, frightened by the misfortune of some neighboring Church with a bad Pastor who was unwilling to follow his departed usefulness — holding on to his legal settlement as a drowning man grips the rope which he took overboard with him in his fall — they think it may be a more excellent way to 'hire a stated supply' for the Pulpit, as they 'hire a stated supply' for the farm-yard or the meadow; both preacher and ploughman to go when wages are stopped, or when they can 'do better' elsewhere. This mercenary practice has — strangely enough — been favored by some ministers, who think to make it convenient to leave when a 'field of broader usefulness' opens elsewhere, and who esteem it a convenience to be hampered by no necessity for advice of Council, as to staying or going.

All this is uncongregational, and unscriptural, and — as facts abundantly are testifying — evil for the churches; and for the ministry, as well. The New Testament idea of a Christian Church is of a brotherhood guided and led by one of its own members, in whom all have so much confidence and love as to entrust him, under Christ, with the responsibility of the Pastoral office; — one whose interests will be

ferred; and that, even while in office, he was a layman to all the world except his own congregation, and had no right to exercise any clerical functions elsewhere."—Palfrey's *History of New England*, Vol. ii. p. 39.

identical with theirs, and who will *'dwell* among his own people;' who will be such a Shepherd of the flock that the sheep will follow him because they *know his voice.* 'But he that is an hireling and not the Shepherd, *whose own* the sheep are not, seeth the wolf coming and leaveth the sheep and fleeth; and the wolf catcheth them, and scattereth the sheep. The hireling fleeth *because he is an hireling, and careth not for the sheep.*' The more feeble a flock may be, the more it needs the tender care of a *shepherd*, who loves it because it is his own, and who is even willing to give his life for the sheep. And the more feeble a Church may be, the more it needs the service of a *Pastor;* who will make its lot his own, who is willing to spend and be spent for it, who is not mainly occupied in looking out for a better place for himself elsewhere, but whose whole soul is intent upon the growth in grace of the people of God and the conversion of sinners there, until Zion shall find enlargement and the little one became a thousand, through the affluent descent of that celestial influence which alone can make a Church rich, and add no sorrow thereto.

It is readily conceded that exceptional cases may exist, where a minister may rightly labor with a Church temporarily, without the intention, on either side, of a permanent union. But it is questionable even then, if it would not be better for that minister to remove his relation to that Church, and to be elected by it its Pastor, for the time that he may remain; throwing in his lot heartily with them, and being one with them, so long as his labor is there. It cannot, we think, be questioned that the Divine idea of churches is of a brotherhood led by a Pastor; and that God may much more reasonably be expected to further, with his continual help, a Church which in this respect complies with the spirit of his Word, than one which ignores, or tramples on it. And as for the 'Stated Supplies' themselves, it may be commended to their earnest and prayerful thought, whether the old-fashioned Congregational pastorate is not more favorable to the permanence, happiness, and usefulness of the relation of a minister to his Church, than this illogical, unscriptural, and, to say the least, practically doubtful modern practice? Meanwhile it is clear that so long as a 'Stated Supply' is neither an officer nor a member of the Church to which he temporarily ministers, he is not in any Congregational sense its Pastor, and has no right to represent it, as such, in Councils to which that Church may be invited to send its 'Pastor and Delegate;' and, since he derives no ministerial character from any vote or action of the Church to which he preaches, he is not, in any proper official sense, a minister of Christ at all; as, if he has never received Ordination from any Church, he never was officially a minister, and if he was ever ordained over some other Church, his dismissal from it has reduced him again to the position of a layman — having only that right to preach which any gifted layman has, after the approval of his gifts by some 'licensing' body.

But suppose him to have been 'Ordained as an Evangelist,' — would not *that* give him power to exercise his ministry everywhere and always, without action from any particular Church? To this we reply that, strictly speaking, on pure Congregational principles there is no such thing as 'ordaining' men as 'Evangelists.' Ordination is the act by which — usually through a Council — a Church solemnly inducts to his position the Pastor whom it has previously elected over itself.[1] Congregationalism knows of no other ordination than this. Our Fathers knew of none other.[2] There is neither Scriptural jus-

---

[1] See pages 137-143.

[2] Hooker says, "There ought to be no ordination of a minister at large, namely, such as should make him Pastor without a people."— *Survey*, etc. Preface, p. xvi.

Isaac Chauncy says, "Christ never constituted such a ministry, but what were set in a particular Church by election."—*Divine Institution of Congregational Churches*. (London, 1697). p. 18.

John Owen (in his *True Nature of a Gospel Church*), argues at length that "no Church whatever hath power to ordain men ministers for the conversion of infidels" [*i. e.* Heathen], "antecedently unto any designation by divine providence thereunto." He further argues that no man can be ordained but unto a determinate office over some particular Church, because, (1.) it is against the practice of the Apostles; (2.) it was absolutely forbidden in the ancient Church, by the Council of Chalcedon; (3.) such ordination wants an essential constitutive cause, and is therefore invalid; (4.) it makes a *relate* without a *correlate*, which is impossible; (5.) it is inconsistent with the whole nature and end of the Pastoral office.—*Works*, Vol. xvi. pp. 92-94.

Increase Mather (in his *Order of the Churches in New England vindicated*) answers, in the negative, the question whether "a man may be ordained a Pastor except to a particular Church, and in the presence of that Church?" on these grounds; (1.) there is no instance of any such ordination in Scripture; (2.) Pastor and flock are relates, and therefore one cannot be without the other; (3.) a Pastor is under obligation to feed every one that is of the flock which he is a Pastor unto (Acts xx: 28, Heb. xiii: 17), which would be impossible; (4.) if a man is Pastor of the Church universal, no particular Church has any jurisdiction over him; (5.) ancient experiment proved the inexpediency of such general ordinations, and led to their suppression; (6.) they are contrary to the judgment of the most eminent divines, and the practice of the best Reformed churches.—*Order*, etc. pp. 101-109.

The practical question as to what should be done in the case of missionaries to the Indians, early arose in New England, and the manner of its answer shows the conscientious convictions of our Fathers. Stephen Badger was ordained a missionary to the Indians, at Natick, but he

tification nor suggested need of any other. The supposed need, in the case of 'Evangelists' and Missionaries, grows out of the assumption that only an ordained person has the right to administer Baptism and the Lord's Supper. But that assumption is a legacy of Popery which Congregationalism will do well to decline; since the Bible does neither affirm nor endorse it.[1] Scripturally, one of the Deacons or

---

was called and ordained in connection with a Church gathered there. The officers of the churches of the converted Indians at Martha's Vineyard were ordained only after choice of those churches In 1733, 1735, 1754, and 1762, missionaries were ordained at Boston and Deerfield, to labor among the Indians. Some who took part in them seem to have had scruples which they quieted on the theory that the action was only anticipatory of that which would come from the churches which would be gathered; and this is the only logical ground on which a Congregationalist can assist in such an ordination. But such an *Evangelical fiction* is needless, and therefore indefensible. — See Upham's *Ratio Disciplinæ*, pp 130–137; Cumming's *Congregational Dictionary*, pp 170, 276–279.

[1] The great command of Christ to *baptize* all nations, was indeed addressed to "the eleven" Apostles, but not in such a sense as to indicate that they alone should have the right to baptize. It is clear, (from John iv: 2, and Acts ii: 41,) that the "disciples" baptized. Philip the Deacon baptized the Eunuch. Ananias seems to have baptized Paul. Peter did not himself baptize Cornelius and his company (Acts x: 48). Paul (1 Cor. i: 14-17) was accustomed to leave his converts to be baptized by others. There is not — we make bold to say — a single passage in the New Testament which, directly or indirectly, lays down as a precept, or portrays even in the form of an example, the duty of baptizing, as one that inheres in the Pastor of a Church. Doddridge, indeed, says, (*Lectures on Divinity*, Lect. cc., Sec. x. 3) "it is fit that baptism should be administered only by the teachers and ministers of the Church *where their assistance can be had*, not only because it appears that these were the persons by whom it was administered in the New Testament, but because (*cæteris paribus*) they must be most capable of judging who are the fit subjects of it " But this, in the first place, concedes all that we claim — for we only hold that baptism may be administered by duly authorized laymen, *when the assistance of a Pastor cannot be had;* while, in the second place, it makes a questionable inference from the New Testament — since there is no evidence that all of the disciples who baptized, were " teachers and ministers " of churches ; and, in the third place, it rests upon an argument without practical foundation — inasmuch as it is the business of the administrator of Baptism, to baptize only those whom the Church directs him to seal with that ordinance ; as being either the infant children of believers whose right is recognized in its articles of faith and covenant, or individuals whom it has voted to be suitable candidates for its membership — *the Church* thus always assuming judgment " who are the fit subjects " of the ordinance

As to the Lord's Supper, there is no precept from the lips of Christ himself prescribing any person or persons, as the proper officiators His words were (Paul says) to the whole body, " this do, in remembrance of me." Nor is there a word in Paul's description of the scene, or comments upon it, to imply that, in his apprehension, the validity or propriety of the ordinance depended, in any manner, upon the person who was the medium of the words said, and the actions done All the stress is laid on the *social character* of the rite, as one in which the whole body of believers join ; — " this do *ye*." " as often as ye eat and drink," etc., " ye do shew the Lord's death till he come," " when ye come together to eat, tarry one for another," " that ye come not together unto condemnation," etc It would, of course, be natural for the Pastor to officiate, where there was a Pastor, but no law of that sort is enacted, no advice thereto given.

In conformity with this freedom, was the practice of the early Church. Dr. Coleman says, (*Ancient Christianity*, p. 390) " the duty of administering the ordinance [of Baptism] does not

any brother of the Church, whom it may authorize for the purpose, is competent — in the absence of its Pastor — to baptize, or to preside

---

appear to have been restricted to any officer of the Church.... Lay baptism, of which frequent mention is made in the early history of the Church, was undoubtedly treated as valid by the laws and usages of the ancient Church." So he says (p. 427) of the Lord's Supper — "nothing is said in the New Testament respecting the person whose prerogative it is to administer this sacrament.... According to the earliest documents of the 2d and 3d centuries, it was the appropriate office of the president of the assembly to administer the Eucharist." Tertullian (A. D. 200) asserts the *right* of the lay members of the Church both to baptize and to administer the Lord's Supper, (*De Exhort. Cast.* Opera. Ed. Lipsiæ, Vol. ii. p. 105) See also, to the same purport, Erasmus (*Ed.* Lib. xxvi. Vol. iii.), and Grotius (*De Cana. Ad. ubi pastores non Sunt* Opera. Vol. iv. p. 607

A few more modern endorsements of the opinions here advocated will now be quoted.

"We nowhere read in Scripture of the Lord's Supper being distributed to the first Christians by an appointed minister; we are only told that they partook of it in common, and that frequently, and in private houses. (Acts ii : 42.) I know no reason, therefore, why ministers refuse to permit the celebration of the Lord's Supper, except where they themselves are allowed to administer it; for if it be alleged that Christ gave the bread and wine to his disciples, it may be replied, first, that we nowhere read of his giving them to each individually — and, secondly, that he was then acting in the character, not of a minister, but of the founder of a new institution."—John Milton *Christian Doctrine,* (Sumner's translation), p. 445.

"When a pastor died, or was removed, the Church was not obliged to desist from commemorating the Lord's death, any more than from receiving or excluding members; and it was as lawful for them to appoint a Deacon, or any senior member, to preside in the one case, as in the other."—Andrew Fuller. *Works,* Vol. v. p. 285.

"What they conceive to be in that ordinance especially — either in the blessing and giving thanks which accompanies it, or in the distribution of the bread and wine among the disciples, which makes the presence of Elders [Pastors] more necessary in it than in praise, or prayer, or reading, or mutual exhortation, etc., it is hard to say. But this is certain, that one of the main pillars of *clerical* assumption is the idea that men — possessing a certain function, distinct from the mass of the disciples — are necessary to *administer* the Supper of the Lord "— John Walker. *Remains,* etc., Vol. i. p. 343.

"It is supposed by some that none may *in any case* administer it [the Lord's Supper] except an ordained Elder Viewing the ordinance in the light of the New Testament, it does not seem to us that it would be necessarily desecrated if observed in the absence of Pastors Others may preside, without impairing the value of it to the recipients; and without the guilt of presumption It may be as worthily received in the absence of a presiding office-bearer, as in his presence. When an Elder is present, he properly presides at the ordinance, inasmuch as he is the ruler of the Church. Entrusted with the constant oversight of the society, he is perpetual President, at every meeting of the brethren. This is involved in his office of ruling, or governing. But yet no virtue is transferred from the individual who thus presides — whether he be styled clergyman, priest, or elder — to the communicant. He simply invokes the Divine blessing, and distributes the bread and wine; addressing, perhaps, a few words of exhortation to the assembled Church. Thus, when a Church has no Elders, the members may legitimately partake of the Supper. An Elder's presence is not essential to the validity of it. It is *desirable*, because the presumption is that such an one is better qualified to lead the devotions of the brethren more profitably than an individual selected from among themselves. Hence it may be *most advantageous* to have an official person presiding. But it is certainly unnecessary to send for the Elder of another Church; for such an one bears no *official* relation to any society except his own. Standing among the brethren of another Church, he occupies the same position with one of the brethren themselves. All that he brings with him is the experience he has gained in profitably presiding at the ordinance in his own Church. When a Church,

at the remembrance of Christ in the Lord's Supper. This being so, there is no need for the missionary to the Heathen, abroad or at home, to receive ordination before he commences his work. Let him go on the ground, and gather together there a Church, and then let them call, and ordain him, as their Pastor — with counsel from other churches if they can get it, without it if need be — and then he will be Scripturally, and Congregationally, their Pastor and minister. Of course there is no objection to his being "consecrated and set apart" to his work as a missionary, before his departure, by the Church of which he has been a member, if they do not mistake the nature of that service as if it were strictly ordination — which, (however pleasant and edifying and desirable such a service may seem in itself,) it cannot be.

If these principles are true, it follows that one who has been 'ordained as an Evangelist,' stands, in the matter of his official relation to the churches of Christ, exactly where he stood before that ceremony. He has the same right to preach which any layman has, whose gifts and graces invite and warrant the confidence of good people, that God calls him to the pulpit; he has the same right to baptize and to administer the Lord's Supper in emergencies where any Church may be disposed, in the absence of a Pastor, to authorize him by its vote to do so, which he had before, or which any other layman would have under similar circumstances — and no more.

---

therefore, is without Elders, or Pastors, let them by all means partake of the Sacred Supper. It is their duty and privilege to do so. To neglect it is highly culpable. A Deacon selected by the brethren may preside. This is sufficient . The view now given is in accordance with the New Testament. From the 1st Epistle to the Corinthians, we infer that the Church at Corinth had no office-bearers at the time when Paul wrote to them. He regarded the ordinance of the Supper as peculiarly belonging to the disciples, to be attended to by them, even in the absence of ordinary pastors .... The New Testament intimates, in other places, that the first churches partook of the Supper before they had Pastors .... There is, besides, nothing in the *nature* of the Lord's Supper which would render the presence of an Elder essential to its right observance. The ordinance is simple. It is chiefly commemoratlve." .... So "there is no one passage in all the New Testament, which proves that it is the *exclusive* prerogative of the Elders to baptize. And yet the notion is tenaciously held. Coming, as it does, from the Church of Rome, and received from that source by the Protestant Episcopal Church, it has taken hold of other denominations."—Davidson. *Eccles. Polity of New Test.* pp. 280, 283–286.

Dr Watts (in his *Foundation of a Christian Church*) says, "The Church may appoint private members to administer seals [Baptism and the Lord's Supper] rather than to neglect them."— *Works*, Vol. iii. p. 222.

Samuel Mather quotes approvingly Fabritius, where he says, "If any man, even a Laic, be appointed by the Church to administer the Sacrament, if he does it, he does nothing but his duty, and neither offends against the faith, nor against good order "—*Apology*, p 61

His 'ordination' service may have been an edifying and profitable one in its exercises and influence, but it has made him no less a layman, and no more a minister than it found him; simply because it was not the act of a Church deputing to a Council its power to solemnize his entrance to the Pastoral office over it, to which its vote had previously called him; and that is the only kind of ordination which the Bible, or Congregationalism, knows or warrants.[1] Of course, then, a 'Stated Supply' gains no official rank, or power, from the fact that he may have commenced his career by being 'ordained as an Evangelist.'[2]

---

[1] "Those notions which conceive of it [ordination] as some mysterious gift or prerogative — in fact degrade it to a cabalistic process, and are neither more nor less than the disguised remnants of popery."—*Bibliotheca Sacra*, Vol. v. (1848.) p 517.

For light upon the process by which the hierarchal element gradually invaded and overthrew the primitive simplicity and purity of the faith in the particulars above-mentioned, introducing the fiction of mystic grace in ordination, and making Baptism and the Eucharist to depend upon priestly administration, see Neander's *History of the Christian Religion and Church*, Vol. i. pp. 182-204, and 304-332; also Schaff's *History of the Christian Church*, pp. 130, 131; and Shedd's *Guericke*, pp. 139-145. See also, particularly, Dr. Colman's *Ancient Christianity*, pp. 362-450.

[2] Having read the proof-sheets of these last nine pages to a valued friend learned in Congregationalism, he objected to our doctrine of the demission of the ministry — upon dismission from the Pastorship of a particular Church — acknowledging that we were correct in our representation of the views of the founders of New England Congregationalism in that particular; but suggesting that it might be a more excellent way upon which our time has fallen; an improvement upon the rigid practice of the past, which it might be wiser to cherish, than to condemn.

But can an illogical inference from the fundamental principles of a system be safely engrafted upon that system? If suffered to root itself in the popular conviction as true and wise, must it not inevitably react to undermine and uproot such first principles as cannot be true if it is true? 'It is a poor rule that will not work both ways.' If it become good Congregationalism to hold that ordination impresses upon a man the indelible character of a minister, no matter into what secularities his subsequent life may plunge itself, so long as he avoids that moral delinquency which would lead to formal deposition; must not the people be educated by that concession to understand that ordination is really, for substance, all that is claimed by the Papists and Episcopalians, and that to be a minister is, after all, to be an official personage, irrespective of all Church action and consent, or even Church existence? And is it for the interests of Congregationalism, or of the cause of piety, for such unscriptural notions to find a lodgment in the community?

And — wholly aside from all the bearings of the matter as a question of principle — is it not clear that in point of practice, the prevalence of such notions is damaging to the true dignity of the ministry, the best welfare of the churches, and the common fame of Christianity? We can easily recall to mind more than one person, once a settled pastor, but now a farmer, or a merchant, or a physician, or a lawyer, or the keeper of a boarding-house — six days in the week perhaps only discernible from other laymen by the superior whiteness of his cravat, and the inferior tenderness of his conscience in all little matters where money is to be made in bargaining, and on the seventh, always willing to supplement his six days' earnings by the Sabbath day's wages of some "vacant" pulpit — whose general course in this regard is *not* a credit to the profession to which he still claims (unscripturally and uncongregationally) to belong. Nor should we have to travel far to identify churches which have been brought almost to the

Such we understand to be the necessary results of the first principles of our faith in their application to these questions. It is not denied that the present practice of the denomination varies, more or less widely, in some particulars, from them. But it is firmly believed that all such variance is the result of illogical and inexpedient retrocession from pure Congregationalism, in the way of concession to the influences of Presbyterianism and the Papacy; which every lover of the purity and simplicity of the 'faith once delivered to the saints,' is called upon to deplore and resist.

---

verge of extinction by that wicked economy which has led them to drag on a lingering existence, year after year, with the "Stated Supply" of two heartless (and yellow) sermons on the Sabbath, from some layman, who, because he has a barrel of them, which only, now, costs him house-room, and because he earns his living at some secular employment during the week, can afford to administer them "cheaper" than the Church could support a Pastor; and whom the Church suppose, because he was once a minister, to be a minister still. Nor would it be difficult to show that the cause of Christ has sorely suffered from such a mean and mercenary procedure. Here is a case, we must feel, demanding the zeal of those who inquire affectingly for "the old paths."

Let nothing here said be construed, however, to the disparagement of those who are evidently called of God to serve the churches in some other capacity than that of Pastors; as Professors in Theological Seminaries, or Colleges, Secretaries and Agents of Benevolent Societies, and the like. Though neither Pastors nor Deacons, they yet have some special and creditable relation to the churches collectively — in the case of those acting as instructors, not wholly unlike that of the 'Teacher' of the early days of New England. While it may be difficult, on Scriptural principles, to class and name them, it is not difficult to appreciate their indispensableness to the general cause.

CHAPTER III.

HOW CONGREGATIONALISM WORKS.

HAVING thus considered that groundwork of principles on which the Puritan system rests, we pass next to some brief consideration of the practical application of those principles in the various processes of Church life and action; endeavoring to set forth, under its several heads, what we understand to be the right method of doing all Church work — in carrying out Christ's way of Congregationalism for his people.

SECTION 1. *How to form a Church.*

That which constitutes isolated individual believers a Church, is their solemn agreement together to become a Church, by covenanting with God and each other to "walk in all his ways made known, or to be made known unto them, according to their best endeavors, whatsoever it shall cost them — the Lord assisting them."

The first question must always be — "is it expedient to form a Church in this place?" Three things may usually be considered essential to an affirmative answer to this question, namely: (1.) the absence of needful Church privileges; (2.) the interest of a sufficient number of suitable persons in the movement; (3.) a reasonable prospect of permanence and self-support for the enterprise. With regard to the first, it may be said, in general, that the convenience of professing Christians is one element in its decision, and the welfare of the impenitent, and the need of Church labor among the people, is another, and a very important one. For example, in the outskirts of cities, and large towns, it may often be the duty of professing Christians who might themselves be quite conveniently accommodated with Church privileges in connection with existing organizations, to associate together to form a new Church, in order — as Home missionaries — to bring the ordinances of the Gospel to bear upon a destitute portion of the community. With regard to the second, no definite number can be fixed upon as absolutely essential to the formation of a Church; but if the Great Head clearly press present duty, and open a reasonable prospect of future enlargement, where only 'two or three agree as touching this thing,' and are 'gathered together in His name,' they need not fear that He will not be in the midst of them.[1] With regard to the third point, we think it is clear that — in all ordinary cases — there ought to be a fair prospect that the demand for a Church organization will be a permanent one, and that a new enterprise may reasonably anticipate self-support. It seems to us that the formation of a Christian Church is too solemn a thing to be associated with any movement that, on the face of it, must be spasmodic and temporary.

These questions having been affirmatively settled — they ought to be settled with prayer and fasting — those persons who intend to become associated in the movement, who are members of other churches, should apply to them for letters of dismission and recommendation, for the purpose of aiding in the formation of the proposed new Church.[2] It would be well also for them to appoint a committee

---

[1] Our Fathers generally held that *seven* was the least number who could rightly associate to form a Church (See Cotton Mather's *Ratio*, Art. I. Sec. 1) This was not, however, from any absurd and superstitious reverence for the number seven, as Mr. Peter Oliver so gratuitously suggests, in his pert and violent *Puritan Commonwealth*, (p. 155) but because, according to their calculation, the directions of our Saviour in the 18th of Matthew, in regard to Church discipline, could not be literally carried out with a less number; namely, the offender, the complainant, the two witnesses, and two members with the moderator, who might constitute the body to hear and try the case — making *seven* in all. (See also Cotton's *Way*, p. 53, and Mather and Tompson's *Answer to Herle*, in Hanbury, Vol. ii. p. 172.) John Robinson, however, held that "two or three" were sufficient, in necessity (*Answer to Bernard*, Works, Vol. ii. p. 232.)

[2] The following would be an appropriate form of request for a letter of this description:

To the ——— Church in ———
  Dear Brethren:
      Whereas the Providence of God has led me to this place, and seems to make it my duty to become associated with other Christians here in the formation of a Congregational Church, this is to request you to give me such a letter of dismission and recommendation as may be suitable in these circumstances.
              Faithfully and Affectionately,
                  Your brother,
(Date, and place of date.)   A——— B———.

If it should so happen that any of the proposed members of the new Church are members

of (say, three) brethren to prepare a list of all proposing themselves as members, and a form of Confession of Faith and Covenant, to be the basis of their union.

If they are so situated — as they might be in some extreme border wilderness — that it is impossible for them to secure the counsel and coöperation of existing Congregational churches in the act of their formation; they may then, on receipt of letters dismissing those who have been members of other churches, proceed, by solemn vote, to associate themselves as a Christian Church upon the basis of the Articles of Faith and Covenant to which they have agreed, and may then go on to elect necessary officers. Such a Church, so constituted without the concurrent advice and tendered fellowship of other Congregational churches, is a Congregational Church, if its Independency is a mere necessity of position and circumstance — to be removed whenever other churches come near enough to it to be reached by the right-hand of its fellowship.

In all ordinary cases, however, the next step after the appointment of the Committee to prepare the Articles of Faith and Covenant,[1]

---

of churches in other denominations, — whose practice may not be to give letters to their members who ask for them under such circumstances, it might be well for the phraseology of the above letter to be modified by the insertion of the following clause in place of what comes after "*this is*, etc." in the third line, so as to make it read: —

"*to notify you of the same, and respectfully to request you take such action, under the circumstances, as may seem to you expedient.*"

If no answer should be received to such a request within a reasonable time, it might be repeated, so as to make sure against accidents by mail, and if no notice were taken of the repeated request, the person asking for a letter — having done his duty in the premises — might then report the facts to the Council called to advise with reference to the formation of the Church, or to the Church, if it had been already formed, and the way would be open for his reception, by special vote, without any letter.

It would be a violation of Christian courtesy, and of covenant, however, for a member of such a Church — even if he were *sure*, beforehand, that no notice would be taken of his request for dismission to a Congregational Church — to join another Church without first asking to be released from his previous relation. He ought to do *his* duty, and leave the Church to do what they think is theirs; and no expectation of refusal on their part can excuse neglect on his.

[1] The following forms of Articles of Faith and Covenant, are submitted as brief and pertinent — in case aid is desired in drawing them up:

ARTICLES OF FAITH.

1 We believe that the Scriptures of the Old and New Testaments are the word of God, and the only infallible rule of faith and practice, and — in accordance with the teachings of those Scriptures: —

2. We believe in ONE GOD — subsisting in three persons, the Father, the Son, and the Holy Ghost — eternal, unchangeable, and omnipresent, infinite in power, wisdom, and holiness; the

would be the appointment of another — or the designation to the same committee of the new duty — to call a Council of the neighboring

Creator and Preserver of all things, whose purposes and providence extend to all events, and who exercises a righteous moral government over all his intelligent creatures.

3. We believe that man was originally holy ; that our first parents disobeyed the command of God ; and that, in consequence of their apostasy, all their descendants do also transgress His law, and come under its just condemnation.

4. We believe that God has provided a way of salvation for all mankind ; that the Lord Jesus Christ, the Son of God, having taken upon himself our nature, has, by his voluntary sufferings and death, made an atonement for sin ; and that every one who, with repentance for sin, receives Christ as a Saviour, will be pardoned, justified, and saved through that faith alone.

5. We believe that while salvation is thus freely offered to all men, none do truly repent and believe in Christ but those who, according to the sovereign grace and eternal purposes of God, are renewed and sanctified by His Holy Spirit, in obeying the Gospel ; and that none who are thus renewed and chosen to eternal life, will ever be permitted so to fall away as finally to perish.

6. We believe that the Christian Sabbath, the Church, and the ordinances of Baptism and the Lord's Supper, are of divine appointment, and the duties connected with them, of perpetual obligation ; but that only members in good standing of the visible Church, have a right to partake of the Lord's Supper ; and that only they, and their households, can be admitted to the ordinance of Baptism.

7 We believe that there will be a resurrection of all the dead ; and that God will, after that, judge all men — manifesting the glory of his mercy, in the award of eternal salvation to his people, and of his justice, in the everlasting condemnation of the wicked.

COVENANT.

We, who are called of God to join ourselves into a Church state, in deep sense of our unworthiness thereof, disability thereto, and aptness to forsake the Lord, and neglect our duty to him and to each other, do hereby — in the name of Jesus Christ our Lord, and trusting in his gracious help — solemnly covenant and agree, with Him and with each other, to walk together as a Church of Christ, according to all those holy rules of God's Word given to a Church rightly established, so far as we know them, or may gain further light upon them. And, particularly, we covenant and agree : —

To consecrate ourselves, our offspring, our worldly goods, and all that we have, and are, unto the Triune God, as the supreme object of our love and our chosen portion, for this world, and for that which is to come ;

To give diligent heed to His word and ordinances ;

To maintain His worship in the family ;

To seek in all things His glory, and the good of men, and to endeavor to live a holy and peaceable life in all godliness and honesty ;

To contribute from our substance, and by our active labors and continual prayers, to the work of this Church ;

To submit to its Gospel discipline ;

To labor for its growth, and peace, and purity ;

To walk with each other in Christian fidelity and tenderness ;

And, finally, to hold and promote suitable fellowship with all sister churches of the common Head, especially with those among whom the Lord hath set us, that the Lord may be one, and his name one, in all his churches throughout all generations, to his eternal glory in Christ Jesus.

And now the good Lord be merciful unto us, pardoning, according to the riches of his grace, as all our past sins, so especially our Church sins, in negligence and unfaithfulness of former vows, and accept, as a sweet savor in Christ Jesus, this our offering up of ourselves unto him in

churches, to advise the brethren and sisters who propose to form the new Church, whether — in the judgment of the Council — the cause of Christ will be promoted by their proceeding according to their plan,[1] and of laying the whole subject before the Council when assembled. It would be a part of the duty of this committee, also, to request some member of the Council to come prepared to preach a sermon appropriate to the occasion, if the Council should advise them to proceed; and to designate some brother of the Church to receive the right hand of fellowship from the other churches, which the Council — in that case — will tender them.

The Council being assembled, as invited, is organized by being called to order by some one of its older members, who reads the Letter Missive which is the authority for their procedure, and nominates a Moderator — sometimes calls for a ballot for one — who, being elected by the Council, assumes the chair, opens the session with prayer, calls for the election of Scribe (sometimes, in large Coun-

---

this work; filling this place with his glory, making us faithful to himself and to each other so long as this transitory life shall last, and, after that he has kept us from falling, presenting us faultless before the presence of his glory with exceeding joy.* Amen!

[1] The following would be a proper form of Letter for calling such a Council:

To the Congregational Church of Christ in ———.
Dear Brethren:

The Great Head of the Church having inclined a number of believers here to think that it is our duty to become associated as a Congregational Church, we respectfully request you, by your Pastor, and a delegate, to meet in Council at ——— in this place, on the ——— of ———, at ——— o'clock in the ——— to consider the expediency of the course proposed by us, and advise us in reference thereto; and should the formation of such a Church be deemed expedient, to assist in the public service appropriate to its formation and recognition.

Wishing you grace, mercy, and peace,
We subscribe ourselves,
Your brethren in Christ,

———————— } Committee of
———————— } those proposing to
  } become a Church.

(Date, and place of date.)

N. B. The Churches invited to sit in this Council are the following; viz: —
Congregational Church in ———. Rev. Mr. ——— Pastor.
  "   "   " ———.   "   "   ———   " etc., etc.

* The general scope, and some of the specific clauses of this Covenant, are taken from the original covenant of the Old South Church in Boston, in use by it for more than one hundred years. (See Wisner's *History of the Old South Church*, p. 8, and p. 76.)

cils, for that of Assistant Scribe) and, the Council thus being fully organized and ready to proceed to its business, the committee who signed the Letter Missive should present to it a list of those who are willing to become members of the new Church, and state briefly, yet fully, the reasons which have led them to desire to take such a step, and to decide that such a course is their duty, and the demand of the Great Head upon them — answering any and all questions connected therewith, which any member of the Council may desire to ask. All the facts in the case being in, the Council would then — if there is any call for discussion upon the matter, asking all others (including, of course, those who seek their advice) to withdraw, that the discussion may proceed most freely — vote either that it is, or is not, of opinion that the proposed movement is wise, and one which its members are prepared to advise and sustain by their fellowship. This vote being favorable, the Council would then proceed to hear the Articles of Faith and Covenant, and to examine candidates for membership in the new Church, as to the regularity of their letters of dismission, or the fact of their personal piety, if they present themselves as new members. If it be satisfied that a Church ought to be formed; that it ought to be formed upon the basis of these Articles and Covenant; and that these applicants are suitable persons to become its members; the Council will then vote to advise these persons to proceed to form the proposed Church, and will appoint some of its own number to take such part in the public service of the occasion as may be desired, and desirable; the more important services usually performed by members of the Council, being the following; namely: (1.) Invocation and Reading of appropriate Selections from the Scriptures, (2.) Sermon, (3.) Reading of the Articles of Faith and Covenant, (4.) Prayer of Recognition and Consecration, (usually by the Moderator), (5.) Right Hand of Fellowship to the new Church, (6.) Address to the Church, (7.) Concluding Prayer, (8.) Benediction. These preliminary arrangements being completed, at the appointed hour, these services would be publicly performed; the members who are to form the new Church, after the reading of the Articles and Covenant, assenting to the same, by solemn vote (all rising) — thus, in accordance with the advice of the Council, constituting themselves a Church, by their own act.

If it were so to happen that the Council should not agree in approval of the Articles, or Covenant, or of some portion of the procedure of the brethen calling them together, it would so report, and conference would be had with a view to the adjustment of the difficulty. And if the Council should, in the end, vote itself unable, for any reason, to advise the formation of the Church, it would remain for the applicants to consider the matter, with much humility and prayerfulness, and either to acquiesce in the opinion of the Council, and give up their intention; to modify it in such a manner as to remove the objection; or — if that seems to them impossible — to proceed (as — if they are unconvinced by the adverse opinion of the Council, and still feel bound in conscience to go forward — they have the right to do) to organize themselves into a Church, without the aid and recognition of a Council; in which case they would remain an Independent Church, until such time as their neighbor Congregational churches should receive them into their fellowship.

SECTION 2. *How to choose and induct Church officers.*

(1.) *Choice of lesser officers.* As an organized body cannot exist and act without officers, it will be the first duty of the Church, after its constitution, to elect those officers without whom it cannot commence its proper work. A moderator is the first necessity, and some brother of age and experience will naturally call the Church to order, and call for the choice of such a moderator — either by nomination, or by ballot; counting and declaring the vote, after which the elected moderator would take his seat. The next business would properly be the choice of a clerk, whose duty of record would run back to include a brief, yet accurate minute of those preliminary steps by which the formation of the Church has been initiated; and a treasurer, to take charge of all monies belonging to the body. The choice of a committee would naturally be next in order, who should have in charge the whole matter of procuring a suitable place for public worship, and a minister to conduct that worship — including conference with the " Society," (if one exists, or is to be formed) or the securing by some other method, of the amount that may be needful to defray the necessary expenses of worship, and of Church life. It would be well, also, for steps to be immediately taken looking toward the election of two or more Deacons — say the assignment of some future day for that election, at an interval long enough to allow of that preparation of thought, and prayer, and mutual conference, so desirable before action involving so much the peace and prosperity of the organization. If deemed expedient, an Examining Committee — to confer with applicants for membership, make inquiry in regard to their qualifications, and recommend such as seem to them qualified to the Church for admission — might also be soon chosen; though in small churches it is more usual, and perhaps quite as expedient, for this duty to be done in committee of the whole.

(2.) *Choice and induction of Deacons.* When the occasion previously designated for the duty has arrived — the Church being assembled with full ranks, and a moderator being chosen — it would be well for the moderator — stating the business assigned to the hour — to read from the Word of God the first seven verses of the 6th chapter of Acts, the six verses following the seventh verse of the 3d chapter of Paul's first Epistle to Timothy, with any other passages which seem to be appropriate to the occasion — for wisdom, and for comfort; and then to invoke — or to call upon some brother to invoke — the special blessing and direction of the Great Head of the Church upon them in their performance of the work to which they are called; that they may choose for their office-bearers, good men, full of the Holy Ghost, and of faith, who may not only use the office of a Deacon well, but by whom much people may be added unto the Lord.

Such an election should always take place by ballot, in order that each brother may be able to indicate his real choice in the freest possible manner. While it is very desirable that the result of such a balloting should be unanimous, and while few candidates would think it wise to accept such an office by the choice only of a bare majority, it will yet often happen that no one person will so concentrate the suffrages of all, as to give him the clean record of an election without any opposing vote — so that to take the ground that absolute unanimity is essential to acceptance, would often be to keep the office vacant.

The election having been made, and the brother (or brethren) chosen having signified a readiness to accept the trust, there may appropriately be some formal entrance upon the office. The record in the Acts states that the Apostles prayed, and 'laid their hands on' those who were first chosen Deacons in the Church at Jerusalem.

Some have supposed this to involve a regular public service of formal ordination. But we think it is clear[1] that the intent of that precedent will be better followed, by a simple recognition of the new officer (or officers) in prayer, at the first communion season following — or on some other suitable and convenient occasion; in connection with which public recognition, let the duties of the office be commenced.

After the induction of Deacons, it will be appropriate for one of them to act as the treasurer of the Church — either with or without special designation to that trust; inasmuch as the care of the secularities of the body inheres in their office.

It is usual in many churches, also, for the Deacons, in the absence of a Pastor, to preside over all meetings, according to their seniority in election — though some churches prefer (and every Church — unless it deprive itself of the right, by some standing rule which cannot be set aside — has always the right) to elect, from the membership at large, a moderator for every business meeting at which its Pastor is not present. Sometimes this right is a very important one to be exercised, and it is well always to remember that by the common law of Congregationalism, the Pastor is the only official standing moderator of a Church, so that unless, by a special statute of its own, the Church entrust the moderatorship to the Deacons, in the Pastor's absence, it reverts always to the hands of the body, — which should choose a moderator for every meeting, either by nomination, or by ballot.

It is usual, moreover, for the Deacons to have the oversight, on the part of the Church, of the supply of the pulpit, in the temporary absence of the Pastor. When there is an Ecclesiastical Society connected with the Church, a committee appointed by it might coöperate with the Deacons to this end, and where a new Pastor is to be sought, the Church might well appoint a special committee (upon which, however, it would naturally place its Deacons) to act with the Parish committee, in bringing about the settlement of a suitable Pastor.

(3.) *Choice and induction of a Pastor.* The first public step toward the choice of a Pastor is usually a report to the Church, by the committee previously appointed to have the matter in charge, of the name of some minister of the Gospel, who, in their judgment,

---

[1] See page 140; also Tracy's Report, in the appendix of Punchard's *View*, pp. 340–8.

might be obtained, and would be a worthy incumbent of the office. Such report being made, time enough should be taken to allow all the members of the Church opportunity to make suitable inquiry in regard to the candidate, when — after a day of fasting and prayer for the special direction of the Great Head of the Church — the question is put to vote by ballot. The ballot may be either 'yea,' or 'nay,' upon the name reported by the committee, or may be by names upon the ballots, in which case, a negative vote for this candidate would be a positive vote for another. Perfect — or sufficient — unanimity manifesting itself in the result, the next step would be the appointment of a committee to make known this vote to the Ecclesiastical Society with which the Church is associated (if there be one), and to ask a concurrent vote from its members, fixing upon the yearly salary to be offered to the candidate. Should that Society concur, and vote to offer the candidate a reasonable stipend, and appoint a committee to coöperate with the committee of the Church in communicating these facts to the Pastor elect, the next step would be for those committees to forward to the candidate a 'call' to become their Pastor, covering the votes passed, and urging his acceptance of the invitation conveyed in them.[1]

---

[1] The following may suggest a proper form of 'Call.' Those portions marked in brackets are to be modified according to the facts in the case, as to whether the candidate has been ordained or not, so as to be known as 'Rev.' or merely as 'Mr.' and is now to be 'ordained' or 'installed ;' and as to whether there is an Ecclesiastical Society acting with the Church, or not.

Rev. [*Mr.*] *A—— B——.*
Dear Sir:
The undersigned, on behalf of the Congregational Church of Christ in A—— [*and the Ecclesiastical Society connected therewith*] *beg leave respectfully to submit to your consideration the following certified copies of recent votes of that Church,* [*and Society*].

At a regularly called meeting of the Congregational Church in A——, on the —— day of —— it was unanimously [*or state the vote*]

Voted, That the Rev. [*Mr.*] *A—— B—— be invited to become the Pastor and Teacher of this Church.*

Voted, That Brethren A—— B——, C—— D——, and E—— F——, be a committee to communicate these votes to Rev. [*Mr.*] *A—— B——; to urge him to comply with the request which they contain; and to make all arrangements which may become necessary to carry out the wishes of the Church in the premises.*

A true copy of record.
(*Signed.*)
——————— *Moderator.*
——————— *Scribe.*

[*At a legal meeting of the Ecclesiastical Society connected with the Congregational Church in A——, on the —— day of ——, it was unanimously* [*or otherwise*]

Should the Society fail to concur, and prefer some other candidate, the Church committee would report that fact back, and it would then become necessary for conference between the Church and Society, and for such modification of the action of one, or both, as the best interests of all should seem to demand.

Should there be no Ecclesiastical Society in connection with the Church, the Church itself would vote what it felt to be a suitable salary to the candidate, should he become their Pastor, and proceed by its committee to forward the 'call,' covering its votes, to the Pastor elect.

On receipt of his acceptance, the next step is for the committee of the Church (with that of the Society — if there be a Society), in conference with the Pastor elect, to agree upon the churches which shall be invited to meet in Council for the purpose of the examination of the candidate, and, if they are satisfied with his character and qualifications, and with the doings of the people, of tendering the fellowship of the churches in the ordination [or installation] service,

---

Voted, That the Rev. [Mr.] A—— B—— be invited to become the minister of this people;

Voted, That, in case of his acceptance of this invitation, with that extended by the Church, this Society will pay Mr. A—— B—— the annual sum of —— dollars, in quarterly instalments, on the first days of January, April, July, and October, in each year, so long as the relation shall continue.

Voted, That Mr. A—— B—— be offered a vacation of —— weeks, during which this Society will supply the pulpit, under the direction of the Deacons of the Church.

Voted, That Messrs. G—— H——, and I—— J——, be a Committee to act with the Committee of the Church in this matter.

A true copy of record.
(Signed.)
——————— *Moderator.*
——————— *Clerk.*]

Allow us, Dear Sir, to add to the invitation contained in these votes, the expression of our earnest hope that you will feel it to be the desire of the Great Head of the Church that you should accept this call to be our Pastor, and name an early day for the [Ordination] *Installation service.*

Praying God to bless you, and all who love our Lord Jesus Christ in sincerity,
We subscribe ourselves,
Yours in the Gospel,

A——	B——	
C——	D——	Committee of
E——	F——	Church [and
G——	H——	Society.]
I——	J——	

[*Date, and place of date.*]

and send out the Letter Missive to them.[1] These are usually the neighboring Congregational churches, adding, sometimes, remoter churches, whose Pastors it is desired should perform some part of the public service of the occasion.

The Council having assembled and organized itself by the choice of Moderator and Scribe, it is then the business of that committee to lay before it, (1.) all the records of the Church relating to the proposed Pastoral union; (2.) all the records of the Society (if there be one) to the same purport; (3.) all the communications received from the Pastor elect, in reference to the acceptance of their invitation, with any other documentary, or other facts, bearing upon the matter before the Council. If the Council is satisfied with these, as being regular and suitable, it will so declare itself by vote, and proceed next to examine the fitness of the candidate for the place.

That examination will respect, (1.) his evidence of being in good standing in some Christian Church, and his intention to become a member of the Church over which it is proposed to ordain him — if he is not already so; (2.) his evidence of approval to preach the

---

[1] The following would be an appropriate form for such a Letter Missive: —

The Congregational Church in A——— to the Congregational Church in B———, sendeth greeting;

Dear Brethren:

The Great Head of the Church has kindly united us, and the Congregation statedly worshipping with us, in the choice of Mr. [Rev.] A——— B——— as our Pastor and Teacher, and he has accepted our invitation to that office. We, therefore, affectionately request your attendance by your Pastor and a delegate, at ———, on the ——— day of ——— next, at ——— o'clock in the ———, to examine the candidate, review our proceedings, and advise us in reference to the same; and if judged expedient, to assist in the Ordination [Installation] service.

Wishing you grace, mercy, and peace,
We are fraternally yours,

————————— } *Committee of*
————————— } *the Church.*

[*Date, and place of date.*] [——————— } *Committee of*
                             ——————— } *the Society.*]

The other Churches invited to this Council are as follows:
[Name them all]

It is proper also to append to those letters sent to churches whose Pastors are desired to take part in the public service, a postscript, notifying them of that fact — that such Pastors may have suitable time for preparation.

Gospel, from some customary body; (3.) his evidence (if he has been before settled as a Pastor) of orderly dismission from his former charge, and his commendation by the dismissing Council as a suitable candidate for another settlement; (4.) his religious experience, and the quality of motive which leads him to the ministry; (5.) the sufficiency of his literary acquisitions, and the Scriptural soundness of his theological faith. It is usual for this examination, so far as it involves categorical inquisition, to be mainly conducted by the Moderator, but to be completed by the calling of the roll of the Council, and by giving to each of its clerical and lay members, the opportunity to question the candidate.

This examination — which is always public — being concluded, the Council vote "to be by themselves," when the candidate, and the committee calling the Council, should retire, with all others not members — to give opportunity for the fullest confidential conference. Being satisfied upon all the points before them, the Council would so declare itself by vote, and — calling in the candidate and the committee — would proceed, in conference with them, to assign the parts in the public service; which are usually, (except singing), (1.) Preliminary statement by the Moderator, (2.) Reading of the Result of the Council, by the Scribe, (3.) Invocation and Reading the Scriptures, (4.) Sermon, (5.) Installing [or Ordaining] Prayer, [with, or without, the Imposition of hands, as the candidate has, or has not, been settled before], (6.) Right Hand of Fellowship, (7.) Charge to the Pastor, (8.) Address to the People, (9.) Concluding Prayer, (10.) Benediction, by the new Pastor.[1]

The Church having thus chosen its Pastor, and ordained him, through the fraternal hands of the delegates of its sister churches, he is now fully set over them in the Lord.

SECTION 3. *How to transact the regular business of a Church.*

(1.) *Standing Rules.* It is well for every Church — however

---

[1] It is vital to the best effect of a service of this description that each of these parts should be brief, and be confined strictly to its own sphere. We have heard, for example, sermons which included the Right Hand of Fellowship and Charge, and an Address to the people; and Invocations and Concluding Prayers, both of which invaded each other's province, and left little that was special for the prayer of Ordination. Weariness is the inevitable result. But if each is brief and pertinent, the general effect may be admirable.

small — to adopt some few standing rules which may give definiteness to its procedure, and, by pointing out beforehand right ways for the performance of all necessary business, avoid that trouble which sometimes arises from doing simple things in a mistaken manner. These may sometimes be very few; in other cases, the best interests of all concerned would be promoted by their greater fullness.[1]

---

[1] The following are suggested as adapted to meet the case of a Church desiring a full and careful code.

STANDING RULES.

This Church is Congregational in its recognition of the fellowship and fraternity of the churches, yet Independent in assuming, under Christ — after advice from others, when desired — the sole responsibility of its own actions. It will, accordingly, extend to sister churches, and expect from them, that communion, council, and aid, which the law of Christ demands; while it controls the administration of its own affairs according to its own understanding of the word of God. And to promote good order in its life, it adopts the following rules of action:—

1. The Pastor of this Church shall be a member of it, and shall be its standing Moderator.
2. In the absence of the Pastor, or in any case when he may become a party in interest to Church action, so as to make it improper for him to act as moderator, a moderator *pro tempore* shall be chosen — by ballot when any three brethren so request, otherwise by nomination.
3. The annual meeting of the Church shall be held in the month of ———, on such day as the Pastor and Deacons may appoint.
4. Business may be done at the close of any regular Church prayer-meeting; and a special business meeting *may* be called at any time, when in the opinion of the Pastor and Deacons, it may be expedient; and *shall* be called, on the written application to the Pastor — or, in his absence, the Senior Deacon — of five members. *Male* members of the Church only are entitled to vote upon the business before it. *Ten* male members shall constitute a *quorum*.
5. Special business meetings shall always be notified from the desk on the Sabbath, or by written notice served upon every resident member, at least two days before the time of meeting.
6. All meetings for business shall be opened with prayer.
7. At the annual meeting, the following elections shall be made for the ensuing year — all officers to serve — during good behavior — until others shall be regularly chosen in their places.
(1.) A Clerk,* who shall keep the records of the Church.
(2.) An Examining Committee — of which the Pastor and Deacons shall be *ex officio* members, who shall examine all applicants for admission to the Church, and present to the Church a written report of the names of those whom they approve; any candidate whom they may not recommend, having the right of appeal to the whole Church. This Committee shall also act as a Committee of preliminary inquiry in regard to all cases of discipline, and shall make a report to the Church of its condition, and of their doings, with a list of all absent members, at the annual meeting.
(3.) A Treasurer, who shall take charge of all Church monies, and contributions for charitable purposes, and make a full written report of the same at the annual meeting.
(4.) An Auditor, who shall supervise the Treasurer's annual account, and report thereon.
(5.) A Committee of Collections for religious and charitable objects, whose duty it shall be

---

* It is always better that the *Pastor* should *not* be Clerk of his own Church. We have seen so many cases of difficulty arising from alleged falsification of the record, or imperfection in it, at the hands of a Pastor, who was Clerk, and with whom there was trouble, as to convince us that no Pastor should run into such needless danger. It is, of course, often convenient for the Pastor to have the records "handy," but that can be secured by requiring the Clerk to keep them where they will be accessible to *all* who need to see them.

(2.) *Rules of order.* The best definition which we know of Congregationalism, as a working system, is that it is Christian common

— under direction of the Church — to collect and pay over to the Treasurer such gifts of the Church and Congregation to benevolent purposes as may not be raised through the contribution-box; who shall annually report their doings.

8. The order of procedure at the annual meeting shall be as follows :—
(1.) Prayer.
(2.) Reading the record of the last annual business meeting.
(3.) Choice of the Clerk — by ballot.
(4.) Reports of the Treasurer and Auditor.
(5.) Action on these reports.
(6.) Choice of the Treasurer — by ballot.
(7.) Choice of the Auditor.
(8.) Report of the Examining Committee.
(9.) Action on that report.
(10.) Fixing the number of the Examining Committee for the ensuing year.
(11.) Choice of Examining Committee — by ballot.
(12.) Report of the Committee on Collections.
(13.) Action on that report.
(14.) Choice of Committee on Collections.
(15.) Deferred business.
(16.) New business.
(17.) Adjournment.

9. Candidates for admission shall be propounded before the Church and Congregation —— weeks previous to their admission.

10. All persons admitted to the Church shall affix to the Confession of Faith and Covenant their full names — in a book to be kept for that purpose.

11. The Lord's Supper shall be observed on the —— Sabbath of the months of —— in every year.

12. The regular weekly meeting of the Church for prayer and conference shall be held on —— evening; and the —— evening last preceding each communion season shall be especially devoted to preparation for the proper reception of that ordinance; and at its close a contribution shall be taken for Church expenses, and the relief of the poor, under the direction of the Deacons.

13. The necessary expenses of the Pastor in attendance upon all Ecclesiastical Councils, as a representative of the Church, shall be paid by the Treasurer from the funds of the Church.

14. Delegates to Ecclesiastical Councils shall make brief report of their doings, and of the action of the Council, at the meeting of the Church next following.

15. Members of this Church removing elsewhere, will be expected to take letters of dismission and recommendation to the Church with which they worship, *within one year* from the time of their change of residence, or render reasonable excuse for not doing so.

16. All letters of dismission given by this Church shall be valid *six months only* from their date; and no member who has received such a letter shall vote in business meetings of the Church, except on return of the letter.

17. Members of this Church who have habitually absented themselves from its worship and ordinances for *one year*, without rendering satisfactory excuse, shall be debarred from voting with the Church, so long as such habitual absence continues.

18. When any officer of this Church shall cease statedly to worship with us, his office shall be vacated from the time of his departure.

19. When any member of a sister Church shall statedly worship and commune with this Church for more than *one year*, without removing his relation to us, it shall be the duty of the Examining Committee to notify the Church to which he belongs, of that fact.

sense applied to Church matters. And since a Congregational Church is simply a pure democracy, those common rules by which democratic assemblies are usually governed — by which order is maintained, and each member quietly secures his full rights of debate, and of decision — exactly apply to the government of Congregational churches in the doing of their Church work. As differences of opinion sometimes arise, however, when sudden points require adjustment, and an unpractised moderator may be in the chair; it may be well briefly to lay down here the substance of those rules which are most essential, and whose strict observance will conduct any assembly to a satisfactory result.[1]

(*a.*) *Coming to order.* If the Church have a Pastor, or other standing moderator (by its rules), and he is present; it is his duty to request the Church to come to order. If it have none, or he is absent, the senior Deacon, or some one of the older male members, may call the membership to order, and call for the choice of a mod-

---

20. At their first meeting after each communion season, it shall be the duty of the Examining Committee to examine all entries made in the Church record by the Clerk, since the Communion preceding the last, and, if found correct, approve them; an entry of such approval to be made upon the record, signed by the Chairman of the Committee.

21. The following shall be deemed the regular course of procedure in all cases of discipline:—

(1.) The brother offended or aggrieved, should seek the removal of the offence, in the spirit of the Gospel, by fraternal conference with the offender alone.

(2.) Failing in the removal of his difficulty thus, he should take with him one or two judicious brethren, and with their mediation, strive for Christian satisfaction.

(3.) This proving in vain, he should bring the matter to the notice of the Examining Committee, who shall endeavor to bring about a reconciliation, and who (if this cannot be effected, or does not result in harmony) shall prefer a formal complaint before the Church against the offending brother.

(4.) If the Church entertain the complaint, they shall appoint a time for a hearing of the case, and summon the offender to be present at that hearing, furnishing him — at least one week before the time of the hearing — with a copy of the charges against him, together with the names of the witnesses who will be relied on for proof.

(5.) If, on such hearing, the Church are satisfied of the guilt of the party accused, they may vote to admonish him publicly, to suspend him for some definite period from the privileges of the Church, or to excommunicate him from its membership; according to the aggravation of the offence, and the state of mind in which he is.

(6.) No such vote of censure shall be passed, except by the concurrent vote of two-thirds of the male members present at a regular meeting.

(7.) In case of the excommunication of any member, public notice shall be given of the fact.

22. No alteration shall be made in the foregoing rules, unless at a regular meeting of the Church, after notice of the proposed change at a previous regular meeting, and by vote of three-fourths of the members present. This rule shall not, however, be so construed, as to forbid the temporary suspension of any rule, when the Church shall see fit *unanimously* to order such suspension.

[1] So far as any manual has been referred to in this connection, it is Cushing's well-known *Manual of Parliamentary Debate.*

erator, in the usual manner. On his election, the moderator will take the chair, and inquire if the standing Clerk be present; if not, a Clerk *pro tempore* should next be chosen, to insure proper record of all business done. The moderator will then entertain and put all motions, decide all questions of order, announce all votes, and, in a word, preside over the meeting.

(*b.*) *Motions.* Every item of business should be introduced in the form of *a motion;* which is simply a proposal to proceed to the doing of that business — put into a succinct and suitable form of words. All such motions, and all remarks upon them, should be addressed to the moderator. If a member wishes the Church to do any particular thing, he should, therefore, *move* that the Church do that thing. Any member has a right to make any motion, not against the rules, but, to protect the Church from having its time wasted upon foolish and impertinent propositions, it is required that every motion be *seconded* — so as to be endorsed by *two* responsible parties — before it can claim discussion and decision. After having made his motion, and it has been seconded, the mover will naturally proceed to set forth such reasons as prevail with him to decide that it is expedient for the Church to follow the course suggested by him. Others may follow, in approval or condemnation of his view. All must discuss only the specific question that awaits their decision in that motion. If any speaker wanders to disconnected subjects, or if members interrupt each other, or violate the rules of courteous debate, it is the business of the moderator to call them to order, for so doing. The proper time — unless some specialty (like the assignment of a fixed hour to close the debate, or something of that sort) interpose itself to modify the case — to take the vote upon the question under discussion, is when all who desire to say any thing, for or against it, have spoken, and thus the debate has closed itself.

Any member has always the right to demand that any motion be reduced to writing, by its mover, for more definite understanding. The moderator is obliged to put all motions to vote — however distasteful they may be to himself, personally — unless they are clearly against the standing rules of the Church, or the common law of deliberative bodies.[1] No new motion can be entertained while one is

---

[1] Moderators — especially if they are Pastors, in times of trouble and excitement — sometimes assume a right to veto Church action, to embarrass the movements of the Church, to

yet under debate, except it be of the nature of an amendment to it, or what is called a privileged motion; and no speaking is in order in a business meeting that is not upon some motion previously made, remaining undecided, except that a member who is about to make a motion, may preface it with an explanation.

(c.) *Amendments.* Any proposition to modify the motion which is under discussion, by striking out words from it, or by adding words to it, or both, in order to bring it more nearly into harmony with the views of the membership, is always in order, except when some privileged question is interposed, or when its insertion would too much complicate the question. The former bar will soon be considered. The latter is easily explained. An amendment to a simple motion is in order. So is an amendment to that amendment. But there the direct right to amend ceases, since an amendment to an amendment to an amendment, would so pile questions upon each other, as to lead to confusion. The line must be drawn somewhere, and, by common consent of legislative bodies, it has been drawn here. If it is desired to amend the amendment of an amendment, it must be done indirectly, by voting down the proposed amendment to the amendment, and then moving the new proposition in its place, as a new amendment to the

---

refuse to put motions which are distasteful to themselves, or even to adjourn the meeting at their pleasure, or declare it adjourned at the call of some friend for such adjournment, without putting the vote to the test of the 'contrary minds.' All this is an absurd and wholly inexcusable violation of the proprieties of the case. The moderator — and if he is moderator in virtue of being Pastor, it makes no difference — derives all his power from the body over which he presides, and he has no more right than any other individual, to interfere with the due course of business. His duty cannot be better condensed than it has been by the standard writer on parliamentary usage (Cushing's *Manual*, Sec 27), viz: "to represent and stand for the Assembly — declaring its will, *and, in all things, obeying, implicitly, its commands.*"

But, it may be asked, what ought a moderator to do, in case he should see the course of Church action going — in his judgment — wholly wrong, even to that extent that it is likely to commit *him* to what will be against his conscience? The answer is easy. Let him explain, as clearly as he can, to the body, the wrong they are about to do; if that is not enough, let him solemnly protest against it, and even — if, in his judgment, the gravity of the case calls for so extreme a course — let him retire respectfully from the chair, leaving it to be filled by the choice of another moderator by the Church. This will clear *his* skirts of complicity with the result, while, at the same time, it preserves the rights of the Church, and the good order of the whole transaction; while it cannot help being much more effectual in its tendency to restrain the body from rushing to any wrong result, than any arbitrary and unwarrantable interference, of the nature of an attempted veto, or an enforced adjournment; which must almost certainly react to confirm the majority in their ill judgment. There is absolutely no justification in Congregational usage, or in common sense, for that ministerial folly which seeks to 'lord it over God's heritage,' by assuming to veto Church votes, or to adjourn Church meetings, or arbitrarily to dictate, in any manner, to a Church, the course it should pursue.

amendment. In this case, he who desires to move such new amendment in place of the one before the meeting, may give notice that if the amendment to the amendment on which the question now rests shall be voted down, he will move this new proposition in its place, — thus enabling members to vote understandingly.

Any amendment must be 'seconded,' like an original motion, before it can claim the consideration of the assembly. It is usual, however, where the mover and seconder of the original motion, or of an amendment which an amendment is proposed to modify, 'accepts' the new amendment, for it to be quietly incorporated — without vote — into the question as it stands, awaiting decision.

It is not necessary that an amendment should be cordial in its tone toward the proposition which it proposes to amend. It has long been considered allowable, by parliamentary usage, to propose to amend a motion in a manner that would so entirely alter its nature, as to compel its friends to vote against it, should it be so amended; or to amend it by striking out all after the words "Resolved that," or "Voted that," and inserting a proposition of a wholly different tenor.[1]

An amendment — or an original motion — that has been regularly made, seconded, and proposed from the chair, is thereby put into the possession of the assembly, and cannot be withdrawn by the mover, except by general consent, or by a vote giving him leave so to do.

The motions for the "previous question," and "to lie on the table," cannot be amended, because their nature does not admit of any change.

(d.) *Privileged motions* There are certain motions which, on account of their superior importance, are entitled to supplant any other motion that may be under consideration, so as to be first acted on, and decided, by the body; and which may, therefore, be made *at any time*. Privileged motions in a Church meeting, would be the following: —

---

[1] In the House of Commons, April 10, 1744, a resolution was moved, declaring "that the issuing and paying to the Duke of Aremberg the sum of £40,000 to put the Austrian troops in motion, in the year 1742, was a dangerous misapplication of public money, and destructive of the rights of Parliament." The object of the motion, of course, was to censure the British ministry. Their friends being in a majority in the House, preferred — instead of voting the proposition down — to turn it into a direct resolution of approval of the course referred to; and they accordingly moved to amend, by leaving out the words "a dangerous misapplication," etc., to the end, and inserting, instead, the words "necessary for putting the said troops in motion, and of great consequence to the common cause." This amendment was adopted, and the motion as amended was passed — in a form the precise opposite, in sense, of its mover's design — See *Cushing*, p. 75.

(*aa.*) *The previous question.* The object of this motion is to bring debate upon the motion under consideration to an end — if commenced — or to suppress it altogether. It cannot itself be debated. Its form is, " shall the main question be now put ? " If decided in the negative, debate may be resumed. If decided affirmatively, the question before the body must be put to an immediate vote.

(*bb.*) *The motion to withdraw the question under discussion, by its mover.* When the mover of a question wishes to withdraw it, for any reason, and has asked — but failed to obtain — the general consent to do so, he may move for leave to withdraw it, and his motion will take precedence of the question itself. It may itself, however, be debated.

(*cc.*) *The motion to lay on the table.* The object of this, is to lay aside the subject to which it is applied, for the present; leaving it where it may be brought up for consideration at any convenient time. It is itself debatable.

(*dd.*) *The motion to commit the question to a committee.* The object of this is to obtain more light upon the question; to amend its form, if defective; to incorporate additional provisions, if needful; and in general, to put into a form more satisfactory than its present. It may be committed with, or without, instructions to the committee, as to the precise manner in which their function shall be discharged. This motion may be debated.

(*ee.*) *The motion to postpone to a fixed time.* The object of this motion is to gain time for all the delay that may be desired for more light upon the question, or for any other reason, yet to fix the date when the subject shall recur. This motion may be debated.

(*ff.*) *The motion to postpone indefinitely.* The object of this motion is to suppress the question to which it is applied, without committing the body to it by direct vote. If negatived, the matter stands where it stood before it was proposed. If carried, the effect is to quash entirely the motion so postponed. This motion may be itself debated.

(*gg.*) *The motion to adjourn.* This motion is always in order, except when a member is speaking — when no motion can be made without his consent, and no interruption is to be tolerated, except a valid call to order (if the speaker is out of order in his remarks), the adjustment of which gives him the floor again. The motion to adjourn, in its simple form, takes precedence of all others. If no motion is before the body when the motion to adjourn is made, it is susceptible of amendment, like other questions. But if it is itself made with a view to supersede some question before the body, it cannot be itself amended. It is then undebatable.

The effect of the adoption of a simple motion to adjourn, in the case of a body not holding regular sessions from day to day, would be equivalent to a dissolution. Otherwise it would adjourn the body to the next regular sitting day. In either case, the previous adoption of a resolution that "when the body adjourn, it adjourn to some other future time fixed," would modify the case. But the motion to adjourn to some future time fixed, is not a privileged question.

An adjourned meeting is a continuation of the previous meeting — legally the same meeting — so that the same officers hold over. When a question has been interrupted, however, while under discussion, and before a vote has been taken upon it, by a motion to adjourn, the vote to adjourn takes it from before the meeting, so that it will not be under consideration at the adjourned meeting, unless brought up afresh.

(*e.*) *Voting.* When a motion has been made and seconded, if no alteration is proposed, or it admits of none, or has been amended, and the debate upon it appears to have reached its close, the presiding officer inquires whether the body is "ready for the question?" Such being the fact, he should then clearly restate that question, so that no member can possibly fail to understand it, and then say, "as many of you as are in favor of the passage of this motion, will please say *aye*," [or hold up the right hand]; then "as many of you as are of the contrary opinion will please to say *no*," [or hold up the right hand]. Then, judging the quality of the vote by eye and ear, he should announce it accordingly, "the ayes have it," or "the noes have it," — or by some equivalent phraseology — as the case may be. If members are equally divided, the presiding officer has the right to give his casting vote, but is not obliged to do so. If he does not vote, the motion does not prevail.

When the vote is declared, any member who thinks the moderator to be in error, has the right immediately to demand that the vote be taken again, by saying "I doubt the vote." It must then be put again, and the votes carefully counted. Where excitement exists, and the vote is close, it is sometimes well for the moderator to appoint a teller from each party, to count and report the vote.

Debate may be renewed—unless 'the previous question' has been voted — at any stage before the *negative* vote is called for—in any form of voting where the affirmative is first taken. But if debate should be reöpened after the affirmative has been called, in whole or in part, the affirmative vote must be taken over again when debate has again ceased. In taking the yeas and nays, where both affirmative and negative are called together, debate is not in order after the call has been commenced.

In voting, the motion *last made* is always the one for decision, so that when an amendment has been offered to an amendment, the order of voting on them will be the *reverse* of the order in which they were presented. If several *sums* are proposed, the question is put with regard to the *largest*, first; if several times, the *longest*.

(*f.*) *Reconsideration.* Although it is a fundamental article of parliamentary law, that a question once settled by a body, remains settled, and cannot be again brought into judgment before the same body; yet, as a means of relief from embarrassment, or to enable advantage to be taken of some new light upon the matter, it has now become a well settled principle that a vote once passed may be reconsidered. Where no special rule regulates the matter, a motion to reconsider a vote once passed, may be made, and seconded, and considered, and acted upon, in the same way as any other motion. It is usual in legislative bodies, however, to limit the conditions of this motion so far, at least, as to require that it shall be made by some one who voted with the majority, on the question; sometimes, also, it is made essential that as many members shall be present, as were present when the vote was passed.

The effect of the passage of a motion to reconsider a vote, is not to *reverse that vote*, but simply *to annul its adoption*, so that the motion comes back under discussion again, and is the motion before the body requiring disposal first of all — the whole matter standing where it did before any vote at all was taken on it.

(*g*) *Questions of Order.* It is the duty of the moderator to enforce the rules of the body, or, if it have no special rules of order, to enforce those which commonly govern similar bodies. If any member interrupts another while speaking; or proposes a motion that is out of order; or insists on debating an undebatable question; or wanders from the matter in hand into irrelevances, or impertinences, or personalities, it is the *duty* of the moderator, and the right of any member, immediately to call him to order. Should any question of fact as to whether any given conduct *is* out of order, arise, it is the duty of the moderator to decide the question, and to enforce his decision. If any member, however, thinks his decision incorrect, he may object to it, and appeal the matter to the assembly. The moderator would then state this as the question: "shall the decision of the chair be sustained?" This question may then be debated and decided by the assembly, in the same manner as any other, only that the moderator here has the unusual right to share in the debate; the decision of the body being final.

(*h.*) *Committees.* It is very often a matter of convenience to place business in the hands of a select number of individuals to be, by them, conducted through its preliminary stages. Much time may thus be saved, and information may often be obtained, and action initiated, with more ease and freedom than would be possible, if the work were undertaken by the whole body.

(*aa.*) *Special Committees.* The first thing to be done after the vote to refer any matter to a special committee, is to fix upon the number; which is usually three, five, seven, or some odd number — to ensure a majority in case of difference of opinion among its members. The number being fixed, there are four modes of selecting the individuals who shall compose it: (1.) by ballot; (2.) by nomination from a nominating committee appointed for that purpose by the chair; (3.) by direct nomination from the chair; (4.) by nomination from the membership at large — all such nominations requiring a confirmatory vote from the body. The first named member usually acts as chairman of the committee; though every committee has, if it please to exercise it, the right to select its own chairman.

(*bb.*) *Standing Committees.* These are yearly appointed to meet certain constantly occurring necessities — usually by ballot.

(*cc.*) *Committee of the whole.* It is sometimes a convenience for the whole body to release itself, for the time being, from those strict rules which govern its ordinary debates, so as to discuss some topic before it, in the freest and fullest informal manner. It then — on motion made, seconded, and carried — resolves itself into a committee of the whole; when the Moderator nominates some member as Chairman and retires, himself, to the floor. The main points in which procedure in committee of the whole differs from the ordinary routine of the assembly are, (1.) the previous question cannot be moved; (2.) the committee cannot adjourn, as a committee, to another time and place, but must report its unfinished procedure to the body, and ask leave to sit again ; (3.) every member has the right to speak as often as he can obtain the floor; (4.) the committee of the whole cannot refer any thing to a sub-committee; (5.) the presiding officer can take part in the debate and procedure, like any other member. When the committee of the whole have gone through with their work, they vote to rise, the moderator of the body resumes his seat, and the chairman of the late committee of the whole makes report of its doings.

(*i.*) *Reports.* When any committee presents a report, the vote to *accept* it, takes it out of the hands of the committee, and places it upon the table of the body — where it can be called up, at any time, for further action — and discharges the committee. When the report is taken from the table and considered, it may be rejected, re-committed, (to the same, or to a new committee — with, or without instructions) or adopted. Its *adoption* makes whatever propositions it may contain, the judgment and act of the body; and it would often be better (because more perspicuous) to bring the matter directly to a vote upon those propositions; rather than to reach the same result indirectly, upon the question of 'adoption.'

(*j.*) *Closing a meeting.* Business being completed, the moderator may call for a motion of adjournment, or of dissolution — which is better, where the same meeting is not to be continued. "Adjournment *sine die,*" is, strictly, a contradiction in terms. If a vote has previously been passed, that, at a given hour, the body shall be adjourned to some future time fixed; the moderator, on the arrival of that hour, would pronounce the meeting adjourned, in accordance with the terms of the vote.

(3.) *Admitting members.* It is usual for a Church to fix some regular seasons for attention to requests for admission by persons desiring to become members. Some churches which are small in numbers, and situated in a sparse population where additions are infrequent, leave the matter in the hands of the pastor to request them to remain after any Preparatory Lecture when a candidate may desire examination. The proper course then, is, for the candidate to make known his desire to the Pastor, who — if, on inquiry, he is satisfied of the probable fitness of the applicant — will request the Church (sometimes merely the male members, but usually all) to remain after the next Lecture, or appoint a special meeting for the purpose; when the application is made, and the examination is conducted by the Pastor in presence of all, any member having the right to interpose an inquiry at any point. The candidate retiring, the question is then put, whether he shall be "propounded for admission?" If this is carried, the candidate's name is announced to the congregation, two weeks, or more, before the date of intended admission, so that if any person has complaint to make, affecting his Christian character, there may be seasonable opportunity to lay it before the Church. No such objection being made, the final question of his admission comes before the Church, usually at the close of the next Preparatory Lecture, when a majority vote will admit him — which vote is, however, usually unanimous, because if any member has any good ground of objection, it has been mentioned, and had its due weight beforehand.

Larger churches, and churches where requests for admission are more frequent, and in communities where a more thorough examination is sometimes expedient than can well be managed before the whole Church, usually find it most expedient to depute these preliminaries to an "Examining Committee." notice of whose regular meetings is publicly given. Candidates then present themselves before that Committee, who examine them — sometimes appointing a sub-committee to make special and rigid inquiry in doubtful cases — and who report to the Church the names of such candidates as they are prepared to recommend for admission. These candidates are then propounded — usually without a vote to that effect by the Church (the vote in committee being equivalent, in effect, to the vote to propound where the whole Church examine); and at the close of the Preparatory Lecture, or at some other regular time, the question of the admission of the propounded candidates is put to the vote of the whole Church.

Candidates bringing letters from other churches are often examined — though hardly so rigidly as others — for admission; nor is such examination considered any token of disrespect, or hint of unsoundness in the faith, toward the sister Church whose letters of dismission and recommendation they bear. It is sometimes made specially important, by the length of time that has elapsed since the dismissing Church has had direct cognizance of the Christian walk of the party to the letter — by reason of his long absence from its direct watch and care.

The public admission of members who have been received by vote, usually takes place just before the Communion service, when the new members range themselves before the pulpit, and give their public assent to the Articles of Faith and Covenant, as they are read by the Pastor. Baptism is usually administered to those who have not received it, after the reading of the Articles, and before assent is given to the Covenant. The signature of every new member to the Articles and Covenant in the book kept for that purpose, should follow, at the first convenient moment. Some Pastors make a brief address, and give the right hand of fellowship to new members, as a part of the public service of their admission.

(4.) *Dismissing members.* When members remove their residence to the nearer neighborhood of a sister Church, or when, for any good reason, it seems to them expedient to transfer their regular attendance to the ministrations and worship of a sister Church, they ought to ask, and the Church ought to grant them, letters of dismission and recommendation.[1] It is well that this request should be in writ-

---

[1] It is evidently — as a rule — better for a Christian to be in direct fellowship with the Church with which he statedly worships, and so under its immediate watch and care. He will not only be more careful in his walk and conversation, but he will feel more at home, and so both do, and enjoy more. It is always a bad sign when such a professor hangs off from the removal of his Church relation, and makes excuses — that 'he has n't made up his mind how long he shall stay;' 'he may return to his old home,' etc. His heart is either very cold, or he is afraid to risk that attention to his actual character which his request for a letter would draw after it, at both his old and new home, or he grievously over-estimates the trouble of the transfer. When, then, an absent member has so far overcome the temptation to 'keep dark,' as a Christian in his new home, as to write for a letter of dismission; his Church ought, by all means, to encourage the removal of his relation. Grant that they fear that his Christian character has been in eclipse, and has failed to honor the Saviour; his very request is an encouraging sign of a reawakened conscience; and — at all events — his recovery to a consistent and earnest walk with God, will be more likely under the proposed new relation, than in the mere formal continuance of the old. Unless, then — as we have said above — some *charge* is on the table affecting his Christian character, and involving a process of discipline — it is usually best that his request should be complied with. In fact such a member has a *right* to claim to be either disciplined, or dismissed, as — technically — in " good and regular standing;" which means simply that he is a member against whom no charge of unchristian conduct is made.

That is a very weak-minded error into which some churches — in both city and country — have been led, of disfavoring the desire of absent members to be dismissed, because such dis-

ing.¹ On its reception, the Pastor will read it to the Church, at the first meeting when business is in order, when — if no charge is before the Church, affecting the Christian character of the applicant, and no reason is known why the request is not a proper one — some brother usually moves (and another seconds it) that the request be granted. If this motion pass, it becomes the duty of the Clerk of the Church immediately to fill out a letter of dismission and recommendation in some ordinary form, and forward it to the party to whom it has been granted.²

---

mission would reduce the numbers of the Church, and so *detract from its apparent consequence in the annual statistical returns!* If the annual report of more Church members, by a large fraction, than the average number of its Sabbath congregation, does not involve a Church — or its Pastor — in some sort of false pretence; there must be a very curious and abnormal state of things in that community!

¹ This would be a suitable form for such a request:

To the Congregational Church in ———.
Dear Brethren.
  Having, in the Providence of God, been led to remove my residence to this place, and having been led to think it my duty to remove my Church relation to the ——— Congregational Church here; this is to request you to grant me a letter of dismission from your body, and of recommendation to its fellowship.
       Wishing you grace, mercy, and peace,
           I subscribe myself,
       Affectionately, your Brother in Christ,
[Date and place of date.]   A——— B———.

² The following is a good form for a letter of dismission and recommendation:

The Congregational Church in ——— to the Congregational Church in ———, sendeth greeting:
Dear Brethren:
  The bearer, Bro. A——— B———, is a member with us in good and regular standing. He has desired a letter of dismission from us, and of recommendation to your Christian fellowship, and we have granted his request; so that, when received by you, his membership with us will cease.
       Wishing you grace, mercy, and peace,
           We are yours in the Lord,
                 By the hand of
[Date and place of date.]   C——— D———, Church Clerk.

  N. B. Please to inform us, by a return of the accompanying certificate — or in some other way, of our brother's reception by you.

  This is to certify that A——— B——— was received a member of the Congregational Church in ———, on the ——— of ———, by letter from the Congregational Church in ———.
                 Attest.
[Date and place of date.]   E——— F——— Church Clerk.

Sometimes, churches — by standing rule — commit all such requests to a committee, whose duty it is to inquire into the circumstances of the case, and report whether any reason exists why the request should not be complied with. Other churches require that such an application lie upon the table one or two weeks, before action; to give time for inquiry, and to guard against precipitancy.

If a member should request dismission to some Unevangelical Body, it would become the duty of the Church to attempt to dissuade him from such a course, and, if he persists, to make him a subject of discipline, in some form. No Church can give letters to a body with which it is not in full and fraternal fellowship. Neither can a Church dismiss to no Church; that is, terminate a member's relation without censure, and without transfer [1]

If a member of the Church proposes to be absent on a long journey, or permanently to remove his residence, but is uncertain whither, or doubtful as to what Church in the place of his new abode he may, on further acquaintance, think it best to join; he should take with him a certificate of his good standing in the Church, which will introduce him to Christian communion wherever he may go, and postpone asking for a letter of dismission and recommendation until he ascertains to what particular Church his duty calls him.[2] It is neither good Congregation-

---

[When this form is printed, the foregoing certificate may be printed on the second leaf of the sheet, so as to be readily torn off, filled and returned. If a *postage stamp* were enclosed with this certificate, it might facilitate its return, and — since the good of the certificate is mainly for the dismissing Church, that it may keep its record exact — that slight expenditure really belongs to it.]

[1] Sometimes persons who have become convinced that they were deceived in regard to their own condition when they joined the Church, and that they really are not Christians, ask to be dismissed, or dropped, or to have their relation terminated, in some way, without discipline. Compliance with such a request is simply impossible. Union to the Church is an act of triple covenant, namely: between the individual, the Church, and the Great Head of the Church; and no request of the first party, or consent of the second, can discharge that first party from his obligation to the third party. He has solemnly promised to be the Lord's, and covenanted with the Lord that he will be His, and no vote of the Church can make void that obligation.

Is it asked, what shall the man do who finds himself in the Church, without being, in his own conviction, a child of God? We answer, he has *promised* to be a child of God — let him keep his promise. If he is not now worthy to be a Church member, he has sworn to be worthy — let him keep his oath; for no power on earth can discharge him from it, and he must either keep it, or go up to the judgment seat, and answer, in addition to all his other sins, for that great guilt of vowing unto the Lord, and failing to redeem his vow. Cambridge Platform says, explicitly, "the Church cannot make a member no member, but by excommunication." (Chap. xiii. Sec. 7.)

[2] A letter of this description may be given by the Pastor, or the Clerk, without special vote of the Church. The following would be a suitable form:

alism, nor good common sense, for a Church to grant one of its members a "general letter" of dismission " to any Church to which the Providence of God may lead him." Such a Church is very apt to prove no Church, and such a letter to lead to confusion, and the losing sight of members through unprofitable and ungodly years; and the Church member who cannot afford a new postage stamp to ask for a special letter, when he has found out to what particular Church it should be directed, deserves no letter at all.

It is, for many reasons, often a wise course to superscribe and send the letter of dismission to the Pastor of the Church to which it is directed, rather than to the individual asking for it. It notifies the Pastor, at once, that there is such a member of his flock proposing union to his Church, and smoothes the way to a pleasant introduction of acquaintance between the two — where none has been formed; while it facilitates the speedy use of the letter, in the union of the member dismissed by it to the Church of his new home.

All dismissed members remain members still of the dismissing Church, until that relation is terminated by their actual reception into that to which they have been dismissed; though some churches, by special rule, withdraw from such dismissed members the right of voting (unless they return their letter.) When the tenure of a letter of dismission is limited to one year, or six months, as it often is, by standing rule, and the letter lies unused during that time, it becomes null; and the member falls back into full membership in the Church which gave it, and must get a new letter; while he becomes the subject of inquiry and of discipline, if he has *improperly* failed to use his letter during its validity.

(5.) *Disciplining members.* Since " it must needs be that offences come," it is necessary that some regular method of procedure in re-

---

**To all who love our Lord Jesus Christ in sincerity.*
   Dear Brethren:
   Let this certify that the bearer, A—— B——, is a member, in good and regular standing, of the Congregational Church in ——; and, as such, is affectionately commended to the Christian fellowship of any Church of Christ with which he may desire to commune, and to the kind offices of all the people of God.
   Witness my hand,

—————— { Pastor [or Clerk] of the Congregational Church in ——.

[*Date, and place of date.*]

gard to them should be followed by the Church; and our Saviour, in the 18th of Matthew, laid down the general principles on which Church discipline should be founded.[1] The more faithfully any Church can succeed in carrying them out, the more healthful and useful will be the results of its action. Four classes will include all those offences with which churches are called to deal, namely: private offences where but one individual is concerned; private offences between two or more; matters of public and notorious scandal; and departures from the covenant, on the part of those whose lives are otherwise blameless.

(*a.*) *Private offences where only one individual is concerned.* Such an offence would be an instance of drunkenness, or profaneness, or falsehood, or of any unchristian conduct, on the part of an individual Church member, where it is known only to another, or at most to a very few — the body of the Church, and the community, being ignorant of it. In such a case it becomes, by the mutual covenant between them, the duty of the brother who knows it, and is grieved by it (not because it is an offence against him, but because it is an offence against God, which has been forced upon his cognizance,)[2] to go to his erring brother alone, and confidentially, and seek to bring him to repentance. Should he be successful — the offender acknowledging and bewailing his guilt, and promising repentance toward God, and reformation of life — that would end the matter. Should the result be otherwise, the brother should take — confidentially as before — two or three judicious brethren with him, and all of them together should labor to bring the offender to penitence and reformation. If now successful, this will end the matter. If the offender continue obdurate, and furnish new proof of the unchristian posture of his heart, nothing remains but to 'tell it unto the Church.' Yet this may wisely be done in a cautious and unhasty way, giving the offender time to think the matter over in all its aspects, if perchance he .

---

[1] See pp. 41, 42.
[2] Let it be said here, once for all, in answer to all inquiries as to whose duty it is to commence Christian labor with an offender; It is often assumed that Christ's "If thy brother trespass against thee," etc., refers exclusively to a personal quarrel between the two, so that it is nobody's business to try to reclaim an offender but the brother with whom he had the quarrel — very likely the last man to try it, or to succeed in it. But the mutual covenant between all the membership, makes the quarrel of one brother with another *a trespass against the peace of all*, so that *any* brother having cognizance of the fact *may* go, and *ought* to go, and labor to have the wrong righted, and the scandal removed.

may come to a better mind — since the first object of all Church discipline must always be the reformation of the guilty. To favor this wise delay, many churches make it a standing rule,[1] that all complaints, in cases of discipline, be made first to the Examining Committee;[2] that they may review the facts, with the steps already taken, and privately endeavor to bring the offender to that state of mind and heart, which his covenant vows demand. Failing in this, the Committee would bring the matter to the attention of the Church, by entering a formal complaint, charging definitely upon the offender the offence committed, and stating the evidence by which the charge can be substantiated.[3] If the Church vote to entertain this complaint,

---

[1] See page 175, (note), Art. 21. (3.)

[2] Where there is no Examining Committee, and no Committee of any kind charged with the care of cases of discipline in their early stages, the complainant would most naturally carry his complaint to the Pastor and Deacons, who might bring it before the Church themselves, or secure some brother to do so, and have it referred to a special committee for investigation — on whose report the Church would drop the matter, or proceed to ultimate it by a regular charge, and trial. The advantage of having some Standing Committee before whom such cases may be quietly brought, is that, in a majority of cases — we might say in all cases, where misapprehension, and not a chronically unchristian state of the soul is the cause of the difficulty — the whole trouble may be settled without any public cognizance of the Church, with its inevitable attendant scandal, to the cause. The raising of a special committee to investigate a case that might be so settled by a standing committee, is, of itself, an evil.

[3] Such a complaint might take some such form as this:

To the Congregational Church in ———.

Dear Brethren:

It becomes our painful duty to bring to your notice the offence of a brother, and to ask you to deal with it according to the law of Christ. Having become satisfied of his guilt, and having failed — in the use of the first steps of Gospel discipline — to bring him to a better mind, we are compelled, in great sorrow of heart, and with the earnest prayer that the Great Head of the Church may bless this labor to the restoration of our erring brother, to make the following complaint against him.

We charge Brother A—— B—— with being guilty of the sin of ——; and particularly on the —— day of —— last, [and at other times]; and of denying the same, [or remaining obdurate in regard to the same] : in violation of his duty as a Christian, and of his covenant vows.

Brothers C—— D—— and E—— F——, are witnesses of the subject-matter of this complaint.

We respectfully ask you to entertain this charge, and to proceed to try the same, according to the rules of this Church, and the law of Christ.

Your brethren,

_____ } *Examining Committee of the Congregational Church in* ———.

(*Date.*)

they will then appoint a time for a hearing of the case, and summon the offender to be present and take his trial upon the charge preferred against him — furnishing him seasonably with a copy of the charge, and with the names of the witnesses on whom reliance will be had for proof.[1] If, at this hearing, he should acknowledge his guilt, the matter could be settled by his making a public confession of his sin; (his private confession to the party who labored with him, would not now suffice, because the offence has been made public, and the confession must be as public as the scandal), and asking forgiveness of God, and of the Church. If he should deny his offence, or seem insensible to it, and remain obdurate, while the Church become satisfied of his guilt, they must vote to admonish him, to suspend him for some definite period from Church privileges, or to excommunicate him altogether, according to the aggravation of his offence, the state of mind in which he is, and their conviction of the requisitions of the general good. It is usual, however — for better security against hasty and unjust action — to demand the concurrence of two-thirds, or three-fourths, of all the male members present, for the passage of any such vote of censure.

Such *admonition* would have no effect upon his Church privileges. *Suspension* would deprive him of them all during the period of its continuance. Should that be for some definite period of time — as six months, or one year — and no action then be taken, his sentence of suspension having terminated itself, his full Church privileges would revert to him. Should his suspension, however, have been made operative "until he shall show penitence, and ask to be restored," it would continue indefinitely until terminated by vote — consequent upon his confession and desire for restoration ; or upon renewed evidence of his hardness of heart, leading the Church to feel that he ought to be excommunicated. *Excommunication* would cut him off ignominiously from all relation of privilege to the Church, while it would leave upon him all relations of duty, inasmuch as he has for-

---

[1] It is usual to hold the confession of the party accused, the concurrence of two or more competent witnesses (Matt. xviii: 16), or circumstantial evidence to the same amount, to be sufficient for conviction. One witness — without added circumstantial evidence enough to amount to the testimony of a second witness — would *not* justify discipline. Witnesses, however, need not be themselves Church members, to be competent. Any whom a court of justice would receive, the Church may — reserving the right to take all testimony at its own estimate of value.

feited all privilege by his own misconduct, while he cannot forfeit the claims of duty which rest upon him in virtue of his covenant with God — a covenant from which God never will release him. Hence, he remains *an excommunicated Church member*, not a non-Church member; as the criminal imprisoned for life ceases not to be a member of human society, but is an imprisoned member. And, as such a prisoner resumes his *status* in society when he is "pardoned out;" so, should an excommunicated Church member repent, and ask to be forgiven, the lifting of the sentence of excommunication from him, on his humble confession, would at once restore him to 'good and regular standing' in the Church without his needing to be admitted 'by profession,' *de novo*.[1]

Public notice ought to be given to the congregation usually worshipping with a Church, of any vote of extreme censure; because the scandal which rendered it necessary, has become public, and the cause of Christ is entitled to the public benefit of its acts of self-purification.

(*b.*) *Private offences between two or more.* These are, perhaps, the commonest form of Church offence; as when two members "have a difficulty," or when one member "has a difficulty" with a non-Church member — when the matter has not been noised abroad so as to become a public scandal. In the former case, one or the other of the two who are aggrieved, would naturally commence to labor with the other, and, failing to secure satisfaction — upon the attempt to do

---

[1] It used to be held that excommunication was a delivery to Satan, and that the meaning of " let him be unto thee as an heathen man, and a publican," required civil and social non-intercourse. (See Cummings' *Congregational Dictionary*, pp. 171-181.) It was held, of course, that the act put one out of the Church in such a manner as to " make a member no member." But Samuel Mather sets the matter right (in his *Apology*, p 108), where he says, the churches pretend to no more power and jurisdiction over their members " than a society of discreet and grave Philosophers over such as are admitted into their society, whom they see meet to admit when they are duly qualified; and they think themselves obliged to censure, and exclude from their society, when they have forfeited the privileges of it by their exotic sentiments or indecent carriages. 'Tis true, some of our Congregational brethren, who verge toward Presbyterianism, pretend to much more in their discipline than that for which I have been pleading; but all such as are thoroughly Congregational will be content with this. I must confess, that this is all the power to which the churches have any rightful claim; and, I conceive, all that they pretended to exercise in the early times of Christianity." So Hornius says (*Hist. Eccles.* p. 145,) of the excommunications of the Apostolic Church, "neque vero excommunicatio aliud tum erat quam *separatio, non-communio, renunciatio communionis;* non vero damnatio, execratio," etc. *Alford's* comment. on Matt. xviii: 17, is " let him no longer be accounted as a brother, but as one of those without — as the Jews accounted Gentiles and Publicans Yet even then not with hatred; (See 1 Cor. v: 11, and compare 2 Cor ii. 6, 7, and 2 Thess iii: 14 15)." Vol. i. p. 177.

so in the presence of witnesses — would bring it to the notice of the Examining Committee (or the Pastor and Deacons), who would proceed as before. If neither of the two commence to labor with the other, it would be the duty of any brother who should become cognizant of their disagreement, to commence labor with both of them, for its removal; and to pursue it until the end should be reached. There is no greater hindrance within the Church to the progress of the Redeemer's kingdom, than the sullen, or violent, differences of those who have covenanted to walk with each other in all brotherly love and fellowship, but who fall out by the way, and even stay away from the table of the Lord, because they will not partake with their enemy. Such a scandalous state of things should not be suffered to exist, and the surest way to end it, is for the first brother who gets knowledge of such a quarrel, to commence Gospel labor with both parties to it, and to pursue that labor until the breach is healed, or the Church purified by the excision of the offenders.

In the latter case referred to, the party to the difficulty who is not a Church member may properly tell his grievance to some one who is; who may undertake the work of reconciliation, and of the discipline of his brother — if he seems to deserve it.

(c.) *Matters of public scandal.* It has been said by some Congregational authorities, that in matters of open and notorious offence on the part of a Church member (as where he should have committed murder, or eloped with the wife of another, etc.,) there is no need of any preliminary and private steps, but the Church ought to purify itself by the instant expulsion of the criminal. But this forgets that the first aim of Church discipline must *always* be the reformation of the offender, and that the 'blood of Jesus Christ cleanseth from *all* sin.' And although the Cambridge Platform (Chap. xiv. Sec. 3) warrants such a course, it seems to us that nothing can be lost, while much *may* be gained by adhering rigorously, *in all cases*, to the rule that the Church will not entertain a complaint against one of its members, except in the regular way, and on assurance that the 'private steps' have been rightly taken.[1] The only difference which we

---

[1] We say "rightly taken," because we have known the most absurd misapprehension to exist in regard to those steps. We have known one Church member, who 'had a difficulty' with a brother, to have a conversation with him which contained not the most distant allusion to their 'difficulty,' nor the faintest attempt to reconcile it on Gospel principles, and then to turn back

should allow, then, between procedure in cases of open scandal, and those of a private nature, is that in them it would be the duty of the Examining Committee (or, in their absence, of the Pastor and Deacons) to commence their labor preparatory to discipline, without waiting for complaint from any individual.

(*d.*) *Violations of the Articles of Faith and Covenant.* This class of offences sometimes grievously perplexes a Church. Where a man of irreproachable — even of an eminently useful, and beautiful — life, gradually, under the influence of friends, or it may be of mental idiosyncracy, strongly inclining him toward some plausible error, departs from the faith once delivered to saints until he holds and advocates doctrines destructive of the creed of the Church with which he is in covenant relation, that Church must necessarily take cognizance of the change. It has covenanted to 'watch over him' and to 'seek his edification.' No charge can be made against his moral character; perhaps, even, those who know him best are confident that he is still a true disciple of the Saviour. Under these peculiarly trying circumstances, what shall be done?

In reply, it is clear that not all who are hopefully Christians, can rightly belong to any given Church, but only those who, as Christians, hold, for substance, the faith *as the Church holds it.* Baptists and Methodists, though ever so eminent as Christians, could not walk with a Church holding the ordinary Pædo-baptist, and Predestinarian Congregational creed. It is not a necessary conclusion, therefore, that the withdrawal by a Church, of its fellowship, from a person whose faith has lapsed from the articles of its creed, is necessarily a remission of him to hopeless destruction, or even to uncovenanted mercy. The Church is responsible before God to walk according to

---

as he was walking away, and tell him 'he might please to consider that the first step according to the 18th of Matthew, had been taken with him!' And we have known the second man, thereafter, to dodge the first, as if he were an assassin waiting to fire the pistol of the 'second step' at him, and the first — after long patience — to corner his victim, and follow his opening salutation with the words, 'I hereby notify you that I have taken the second step, in the presence of these witnesses, and shall immediately enter a complaint before the Church against you!'

All such formal and merely technical procedure disgracefully violates the Saviour's intent — who had in mind, evidently, a tender fraternal conference in the use of every means of persuasion from error, in the first place; and, in the second, the seconding of that by the added entreaty and influence of the 'one or two more' — who might also serve as witnesses of the subsequent reconciliation, or renewal of the offence.

its covenant with Him; and the individual is responsible before God for his own belief, whatever it may be. Each must do its own duty.

The first step in such a case, should then be careful, and faithful, and most fraternal labor with the individual — either by some brother specially interested in him, and grieved by his position, or by the Pastor — in the hope to persuade him to return whence he has strayed. This failing, a regular process of discipline must issue, in ordinary form (which will most likely be cut short by the frank avowal on the part of the individual, of his changed belief) ultimating in final separation from the Church. Some would argue from Paul's use of the phrase "*withdraw yourselves* from every brother that walketh disorderly, and not after the tradition which he received of us," (2 Thess. iii: 6) that the proper Church act in this case would be called "withdrawal of fellowship," rather than excommunication; urging that the latter implies forfeiture of *Christian* standing, the former only forfeiture of *Church* standing. Mr. Punchard ably argues thus, in the appendix of his *View of Congregationalism* (pp. 329–336), but acknowledges a lack of Congregational authorities in support of his position. The truth would seem to be that there is little, if any, difference between the two methods of cutting off a member — in their practical results, and that if it would make it easier for any Church to discharge its painful duty by calling the act of excision by the milder name, there can be no objection to its doing so. Whether it do so, or not, all who are cognizant of the transaction, will always understand the difference between expulsion for a faith against the covenant, and for a life against the Gospel.

Other cases of violation of covenant sometimes arise — as when members remove, and are gone years without taking letters of dismission; or when they, for some fickle reason, neglect their own spiritual home, and wander about from Church to Church, in the vicinity, ever on the watch for the last new pulpit light, etc. Such cases must be dealt with tenderly, and always in the loving aim of reclamation; yet, where worst comes to worst, they should not be spared from the extreme sentence of the law of Christ.

SECTION 4. *How to vacate Church offices.*

The general understanding with which the lesser officers of a Congregational Church are chosen, is that they will serve until the next annual meeting; or — if that meeting should not take place at the usual time — until others are chosen in their places. With regard to Deacons and Pastors, the understanding is, usually, that they will serve during good behavior, or until such time as the best interests of the Church may require their removal; though, of late years, some churches have introduced the custom of choosing Deacons for a term of years, taking care that they shall be so chosen that all shall not retire, or take their chance of reëlection, at the same time. Cases sometimes occur, however, when the best interests of the Church demand the removal of an officer, while his official term is unexpired, and when he himself is not forward to move in the matter. It is important to the welfare of the Church that whatever steps may be taken, in such a case, should be taken prudently.

(*a.*) *How to vacate lesser Church offices.* It may often be best, where it is unquestionably the desire of the majority of the Church that such an officer should retire from his official position, to allow him to serve out the remainder of his term until the annual meeting, rather than to risk 'hard feeling' in his removal. But there may be cases where the longer continuance of a brother in office would clearly be so detrimental to the Church, that less harm would result from his removal, than from his continuance. In such a case, the Church should pass a vote requesting him to resign his office, and, if that prove ineffectual, a second vote, removing him from that office — which it may then proceed to fill. The claim that a man once chosen *has a right to his office* during the whole term for which he was expected to hold it when elected, and in expectation of which he based his acceptance, is good only while the state of things in which he was elected remains essentially unchanged. If he has developed traits of character which were unsuspected before, and which, if known, would have prevented his election; that changes the whole aspect of the matter, and terminates his right. Or, if any circumstances have arisen, affecting his usefulness, which the Church did not anticipate when electing him, and which, if anticipated, would have made his election impossible, that terminates his right. The general principle which must always govern, in such a case, is that the welfare of the Church is of more importance than the pride or the desire of office of an individual, and that the power which set up — always supposing it has not hampered itself by any organic law which would take away its power temporarily from itself — has the power to set down; and is solemnly bound to administer its affairs in the interest of Christ and his cause, and not of any person, or persons, whatsoever.

(*b.*) *How to vacate the Deaconship.* The principles just referred to apply with even augmented force in the case of the Deacons of a Church, especially when they are chosen for life. It has not been an unheard-of thing among us, for Deacons to have officially 'outlived their usefulness,' and for churches to be greatly troubled with them, and still more troubled to know how to be rid of them. This has been sometimes specially the case where Deacons have mistaken the nature of the trust confided to them by the Church, and supposed themselves — instead of being merely its servants, appointed to take care of its temporalities, to comfort and help its poor members, and to minister at the communion table — to be an oligarchy for its supreme control, including the management of the Pastor — whose 'usefulness' in their judgment, is measured directly by the degree of his subserviency to their dictation.

It is impossible to deny that a Deacon has no moral right to continuance in his office, when that continuance is not for the best good of the Church — because he was chosen for its help, and not for its hindrance. And if he has, then, no moral right to continuance in office, the Church has no moral right to let him continue in it; and if they have no moral right to let him continue in his office, they are morally bound to remove him from it.

When such a case unfortunately exists, where a decided majority of the Church are of opinion that the longer continuance of a Deacon in office is not for the good of the Church, the first appropriate step would be, for some influential members of the Church to converse with him privately, and inform him of the feeling of the Church, and urge him to resign his office. If he should doubt the truth of their representation, or refuse, altogether, to do any thing about it, it would be wise for one of these brethren to bring the matter before the Church, and for the Church to pass a vote requesting him to resign, and to appoint a committee to endeavor to induce him to comply with that request. This failing to produce the desired result, the way is then open for the Church to pass a vote removing him from office, and to make arrangements to fill the vacancy thus created.

Such a vote is not a vote of censure upon such a Deacon's Christian character, but merely a declaration on the part of the Church, that however good a Christian he may be, he is not the most desirable man for the office of a Deacon with them. We have known a Deacon so deposed to endeavor to persist in serving, on the ground that he was chosen for life, and that the office could not be taken from him except for some disciplinable offence, destructive of his Christian character; and claiming that such a vote of deposition was an attempt to discipline him in an unconstitutional manner. This absurdly confuses Christian character, with fitness for important office in the Church. Such a Deacon, so deposed, has no more ground of complaint against the Church for an attack upon his personal piety in the vote of deposition, than each of the 'ninety and nine just persons' who were not chosen Deacon, when he was chosen, have, that their non-choice was an attack upon *their* personal piety. True, a Deacon in such circumstances needs to use great caution, or he will be betrayed into saying and doing things which will furnish just ground of complaint against his Christian character.

So, on the other hand, we have known a Church to suffer for years under the malign influence of a Deacon who, though nobody doubted that he would go to Heaven when he died, continued, yet, to make himself so unlovely in his office, that there would have been a general willingness on the part of the Church to have him go, if the Lord wanted him; because it labored under the impression that having once chosen him, he could not be removed except he committed some 'disciplinable offence.' But nothing can be clearer — in point of principle — than that a Church not only has the right, but, in ordinary cases, is bound to exercise the right, by majority vote, to remove a Deacon whenever the Church feels that its good clearly requires such removal — and to base their action distinctly on that ground as its justifying cause.

(*c.*) *How to vacate the Pastorship.* It is a little remarkable that those very Deacons who — being chosen for life, or good behavior — fail to see the right of the Church to remove them except they have committed some disciplinable offence, are yet usually prompt to recognize the propriety of the removal of a Pastor — chosen on the same tenure of office as themselves — when the Church desire him to go, even when he hath not 'committed things, worthy of stripes!' So far as the Church officer-ship of the Pastorship is concerned, however, the same principles apply to both cases. And when the decided majority of a Church have become conscientiously persuaded that the good of the cause of Christ requires their Pastor's removal, it is both their right and their duty to move in the matter. The process of the dissolution of the Pastoral office is, however, complicated: first, by the fact that, as the public officer of the Church, through whom especially it comes into contact with other churches — and who was inducted by their advice — the fellowship of the churches requires that their advice should be taken also upon the question of his removal; and second, by the fact of a contract[1] between the two parties, of which the law takes cognizance, and which it holds itself bound to enforce.

The first appropriate step would be that of private conference with the Pastor, in which, in the freest, frankest, fullest, and most Christian manner, prominent members of the Church should acquaint him with the judgment of the body upon the matter; stating all the reasons which lead them to believe that the common good would be promoted by his removal. They ought, at such a time, moreover, to remember that they are asking their Pastor to make a sacrifice of reputation, and probably of worldly goods, for their advantage; and, since it is almost inevitable that a large share of the blame of the existing state of things rests upon them, they ought, in a generous spirit, to offer to share with him — so far as their pecuniary aid can go — the inconvenience and loss to which they ask him to submit for their sake. A little more magnanimity and Christian generosity in this direction would have relieved many a retiring Pastor's heart from great suffering, and would have saved some Churches and Parishes from expensive difficulties in "fighting off" one who so smarted under a sense of injury from them, as pertinaciously to claim the fullest protection of the law for the contract between them.

---

[1] "According to early New England Congregationalism, the pastorate is simply an office in a particular Church, of Divine origin, but to which the Church elects the incumbent as it would any other officer. Ordination was merely inauguration into the office pertaining to that Church, not to a grade of clergy. Removal from office was under the control of the Church, and when effected by vote of the Church, was called "deposition," — a term which is now applied to degradation from the ministry itself. Yet when so performed, it was held that it *ought* not to be done without the advice and approbation of neighboring churches represented in Council. There very soon arose the idea that the relation was really a contract, and that so long as both parties performed their share of the contract, neither party had a right to break it; and when an actual contract for support entered, this theory was confirmed. That the relation is a contract, and determinable for proper causes, and in a proper manner, all agree." — Rev. A. H. Quint. "Connection of Pastor and People." *Cong. Quarterly.* April, 1859. p. 170.

In nine cases out of ten — we might say in *every* case in which the Pastor is a man of both sense and piety — if the state of mind of the majority of the Church is a kind and legitimate one, and one which they ought to have; such a conference will be followed by his resignation. If he lack evidence, however, of the truth of the alleged facts, it may be well for the Church, by formal vote upon a resolution declaring them, to furnish that evidence. And if, admitting the facts, he doubts the expediency of his resignation in consequence, the Church and Parish[1] should then request him to unite with them in submitting the matter of his removal[2] to the consideration and advice of a Mutual Council;[3] distinctly stating to him the several reasons which they propose to lay before that Council.[4] Should he refuse thus to submit the question, the Church and Parish may properly proceed to call an impartial *ex-parte* Council;[5] laying the facts before it,

---

[1] "The offer of a Mutual Council, to be effectual, must have been made by virtue of authority from the *Parish*."—Case of Thompson *v*. Rehoboth, *Mass. Reports*, 7 Pickering, 159.

[2] "When asked to agree in a Mutual Council, the minister ought to have a general statement of the grounds and reasons of the call upon him; not in a precise technical form, but substantially set forth, so that he may exercise his judgment whether to unite in a Council, or not."—*Ibid.*

[3] The following form of Letter Missive would be appropriate for use under these circumstances : —

The Congregational Church in ———— to the Congregational Church in ————, sendeth Greeting.

Dear Brethren:

Whereas, unhappily, a state of things exists among us which, in the judgment of a majority of this Church, and of the Ecclesiastical Society connected therewith, renders it expedient that the relation between the Church and its Pastor should be dissolved · we affectionately invite your attendance by your Pastor and a Delegate, at ————, on the ———— day of ———— at ———— o'clock in the ————, to examine the facts and advise us in the premises.

Wishing you grace, mercy, and peace,

We are yours in the Gospel,

———————————— Pastor.

————————————
———————————— } Committee of the Church and Society.
————————————

(*Date, and place of date.*)

N. B. The other Churches invited to this Council are the Church in ————, Rev. Mr. ———— Pastor; etc. etc.

[4] See Whitmore *v.* Fourth Congregational Society in Plymouth, 2 Gray.

[5] In this case the above letter might be varied so as to read thus : —

Whereas, unhappily, a state of things exists among us which, in the judgment of a

and asking its advice as to the course to be pursued.¹ Such a Council, as its first act after organization, should send a special communication to the Pastor, informing him that they are assembled, and inviting him to make the Council a mutual one by appearing before them, and presenting his view of the case on which their judgment is desired. Should he refuse to comply with their request, they would then go on to obtain the completest view of the facts possible, and base upon them their advice to those who called them together. They should be careful to state distinctly the grounds on which that advice is founded, as the courts may revise their action, and annul it if those grounds are not specified,² or seem to be insufficient to justify the result.³ They may — if they concur in the opinion arrived at by the majority of the Church — express their solemn and decided conviction that the interests of the cause of Christ as connected with that Church seem to them to require a dissolution of the Pastoral relation, and may advise the Church and Parish to urge again upon the Pastor the duty of laying down his office. But such a Council would have no right to declare the pastoral office vacant. Here again it may be repeated, that if the Pastor is a man of sense and piety, he will, in ninety-nine cases out of a hundred, immediately follow the suggestion of the Church and Society, now backed by the moral weight of the solemn judgment of impartial representatives of the churches in Council assembled. He cannot be justified before the Christian public, or the world, if he does not do so.

---

majority of this Church and Society, renders it expedient that the relation between us and our Pastor be dissolved, yet he declines to take action for such dissolution, and refuses to submit the facts to a Mutual Council for advice, although such a Council has been asked for, in the legal and usual manner, by the said Church and Society, we affectionately invite your attendance upon an Ex-parte Council, by your Pastor, etc., etc.

1 "If, in a proper case for the meeting of an Ecclesiastical Council to be mutually chosen, either party should unreasonably and without good cause, refuse their concurrence to a mutual choice, the aggrieved party may choose an impartial Council, and will be justified in conforming to the result."—Avery v. Tyringham, 3 Mass. 160.

Great care should be taken that the members of such an *ex-parte* Council be such as the community will feel to be, and the Pastor himself acknowledge to be, able, candid, and impartial men. "In the case of Thompson v. Rehoboth, a member of a former unfavorable Council was declared to be unqualified to serve again."— Rev. A. H. Quint, *Cong. Quar.*, 1859, p. 174.

² "They [the Council] find only that *some* of the charges were proved, without specifying which of them. Now as some of the charges do not, of themselves, furnish grounds of compulsory removal, it may be, for ought the record shows, that these alone were proved." Thompson v. Rehoboth, 7 Pick. 159. In this case the Court would not allow parole evidence to be introduced to show which were the charges established before the Council.

³ See Stearns v. Bedford, 21 Pick. 114.

. But what shall be done if he is *not* a man of sense and piety, and still obstinately refuses to free the Church from the incubus of his presence?

The answer to this partly depends upon the state of the civil law, and the decisions of the courts. We shall treat of the matter as it is under Massachusetts law, because it is presumed that no State is more stringent in this regard, and therefore that whatever changes may be needful to make those processes which are necessary here applicable elsewhere, will be the easy ones of omission.

By Massachusetts law, the decision of a properly constituted Mutual Council — or of such an impartial and rightly managed *ex-parte* Council, as we have referred to — that the Pastoral relation *ought* to be dissolved, would have precisely this effect ; namely :

1. It would *not* dissolve the contract, and of course would not dismiss the Pastor. But,

2. It would, when accepted and acted upon by the Church and Society, legally justify them in treating him as no longer their Pastor, and would be a good defence in law against any suit which he might bring on a claim for salary subsequent to that result of Council; *provided* that result has been founded upon any reason which the law holds to be valid in such cases.[1]

3. Valid reasons, in the eye of the law, are these three; namely: (*a*) Essential change of doctrinal belief and teaching; (*b*) Wilful neglect of duty; (*c*) Immoral or criminal conduct. These are held to be good and sufficient grounds for forfeiture of the ministerial relation, when fairly made out — as being not "occasional inadvertencies," or "imprudencies," but "of the grosser sort; such as habitual intemperance, lying, unchaste or immodest behavior."[2]

If, then, the advice of Council has been based upon these, or any

---

[1] "The effect of the orderly decision of a Mutual Council, or of a properly constituted *Ex-parte* Council, is simply this: It does not, and cannot dissolve the contract; *but its decision is a legal justification of the party adopting it*."—Rev. A. H Quint. *Cong Quar* (1859) p. 179.

"The effect of the advice of a Council is nothing more than a legal justification of the party who shall adopt it."—Burr *v* Sandwich, 6 Mass 277.

"Either party conforming thereto [that is, to the fair result of a fair Council] will be justified."—Hollis Street *v.* Pierpont, 7 Metcalf. 495.

"These decisions [of Councils] are not conclusive in all respects, as already stated, and they do not operate *ex proprio vigore* as a judgment, but only as a justification of the party conforming to them."—Stearns *v.* Bedford, 21 Pick. 114.

[2] See Sheldon *v.* Easton, 24 Pick. 281 · Burr *v.* Sandwich, 9 Mass. 277 ; and Hollis Street *v.* Pierpont, 7 Metcalf, 495.

one of them, as its strong reason, the Church and Society accepting and acting on it, will be practically freed by it from any further responsibility to the man who has been their Pastor, and can, by vote, declare the office vacant, and proceed to take measures to fill the vacancy.

But if the advice of Council is founded upon something less and other than these reasons, the legal relation will not be affected by it. The mere unacceptableness of a Pastor to his people, or his unpopularity with them, is *not* recognized in law, as, of itself, a sufficient ground of removal; for the law takes it for granted that the Church and Parish have taken time to become thoroughly acquainted with a man before inducting him into such a position. It is distinctly held that having " capriciously and causelessly withdrawn their confidence, they cannot allege their own misconduct, as a ground for their discharge from the contract which they entered into." [1]

But is there no relief for a Church and Parish who find themselves yoked to a Pastor by legal contract, whose continuance they —in their vast majority — deeply and most conscientiously feel to be disastrous to their prosperity; whom they have urged to retire, or even to submit the matter to the advice of a Mutual Council, in vain; and whose further continuance an impartial *ex-parte* Council have advised against and deplored; yet who has not been guilty of any offence which the law, as heretofore administered by the Massachusetts courts, would cognize as justifying them in sundering their contract with him?

We think there is. In the first place it is our very decided impression that a Parish which should make the fair result of a fair Council advising their Pastor's dismission on the ground of general and manifest unfitness for the proper filling of his place — on grounds less than those which the Courts have heretofore required, yet which are morally and religiously sufficient,—their justification for treating him as no longer their Pastor, would *now* find themselves sustained by the Massachusetts courts, in case of his suit for salary. The bench has shown progress in the treatment of these cases. The old decisions which we have cited, were made thirty or forty years ago, under the former *territorial* Parish system. If we mistake not, there

---

[1] See Sheldon v. Easton, 24 Pick. 281.

has been but one case decided under the present Parish arrangement, and every thing indicates an advance toward future decisions of a more equitable and less technical character; so that we can hardly doubt that a new suit would gain a judgment sustaining a Parish against *unreason*, as well as against heresy, neglect of duty, or immorality in its Pastor.

And even in the failure of such an expectation, it certainly could not be the duty of a Church and Parish, to sit down in quiet submission to their own suicide. We think that under those peculiar circumstances, where the matter is reduced, by the Pastor's unreason, to a contest upon the arena of bare legal right, a Parish would be justified in what, under other circumstances cannot too much be condemned; namely, such a *legal* reduction of his salary as may remove *that* inducement for his persistent hold upon the contract. It will do no good to close the meeting-house against him, because the Courts have repeatedly decided [1] that the Pastor who holds himself *at all times ready* to discharge his legal duties, may lawfully claim his salary, even when the 'Parish do not allow him to perform them. But if a Pastor could be so lost to all sense of the decencies — not to say proprieties — of his position, as thus to persist in inflicting his presence upon a loathing people, in the face of the advice of his brethren in Council; we do feel that his people would be justified in all legal efforts, by way of reprisals, to make his position uncomfortable among them — until he should be driven to cut the knot by his reluctant resignation. We thank God, however, for the belief that there cannot be one Congregational minister in ten thousand, who, under any circumstances of sanity, could be brought to allow himself to be thus "an astonishment, a proverb, and a byword" on the earth.

One word in reference to that 'result' of Council which dismisses a Congregational Pastor — as in nearly all cases he is dismissed — by the mutual reference of the question of duty for him, and for his people,

---

[1] In the case of Sheldon *v.* Easton, before cited, the court decided that the plaintiff was entitled to his salary though locked out of the meeting-house, because he had "*at all times been ready to perform all duties to them,*" etc. So the court held, in Thompson *v.* Rehoboth, (5 Pick 470.) that Mr. Thompson was "a minister *de facto*, as well as *de jure*, until lawfully dismissed, and might lawfully claim his salary, on the ground of service, *notwithstanding the meeting-house was shut against him.*" See also Whitney *v.* Brookhouse, 5 Conn 405.

to the representatives of the neighboring Churches. Such a 'result' should contain — always supposing just ground for it in the facts — such an expression of respect for, and confidence in, the Christian character and ministerial qualifications of the retiring Pastor, as may be his credentials to any future field of labor, and the warrant for the action of any Council that may be called to instal him elsewhere.[1]

It is sadly necessary to refer here, also, to the procedure proper by a Church in the possible case of gross heresy, or immorality, on the part of its Pastor. By virtue of his Church-membership with them — or, if not that, by virtue of his Pastorship over them — the unworthy Pastor of a Congregational Church is amenable to its discipline;[2] and it has the inherent right to proceed to his trial and excommunication, as if he were a private member. But because the fellowship of the churches was involved in his settlement, and because of the greater conclusiveness before the general public, of the verdict of an impartial Council over that of a single Church — itself deeply interested; this should always be done with the advice of Council.[3]

The proper course to be pursued, in the melancholy case supposed, would, then, be this: (1) all the preparatory steps should be taken as in the case of a private member, and the case be brought to a

---

[1] The following may be regarded as a suitable common form for such a clause in this 'result:' —

In coming to this result the Council are able to declare, with great satisfaction, that they have found nothing in their investigation of the causes which have led to this dismission, to impair their confidence in the essential integrity of the Christian, or ministerial, character of the retiring Pastor; whom, accordingly, they hereby commend to the confidence of the churches as — in their judgment — an honest, faithful, and useful minister of the Lord Jesus Christ; who carries with him their tender sympathies, and earnest prayers for his future prosperity in the work of the Lord, wherever Providence may assign his labors.

[2] " In case an elder offend incorrigibly, the matter so requiring, as the Church had power to call him to office, so they have power according to order (the Council of other churches, where it may be had, directing thereto) to remove him from his office," etc., etc. — *Cambridge Platform*, chap. x. 6.

See also, Cotton Mather's *Ratio*, Art. ix, sec. 2, p. 162; Sam. Mather's *Apology*, pp. 80-85; Cotton's *Keys*, pp. 81-43; Chauncy's *Divine Institution*, etc., chap. xii. sec. 8; *Hutchinson*, vol. i p. 432; Hooker's *Survey*, Part iii. p. 8; Davenport's *Power*, etc., p. 136; Wise's *Churches' Quarrel*, etc., p. 118; Punchard, p. 209.

[3] The forms of Letter Missive given on p. 200, might be used, without change, for calling such a Council.

judgment before the Church; (2) the Church, instead of passing the vote of excommunication, should vote that they are satisfied of the truth of the charges, but, in view of the importance and solemnity of the subject, will take the advice of sister churches before proceeding further; (3) they should then invite their Pastor to join them in a Council to advise in the premises, and, if he refuse, call one without his concurrence; (4) this Council hears the case, and if satisfied of the Pastor's guilt, and he remain obdurate, or the circumstances of the case are so aggravated that, even if he be now penitent, it is unsuitable for him to retain his official relation, they advise the Church to depose him from his ministry over them — perhaps to excommunicate him from its fellowship; (5) the Church, if they see fit, follow this advice of Council.

This we understand to be the truly Scriptural and Congregational way, though most Consociated Churches have a different practice.[1]

Section 5. *Church and Parish.*

There are three methods under which the ordinary work of an ecclesiastical organization in any given locality may be performed, its offices be sustained, and its labors upon the world around be managed. The Church, in its pure simple New Testament sense, may do the whole; or the Church acting, for all purposes of civil relation, as an Ecclesiastical Society, or Parish, may do the whole; or the Church and a distinct organization called an Ecclesiastical Society, or Parish, may act together, on terms mutually agreed upon. Which of these methods may be best in any specific case, must be determinable, in part, by the law of the State in which the work is to be done.

(1.) *The Church, simply and alone.* This is the New Testament plan; so far as it hints any plan at all. And there is no legal hindrance[2] of which we are aware in any State, which would neces-

---

[1] See Mitchell's *Guide*, pp. 235, 236. Also, *Punchard*, p. 316. See also p. 221.

[2] Churches — as such — are generally recognized as bodies corporate; either by legislative enactment, or by common law, and as such, it is usually held that they may hold property — independently of any Parish — for the purposes for which they are formed. This was the doctrine in Massachusetts until, in the Unitarian controversy, it became important for the Unitarian interests to have a different decision, and then, (as we believe, in the face of the precedents of the past, and of the justice of the case,) Chief Justice Parker decided that " the only circum-

sarily forbid any Church that pleases to do so, from assuming the entire charge of its temporalities, building and owning its own house of worship, pledging and raising all monies needed for the stated support of public worship, and doing all, that, in any case, is done by both Church and Society.[1] In the West, particularly, it is believed that this plan has been extensively tried, and is held to be safe, expedient, and successful.[2] In New England there are few instances of its adoption, as the mixed Parish system here inherited from the past prevails, and the State laws are so adapted to that method, as to work more kindly with it than with any other. Where a Church — in any State — desires to undertake the whole work, without the co-operation of any Parish, it should, by all means, consult some able lawyer familiar with the State law, and govern itself, in the minutiæ of its arrangements, by his advice. No general directions can be given which it would be entirely safe to follow, without special regard to local statutes, which may change in any year.

(2.) *The Church — for all secular purposes — acting as a Parish.* This would involve the existence of a legally formed "Society," or Parish, whose constitution should identify its membership with that of the Church. The result would be, that the same individuals would constitute both the Church and Society, and, when acting in one form, and under one set of By-laws, would be the Church, and, when

---

stance which gives a Church any legal character, is its connection with some regularly constituted Society" [See *Dedham case, Mass. Reports*, Vol. xvi. p. 505, etc.] This decision has never been acquiesced in by Massachusetts Congregationalists, and never will be; and it is hardly too much to say that there can be little doubt of its being overruled whenever any new case shall bring the matter before the bench.

On the general subject, consult "*Legal rights of Churches and Parishes,*" in the appendix to Upham's *Ratio. Disciplinæ*, p. 317; Mass. Reports, Burr *v.* Sandwich, and Baker *v.* Fales; and Dr. Pond's MSS. "*Rights of Congregational Churches in their connection with Parishes,*" in the custody of the Congregational Library Association. Especially read the argument of Hon. Lewis Strong, in the Brookfield case, *Pickering*, vol. x. p. 172, etc.

[1] We presume such a course must involve an assumption on the part of *the Church* of the entire pecuniary responsibility (without reliance upon any systematic aid from non-church-members) and — in some of the States — a relinquishment, on the part of both Church and Pastor, of some legal safeguards; to the end of a more entire dependence upon the Christian honor of all parties.

[2] "There are, at this moment, hundreds of Congregational churches in different parts of our land, which have no connection with incorporate parishes, or religious societies, and never had any. Some of these churches are in the cities and in the older States, others are in the newly settled parts of our country. They own their meeting-houses; they settle and support their ministers; they exist and they flourish without the help or the hindrance of connected Parishes." Dr. Pond's "*Rights of Cong. Churches,*" etc., *cited above*. See also, an article by Rev. H. M. Storrs, [in the *Cong. Quar.*, for 1800, (vol. ii.) pp. 329-336], on "Church and Society." See also the [Kansas] *Congregational Record*, for Oct., 1859, pp. 65-68.

acting in another form, and under another set of By-laws, would be the Parish. The only object of such an *opus operatum* would be to bring the proper secular work of a Parish technically under some State law, while still retaining it exclusively in the hands of the membership of the Church.

(3.) *Church and Parish.* This is the Massachusetts method, and grew out of the peculiar history of its religious affairs. Originally, none but church-members were citizens,[1] so that the town-meetings

---

[1] "To the end the body of the comons may be pserued of honest & good men, it was likewise ordered and agreed that for time to come noe man shalbe admitted to the freedome of this body polliticke, but such as are members of some of the churches within the lymitts of the same." — (May 18, 1631,) *Records of the Colony of Mass. Bay*, vol. 1. p. 87.

The Connecticut Colony passed a similar law, May 19, 1643. See Felt. *Ecclesiastical History of New England*, vol. 1. p. 517.

This fundamental principle explains the law passed at *Newe-Towne* [Cambridge], March 3, 1635–36, as follows: —

"Forasmuch as it hath bene found by sad experience, that much trouble and disturbance hath happened both to the church & civill state by the officers & members of some churches, wch have bene gathered within the limits of this jurisdiccon in an vndue manner & not with such publique approbacon as were meete, it is therefore ordered that all psons are to take notice that this Court doeth not, nor will hereafter, approue of any such companyes of men as shall henceforthe ioyne in any pretended way of church fellowshipp, without they shall first acquainte the magistrates, & the elders of the greatr pte of the churches in this jurisdiccon, with their intencons, & have their approbacon herein. And ffurther, it is ordered, that noe pson, being a member of any churche which shall hereafter be gathered without the approbacon of the magistrates & the greater pte of the said churches, shall be admitted to the ffreedome of this comonwealthe."—*Records of Col. of Mass. Bay*, vol. i. p. 168.

"Whereas the way of God hath always beene to gather his churches out of the world, now the world, or civill state, must be raised out of the churches."—John Winthrop. *Reply to Vane's Answer, etc.*

"None are so fit to be trusted with the liberties of the commonwealth as church-members; for the liberties of the freemen of this commonwealth are such as require men of faithful integrity to God and the State, to preserve the same."—John Cotton. *Answer to Lord Say and Seal, etc.* Hutchinson, vol. i. p. 436.

"Viewed from whatever point of observation, the civil power during those early years was only a convenient, or perhaps we should call it a necessary, arrangement whereby a company of intelligent and pious people grouped into a number of affiliated churches, were working out a great religious problem."—Clark's *Congregational Churches in Mass.*, p. 68.

"The English *Magna Charta* restricted the right of suffrage in the choice of their own representatives in the Commons to *freeholders*. Puritanism restricted the right of suffrage to *Christians*. It tried to evolve a State out of a Church. There have been many more fanciful, many less inspiring aims than this, proposed in the great schemes of men."—*North American Review*, vol. lxxxiv. p. 453.

"The conception, if a delusive and impracticable, was a noble one. Nothing better can be imagined for the welfare of a country than that it shall be ruled on Christian principles; in other words that its rulers shall be Christian men — men of disinterestedness and integrity of the choicest quality that the world knows, — men whose fear of God exalts them above every other fear, and whose controlling love of God and of man, consecrates them to the most generous aims. The conclusive objection to the scheme is one which experience had not yet revealed, for the experiment was now first made."—Palfrey. *Hist. New England*, vol. i. p. 345.

were just church-meetings in another form, and the "General Court" but a delegated mass meeting of the churches. Then the churches not only chose their own ministers, but contracted with and supported them, and built and owned their meeting-houses and parsonages; assessing and collecting money for the same, not merely of church-members, but of others. A few years later, the towns were expressly authorized to assess and collect church dues like other taxes.[1] When, after 1665, other than church-members were admitted to citizenship,[2] the towns still continued to act as Parishes for the support of the minister, while the Church had the sole voice in his selection; until the "Parish controversy" arose, which, after being carried through 1692 – 5, resulted in arranging a concurrent action between the town as a Parish, and the Church, in such elections.[3] Subsequently — in 1833 — after long effort on the part of those who felt aggrieved by the law as it stood, an act was passed severing all connection between Church and State, and introducing the voluntary system. The result of this was to organize the present Parish system, in place of the old, by which the body of male worshippers — under such restrictions as may be agreed upon, (as pew-holders, or as subjects of election by vote, or in some other way) — becomes thus associated to carry forward the secular affairs of the enterprise, in a way of amicable co-operation with the Church.

This general plan, having thus a basis in our history, and existing laws, still remains the usual New England method; having some obvious advantages and disadvantages,[4] but likely — in virtue of pre-

---

"The Church *instructed* the town, and the town *provided for* the Church."—Newman's *Rehoboth in the Past*, p 16.

[1] The usual conditions on which early grants of townships were made, were that a sufficient quantity of land be reserved for the use of a gospel ministry, and of a school.—See Washburn's *History of Leicester, Mass.*, p. 9.

Johnson in his *Wonderworking Providence* (A. D. 1654), says that "it being as unnatural for a right New England man to live without an able ministry, as for a smith to work his iron without a fire," therefore, the people delayed "seating themselves" in a town estate, until they "came to hopes of a competent number of people as might be able to maintain a minister." (p. 177.)

A "meeting-house place" was usually nearly the central lot upon the ground-plan of the town, and among the first town votes involving expenditure were usually those for the erection of a meeting house, and the support of a pastor.

[2] See *Records of the Colony of Mass. Bay*, vol. iv. part ii. pp. 117, 118.

[3] See *Christian Examiner*, 1830, p. 3.

[4] The general ill result of the old town parish system is well stated by Rev. Jacob Scales of Plainfield, N. H., who says, after describing the fortunes of the Church in Henniker, N. H.,

cedent, if nothing more — to hold its own for the present here. Several particulars may be usefully noted, for the benefit of those who desire to know the methods usually pursued under it.

(*a.*) *Organization of a Parish.* State law must always be consulted, to avoid any fatal informality. Some specific form of public notice is required. In Massachusetts, Articles of Association should be signed, and public notice given and filed with the town, or city clerk, and County Register, in which some person is authorized to call the first meeting of the Corporators.[1] The first meeting must be held in rigid conformity to this notice. In New York, trustees — from three to nine — chosen in a specified manner, hold the Parish property; in their corporate name can sue and be sued; have power to build, repair, and alter, the meeting-house (and parsonage); may make rules for managing the temporal affairs of the Society; may dispose of its income at their judgment, and regulate the prices and order the renting, of the pews — but have not power to fix the amount of the Pastor's salary, which is determinable by a majority of legal voters at a meeting called for that purpose.[2]

(*b.*) *By-laws of a Parish, etc.* The first work of such a Parish after organization would be the adoption of some appropriate code of

---

"A voluntary society, united in the bonds of love to the truth, is the main pillar of Congregationalism. The old bonds formed by town lines, pressed together by an equal regard to the welfare of the inhabitants of every class, and of every age, may be firm and strong for some uses. But though they may secure a convenient attention to many temporal things, they uniformly fail in regard to those which relate to spiritual and everlasting interests."—MSS. *History of Cong. in Henniker, N. H.*, in custody of Cong. Library Association, (p. 23.)

On the general subject, consult "Rights of Churches *v.* Parishes," *Spirit of the Pilgrims*, vol. i. pp. 57-74, 113-140; "Difficulties in Parishes," [by Rev. Dr. Walker] *Christian Examiner*, vol. ix. pp. 1-20; "Life and Times of Rev. Isaac Backus," pp. 158-264.

[1] The following are "Articles of Association" actually used for this purpose in a recent case.

The undersigned, all of ———, *in the County of* ———, *in the Commonwealth of* ———, *do hereby associate ourselves together, under the name of the* "——— *Congregational Society," as a Parish, or religious society, at said* ———; *and the purposes for which this corporation is established are the support of the public worship of God, and the promotion of Christian knowledge, and charity, according to the general usages of the Congregational Churches, and Parishes, of Massachusetts.*

Mr. ——— ———, *is authorized to call the first meeting of the corporation.*
(*Date.*)   Signed. ——— ———,
                    ——— ———,
                    ——— ———, etc., etc.

[2] See *Digest of New York Ecclesiastical Laws*, published with the *Manual* of the Plymouth Church, Brooklyn, N. Y.. pp. 27-29.

By-laws, to regulate its future action;[1] after which it would proceed to the election of the officers which those By-laws require, in the

---

[1] The following are By-laws adopted for the government of one of the more recently formed Societies in Massachusetts, and are believed suitably to cover all points needed to be met in such a code.

BY-LAWS OF THE ——— CONGREGATIONAL SOCIETY.

I.

This Society shall consist of the persons who signed the call for its organization; of those who, by special ballot, may become associated with them, until the erection of a meeting-house; and of those who shall hereafter become owners of pews in the meeting-house.

II.

The following officers and standing committees shall be chosen annually, by ballot: —
1. OFFICERS.—First, a Clerk, who shall be sworn to keep the records of the Society, notify its regular meetings, and preside at all meetings, till a moderator be chosen.
Second, a Treasurer, who shall issue the bills of rent or taxes on pews, take charge of all moneys belonging to the Society, disburse the same only under the direction of the Prudential Committee, and report to the Society at the annual meeting.
Third, an Auditor, who shall examine the Treasurer's accounts.
2. STANDING COMMITTEES. — First, a Prudential Committee, consisting of five persons, to take charge of the meeting-house owned or occupied by the Society; to make such repairs as, from time to time, may be necessary; to provide for warming and lighting the house and chapel; to appoint the Sexton, fix his salary, perquisites, and duties; and generally to attend to the concerns of the Society, with authority to expend such sums of money as are not specially appropriated by the Society.
Second, a Committee, consisting of the Treasurer and two other persons, to sell and let pews and sittings.
Third, a Committee, consisting of two persons, to superintend the music, on the part of the Society, to act jointly with a Committee of three persons, to be chosen for this purpose, on the part of the Church; said Committee to expend only such sums of money as may be appropriated for the purpose by the Prudential Committee.

III.

The annual meeting for the choice of officers and standing committees shall be held in the month of ———.

IV.

Every member of the Society shall be entitled to one vote; but no person, and no pew, shall be entitled to more than one vote, on any occasion.

V.

The taxes on pews shall be collected quarterly in the months of ———, ———, ———, and ———, of each year.

VI.

The deeds of pews shall be given on such terms as the Society shall direct, and shall be signed by the Treasurer, countersigned by the Clerk, and sealed with the corporate seal of the Society, which the Treasurer is authorized to affix.

VII.

The Pastor and Deacons of the ——— Church, for the time being, shall grant the use of the meeting-house as they may judge expedient, for all religious meetings properly so called; but for all other meetings and purposes, the right to grant the use of it shall rest with the Prudential Committee.

VIII.

The Clerk shall, on application made to him, in writing, by any five legal voters in the Society, warn a special meeting thereof, by causing notice of the time and place of such meeting to be given from the pulpit on the Sabbath, or by sending written or printed notices of the

manner which they fix, and in all things shape its future course by them.

(c.) *Rules for joint action of the Church and Parish.* These will be next in order of adoption after the Parish is fully organized. They should be brief, and simple, yet sufficient to prevent any possible misunderstanding or collision between the two bodies.[1]

The question sometimes arises as to the *status* of a Pastor concerning whom a difference of opinion exists between the Church and the Parish, to that degree that the Parish vote to terminate his relation, while the Church have taken no action in regard to it; such a contingency being usually unprovided for in any rules of joint action.

---

same to each pew-proprietor; notice, in one of these ways, to be given at least seven days before the meeting.. The notice of a special meeting shall, in all cases, specify the particular business for which the meeting is called.

IX.

No alteration shall be made in these By-laws, unless the same shall be agreed to by *two thirds* of the members of the Society present, at a special meeting regularly notified for that purpose.

[1] The following is a form in use in a recently formed Massachusetts Parish:

RULES FOR JOINT ACTION OF THE ——— CHURCH AND SOCIETY.

I.

Whenever the ——— Church and Society shall be destitute of a settled Pastor, and a new one is to be obtained, a joint Committee of the Church and Society, consisting of seven persons, of whom four shall be chosen by the Church and three by the Society, shall provide a supply for the Pulpit, and take all necessary measures to that end. The Church shall have the right, in all cases, to select a Pastor (or Colleague Pastor, when it may be deemed expedient by the Church and Society to settle a Colleague Pastor), to be proposed to the Society for its concurrence. If it shall concur in said selection with the Church, a call shall be given by the Church and Society jointly, to the person selected; but if the Society do not concur in the selection, the Church shall select again, and so again, from time to time, until the Church and Society shall agree in a choice, and when so agreed, a call shall be given to the person so selected, by the Church and Society as stated above; that is, jointly.

II.

The amount of salary to be given to the Pastor shall be fixed by the Society.

III.

Temporary supply of the pulpit, during the absence or sickness of the Pastor, shall be provided by the Pastor and Deacons of the Church, and the bills of necessary expenses incurred for that purpose shall be submitted to the Prudential Committee of the Society; and, when approved by them, shall be paid by the Treasurer. By the word "Church" herein before used, is meant all male members of the Church in good and regular standing, of the age of twenty-one years and upwards.

IV.

A Committee to regulate the matter of singing and of Church music shall be appointed jointly by the Church and Society (annually), three persons by the former, and two by the latter.

V.

No alteration shall be made in these rules, on the part of either Church or Society, unless the same shall be agreed to by two thirds of the members of each, present at special meetings, regularly notified for that purpose.

Several cases have arisen under the uncongregational and inexpedient "three" or "six months notice system,"[1] where the Parish have given the "notice," without immediate concurrent action on the part of the Church.

It is obvious, to a moment's thought, that the power of the Parish thus to terminate the contract, must depend entirely on the terms of settlement. If the Pastor was settled in the old, and ordinary manner, such a vote of theirs is not worth the paper on which it is written.[2] If he was settled on the "three" or "six months notice" plan, their vote — if the terms of the notice are properly complied with — *does* ultimate his legal relation to them, and terminate his claim for salary; and must almost inevitably draw after it, sooner or later, such action on the part of the Pastor and the Church, as shall complete the severance.[3]

Section 6. *Councils.*

An Ecclesiastical Council is a meeting of churches by their delegates, assembled in response to the invitation of a Church — or of an

---

[1] See p. 144.   [2] See pp. 203, 204.

[3] In the year 1829, Rev S. Nott, Jr., was settled over the Congregational Church in Wareham, Mass., the Parish voting that "the conditions under which the Parish agree to settle Mr. Nott, are that Mr. Nott shall have the liberty of dissolving the contract by giving the Parish six month's notice, and the Parish reserve the liberty of dissolving the contract by giving Mr. Nott six month's notice." On the 7th March, 1842, the Parish, regularly convened, voted to give Mr. Nott, "notice that his connection with said Parish be dissolved at the end of six months from this date."

Concerning this, Messrs. Zechariah Eddy and Timothy G. Coffin — then the two ablest lawyers of Southern Massachusetts (the former a hearty, devout, and eminent Congregationalist) — said, in giving a legal opinion upon the matter, — "Thus *all legal civil relation* between them, was at an end. There was an ecclesiastical relation still remaining, which has indeed a very slight hold upon the Parish, being nothing but what the law of courtesy and Congregational usage provide for the benefit of a Pastor who leaves his people, in order that his ministerial and Christian character may not be thereby injuriously affected. . . . The *Parish* have no reason to wish for an Ecclesiastical Council, in a case like this, when the contract for settlement is dissolved in pursuance of their express agreement with him, and if *he* does waive, or suspend, his request for a Council, no law, human or divine, will allow a man to obtain an advantage from his own negligence or neglect. . . . . . . If he made an agreement which dispensed with the action of the Church, the Church may complain, but *he* is estopped, and his mouth is shut. . . . . . It has been said that an act of the Church, assenting to the vote of the Parish, was necessary. Not so, in respect to this civil, or legal, connection."— See "Legal Opinion." April 30, 1845, pp 189–192. *Sixteen Years Preaching and Procedure at Wareham, &c.* Boston, 1845.

See also the 2d Article in the result of the Manchester (Mass.) Council, Dec. 9, 1857, dismissing Rev Rufus Taylor — where it was held that his civil contract was terminated by his unconditional resignation to the Parish of April 22d previous, and their acceptance of the same on the 6th of May; while he remained the undismissed Pastor of the Church up to the Result of Council reached on the 16th Dec. 1857 — See *Congregationalist*, Jan. 1, 1858.

aggrieved individual member whom his Church has (apparently without sufficient reason) refused to join in such an invitation — where either light or peace is desired, to consider some matter of common concernment, and give advice thereon.* The fundamental idea of a Council is an outgrowth from that of the fellowship of the churches; and the necessity of Councils grows not out of any want of power in each Church to decide finally upon its own affairs, but from the desire of each so to order its doings as to satisfy, and secure the fraternal confidence and coöperation of, all. The following points, it is believed, cover all matters of practical inquiry concerning the calling and ordering of these bodies.

(1.) *Who may call a Council?* A *Church* must always be the party moving to call a Council;[2] with the two exceptions of the formation of a Church, when the individuals desiring to become the Church call it, and of an *Ex-parte* Council, where an aggrieved member expressly bases his call upon the fact that he has asked his Church to convoke a Mutual Council, and has met with what he conceives to be an unjust refusal to do so. The reason of this rule is the simple one that the Christian community cannot hold itself bound to interfere, in cases of private difficulty, with the proper business of a Church. Where two members disagree, it is the duty of their Church to reconcile them; and only when difficulties surmount the wisdom of a Church, so as to give it a claim upon the collective wisdom of its sister churches, can attention be rightly called toward them from without. If, then, at any time, any member, or members, feel that the advice of a Council is needed, they should ask their Church to call one together. In most cases where there is sufficient warrant for such a procedure, the Church will accede to their request. Should it, however, arbitrarily and unjustly refuse to do so, those aggrieved brethren have, then, the right to invite an *Ex-parte* Council — in form and manner as will subsequently appear.

(2.) *How a Council is called?* In the ordinary cases of calling ordaining, and dismissing Councils, it is usual for the Church to ap-

---

1 See page 3. Also, particularly, pp. 59-6.

2 "A party in a Church complaining of another party, cannot demand of the other to join in calling a Council; nor can the two together call one; but they can bring matters directly before their Church; and if that Church sees fit, *it* can call a Council to advise as to its internal difficulties. A Church must, in all cases, be a party concerned."—Rev. A. H. Quint. *Cong. Quar.*, vol. ii. p. 54.

point a Committee to select the churches to be invited, and the form of the letter of invitation. These are reported to the Church, and if adopted the letters are then signed by the Committee, and sent to the selected churches. In case of difficulty, it is usual for each party in difference to select one half of the churches [1] — sometimes both parties uniting upon one Church, whose pastor it is understood would be acceptable to all as moderator.[2]

In a case of difficulty where members feel aggrieved by Church action, and have tried, in vain, to persuade the Church to take action for a Mutual Council, those members may then proceed themselves to send out Letters Missive for an *Ex-parte Council;* stating the case briefly and fairly, and especially recounting their unavailing endeavor for a Mutual Council.

(3.) *Letters Missive.* These have the same relation to the action of the Council that the "warrant" has to that of a town-meeting. They furnish the authority on which the Council meets, define its membership, and limit its powers.[3] The Council, when assembled, has no power to invite any man to sit in consultation with it, who was not invited by the party calling the Council; no right to exclude the delegates of an invited Church; and no right to consider and offer advice upon any subject not fairly embraced in the terms of the Letter Missive.

---

[1] Sometimes, in instances of bitter feeling spreading over the adjacent community, it has been thought wise to secure impartiality by selecting churches mainly from a distance, who must necessarily be, in great part, strangers to the place, the persons, and the perplexity.

[2] In such a case the Council would be under no *obligation* to be governed by this fact in their selection of their moderator, yet — if no special objection were in the way — such a course would be both natural and expedient.

[3] For a suitable form of Letter Missive for the organization of a Church, see page 164; for one suitable to an Ordaining, or Installing Council, see page 171; for one proper for an ordinary Dismissing Council, see page 200; for an *Ex-parte* Council, see page 201.

The following would be a correct form for calling a Mutual Council in a case of Church difficulty not connected directly with the dismission of the Pastor, viz: —

The Congregational Church in —— *to the Congregational Church in* —— *sendeth greeting ·*

Dear Brethren:

Difficulties having arisen between the Pastor and some of the members of this Church [or *between various members of this Church*] [or *between the Church and A. B., a member feeling himself aggrieved and injured by Church action*] *for the adjustment of which we desire your Christian Council, this is to request your attendance, by your Pastor and a delegate, at* —— *on the* —— *of* —— *at* —— *o'clock in the* —— *to advise us on the following points, viz:*

[*here state every material question on which light is desired.*]

(4.) *Quorum.* The common sense rule is that a present majority of all having the right of membership, constitutes a quorum. Thus, if ten churches have been invited to send each a pastor and delegate, *eleven* members would constitute a quorum. If two of those churches have no pastors, and have not been invited to send delegates in their place; *ten* would constitute a quorum. It would be better to make a present majority of the *churches* sent to, the basis of a quorum, provided a return was also made to the old way of *voting by churches;* but until the latter is done, the former would not be just.

(5.) *Organization.* The simple question of organization is, "who bring full credentials in accordance with the terms of the Letters Missive?" This determined, the choice of moderator,[1] of scribe — and sometimes of assistant scribe — is next in order. Then prayer; then a call for the business in due form.

(6.) *Scope of business.* Every Council is necessarily limited to

---

and such other incidental matters as may inseparably belong to these main difficulties between us. *Wishing you grace, mercy, and peace, &c., &c., &c. Signatures, &c.*

The following would be a correct form for the calling of an Ex-parte Council, by an individual [or individuals,] feeling himself aggrieved by Church action for which he can obtain no redress, viz: —

To the Congregational Church in ———.
Dear Brethren:

The undersigned, feeling himself [*themselves*] *aggrieved and injured by recent action of the Congregational Church in* ——— *and having in a legal, usual, and proper manner, earnestly requested it to unite with him* [*them*] *in bringing the matter before a Mutual Council, and been — as it seems to him* [*them*] *— unreasonably refused; desire*[*s*] *to avail himself* [*themselves*] *of the privilege offered by Congregational usage to Church members thus oppressed, by laying his* [*their*] *grievances before an Ex-parte Council, in manner and form, as follows: — [Here insert the grievances desired to be laid before the Council.*]

In view of these facts, the undersigned beg[*s*] *to request of your sense of right, and your Christian sympathy and friendship, your participation, by Pastor and Delegate, in such an Ex-parte Council, called to meet at* ———, *on* ———, *at* ———, *o'clock, in the* ———.

Faithfully, your Brother [*brethren*] *in the Lord,*

[*Signature.*]

(*Date, &c.*)
The Churches invited to sit in Council are the following —[*name all.*]

A form for calling an *Ex-parte* Council with regard to the dismission of a minister who will not unite with his Church to call a mutual one, may be found on page 201.

[1] In Eastern Massachusetts, the Council is usually called to order by one of its oldest clerical members, who reads the Letter Missive and "takes the liberty" to nominate a moderator. In Western Massachusetts it is more usual — if we are rightly informed — to choose the moderator by ballot. This, we submit, is always the better way.

action upon the subjects directly stated in the Letter Missive calling it together. It has no right to go one step in any direction beyond that letter, because the party calling it has expressly asked its advice upon those points and none other, and because the churches have sent its members expressly to consult and advise with reference to those points and none other; and therefore it has been organized and has existence as a Council, for the purpose of consulting and advising upon those points and none other.[1]

(7.) *Method of business.* As there is no code special for Councils, they fall under the ordinary rules governing deliberative bodies. In examining witnesses they should ordinarily receive only such as would be received in a court of justice; as the courts may review their action. If one rule more than another commends itself to such bodies, it is that of the most absolute and scrupulous Christian impartiality. This, with Christian common sense, will carry any Council safely through the most trying experience.

(8.) *Result.* In coming to a result it is usual, after the testimony is all in, and those who called the Council have said all that they wish to say in elucidation of the matters at issue, for the Council to vote to "be by themselves." Privacy thus being secured for their deliberations, it is usual for the Moderator to request the Scribe to call the roll of the Council, giving each Pastor and delegate an opportunity to express, as briefly and clearly as possible, the opinion which he has formed, and the advice which he thinks ought to be given to the parties in interest. When all have spoken, and thus the general drift of the sentiment of the Council has become clear, it is usual for a Committee of three — where there are decidedly two opposing opinions in the Council, this Committee may wisely include one representative of each of these opinions, and one occupying middle ground — to be appointed to draw up a form of result which shall embody the judgment of the Council upon the subjects before them. That report when made, is freely discussed and amended until it is

---

[1] "For example: a Council is called for organizing a new Church, for the alleged reasons that great want of harmony exists in another in the same town; it is then perfectly competent for the Council to inquire as to the existence of the alleged dissensions, and whether they are such as to furnish good reasons for advising a new organization, and whether they are irremovable; but they have no right to proceed to an investigation into the merits or demerits of the dissensions, — because the parties are not before them, and if *they* were, the *case* is not." — Rev. A. H. Quint. "*Authority of Councils.*" Cong. Quar., vol. ii. p. 59.

brought into such a shape that it will secure the unanimous assent of the body, or that of its large majority, when it is formally adopted, authenticated by the signature of the Moderator and Scribe, and communicated to the parties.

The vote is usually taken by calling the roll of members, and determined by their majority. There would, however, be obvious advantages in a return to the method formerly practised, of a vote by churches; each Church giving one vote. In that case any inequality of attendance would be adjusted; sometimes to the great gain of the moral force of the result.

In form, such a "Result" should first contain a correct list of the churches represented, and of the Pastors and delegates comprising the Council; second, a condensed journal of its sittings and procedure; and third, the document containing the conclusion to which it comes.[1]

(9.) *The Force of the Result of a Council.* As all true Congregational Councils are called to give advice, and for this only, it necessarily follows that it is *advice*, purely, which they give.[2] Those who

---

[1] The following may suggest all that is needful as to the exact phraseology of such a "Result."

Pursuant to Letters Missive from the Congregational Church in ———, [*or, name the exact source of the letters*] *an Ecclesiastical Council convened at* ———, *on* ———, *for the purpose of* [*state the object as given in the Letters Missive.*] *The Council was composed of representatives of the churches as follows:* —

From the Congregational Church in ———, *Rev.* ——— ———, *Pastor.*
Bro. ——— ———, *Delegate.*

[*and so arranging the churches either in alphabetical order, or by their seniority of formation.*]

It was organized by the choice of Rev. ——— ———, *Moderator; Rev.* ——— ——— *Scribe,* [*and Rev.* ——— ———, *Assistant Scribe.*] *After Prayer by the Moderator, the parties calling the Council proceeded to lay before it the matters upon which its advice was desired.*

[*here insert briefly the journal of proceedings, sessions, adjournments, etc.,* — *shorn of all trivial matters* — *until the result is reached.*]

After the most patient, thorough, and prayerful examination which they have been able to give the matter submitted to them for action, the Council came [*unanimously*] *to the following Result.*

[*here give, in full, the document finally agreed upon as embodying the advice of Council.*]

Signed, (1.) *Moderator.* (2.) *Scribe.*
(*Date.*)

[2] See this more at large, pp. 64–5. See also, pp. 200–4. See also, S. Mather's *Apology*, p. 118; I. Mather's *Disquisition*, p. 28; John Norton's *Responsio*, pp. 112–119; Pres. Stiles' *Convention Sermon*, p. 46. See also *one* true statement in the famous Dedham "Statement." (1819), viz: "the power of Councils is merely advisory; nor can they *volunteer* that service

have called a Council are morally bound to accept, and act upon, its advice, in good faith, if it commend itself to their conscience as the will of God concerning them. The presumption must always be that the result of every fairly constituted and properly managed Council is binding upon the parties calling it, unless they can show good cause, in conscience, for neglecting it.

But there is, purely speaking, no *authority* in the result of any Council.[1]

By the decisions of the Massachusetts courts, the result of a Council in its legal aspects, may be stated in these four particulars.[2]

1. Such a result is of no force until accepted by the parties.[3]
2. If accepted by one party and not accepted by the other, it will

---

They cannot come till they are asked, nor extend their inquiries beyond the point submitted; and then their decision may be regarded or not, as shall seem best to the party asking." p. 55.
See also some very pungent reasoning on this subject (pp. 31-39), in "a Neighbor's" *Second Treatise on Church Government*, called out by the Bolton case, (1773), with this pertinent statement, (p. 39). "It is the churches' prerogative to judge, and Council's main province *to reflect light in order that churches may judge uprightly.*" See also the admirable reasoning of Gov. Thomas Fitch, in his *Explanation of Say-Brook Platform*, (published anonymously in 1765), *passim*, and specially this passage, (p. 24), " If we conceive of Councils as having *jurisdiction* [properly so termed], and consequently a judicial authority in *any* case, endless disputes will arise, nor will it be possible to reconcile our Ecclesiastical Constitution with itself: such a power in Councils is quite inconsistent with the rights and duties of particular churches, clearly and expressly asserted and maintained by these churches, &c. But if we view Councils as helps, counsellors, advisers, &c., affording light, assistance, &c. for the conviction, peace, and edification of the churches, and the like, our constitution will appear in a good light, consistent with itself, and agreeable both to the principles and genius of the Gospel of Christ."

[1] Sometimes all parties calling a Council enter, before its session, into an agreement to abide by its Result, whatever it may be — thus making it strictly a Board of Referees, rather than a Council. [See Bliss's *Rehoboth*, p. 209, and the *Manchester* (Mass.) *Council*, Dec. 1857.] In that case there will, necessarily, in virtue of the previous agreement, be a binding force in the Result, and the courts will enforce it, in all pecuniary details [see Stearns *v*. Bedford]; but, as a *Reference* and not as a *Council*. Nor is it clear that such agreement beforehand is any suggestion of real Congregationalism. [*Cong. Quarterly*, Jan. 1860, p. 63.] On this point, see *New England's Lamentations*, by Rev. John White, of Gloucester, who says [p. 165, Wise's *Quarrel*, etc.] " Some Councils have perswaded the Church and aggrieved to promise to acquiesce in the determination of the Council before they heard the case, *by which their consciences have been ensnared, and the Council turned into a solemn arbitration. This, therefore, is matter of just lamentation.*"

John Norton, in his *Responsio* [the first Latin work ever written in this country; as his *Orthodox Evangelist* was the first treatise of systematic Divinity ever composed here], takes strong ground as to the duty of a Church to accept the advice of Council, yet even he presupposes the danger of error in such a result, and its consequent invalidity. His reasoning is ingenious: " Errorem Synodi et Ecclesiarum non esse fundamentalem, *quia tum cessarent Ecclesiæ esse Ecclesia, et, consequenter, Synodus non esset legitima.*" p. 112.

[2] See *Congregational Quarterly*, vol. ii. pp. 60-64.

[3] " The result of a Council, of its own intrinsic validity, is never obligatory upon the parties." Stearns *v*. Bedford, 21 Pick. 114.

justify the party adopting it, in acts done in consequence, but will not bind the party rejecting it.¹

3. Such a result is conclusive as to facts — adjudged to be facts by the Council.²

4. The court may, however, revise (all but the facts) the *modus operandi;* to assure itself that all processes have been fair and regular.³

So that the legal aspect of the result of a Council is, in short, this: — if "a Council has been properly called, if the subject-matter is such as should come before a Council, if its members are impartial, if its investigations are fair, if its decision is clear, — then its result, while it must be adopted before it is of any authority, will justify either party conforming thereto."⁴

(10.) *Dissolution.* When a Council has concluded its preliminary sessions, and reached its Result, its function is at an end, and the proper vote to be passed, is that "it be dissolved." It has no longer any legal existence, and can never be recalled.⁵ It has no right to adjourn for a definite period, or "subject to the call of the moderator;" in the view of waiting to see whether the parties it has advised will follow its advice; and with the intention of another session, and another judgment, if they do not follow it. It was not invited to oversee the execution of its advice, but merely to give it, and when once given, it is an impertinence for it to assume to become a tribunal for its enforcement. Such an attempt to assume authority over the churches is a Presbyterian heresy, which Congregationalists should be vigilant to eschew.⁶

---

¹ See page 202, with the legal references there given. See, also, Avery v. Tyringham, 3 Mass. 160.

² Stearns v. Bedford, and Burr v. Sandwich.

³ "The court always look behind the adjudication, and before the result can be received as evidence, or allowed to have any validity, they will examine the proceedings, to ascertain whether there was a suitable case for the convocation of an Ecclesiastical Council; whether the members were properly selected; whether they proceeded impartially in their investigations; whether their adjudication was so formally made that it might be seen that they acted with due regard to the rights of the parties, and that they founded their decision upon grounds which will sustain it." Thompson v. Rehoboth, 7 Pickering.

⁴ *Congregational Quarterly,* vol. ii. p. 62.

⁵ See this point argued in the Result of the famous *Reading* Council, June 15, 1847, p. 14.

⁶ In Felt's *Annals of Salem,* vol. ii. pp. 593-9, is an account of an attempt by a "grand Council," (A. D. 1734-45), to excommunicate Rev. Mr. Fiske and his Church: the Council assembling and reassembling, and appealing to the churches of the Commonwealth to sustain them. Mr. Cummings says, (*Dict.* p. 74,) "Mr. Fiske, the minister, and a majority of his

In very rare instances, we are aware, circumstances may arise which may make it desirable for the same churches to be again convened in Council upon the same subject. But this can only be done by a new Letter Missive,[1] and a course of procedure, in all respects, *de novo.*[2]

SECTION 7. *Consociation.*

A Consociation — in the sense in which the word is now com-

Church, did not approve of this 'third way of communion,' disregarded the sentence, and outlived the storm." The pamphlets published on this controversy, fill a volume, and may be consulted in the *Salem Athenæum.*

[1] "Councils expire when they have given the advice for which they were called."—Cumming's *Cong. Dict.*, p. 128.

"To reassemble, therefore, by their own authority, and without the originating power of a new Letter Missive, and to prosecute inquiries anew in relation to the Church and people, or to do any thing else as a Council, would be considered at variance with Congregational principles."—Upham. *Ratio Disciplinæ*, p. 188.

See the Reading case (1847), for illustration of the bad policy of the reassembling of a Council, where [Protest, p. 75, Appendix to Result], it is said of such a reassembling [April 7, 1847, of a Council which met March 4, 1846], "we deem it an entire perversion of Congregational principles for a Council to retain a permanent authority to inspect the conduct of any Church, or any member of a Church."

[2] Some of the most important published results of Councils of recent days, are that at Salem, Mass., 1849, (Howard Street Church), in which, and in the Review of it [attributed to Rev. S. M. Worcester, D. D.] is thoroughly discussed the question whether a Congregational Church can disband itself by the force of majority vote; that at Reading, Mass., (South Church), 1847, above referred to, in which the claim of a Pastor to negative Church acts is discussed; those at the same place in 1832 and 1834, in which opinion is given on the question of making Infant Baptism imperative upon Congregational Church members; that at Danvers, Mass., 1852, where the "three month's notice" plan is referred to; that at New York (Church of the Puritans), 1859, where arbitrary and summary exclusion from the Church is advised to be null.

For good examples of the Councils that were held in the days of the Unitarian apostacy — and exhibiting the trickiness and dishonesty sometimes practised by the opposers of the Trinity, see the Fitchburg, Mass. case (1801), [Life of Dr. S. Worcester, vol. i. pp 263–356]; the Dorchester case (1811-12), [reviewed in the *Panoplist*, 1814, pp. 256-307]; the Princeton case (1817), [reviewed in the *Panoplist*, 1817, pp. 264-273]; the Sandwich case (1817), [result published in the *Panoplist*, 1817, pp. 274-279]; the Dedham case (1818), [reviewed by Judge Stebbins, in the *Spirit of the Pilgrims*, 1829, pp. 329-331]; the Groton case (1826), [reviewed in the *Spirit of the Pilgrims*, 1829, pp. 370-403]; and the Cambridge case (1827-29), [reviewed in the *Spirit of the Pilgrims*, 1829, pp. 559-571].

For fine specimens of the older method of Councils in New England called to advise in reference to matters of doctrine in the alleged heresy of ministers, see *Report of a Conference held at Westford*, [Mass.], Dec. 4, 1781, in *Congregational Quarterly*, 1861, pp. 268-278, and *Result of a Council of Churches at Grafton*, Mass., Oct. 2, 1744, in the collections of the Congregational Library Association. It is noticeable in these old results, that the names of the Pastors and Delegates are not given (with the exception of the Moderator, and Scribe); the stress then being laid upon the assumed presence of the *churches*, and not on the personal dignity, or sagacity, of the *individuals* composing the Council.

In the rich collections of the Massachusetts Historical Society, and of the Salem Athenæum, may be found many curious documents illustrating the ancient ways in these particulars.

monly used[1] — is a Standing Council,[2] which some Congregational churches, and especially those of Connecticut, have substituted for the common Method of Councils.[3] Strictly it is, with

---

[1] Our fathers talked about the "Consociation of Churches," when they only meant by it their *fellowship*. Peter Thacher and John Webb, in their "*Brief Declaration*," [Boston, 1720], say, (p. 6), "as to the *Consociation of Churches*, we find our Synods speaking very honorably of it, and with great Light and Force urging the strict Union and holy Communion of all particular Churches one with another, in all the proper acts of that communion; such as Mutual Direction, Prayer, Admonition, &c." They then go on (pp. 7, 8) to show that this involves no *control* over the churches, but simply good fellowship between them.

[2] "The Consociation is a Standing Council, both judicial and advisory, competent to ordain, dismiss, and discipline Pastors; to unite, organize, and discipline churches; to revise the decisions of the constituent Churches, and to consult their general welfare." *Rule IV.* of Litchfield North Consociation, Conn. *Historical Sketch*, p. 82.

[3] It is usual to claim Hooker as the originator of this plan of judicature. Dr. Hawes says, [*Contributions to the Ecclesiastical History of Connecticut*, p. 87], "he was the father of the system of Consociation. It was a favorite and oft repeated remark of his — 'we must have the Consociation of the Churches, or we are ruined.'" But Hooker appears to have used the term in its ancient and loose, rather than its modern and technical sense, as he repeatedly repudiates the idea of any control over the churches from without. He says, [*Survey*, Part iv. p. 19], "the truth is, a particular Congregation is the highest tribunal, unto which the grieved party may appeal. . . . If difficulties arise in the proceeding, the council of other churches should be sought to clear the truth; but *the power of censure rests still in the Congregation, where Christ placed it*." Again he says, [p. 51], "If Synods and such meetings be attended only in way of consultation, *as having no other power, nor meeting for any other end;* then, as they are lawful, so the root of them lies in a common principle, &c."

About 1656-1662, a movement was made in both Connecticut and Massachusetts toward Consociation. [See Trumbull's *Connecticut*, vol. 1. ch. xiii.; *New Haven Colonial Records*, vol. ii. pp. 196-7, and *Records of Massachusetts Colony*, vol. iv. part 2, pp. 88, 60, 62.] The Connecticut Synod failed of a majority for the plan, John Davenport vigorously opposing it there, and afterward in Boston. The Boston Synod recommended it; first ameliorating it of juridical power. But the matter then died away for the time in both Colonies. About the beginning of the 18th Century [see Pres. Stiles' *Convention Sermon*, pp. 68, 69; *Trumbull*, vol. 1 pp. 478-488, Wise's *Quarrel*, *passim*; Cotton Mather's *Ratio*, pp. 182-184, and *Magnalia*, 5th Book, *Congregational Quarterly*, vol. 1. p. 49], under the leadership of Pierpont in Connecticut, and of Cotton Mather in Massachusetts, the effort was renewed. The Saybrook Synod adopted their famous "Platform" (1708); and the "Boston Association" (1705) proposed a system of Consociation. Butler's *History of Groton*, Mass. [p. 169], contains the record of a proposition to the Church in Groton to unite in a Consociation, which had been proposed by an Association, met at Marlborough, July 16, 1707; which proposition was adopted, *nem. con.* by the Groton Church, July 21, 1707 But I have met with no further record of that movement. In Massachusetts, the general plan was violently assailed by John Wise, and others, and found little favor. There are frequent traces of an impulse in this direction, however, in after years In 1782, William Homes, of Chilmark, published his "*Proposals of some things to be done in our administering Ecclesiastical Government, whereby it may more effectually reach its end in some respects,*" etc., in which he advocates a Consociation under the name of *an Ecclesiastical Council or Presbytery*, (pp. 6-30). His *Proposals* came to a second edition some fifty years after, [*Newburyport*, 1774, pp. 43], but never came to any thing else. The Records of the *Mendon Association* show that a proposition was entertained and digested in 1756, by its members, for a Consociation; and that they proposed it to their churches. Mention is again made of the subject in the records of 1757, but then it drops into oblivion, and there is no trace of any movement of the churches in response. [*Hist. Mendon Association*, pp. 47-52.] In 1774, Dr. Whitaker, of the Taberna-

those who accept the plan, the highest Ecclesiastical judicature.[1]

A Consociation is usually composed of the Pastor and one Messenger from each of the Congregational churches of a County, or of half

---

cle Church in Salem, "confuted" John Wise (now in his grave forty-nine years) in a vigorous attempt [*A confutation of two Tracts, entitled 'A Vindication of the New England Churches,' and ' The Churches Quarrel Espoused,' written by the Rev. John Wise, &c.* Boston: Isaiah Thomas. 1774. pp. 98] to commend Presbyterianism to Massachusetts; but the pernicious old Puritan would n't stay confuted, and the churches remained obstinately deaf to the voice of the charmer. In 1814, the plan was again urged in the General Association of Massachusetts, in the form of appointing a Committee to examine an "Ancient Document," found among Cotton Mather's papers, on the question "what further steps are to be taken, that Councils may have due constitution and efficacy." The Committee (of Drs. Morse, Austin, Woods, Worcester, and Lyman, and Rev. Messrs. Hale and Cooley), reported, in 1815, proposing the establishment of Consociations. The matter was laid over to the next session, and then resulted in a vote that they "had no objection to" the organization of Consociations, wherever ministers and churches were so inclined. But so decided was now the repugnance of the Massachusetts churches to the system, that even this qualified endorsement led to the withdrawal of several of the District Associations from the State Body, and the whole project was again abandoned. [See *Panoplist,* 1814, pp. 320-8; 1815, pp. 359-73; and 1816, p. 369.] A committee, consisting of Rev. Drs. Woods, Humphrey, Snell, Shepard, Cooley, and Storrs, and Rev. Parsons Cooke, was appointed at a public meeting in Boston, May 29, 1844, to "take into consideration what measures are necessary for the reaffirmation and maintenance of the principles and spirit of Congregationalism." Their report was made in 1846, "to the Congregational Ministers and Churches in Massachusetts." Dr. Clark says [*Cong. Churches of Mass.*, p. 283.] "though the whole subject of Church-Government was laid open by the committee, their leading object evidently was to magnify the office-work of Councils, and to strengthen the authority of their decisions." This new attempt, however, fell still-born from the press which printed the report, and now, after the lapse of sixteen years, the churches hardly remember that such a movement ever took place.

In Connecticut, the Saybrook "Articles" — which were practically a compromise between the Presbyterian and Congregational interests [Bacon's *Historical Discourses,* p. 191], and are obviously susceptible of a strict construction, elevating the Consociation into a virtual Presbytery; and of a looser construction, making it merely a stated Council — were, gradually, and with some jealousy, adopted by the churches; the New Haven Association (where Davenport's influence was still felt), refusing to accept the Platform, till they had put upon record their understanding of it. Among the majority of the churches of the State, the strict, or Presbyterian, construction of the Articles prevailed for many years, and was used to prevent the formation of "New Light" churches in the days of Whitfield. [*Cont. Eccl. Hist. Conn.*, p. 122.] After the first half century, or more, the Congregational construction of its articles became more general, and so remains.

[1] "When any case is orderly brought before any council of the churches [i. e., any Consociation], it shall there be heard and determined, which (unless orderly removed from thence), shall be a final issue; and all parties therein concerned shall sit down and be determined thereby."— Art. V., *Saybrook Platform. Trumbull,* vol. i. p. 484.

"The churches of Connecticut have adopted the Consociating principle, as best supported by God's word, and established the Consociation, as *the highest Ecclesiastical judicature.*" — John Elliott's *Sermon* at Guilford, 1817. p. 7.

"Y[e] pastors met in our Consociation have power, with y[e] consent of y[e] Messengers of our Churches chosen, and attending, *authoritatively, juridically and decisively to determine Ecclesiastical affairs, &c.*"— Art. II., Old Consociation of Fairfield Co., Conn. *Cont. Eccl. Hist. Conn.,* p. 356.

a County, where the territory is too large for convenience in one. This body meets at stated periods. Whenever any special need for advice arises in one of the Consociated churches, provision is also made for calling it together — though not always the whole of it is required to be assembled.[1] The advice of Consociation is strictly, and according to the Say-Brook Platform, and the ancient understanding, in the nature of an authoritative adjudication, and must be followed, on pain of being "reputed guilty of scandalous contempt, and dealt with as the rule of God's word in such case doth provide, and the sentence of non-communion shall be declared against such Pastor and Church. And the churches are to approve of the said sentence, by withdrawing from the communion of the Pastor, and Church, which so refuseth to be healed."[2]

It is but just to add that there has always been a Low Church as well as a High Church theory of this system;[3] and that practically at the present day, Consociation amounts, in many places, to nothing more than a Council of the *neighboring* churches.

The churches of Connecticut[4] appear to be strongly attached to this way of Church fellowship; but although advocated by many eminent men,[5] it is difficult to see that it offers, or secures,[6] any ad-

---

[1] See *Cont. Eccl. Hist. Conn.*, p. 833.
[2] Say-Brook Platform, Art. IV. *Trumbull*, l. p. 484.
[3] See *Trumbull*, l. p. 487. See also Bacon's *Historical Discourse*, (pp. 41-70. *Cont. Eccl. Hist. Conn.*) See also Gov. Fitch's clear, candid, and forcible *Explanation of Say-Brook Platform*, (pp. 89, small 4to., Hartford, 1765], *passim.*
[4] *Cont. Eccl. Hist. Conn.*, pp. 70, 87, 126, 127, 305, 317, 333, 419, 444.
[5] See Dr. Dwight. *Sermon* clxii. Dr. Woods also favored this plan. He said, " the best way, I think, would be for the ministers in their District Associations to form small Consociations ; and, once formed, their benefits would be so obvious, that I think they would be generally and gladly adopted." [MS. *Lectures.*] See also his *Works*, vol. iii. pp. 578-583. There is a passage worth reading in this connection, in Turell's *Life* of Dr. Coleman, [Boston, 1748], pp. 98-108.
[6] The Records of Consociationism in Connecticut show that its decisions are not always more just, or effectual, than those of Councils. The Rev. Mr. Robbins, of Branford, was excluded [1742] from the New Haven Consociation, and deposed — for preaching to a Baptist Church. He quietly went on with his work, and after about seven years was invited back to Consociation. [*Trumbull*, vol. ii. pp. 196-233]. Dr. Bacon says of Consociation — "that it had any efficacy at all in preventing, or in adjusting those local controversies which are inevitably incident to the government of all self-governed churches, does not appear in all the history of its first half-century." [*Cont. Eccl. Hist. Conn.*, p. 38.] He says indeed [*Hist. Discourses*, p. 192], " for the first half-century, or more, the Saybrook Platform *made more quarrels than it healed.*" In the famous " Wallingford case," Rev. Mr. Dana was settled by an " Old Light " Council [1758], in the face of the remonstrance of the New Haven Consociation. The Consociation convoked to its aid that of Hartford South, and casting out Mr. Dana and his Church, recognized a minority opposed to him as " the Church." That minority, after keeping up worship a little

vantage sufficient to offset the Presbyterian tendencies which inhere in it.[1] Nor is it to be wondered at that Congregational churches, in general, prefer a method more purely an outgrowth of their fundamental principles.[2]

In consociated churches, the trial and deposition of ministers is done by the Consociation.[3]

SECTION 8. *Association.*

An Association, is a meeting of Pastors in the aim to help each other in their common work. Such meetings have existed in New England since a very early date.[4] The Pastors of ten, twenty, or thirty neighboring churches — grouped, and limited, by considerations of mutual convenience — come together thus, twice, thrice, or four times a year, and spend a day, or more, in exercises for intellectual, spiritual, and professional improvement. As a matter of convenience, advantage has been taken of these regular assemblages of the Pastors, by candidates for the Pulpit, to present themselves, after thorough training, for examination for a certificate of approval — in common parlance, "for licensure."[5]

---

more than twenty years, "caved in," and went back. [*Trumbull*, vol. ii. pp. 480-526.] See Dr. Bacon's *Norwich Historical Discourse*, pp. 51-56, for allusion to many such cases.

Particularly mournful is the Rev. Levi Nelson's recent [1854] exposition of "*The trials of a Church and Pastor in attempting to maintain Gospel Discipline under Consociational interference*," in Lisbon, Conn. [See his pamphlet, pp. 50, 8vo.]

[1] The one good thing in Mr. Lesley's "address to the Suffolk North Association," [Boston, 1849, pp. 130], is where he calls Consociationism the "*railed Presbyterianism* of the New Haven and Hartford Colony." (p. 43.) As long ago as 1772, John Cotton, of Plymouth, accused the Rev. Chandler Robbins of attempting to bring in "the Connecticut discipline;" adding, in a note, "Scarce any are ignorant that the discipline in Connecticut *verges towards Presbyterianism*." See his *General Practice of the Churches of New England, relating to Baptism, vindicated.* [Boston. E. Russell. 12mo. pp. 73. p. 71.]

[2] "A Congregational Church holding that mode of Church government, cannot, while such, become consociated."—*Address to the Rev. Moses C. Welch.* [Windham. 1794. p. 32.]

"Consociationism leads to Presbyterianism; Presbyterianism leads to Episcopacy; Episcopacy leads to Roman Catholicism; and Roman Catholicism is an ultimate fact."—Dr. Emmons. *Park's Memoir*, p. 163.

[3] See page 206.

[4] President Stiles [*Convention Sermon*, p. 68] fixes the earliest date, in his knowledge, of such a meeting, in New England, at about 1670. The Library of the *Mass. Historical Society* contains the MS. record of "Cambridge Association," formed at the house of Charles Morton, in Charlestown, Mass., Oct. 13, 1690. This was the Association which Cotton Mather so often refers to in his *Magnalia*, and this MS. contains the originals of most of the votes reported by him.

[5] The theory of New England Congregationalism has always been that a Church of Christ is the only body possessing authority to empower any person to preach the Gospel. But as

In some of the States, delegates from these District Bodies meet once a year to constitute a General Association of the State; the printed report of whose annual meeting is made to include the statistics of the Congregational churches in that Commonwealth.[1]

While these Associations are very helpful to Pastors, and through

---

It is an important aid to the churches in this work to have beforehand the carefully formed judgment of Pastors in reference to the qualifications of candidates, the practice has grown up of having all candidates present themselves to some ministerial association for thorough examination as to their fitness — in learning and piety — to preach; and, on the part of the churches, of entertaining no candidate who does not bring, from some recognized and respectable body of ministers, a certificate of their approbation as a fit occupant of the pulpit. Such a certificate is not a *license* to preach. It confers no power, and ought not to be so named. It is merely a letter of commendation, designed favorably to introduce its holder to the churches. Any one of them, that pleases to do so, on the strength of the letter, and its own subsequent investigation, has power to *license* the candidate, by making him its Pastor; with the counsel of others.

David Thurston was the first commended by the Mendon Association, Nov. 6, 1751. The late Thomas Gray, D. D., of Roxbury [3d Church] was the first "approbated" in this way, by the Boston Association, in 1792. The Mendon Association, now in its second century, has always scrupulously refused to use the term "license," and therein deserves the commendation of all true Congregationalists. See *Centurial History of Mendon Association*. [Boston, 1853] p 75

In 1651, the Church in Malden was *fined* £50, by the Massachusetts General Court, for settling a minister without previous approbation; and in 1653, the Court forbade the "new" Church, in Boston, to settle "Mr. Powell," because they thought him too unlearned, and ordered that no one should be allowed to preach who was not approved by "the elders of the four next churches, or the County Court;" but the order was repealed at the next session, on petition from members of the Church and town of Woburn, as being an infringement on the liberties of the churches. [See *Records Mass. Colony*, vol. iii. pp. 237, 250, 293, 294, 317, 331, 359; and *Mass. Hist. Coll.*, 3d series, vol. i. pp. 38-45, where the petition is given in full, with signatures.]

[1] New Hampshire, Massachusetts, and Connecticut, have General Associations based purely on delegations from local clerical Associations. Vermont, New York, Illinois, Michigan, Wisconsin, Iowa, and California have substantially such bodies, with a lay element superadded. In Rhode Island, Indiana, Minnesota, Nebraska, and Oregon, the State bodies seem to be made up of Pastors and delegates coming directly from the churches, without delegation from any intermediate body whatever. An effort was made, in 1818, — under the pressure of the Unitarian movement, and its admonitions to the friends of Orthodoxy to strengthen themselves in every possible manner — to unite all the General Associations of New England into one Grand Unity, by means of a sort of "Committee of Union." Naturally enough, this plan came from Consociational Connecticut. The General Association of Massachusetts appointed Drs. Worcester and Hyde and Rev. Thomas Snell to meet committees of conference from other State Bodies in regard to it. They reported (1819) in favor of the plan, and advised that a "Committee of Union" meet annually on the 3d Wednesday of October. This "Committee" met accordingly in Hartford, in the October following — Drs. Flint of Hartford, and Lyman Beecher (then of Litchfield). representing Connecticut; Dr. Hyde and Mr Snell representing Massachusetts, and New Hampshire and Vermont declining to go into the arrangement. Dr. Hyde was chairman and Dr Flint scribe, and Dr. Hyde preached, and two days were devoted to "business" — such as it was; Dr. Beecher being appointed to preach next year. But, in 1821, this "Committee" had good sense enough to see that they were ineffectually endeavoring to attach a fifth — superfluous and so pernicious — wheel to the denominational coach, and they accordingly recommended their own dissolution. The recommendation was adopted, and the scheme was decently and speedily buried in oblivion, the only monumental erection to keep alive its memory that we recall in print, being a page in the *Cong Quarterly*, for Jan 1859, (p 48).

them to their flocks, it is a fundamental principle, usually, if not universally, expressed in their constitutions, that they have no direct connection with the churches, and no claim to any shadow of authority over them.

SECTION 9. *Conferences.*

A Conference is an assemblage of Pastors and delegates of churches, assembled, not, like a Council, on the special call of a sister Church for some isolated service toward light and peace, but in virtue of a Constitution providing for periodical meetings, for mutual prayer, communion, advice, and helpfulness.[1] As in the case of Pastoral Associations, the size, boundaries, etc., of these Conferences, are dictated by convenience.

As with Associations, a distinct disavowal of all ecclesiastical control, is usually, and very properly, a fundamental article of their confederation.

In some of the States, delegations from these local conferences meet annually, in a General Conference representing all the Congregational churches in the State;[2] and their "minutes" carry the annual statistics.

SECTION 10. *Church Extension.*

Where population is steadily increasing, it is necessary that religious privileges should perpetually be enlarged by the establishment of new centres of hallowing influence; that the Gospel may keep pace with the need for it. The peculiar fitness of Congregationalism — notwithstanding its lack of organization outside of the local Church — to extend itself, will be more particularly discussed here-

---

[1] The New England Synod of 1662, seem to have had Church Conferences in mind in some of their suggestions [See *Magnalia*] Book v., vol ii., pp. 300-301.] Increase Mather, in his *First Principles of New England*, cites a plan which he says John Cotton drew up just before his death, defining and recommending this practice of the conference of churches. Upham [*Ratio Disciplinæ*, p. 246,] however thinks that the first efficient measures to carry out this plan, took place in the County of York, Me., 1822-3; whence the system spread over Maine, and thence largely over the United States.

[2] In Maine and Ohio, the State Body is thus a General Conference, made up of delegates, lay and clerical, from local conferences. Massachusetts has recently formed such a Body, in addition to her General Association.

after.[1] It is enough to say here, that it is — and from the beginning has been[2] — eminently missionary in its spirit; and that — on the common sense principle that "when there is a will there is a way" — it has never found any difficulty in working upon the destitute and dying world; whether in near localities,[3] or distant states,[4] or nations.[5]

This it has found it most suitable and convenient to do by the means of Societies for City, Home, and Foreign Missions, etc., into the hands of whose well-selected officers, and to the care of whose wise and well-studied agencies, the local churches commit their alms.

Of late years the American Congregational Union has been established,[6] in order to be the medium of conveying aid from these Congregational churches who have some strength to spare, to their feebler brethren; and has accomplished incalculable good in the way of helping young churches at the West to their first houses of worship — without which they can accomplish little; hardly hope even to keep themselves alive.

It is greatly to be hoped that Congregationalists everywhere will increasingly perceive, and use, the benefit of these helps toward a fit obedience to the Saviour's last command.

---

[1] See page 238.

[2] See Acts viii: 1, 14, 26; x: 19; xi: 19–29; xiii: 2, 8, 45–51; xiv: 21, 22, etc.

Very touching are Gov. Bradford's words in regard to the motives of the Leyden Pilgrims in coming hither: "lastly, (and which was not least,) a great hope & inward zeall they had of laying some good foundation, or at least to make some way thereunto, for yᵉ propagating & advancing yᵉ gospell of yᵉ kingdom of Christ in those remote parts of yᵉ world; yea, though they should be but even as stepping-stones unto others for yᵉ performing of so great a work." — *Plimouth Plantation*, p. 24.

[3] Our fathers began by colonizing new churches from those already vigorous. Three churches (Duxbury, Marshfield, and Eastham), were colonized from the Mother Church at Plymouth in the space of twenty-six years. Branch churches were also formed in destitute localities, and sustained by sap from the trunk. [See *Early Methods of Church Extension*, Cong. Quar., vol. i. pp. 53–59.] See also Clark's *Congregational Churches in Massachusetts* [pp. 95, 96], for a discussion of these branch churches. [He says it was our fathers' "mode of conducting domestic missions, and may be regarded as the first form which this enterprise took in New England." He adds that "as the members of a branch were still enrolled with the Church from which it sprung, till a formal separation was effected, so its minister was included in the Eldership of the other, and was often sent with the Pastor to sit in Ecclesiastical councils.

[4] The *American Home Missionary Society* was Congregational in its origin, and soon will be in its entire quality. [See *Puritans and Presbyterians*, Cong. Quar., vol iv. pp. 38–57.]

[5] The *American Board of Commissioners for Foreign Missions* was founded by the Mass. General Association, in 1819. [See Cong. Quar., vol. i. pp., 46–48.]

[6] The *Union* was formed at New York City in May, 1853. Its receipts reported May, 1861, for the year then closed, were $14,048.80, and with this it had helped — in the twelve months — *thirty-nine* feeble Congregational churches to enter houses of worship free of debt.

SECTION 11. *Denominational Relations.*

Congregationalists have some peculiar advantages in the matter of denominational relations, arising from the simplicity, breadth, and catholicity of their first principles. Believing that the vitality of the Church organism does not reside in the outward form, but in the inward substance, they are not compelled to unchurch any body of sincere believers, banded under whatsoever form differing from that which is usual to themselves. While they have their own decided preferences, both as to the manner of all church work, and the fashion of all public worship, they are not compelled by fealty to their own fundamentals, proudly, or sadly, to cast all who differ from them upon the "uncovenanted mercies" of the Lord. They rather — while they seek to conserve among themselves and promote among others what they esteem to be the faith once delivered to the saints, — trust and believe that "God is no respecter of persons: but in every [denomi]nation, he that feareth Him, and worketh righteousness, is accepted with Him."[1] They therefore hold out the hand of Christian fellowship — as Paul did[2] — to all those "that in every place call upon the name of Jesus Christ our Lord, both theirs and ours;" and delight to work with them in missions, moral reforms, and all practical ways of coöperation.

It is usual for Congregational ministers to tender the exchange of pulpit services, and the interchange of all manner of Christian courtesies, with ministers of all other denominations;[3] except those from whom they are necessarily debarred by the fact of their "not holding the Head, from which all the body by joints and bands having nourishment ministered, and knit together, increaseth with the increase of God."[4] And Congregational Churches endorse and enjoy this action of their Pastors; and are always ready, for their own part, to prove their fellowship with all other branches of the invisible Holy Church universal, by dismissing members in good standing to them, and re-

---

[1] Acts x: 34, 35.
[2] 1 Cor. i: 2.
[3] It is not the fault of Congregational Pastors that their kindly fraternity does not practically include *all* who agree with them in doctrinal essentials. And we have occasion to know that *some* Episcopalians mourn over that exclusiveness in their system, which prevents them from meeting our courtesies with a cordial return.
[4] Coloss. ii: 19.

ceiving such members from them, when Providence shapes the way of duty in that direction.[1]

Aside from this informal reciprocation of Christian courtesies with other denominations of believers, there has been to some extent an endeavor to further a more formal intercourse, by means of the interchange of delegated attendance upon the meetings of State or National associations. Experience has, perhaps, thrown doubt[2] upon the question whether such delegations promise enough of practical good to insure the perseverance of this method of manifesting Congregational good-will to "them that have obtained like precious faith with us through the righteousness of God and our Saviour Jesus Christ,"[3] but who do not "walk according to this rule."[4]

Section 12. *How to Dissolve a Church.*

In the Providence of God it may sometimes happen that — by the gradual depopulation of the locality where it was planted, or by the emigration of its members, and of that portion of the population among whom it can hopefully work, or for other reasons—the extinction of a given local Church becomes an inevitable necessity; so that the question arises: what steps are orderly for its dissolution?

It was formed by the covenant of its members, each with all the others; (usually) in connection with advice from other churches, through the medium of a Council.[5] It should be disbanded by a process which, to all intents and purposes, will reverse this. It is well, (but not essential) that a Council be called, and the state of the facts laid before it, so that sister Churches may have full and seasonable cognizance of a movement of so much consequence, and may have the opportunity to proffer aid, if aid may wisely be tendered to avert the catastrophe. Such a Council[6] having advised to a dissolution,

---

[1] See pp. 161, 162, (note) for some practical suggestions in regard to the procedure called for where embarrassment arises from the fact that some denominations to which we give our members letters, will not grant their members letters to us, in reversed circumstances.

[2] The Massachusetts General Association entered into correspondence with the General Assembly of the Presbyterian Church in 1811, and after the disruption of that Assembly, continued the correspondence with both branches, until 1856, when, both parties consenting, that with the Old School section was dropped. The correspondence with the New School Assembly still has a name to live.

[3] 2 Pet. 1: 1. [4] Gal. vi: 16. [5] See pp. 160–166.

[6] The form of Letter Missive given on p. 200, would be made suitable for the calling of such

the question would then come before the Church:[1] shall we follow this advice, and shall this Church organization be dissolved? A unanimous vote in the affirmative (which should include the grant of authority to the officers, or to a special committee, to give to all the members letters of dismission to such sister Churches as they may wish to join) would annul the covenant, and terminate the organization — when the conditions implied in the vote should have been performed.[2] So far as we know, there has never been any difference of judgment as to the conclusion that such unanimous consent as this, releases every member from his covenant obligation to that particular organism, and releases that Church from its converse relation to every member, and so allows the body to drop quietly into nonexistence, its constituent elements rearranging themselves in such other combinations as the general good may dictate, and so keeping good their covenant with God; which binds them irrevocably to *some* Church, but not, necessarily, to *that* Church.[3]

---

a Council, by the simple substitution of the clause, "*that the Church should be dissolved,*" for "*that the relation between the Church and its Pastor should be dissolved.*"

[1] Of course, it would be before the Church, and the Church would have a perfect [abstract] right to discuss and decide it, if no Council were held; or even if the advice of the Council should be against disbandment.

[2] It seems to us that there has been a little hypercriticism sometimes applied to this question. Thus, in the Result of the *Howard Street Council*, at Salem, Dec. 4, 1849, it is urged [p. 22] that the vote dissolved the Church at once, and before any letters could be granted, so that there was, in fact, no Howard Street Church, from which the members could go, when they had their letters, and were ready to start. But such a vote of disbandment must necessarily reserve its force until its conditions have been complied with; and therefore there must have been a Howard Street Church, at all events — if every member had taken letters — until every member *had* taken and used them, and then the suspended force of the vote would ultimate, and the organism cease.

A proper form of letter of dismission in such a case, might be the following:

To the Congregational Church in ———,
  Greeting:

Whereas, the Providence of God has made it necessary — in the judgment of its members — for the Congregational Church in ———, to cease to exist, and whereas it has unanimously voted that its existence, as a separate branch of Christ's body, shall cease, whenever its members shall all have been received into the fellowship of those Churches to which they are respectively commended, as in good and regular standing: this is to certify you that the bearer, Brother [or Sister] ——— is thus commended to your Christian care and fellowship.

(Signed.) ——————— ⎫ Committee
         ——————— ⎬ authorized by
                    the Church
(Date.) ——————— ⎭ to issue Letters.

[3] We suppose that the great majority of the more than sixty Congregational churches which

The difficulty which has not unfrequently made this a vexed question, lies in another (always possible) aspect of the case — when there is not entire unanimity in the movement, and the dissolution of the Church is resisted by a minority of its members, who claim that their right in the organism, and its responsibility in covenant to them, are such as cannot be vacated by the mere vote of a majority.

It is urged, on the one hand, that the very nature of a covenant implies the mutual establishment of rights which cannot be resumed without the consent of all parties; that as every Church exists by the personal covenant of each with each, it can cease to exist only when each releases each from that covenant;[1] and that the right to the permanent enjoyment of Church privileges in that particular organization being the consideration on which the covenant was made, it is unjust and oppressive to take away that consideration without consent. On the other hand, it is urged that, as a Congregational Church is a democracy, the common law of the power of the majority ought to apply to it; that every member comes into covenant with it on that express understanding, and so has no ground of complaint if he is unchurched by it;[2] and that to take the ground that unanimous assent is requisite for the dissolution of a Church, is to put the final decision always into the hands of that *one* factious and unreasonable member, who contrives to slip into almost every Church.

We suggest that the true ground lies between these two extremes. There can be no doubt that the common rule of majority action is measurably limited by the covenant, when it comes to touch the fundamental matter of the very existence of the body. On the other hand, it is equally clear that the welfare of a whole Church should not be left where it can hang upon the unreasonable and contumacious conduct of a solitary member. We hold, then, that if a Church ought to be dissolved, it should be done by the unanimous consent of all its members, who are in good and regular standing; and only for reasons so grave and clear that they *ought* to carry the consent of every such member. And if a majority of one, or more, unreasonably and

---

have become extinct in Massachusetts — nine of them in Boston — since its settlement; have gone through with this process — the movement not taking place until, by unanimous consent, it was the only wise thing to be done.

[1] See *Result of Howard Street Council* (Salem, 1850, pp. 64), p. 26.
[2] See *Review* of that Result (Boston, 1850, pp. 140), p. 61.

contumaciously refuses consent; that minority becomes guilty of an offense, and for that offense (unrepented of) should be labored with — as if guilty of any other — until brought to a better mind, or cast out from membership, when — in either event — the way is opened for the regular dissolution of the body by unanimous assent.[1]

---

[1] For various considerations affecting this general subject, see the *Result of Council* before cited, and its *Review, in extenso;* also Clark's *Congregational Churches of Massachusetts,* p. 281. A Council, held April 14, 1847, called to dismiss Rev. Joel Mann, from the Howard Street Church, in Salem, advised the disbandment of the Church, as well as his dismission. May 4, 1847, the Church voted, 17 to 10, to disband. The minority resisted, and continue as the Church to this day. A Council convened in Poughkeepsie, N. Y., March 31, 1857, advised the disbandment and reorganization of that Church, expressly to drop out some alien elements. Dec. 15, 1857, the Church voted, 16 to 7, to follow the advice of Council. The minority acquiesced, and the Church was reorganized. But the effect of the procedure was not considered happy, by those best acquainted with the facts.

I append here the judgment on this question of one of the clearest and ablest of our New England thinkers, recently called home — Rev. Worthington Smith, D D., late President of the University of Vermont. He says:

"My own observation has convinced me that it is no easy matter to terminate a Church corporation. However loosely organized, and, I might almost say, however corrupt, it has a wonderful tenacity of life. It ought not to be attempted unless we are quite sure of success. Let the Church edifice be disposed of and vacated, Church furniture sold, and the avails given to the poor, and letters of recommendation voted, before the *power* shall pass out of the hands of the Church.

"I am not clear that it is proper to disband a Church that has not forfeited its claims to visibility, except it is by the *unanimous consent* of its members. The word *voluntary,* as applied to Church organization, has an equivocal, if not a malignant import, and should be used in a guarded sense, or not used at all. The Church is as much the imperative state of a Christian people as the state of laws and society is the imperative state of rational beings. Church associations are of the nature of *a contract,* and they are understood to be permanent. Rights are created by these associations, or at least recognized by them; and these rights are to be respected, until at least they are voluntarily surrendered. If, without common consent, a Church is disbanded, some are forced into other churches against their will, or they are left by the wayside, deserted of those who engaged to watch over them, and to walk with them in all the commandments and ordinances of the Lord. I have no difficulty in regard to the union of the churches, or the *distribution* of the members of one Church among many, provided it is done with the concurrence of those interested. I do not say that any one is obliged to *remain* in a Church because it is reduced in numbers; for the liberty of transferring one's relations to another Church is understood when he joins a Church; but I know of no liberty he has, on leaving a Church, to pull down the house where others have found a refuge, and would still seek one " — *Memoir,* by Rev. J. Torrey, D. D. (Boston, 1861. 12mo, pp. 368,) p. 70.

On the other side the reader is referred to the following opinion of Rev. Calvin Hitchcock, D. D., who warmly urges: —

"Church covenants have been revised and altered in numerous instances, and since the days of Jonathan Edwards, some scores of 'half-way covenants' have been dissolved. Was not this done by majorities? Was Edwards obliged to wait till every man in the Church would agree to abolish a half-way covenant, before the thing could be done? . . . . It belongs to the very genius of Congregationalism to have the right to modify a covenant, because it arose, and has lived, in opposition to an established religion. If we may not modify a covenant, we have as truly an established religion as any in the world. Any obstruction which we throw in the way of so doing, would be suicidal. If the next generation shall introduce un-

SECTION 13.—*The Restoration of Offenders.*

The intent and hope of Church discipline is always of reclamation.

We have already intimated[1] that the lifting of the sentence of suspension, or exclusion, from a censured member by vote of the Church, consequent upon their acceptance of his manifested penitence with its accompanying works, will restore him to the possession of all which he had forfeited. The thus restored excommunicant does not need to "join the Church" as if *de novo*, because he has always remained a member, though under censure.

The only question relevant to this heading which needs consideration here, is this: Suppose a minister who for any reason has been deposed, to desire — and in the judgment of charity, to deserve — to be restored; what steps are orderly to that end?

We have explained[2] what we conceive to be the proper Congregational method for the deposition of an unworthy Pastor, as being by the action of his Church in connection with the advice of an Ecclesiastical Council. If such a deposed minister, becoming penitent and worthy, wishes to resume the Pastoral office, and any Church shall judge it suitable that he should do so, and desire him for its Pastor, it may proceed to call him to that office, as it would invite any unor-

---

christian covenants, and some future Edwards shall be raised up to reform churches, shall we hamper him with the rule that on such a subject, a majority shall not govern, and all the stereotype heresy and petrified folly which a godless generation shall have thrust into Church covenants, must stand till every member of the Church shall agree to their removal? . . . . . *It is self-evident that any authority which can modify a covenant, can abolish it.* The Apostle appealed to our common sense when he declared that only such things as cannot be shaken are the things that remain. I therefore enter my remonstrance against the proposed rule, that no Church can be dissolved until every member consents." — *Remonstrance,* Review of Howard Street Council, p. 140.

I add an extract in the same line of thought from another eminent living New England Congregationalist — Rev. N. Bouton, D. D., of Concord, N. H. He says: —

"1. There may be good and sufficient reasons why a particular local Church should be dissolved. 2. Of these reasons, a majority have the right to judge. 3. The minority have the right to *protest,* and, if they wish it, to have the advice of Council, *before the act,* or, if aggrieved by the act of the majority, have a right to appeal to a Council. . . . . But to claim that they are the identical Church which was disbanded by vote of the majority, in accordance with the advice of a Council, seems to me preposterous. On that principle a single member may claim to be " the Church " in opposition to the disbanding vote of ninety-nine, and contrary also to the advice of a Council thereunto." — *Review of Howard Street Council,* p. 102.

[1] See page 192.   [2] See page 206.

dained man, and then call an Ecclesiastical Council to advise with them. That Council will naturally desire to be exceedingly thorough in its inquiries, and should proceed only on the best evidence.[1] But if its members are satisfied that it is for the good of Christ's cause that this once deposed Pastor should be set over this Church in the Lord, they will so advise, and the subsequent co-action of Church and Council in ordaining him as Pastor will, in effect, be his restoration to the ministry.[2]

---

[1] "A deposed minister is restored by becoming a pastor of a Church; and whoever is competent to install is also competent to remove a censure, at least to the extent to which its authority is recognized; and the authority of no Ecclesiastical Council can extend beyond their limits. . . . . . . An installing body ought to be satisfied with the qualifications and fitness of the candidate; and, if they restore to office one who has been deposed, it must be on their own responsibility, and for reasons that will commend themselves, first or last, to the religious public, or they become liable to reproval themselves." *Worthington Smith, D. D.*, Torrey's Memoir, p. 76.

[2] Rev. Thomas Cheever [son of the famous Master Ezekiel] was deposed from the pastorship of the Congregational Church in Malden, Mass., May 20, 1686, by a Council, and, nearly thirty years after, restored by a Council which ordained him first pastor of the new Church at Rumney Marsh [Chelsea], Mass., October 19, 1715.

The case of the Rev. J. H. Fairchild is slightly exceptional. He was conditionally deposed by a Council which met at Exeter, N. H., July 24, 1844; their language being, "unless he can present a clearer vindication of himself before some tribunal more competent than ourselves to compel the attendance of witnesses, and the utterance of all the truth; *and till such act be done;* he ought not, and so far as our decision goes, does not, longer hold the place of a minister in the Church of Christ." When acquitted by the civil court of the infamous charge in reference to which the Council had acted, Mr. Fairchild assumed that the deposing clause of the Result of Council had expired by its own limitation, and thenceforth resumed his ministry. We think he was right in his judgment; which was, at the time, sustained by Drs. French, Cogswell, Bouton, Richards, Woods, Burgess, Perry, Ely, Blanchard, Vaill, Cummings, and other eminent Congregationalists; and subsequently fully endorsed by the Council which installed him over the " Payson Church," in South Boston, November 19, 1854. See *Life of Rev. J. H. Fairchild*, pp. 53-110.

CHAPTER IV.

WHY CONGREGATIONALISM IS BETTER THAN ANY OTHER FORM OF CHURCH GOVERNMENT.

We hold that this Congregational system, which we have shown to be founded both upon Scripture and common sense, is essentially superior to any other form of Church government; in what it is, and what it is fitted to be and to do in the world. We speak of its natural tendencies and legitimate possibilities. We do not affirm that it has ever yet done itself full justice; nor that other forms of Church life may not sometimes have seemed to earn preëminence over it. But we do insist that, taking the ages through, and fairly considering the relation which it holds to the nature of individual man, the tendencies of human society, the necessities of the world, and the needs and aims of the cause of Christ, it is best, and can justify its claim to be such.

We now proceed briefly to hint the grounds of that claim, in its most important particulars.

SECTION 1. *It is more in accordance with the mind of Christ than any other.*

We do not affirm that Christ will not aid his people in working through any other system. He will do so; has always wrought through all faithful men, however mistaken might be a portion of their views; however inexpedient a moiety of their life. But He prefers that which is best, and will most bless that which most deserves his blessing. And three considerations indicate His preference for our simple polity.

(1) *It is the New Testament Polity.* We have seen very fully in the preceding pages, that it is the only form of Church government which can exactly respond to the few precepts on that subject which fell

from Christ's own lips;[1] that it is the form which the Apostles impressed upon the early Church in the days of its purity;[2] and that it is the form which nearest answers to their epistolary counsels.[3]

(2) *It is the Polity with which the Great Head of the Church has connected the most remarkable displays of his grace.* The Reformation, though it did not at once consistently develop into Congregationalism, was yet founded upon our fundamental doctrine, and derived its life from it,[4] and modern revivals and modern missions, where they have not been a direct outgrowth from our system, have been indirect results of its essential principles. Furthermore it will, if we mistake not, become clear to every reflecting mind that those seasons of special activity and progress which, by the grace of God, make occasional oases even in the dryest deserts of the history of the Church, in old time, or new, have been characterized by the temporary approach on the part of other systems to the methods and spirit of our own.[5]

(3) *It is the Polity that most favors that development of deep spirituality mingled with earnest personal activity, which alone can bring on the Millennium.* We merely for completeness name this here; it will be the subject of discussion hereafter.

It is not arrogance, in view of these considerations, for us to claim that Christ specially loves that system which he himself founded, and which is inseparably interwoven with His Word, which he has already peculiarly blessed, and which offers to him the most efficient aid in His desire to see of the travail of his soul and be satisfied.

SECTION 2. *Congregationalism is more practicable in its working than any other system.*

If it be the duty of all who love Christ by the renewing of their

---

[1] See pages 9, 34.   [2] See page 13.   [3] See pages 100-110.   [4] See page 2.
[5] The inherent propensities of every other form of Church government are, so to speak, centripetal — tending to throw life and power continually in from the membership, upon the hierarchy in its high or low type, and so to develop weakness and dependence (and consequently a low spiritual life) in the individual. The inherent impulse of Congregationalism is, so to speak, centrifugal, throwing out life and power into the individuals, and making its membership feel that the great work of Christ rests on them as individuals, and not on "the Church." But the periods of greatest progress of the cause of God on earth, have always been when the many have had a mind to work, and when, therefore, the centrifugal, Congregational has, for the time being, overcome the centripetal, hierarchal, tendency.

mind, in every place, to come out from the world and be separate, and confess Him before men, not forsaking the assembling of themselves together; it becomes a matter of importance that due facilities for entering upon Church relations should be everywhere within reach of the redeemed. If also the Church is the pillar and ground of God's truth, the salt by which the putrescent moral tendencies of men are to be counteracted, and the light wherewith the world is to be lighted; the great reforming, regenerating agency by whose activity — divinely furthered and cherished — it is eventually to be brought about that God's will shall be done in earth as it is in heaven; it becomes a matter of moment that her influence should be as easily as possible made operative in every community. And as ages must necessarily pass during which the advancing wave of population is rolling on, before it shall touch every habitable place, so that emigrant peoples will habitually bear an important percentage to the sum total of the race; which emigrant peoples will, on the one hand, specially need, and, on the other hand, be under special disadvantages for receiving, the influence and blessing of the Church; the element of practicableness becomes an important one in weighing the claims of competing forms of Church life; and, other things being equal, that form of Church order which can be easiest reached and handled by a new and remote community — which is most practicable in all communities — must be best.

This superior practicableness is obviously a peculiarity of our system.

(1) *It is so in the formation of churches.* — Wherever any company of persons may be, who are faithful believers in the Gospel, and who desire to bless themselves and serve Christ in and through a Church organization, they may do so in a Congregational form, without any perplexity or delay. They do not need to geographize and journey, to discover some well authenticated aqueduct, bringing the stream of Ecclesiastical life down from the hoary past, to which they must attach themselves, or else be dry; they may dig down anywhere in the sand, with the certainty of finding living water. Suppose they are grouped upon some far Pacific slope, hundreds of miles from any Church, of any name, with communication almost interdicted by the distance and peril of the way; if they are to become

Papal, Patriarchal, Episcopalian,[1] Methodist,[2] or Presbyterian[3] in their spirit and form of Church organization, they must wait and work until they can put themselves into communication with the rest of the world, so as to get hold of the arm of that particular hierarchy which they prefer, and procure its extension to their remote locality, with all due conditions and ceremonies, for such cases made and provided. All this involves delay, trouble, expense; often disappointment and dispersion. Moreover, in its very nature, this necessity of going so far for, and making so much of, mere forms, must tend to magnify forms unduly, and turn their thoughts away from the simplicity of Christ. Still further they are, even when formed, abnormal and incomplete; lacking the aid, for the perfect doing of all their work, of the distant Pope, Bishop, or Presbytery.

But if they wish to become a Congregational Church, they can become such, there by themselves, in a single hour — by solemn vote affiliating for that purpose, and adopting our simple creed — just as those North of England worthies, hunted by the hounds of the Establishment, took refuge in Scrooby, and there, in the very manorhouse of the Archbishop of York, in 1606, formed — without any external help — that Church which, going first to Holland, colonized afterward on the rock of Plymouth. Such a Church, on our principles, is just as perfect in its order, as it could be if all the other churches in the world had helped to make it. It is just as near to Christ, as, and it may be a little nearer than, any other — as the babe lies closer to its mother's breast than the older children. He is just as really its Head, and it is just as truly the channel of his power and grace, as the grandest metropolitan Church can be. And there,

---

[1] On the Episcopalian theory — as in the Papal and Greek — nothing can securely be done in the direction of a Church, except by the agency of a regular priest acting under Episcopal orders, and nobody can be received into the Church by confirmation, but by the hands of the Bishop himself. Humphrey's *History of the Propagation Society*, (p. 11), shows that the first Episcopalian Church in this country was " upon an application made to the Bishop of London, from several of the inhabitants of Boston, in New England, petitioning that a Church should be allowed in that town," an 1 " a Church was allowed."

[2] A Methodist " Society " has the same relation in its origin to an "itinerant," that an Episcopal Church has to a priest.

[3] The Presbyterian rule is, " for the organization of a Church, application should be made to the Presbytery, where the circumstances permit it. If this be not convenient on account of distance, any *ordained minister* is competent to form such an organization. Application must then be made at the earliest practicable moment, to be received into connection with the Presbytery within whose bounds the Church naturally lies." *Handbook of Pres. Church,* p 33.

in its outward feebleness, and in that remoteness, its voice is just as imperative as that of the oldest and numerically strongest body of congenial faith on earth; because Christ says, that "where two or or three are," there he will be, and because the comforting and controlling Spirit can dwell in a little Church just as well as in a large one. And so there it stands — home-made and yet well made — as true a Church as the Great Head anywhere surveys. There it can advance from strength to strength, burdened with no extraneous connections or responsibilities; going to the Bible with humble prayer, and not to General Conference, Convention, or Assembly, to find out what shall be its creed, and what its life. So soon as the growth of a community around it shall evoke the element of the fellowship of the saints, it will affiliate with other Congregational churches as any shall grow up within its neighborhood; and then its entire completeness of relation, without as well as within, will be secured.

There is another feature of the superior practicableness of the Congregational system in the formation of new churches, which was illustrated in the early days of Christianity, and which is now particularly commended to our attention by the present and prospective condition of our own country. It consists in its freedom from all embarrassment in regard to form, where questions of form would be embarrassing; and in its freedom from all entangling alliances and inconvenient precedents, and awkward responsibilities, growing out of the relations of a rigid and wide spread organism to the past. If our Saviour had instituted a technical Church system, having a necessary embodiment in certain usages, and by certain officers, and through certain far reaching relations — a centralized administration with executive branches — its progress would have excited hostility at every step, for it could have taken no step without colliding with existing organizations, social, Ecclesiastical, civil. But a development of Christianity which presented *a faith* to be believed rather than *a form* to be adopted, could glide in between all barriers, and establish itself noiselessly as an *imperium in imperio* everywhere; subsequently embodying its recipients according to local convenience, and perfecting their Church character and relation — and so their thorough organic union to the Great Head — without the need of conspicuous and obnoxious publicity, and premature positive conflict with the things that were.

This flexibility of form, which did such service in the beginning, and has, in our day, so much aided our missionaries in despotic empires, admirably meets, also, the conditions of the newly forming society at the South. Facts are proving that throughout those portions of the rebellious territory which have been recovered by the National Power, and which are beginning to crystallize into civilized society once more, there is a wide spread and bitter prejudice against those old Church organisms which had so much to do in precipitating the reckless and luckless South into the gulf of secession and of suicide. The great territorial Ecclesiastical organizations of the Cotton States were so corrupted by slavery, their deliverances on that subject were so bitter, and their present condition is so unsatisfactory,[1] that they are repudiated and loathed by multitudes who now prefer to connect themselves with a polity which is not merely historically purer in that regard, but whose organic nature makes it impossible that, in any future event, its churches can be made responsible for the sins of some backsliding branch of the same great whole elsewhere.

Moreover it is now easy to establish Congregational churches in the South, because no question is inevitably raised at the outset — reaching back to the former days and touching the raw spot — as to what Presbytery, Conference, or Bishop, now has jurisdiction, and must be propitiated in order to the "regularity" of the act. Bygones are left to be bygones, and out of the old ashes rises a new organism independent of the past, by the simple confederation of kindred believers; whose sufficiency being of God is sufficient unto itself (under Christ) with no thanks due to any hierarchy.

(2) *It is the most practicable system in the matter of the pastorate.* — A Congregational Church freely elects from its own membership,

---

[1] Witness the following testimony from an intelligent Southern observer: — "The apostacy of the Southern churches has been the main strength of the rebellion, stronger even than their cannon, for without such professedly moral sanction, they could scarcely have brought the machinery of war into existence, much less into use. Ecclesiastical systems that for a long time have been drifting from the old paths, and have finally been perverted to the purpose of overthrowing our government, and establishing slavery, will be slow to return to pure Gospel principles. This is especially true of denominations the genius of whose ecclesiastical polity forbids independent local Church action. A local Church bound by the ecclesiastical chain of a great denomination, cannot adjust itself to the present state of things, or take thorough Gospel ground, without being denounced as radical and disorderly, by the body to which it is amenable. The *denomination* must therefore be converted, before the local churches can safely move in view of their systems." — *Congregationalist, Feb.* 24, 1865.

or invites to that membership and then elevates to its pastorship, whatsoever fit person it pleases. It makes such arrangements with him in regard to the matter, as it thinks will be most agreeable to Christ, its great invisible Head, — taking fraternal counsel in the matter from its sister churches, whenever possible.

But the local assemblies of the Papal, Patriarchal, English and Methodist Episcopal churches have no such liberty or power, and scarcely the semblance of it. They must take the person whom the Bishop, or other constituted authority may send; like him or dislike him as they may,[1] and they must wait for him until he is sent. The American Episcopalian and Presbyterian hierarchies allow their local bodies more seeming freedom in this matter, yet retain it essentially in their own control. The Church Wardens of an Episcopalian parish nominate a candidate for its rectorship to its Bishop — who confirms or rejects that nomination at his pleasure.[2] So a Presbyterian Church — under the direction of its Session of Elders, and by "the presence and counsel of some neighboring minister," by commissioners nominates its candidate for the pastoral office to the Presbytery under whose immediate care the candidate may happen to be. If the nominee is unordained, that Presbytery present the call to him, or not, as they please, in view of their judgment of all the circumstances. If the nominee is a pastor already, the Presbytery, upon the whole view of the case, either continue him in his former charge, or translate him, or refer the whole affair to the Synod, as they deem to be most for the peace and edification of the Church.[3]

But it is not alone in its superior ability to secure the filling of its vacant pastorates that our system has practical advantage over others; it has no less preëminence in its method of putting its pas-

---

[1] This needs no proof with regard to the Romish, Greek, and English churches. The Methodist Book of Discipline (*Part* I., *Chap.* IV., *Sect.* 1, *Quest.* 3, *Ans.* 3, and *Sect.* 2, *Quest.* 4, *Ans.* 3,) decrees the appointment of preachers to the hands of the Bishop, and temporarily, in his absence to the Presiding Elder; the congregation having no duty in the matter, but that of submission; for which Dr. Stevens argues as being better than the Congregational system because (1) if left to the societies, the largest societies would choose the most popular men, so that ministerial gifts would not be "distributed;" (2) the less able preachers would be starved out; (3) many societies would choose the same men; (4) it would be fatal to the *itinerancy.* — [*Essay on Church Polity*, p. 156.]

[2] "If the Bishop [or Standing Committee, where there is temporarily no Bishop] be not satisfied, he shall proceed to inquire into the sufficiency of the person so chosen, &c., &c , and shall confirm or reject the appointment, as the issue of that inquiry may be."— [*Canon*, xxx., *Sect.* 2.]

[3] *Book of Pres Church*, *U. S. A.*, Chaps. xv., and xvi.

tors officially in place. As we have already seen,[1] the Congregational conception of ordination (called installation, if repeated in the case of the same individual,) is, that it is the solemn ceremonial act by which a Church places its official head (under Christ) over itself, and therefore that while the counsel of other churches in the matter is desirable and always to be had, and followed, when possible, yet, in all exigencies, the right of ordination is in the hands of the body itself; so that no Church need be hindered and endangered by waiting for external aid, or authority, for that purpose. The Church in Salem ordained its Pastor and Teacher in the month following its disembarking on these shores.[2] The first Church in Boston followed the example, on the 27th August, 1630; the Church having been formed on the 30th July previous.[3] The first Church in Charlestown ordained Rev. Thomas James as its Pastor, on the day of its own formation, 2d Nov. 1632.[4] And so in the case of many other of our early churches.

Necessarily, the case is different with all whose theory of ordination involves certain fixed relations to the past, and to preëxisting organisms. The Episcopalians were greatly troubled, for years, to get ordained ministers for their beginnings here; notwithstanding the important aid received by them from the "Society for the Propagation of the Gospel in Foreign Parts."[5] The Bishop of London

---

[1] See pages 136-145.
[2] Prince's *Annals*, sub. June 24, and July 20, 1629.
[3] *Ibid.* sub. 30 July and 27 Aug., 1630; and Emerson's *First Church in Boston*, p. 11.
[4] Budington's *First Church in Charlestown*, p. 21.
[5] See Humphrey's *History Prop. Soc.*, pp. 24-31, for details of some of these troubles. Bishop Meade says, "immense were the difficulties of getting a full supply of ministers of any character; and of those who came, how few were faithful and duly qualified for the station!" [*Old Churches, Ministers, and Families of Virginia*, 1: 14.] The Churchwardens of St. John's Church, Elizabethtown, N. J., wrote to the Propagation Society, 26 Dec. 1747, mournfully complaining, — "the Dissenters can with great ease be supplyed with a Teacher; but alas! our infelicity is such that we must have recourse to a distant aid." Two years later, 25 Dec. 1749, they write, we "have but a melancholy prospect before us, and can foresee nothing but ruin of our Church. We have already been deprived for about two years of the ordinances of our holy Church, unless occasionally administered by the neighboring clergy, as it could consist with their duty to their respective Parishes." And the next year they say further (29 May, 1750) "as long as the Dissenters in this town have five ministers settled, constantly to officiate, in publick, to visit them in private, ready to serve on any particular occasion, and, in a word, that are always with and among them, and we can have none with us but once in three weeks or a month, who resides at the same time at 20 miles distant, with a ferry between him and us, which makes our dependence upon him at any particular time more uncertain, as long as this is the case, without a prospect of being better provided for, the difference is so great in their favor that most of our people might be persuaded to think it their duty, in that

at first sent over ordained clergymen,[1] but subsequently candidates for orders were raised up here and forwarded to the old country for consecration, though with indifferent success.[2] The question even arose of sending to Denmark for help.[3] At last an attempt was made to procure the right of ordination on this side the sea, and in 1783, Samuel Seabury having been elected Bishop by the Episcopalian clergy of Connecticut, went to London to receive consecration from the hands of the Archbishop of Canterbury. But, after months of

---

condition to join with the Dissenters." [Clark's *Hist. St. John's Church*, pp. 58, 64, 67.] The Virginia "Grand Assembly" passed an act, 17 Feb. 1644 – 5, designed to relieve the difficulties felt in that colony, growing out of their inability to procure ministers properly consecrated, "that where it soe falls out that any minister have induction into two or more cures farr distant one from another, whereby one cure must necessarily be neglected, it shall be lawful for the parishioners of such a cure to make vse of any other minister as a lecturer to baptise or preach," &c., &c. [Hening's *Statutes of Virginia*, 1619 - 1792, i: 289.]

[1] Humphrey's *History*, p. 11; Anderson's *History Col. Church*, i. 261, 410; Stith's *Virginia*, p. 173.

[2] "The exact number of those that have gone home for ordination, from these Northern Colonies is fifty-two. Of these, forty-two have returned safely, and ten have miscarried; the voyage or sickness occasioned by it, having proved fatal to near a fifth part of them." "Two perished in one ship upon the coast of New Jersey, almost in sight of their port." "In several instances our candidates have been carried into captivity — thrown into noisome prisons in an enemy's country — and there languished for many months under the most hideous forms of distress and wretchedness." "The members of the Church of England at *Hebron*, in Connecticut, exerted themselves for near twenty years, and were at great expense in sending home four candidates successively, before they had the satisfaction of enjoying a resident missionary. They first sent home Mr. Dean, in 1745, who was admitted to Holy Orders, and appointed by the Society [Propagation] their missionary for Hebron; but in returning to his mission, and to a wife and several small children who depended upon him for their daily support, he is supposed to have perished at sea, neither the ship nor any person on board having ever been heard from. The next was Mr. Colton; who in 1752, died on his passage from London to New England, and was buried in the ocean. The third candidate sent home by this unfortunate people was Mr. Usher; who, on his way to England, in 1757, was taken by the French, thrown into prison, and at last died in the Castle of Bayonne. The fourth was Mr. Peters; who, in 1759, not long after his arrival in England, was taken with the small-pox, from which he had the good fortune to recover, — and at length, to the great joy of the people, he arrived at Hebron, where he is at present the Society's worthy missionary." — [*The Appeal defended; or the proposed American Episcopate vindicated*, &c., &c., by Thomas Bradbury Chandler, D. D. New York, 1679. 8vo. pp. 268 — pp. 120, 121, 127.] Another difficulty, Dr. Chandler frankly confesses. He says, "a very glaring disadvantage to which the Church in America is manifestly subject, arises from the impossibility that a Bishop residing in England, should be sufficiently acquainted with the characters of those who go home from this country for holy orders. To this it is owing, that ordination has been sometimes fraudulently and surreptitiously obtained by such wretches, as are not only a scandal to the Church, but a disgrace to human nature." [*Appeal*, &c., p. 36. *Appeal defended*, &c., p. 131. See also Clark's *History of St. John's Church*.]

[3] The Theological Faculty of Denmark were consulted, and Count de Rosencrone communicated their favorable reply to the American Minister at St. James, from whom it was sent to Congress, and through them to the States. But no steps were taken further in that direction. [See *Life and Works of John Adams*, viii : 198. Also *Memoirs of Bishop White*, pp. 9, 10; and Hawks, i : 182.]

casuistic delay, his application was refused. He then applied to the non-juring Bishops of Scotland, who gladly made him as much of a Bishop as they could, and he returned home "with authority."[1] But as everything — on the Episcopal theory — hangs on an unmistakable connection with the Apostolical succession (Pope Joan included), and as there were doubts whether this irregularity might not vitiate the grace of the whole American Church,[2] Rev. Samuel Provoost of New York, and Rev. William White, of Philadelphia, were sent to England, and, after special act of Parliament, consecrated at Lambeth, 4th Feb. 1787, by the Archbishop of Canterbury, the Archbishop of York, and the Bishops of Bath and Wells, and Peterborough, assisting.[3]

Thus it was more than a century and a half after the country was settled, and had Episcopalian residents, before those difficulties in the way of the ordination of Episcopal clergymen here which were inseparable from their system,[4] could be removed.

The Presbyterian Church here, had no existence which enabled it to ordain regularly its candidates for the pulpit, until the formation of a Presbytery in 1705, or 1706.[5]

It was eighteen years, also, after Philip Embury gathered the first

---

[1] Hollister's *History of Connecticut*, vol. II., pp. 548–50.

[2] The celebrated Granville Sharp doubted the sufficiency of the Scotch ordinations, and interested himself to dissatisfy American Episcopalians with them, to Bishop Seabury's disadvantage; making President Manning, of Brown University, his correspondent. Sharp had in his possession documents belonging to his ancestor, an Archbishop of York, throwing doubt upon the regularity and validity of the Scotch Episcopate; on the strength of which he labored through Manning with Provoost of New York. The thing resulted in Provoost and White's receiving English consecration. The same qestion of purity now lies, however, at the door of every Episcopal ordination in this country since 1792, for when Bishop Claggett of Maryland was consecrated, in that year, Seabury shared with the other Bishops in the ceremonial; so that, to use the words of Dr. Hawks, [*Contributions to the Ecclesiastical History of the United States*, vol. ii : 312.] "not a Bishop has been consecrated since Bishop Claggett, who must not, to make his consecration canonical, claim the succession, *in part at least*, through the Scottish Episcopate." The most unkindest cut of all is, that this Scotch dilution was thus brought about by the Maryland Church with malice aforethought; expressly "to prevent thereafter forever, the possibility of a question arising in the American Episcopal Church, on the relative validity of the English and Scotch Episcopate." [*Ibid.*, p. 311. For interesting facts with reference to this subject, read *Bishop Seabury and Bishop Provoost, by the Rev. W. S. Perry*, 8vo. pp. 20, 1862, and *Bishop Seabury and the "Episcopal Recorder,"* — *a vindication*. 8vo., pp. 43, 1863, by the same. Consult also Guild's *Life of Manning*, p. 358; *Dr. Hawks*, vol. i., chap. 10; and Anderson's *History of the Colonial Church*, iii : 284.]

[3] Anderson's *History of the Colonial Church*, iii : 285.

[4] "For about two hundred years did the Episcopal Church of Virginia try the experiment of a system whose constitution required such a head [a Bishop] but was actually without it." [Bishop Meade's *Old Churches, Ministers and Families of Virginia*, 1: 15.]

[5] Gillett's *Hist. Pres. Church in U. S. A.*, 1: 18.

Methodist assembly in the city of New York, before, in 1784, Methodism was formally organized here under Mr. Wesley's direction, so that its movements became regular; although in its irregularity it had accumulated 15,000 members, and 83 preachers.[1] So great was the annoyance experienced from this delay, that some of the preachers sought to remedy it by the Congregational ordination of each other;[2] but Mr. Asbury finally succeeded, after indefatigable toil, in bringing back these seceders one by one, in procuring the conferences to pronounce these ordinations invalid, and in so reducing things to "order;" being obliged, however, in doing so, to procure some of the few Episcopalian clergy to travel over large circuits,[3] for the purpose of canonically baptizing the children of the Methodists, and administering to them the eucharist.[4]

It is in place to add here, that the Congregational system has a practicableness in the matter of the pastorate, superior to those which oppose it, not merely in procuring and ordaining, but also — when painfully necessary — in deposing its incumbent. As we have shown,[5] every Congregational Church whose pastor becomes unworthy, through false doctrine or evil life, both may, and ought to, call him to immediate account. If fair investigation of the case compels the conclusion that he has made himself unfit to be continued in his place, it should so far regard the fellowship of the churches as to call a Council, to whose advice the question of their duty should be submitted; after which, no prevalent reason urging a contrary course, it is both their right and duty to depose him from his ministry over them, and cut him off from his membership with them. This is short and simple, yet fair to all parties, and sufficient to all results. Such an offending pastor, as a churchmember, is tried by his peers in the Church; and, as a minister, is tried — to all intents and purposes — by his ministerial peers in Council — so that he has no ground of just complaint. And if it be suggested that he is exposed to the force of local prejudice, in such a local court, it is fair to urge in reply that he also receives the full benefit of all local attachment of friends

---

[1] Stevens's *Memorials of Methodism*, p. 35.
[2] Hawks's *Contributions, &c.*, I : 148 ; *Jarratt's Life*, p. 111.
[3] *Coke and More's Life of Wesley*, p. 351; *Jarratt's Life*, 114.
[4] See Ferris's *Original Settlements on the Delaware*, p. 147, for some details of the difficulty experienced by the early Swedish settlements in this country, in securing a clergy deemed competent by themselves; sending in vain first to Sweden, and then (1691) to Amsterdam.
[5] See p. 205.

and neighbors, and if he cannot justify himself there, with their aid, it must be because he is essentially unjust. It is obvious also that there is much less exposure to circumstantial impediments thrown in the way to postpone or defeat the ends of justice, in this simple system than in any other.

In the Episcopalian Church, deprivation of the clerical office is effected by the sentence of a court, presided over by the Bishop of the Diocese, and if the offender be a Bishop, by trial before a court of Bishops. This brings in the elements of distance, postponement, and uncertainty. The Episcopal Church in Virginia, suffered for nearly two centuries with "unworthy and hireling clergy," whose "irregularities and vices, there was no Ecclesiastical discipline to correct or punish."[1] And in our own day, that Church in this land has borne the disgrace of being practically unable to secure the deposition of Bishops[2] whose absence from that high office, in the general judgment of the Christian community, would have both honored and purified it.

In the Methodist Church, a Bishop is amenable only to the General Conference; though he may be suspended until the time of its meeting by a special court of Presiding and Travelling Elders. An Elder is tried before a court of Travelling Elders, who suspend him, if they think fit, until the next Annual Conference; which fully considers and determines his case; an appeal always lying from the decision of the Annual, to that of the General Conference.[3]

In the Presbyterian Church, process against a minister must be initiated before the Presbytery to which he belongs; the prosecutor being previously warned that if he fails to prove his charges, he himself will come under censure as a slanderer. If condemned, the accused has the right of appeal to the Synod, and thence to the General Assembly. Months and years may thus pass, before the last appeal is reached; which, when it is reached, may be under circumstances most unfortunate, by reason of delay, distance, the absence of witnesses, &c., for the ends of justice.[4]

---

[1] Bishop Meade's *Old Churches, &c.*, 1: 15.
[2] See the *Proceedings of the Court for the trial of Rt. Rev. B. T. Onderdonk, D. D.*, pp. 333. New York, 1845; also the trial of Bishop Doane, as given in his *Life and Writings*, 1: 468-511. The latter gloried in doing what he could to "MAKE THE TRIAL OF A BISHOP HARD," on principle, and for "the safety of the Episcopal order."—*Ibid.* p. 505.
[3] *Book of Discipline*, Part I., Chap. 10.
[4] See the case of Rev. George Bourne, who was deposed, 27 Dec. 1815, by the Lexington

(3.) *Congregationalism is more practicable than any other form of Church government in its methods of worship.*

It is so in that it has no forms which are essential to its good order and well being; but flexibly adapts itself to any just taste, and every providential need.[1] Its worship can be lawfully and acceptably rendered, by chant or song; through an exact and complete liturgy,[2] or in the freest extempore utterance; by a robed officiator, or by one in the layest of all lay attire; under a

> "High-embowed roof,
> With antick pillars massy proof,
> And storied windows richly dight,
> Casting a dim religious light;"

or in the rudest and barest of all conventicle halls. It has absolutely but two forms which approximate toward fixedness, and these are only so far fixed as that, by common consent of propriety and duty, its ministry almost invariably use that formula for baptism,

---

Presbytery, and whose case was not finally settled, on its ultimate appeal to the General Assembly, until the session of 1818; and, on his request to be restored, was in 1824, sent down to the Presbytery of New York, with instructions to "continue the sentence of deposition or restore him, as they may judge proper." [*Assembly's Digest*, ed. 1858, pp. 165-167.] See also the cases of Rev. Samuel Harker, deposed in 1763, after having been in process of trial during five years, [*Digest*, pp. 624-627]; Rev. Hezekiah Balch, who was suspended in 1798 [*Digest*, pp. 629-634]; Rev. William C. Davis, suspended and deposed, Oct. 1811, after having been on trial four years [*Digest*, pp. 646-649]; and Rev. Thomas B. Craighead, suspended by the Synod of Kentucky in 1809, and finally conditionally restored on the decision of the Assembly in 1824; his offence having been committed in and before 1806, and he dying, after *eighteen years* of delay, before the next General Assembly could get a return from the Presbytery of West Tennessee, to whom it had sent down his case.—[*Digest*, pp. 649-655.]

[1] It is sometimes amusing, to those who are irreverent enough to allow themselves to be amused by it, to see the shifts to which some of the sects are put to save their homage to forms. The first holding of an Episcopalian service in a strange locality, involves an amount of solicitude on the part of the partially initiated as to the finding and keeping of their place in the Prayer Book, which is perilous both to gravity and devotion. While the official — not to say heartless — resort to the form of prayer for such cases made and provided, often robs the visit of such a clergyman to the sick room, of all its tender comfort.

[2] Some Congregational churches prefer a liturgy. That in use by the Church under the pastorate of Newman Hall, worshipping in Surrey Chapel, Blackfriars' Road, London, which was originally prepared by Rowland Hill, is an admirable specimen of what such a liturgy may be. It is largely indebted to that of the Church of England, yet briefer, more simple, more humanly touching, and leaving a large margin for the minister's extemporaneous words. [See Rev. W. L. Gage, in the *Congregationalist* for Feb. 10, 1865.] The Leyden Church in Boston printed, in 1846, a manual for their own use, which partook largely of the liturgical element. The "Church of the Pilgrims" in Brooklyn, N. Y., have lately sanctioned a moderate infusion of the same element in their Sabbath service. There is nothing to hinder any Congregational Church which desires to do so, from worshipping God with the aid of the full Episcopalian service, or with that of the Presbyterian, or German Reformed churches, or with any form which it may itself desire. No other Church has absolute freedom in this matter, like it.

which is suggested by Christ's parting words,[1] and that method in the administration of the ordinance of the Lord's Supper which follows most naturally the record of the three Gospels,[2] and of Paul.[3] All else is perfectly free to follow the choice of the local assembly, the convenience of the hour, the suggestion of the *genius loci*, the general judgment of what, on the whole, is best. This combines at once the maximum of practicableness with the minimum of inconvenience.

It is not so tied down to any prescribed ritual growing out of that order of fasts, festivals, and commemoration days, which the Church of the past in its corrupt days established, that it cannot accept and honor any new thought which Providence flashes upon the public mind athwart that order.[4] Nor are its ministers obliged to wait to hear from a "Bishop," before they can offer prayer suitable to a sudden exigence.[5]

(4.) *Congregationalism is more practicable than any other form of Church government in all Church work.*

The proper work of a Church of Christ respects the admission

---

[1] Matt. xxviii: 19.
[2] Matt. xxvi: 26-29; Mark xiv: 22-25; Luke xxii: 19, 20.
[3] 1 Cor. xi: 23-26.
[4] The death of President Lincoln threw the nation into mourning on the Saturday before Easter Sunday for 1865; so that those churches which are bound in the fetters of the "Ecclesiastical Year," were, in a manner, constrained to enter upon the most jubilant services of the whole twelvemonth, while all others were weeping and mourning in their draped and darkened sanctuaries under the dreadful pressure of the most sudden and poignant grief.
[5] On the Saturday of the President's death, some of the Bishops of the Episcopal Church, it is said, issued a form of prayer to be used in all the churches in their dioceses on the next day, with reference to that event; but as it must have been well-nigh a physical impossibility for that form to have seasonably reached their most remote parishes, some of their rectors must have been embarrassed. A curious instance of the infelicity of these rigid rules occured lately in Richmond, Va., since its occupation by the National troops. "General Order, No. 29," enjoined that "in all churches where prayers have heretofore been offered for the so-called President of the Confederate States, a similar mark of respect is hereby ordered to be paid to the President of the United States." The rules of the Episcopal Church prescribe that while *omissions* may be made in its prescribed prayers, no portion of them shall be *changed*, except by authority from the Bishop of the Diocese. The prayers heretofore used included the words "Confederate States," and though the Richmond clergymen were at liberty, and were willing, to omit the objectionable words, they had no authority to substitute therefor the words "United States," and Bishop Johns being in Halifax, no authorization from him could be obtained. In this dilemma, the Episcopal clergymen waited upon General Ord, and stated the case. He blandly replied, that the explanation was quite satisfactory, but the churches must be closed; they were in duty bound to obey their Ecclesiastical, and he his military, superiors. — *Richmond Whig*, 17 April, 1865.

and care of its membership, the Christian culture of that membership, and through them the evangelization of the world around it. The New Testament throws upon the individual members of the Church, as we have seen,[1] the responsibility of keeping the body pure from all who walk disorderly; which necessarily involves the duty on their part both of scrutiny over the admission, and watchfulness over the life, of one another. This duty Congregationalism makes practicable in the simplest and directest form, by committing the admission and discipline of all, to the scrutiny and vote of all. On the other hand, the Episcopal Church admits its members only by act of the Bishop on the certificate of the Rector;[2] the Methodist Church, by the Elder in charge of the circuit, on recommendation of a class leader;[3] and the Presbyterian Church, by vote of its Session — of the Pastor and Ruling Elders;[4] the membership, in such case, having no direct voice, and so no opportunity to discharge

---

[1] See pp. 28, and 189-195.

[2] It will be noted that hopeful piety is not hinted at as a requisite for admission to the Episcopal Church, the rubric being; "so soon as children are come to a competent age, and can say the Creed, the Lord's Prayer, and the Ten Commandments, and can answer the other questions of the short catechism, they shall be brought to the Bishop, and whensoever the Bishop shall give knowledge for children to be brought unto him for their confirmation, the minister of every Parish shall either bring, or send in writing, with his hand subscribed thereunto, the names of all such persons within his Parish, as he shall think fit to be presented to the Bishop to be confirmed." — *Prayer Book; Rubric for Confirmation.*

[3] The Methodist requisite for Church-membership is simply "a desire to flee from the wrath to come, and to be saved from their sins," — such persons are received, as above. See *Book, Part I., Chap. II.,* Sect. 2. The Richmond, Va., *Religious Herald,* of 15 Feb., 1865, stated that the subject of "unconverted Church-membership" was exciting attention among Methodists in North Carolina, and added, "Their Annual Conference for that State, adopted at its last session, a resolution expressing the opinion, that 'unconverted persons are not entitled to membership in the Methodist Protestant Church.' The Quarterly Conference of the Catawba Circuit decided to regard that resolution 'as not binding,' because it 'comes in contact with the second article of the Constitution.'"

[4] The theory of the Presbyterian Church is open to the same objection, of looseness in the admission of members without requiring evidence of regeneration as an indispensable condition; though its practice is believed to be better than its theory in this particular. Their canon is, "children, born within the pale of the visible Church, and dedicated to God in baptism, are under the inspection and government of the Church; and are to be taught to read and repeat the catechism, the Apostle's creed, and the Lord's prayer. They are to be taught to pray, to abhor sin, to fear God, and to obey the Lord Jesus Christ. — And, when they come to years of discretion, *if they be free from scandal, appear sober and steady, and to have sufficient knowledge to discern the Lord's body, they ought to be informed it is their duty and privilege to come to the Lord's supper.* The years of discretion, in young Christians, cannot be precisely fixed. This must be left to the prudence *of the Eldership.* The *officers of the Church* are the judges of the qualifications of those to be admitted to sealing ordinances, &c., &c." — *Directory for Worship,* Chap. ix., Sects. 1, 2.

themselves of their responsibility in regard to the increase of their number.

So in the matter of keeping the Church pure, in all other churches the trial of offences is removed from the people into the hands of the hierarchy; where, if a disagreement occurs, the case is liable to pass on and up until months, and very likely years, may pass before it reaches ultimate decision at the hands of the highest authority — Pope, Patriarch, King, General Convocation, Assembly, or Conference, as the case may be. As we propose, however, to refer to this point more at large again, we do not dwell upon it here.[1]

In the Christian culture of its membership, Congregationalism has superior practicability in the fact, that by its very nature it makes continual appeal to the conscience, the judgment, and the volition and activity of all its constituent individuals; while personal growth in grace requires such continual appeal. In virtue of its fundamental principle, which makes every individual assume, under Christ, his own share of the direct responsibility of the success or failure of the Gospel; its natural effect is to make its members considerate, prayerful, earnest — never allowing them to throw off the blame of failure, or disaster, upon the hierarchy, or "the Church." Its tendency is to bring each of its members into direct contact with all practical duty, and to crowd home continually upon every conscience the fact that Christ expects every one to glorify God in body and spirit, which are His, and to do it in meat and drink and all things — a tendency obviously of the highest value in promoting eminent piety and earnest spirituality.

We would be very far from asserting that other families of believers do not appreciate the importance of entire consecration to God, and do not realize eminent attainments in holiness. What we claim, is that in doing so, they are obliged to work against some of the centripetal and narcotic tendencies of their polities, while we work thus in directest harmony with the individualizing and stimulating qualities of our own.

But this, and the special practicableness of Congregationalism for furthering the work of the Church upon the world, we propose to develop more fully hereafter.[2]

---

[1] See pp. 260, 288.   [2] See p. 273.

SECTION 3. *Congregationalism is better than any other form of Church government, because it tends more to promote general intelligence.*

Its first principles throw it upon the sympathy and respect of the masses, and claim for it their love and support; and in gaining their love and support it works them into its service; and its service is a service of thought, and so of intellectual quickening. The Church, Congregationally administered, calls upon every one of its members, even the humblest, to take a part with every other, in deciding its great questions of faith and duty. It accustoms, therefore, all its members to think, and compare, and choose, and act, under the most inspiring and impressive sanctions. The humblest member of a Congregational Church may, at any time, be called upon to discuss — and perhaps, by his individual vote, to settle — a question, in its temporal and eternal reachings and interests, infinitely graver than any on which our Senators and Representatives are accustomed to vote at Washington. No member can be received, none dismissed, none disciplined, without the question being put to each member of the fraternity: What is right concerning this; what ought to be done; what disposal of it will most please Christ? Thus the habit of acting under responsibility, and with intelligence, is nurtured in the community, and the general mind is quickened, and independent thought and action promoted. Each man is treated as if he were a *man*, full grown, and as if Christ had a work for *him* to do; and as if all his choices and labors were of everlasting account, and he must, therefore, concentrate his whole mind upon the service. That intellectual labor which is done for the membership of the hierarchal churches by their constituted officials,[1] in the way of settling great principles of doctrine and great questions of policy, Congregationalism compels her membership — either in the work of origination, or the question of final concurrence — to do for themselves;[2] and so,

---

[1] When the *man* sinks under the *polity*, he loses somewhat of his impulse to form his own opinions; and is sometimes persuaded to abnegate the right of private judgment."—Prof. Park's *Fitness of the Church to the Constitution of Renewed Men*, p. 47.

[2] "A poor man in an established Church is nothing but a poor man; but with the Dissenters, he is at the same time a moralist, a divine, a metaphysician, and an ecclesiastical politician — in short, a kind of universal scholar and philosopher. He has a character for knowledge to maintain as well as for morals and piety, and soon acquires a degree of acuteness and information, to which his brethren in the establishment can make no pretensions. His acquirements, it is true, may occasionally be attended with some inconvenience — for every good

since they have thus to perform the work of Kings and Bishops and Priests, she makes them to become "a royal priesthood, a holy nation, a peculiar people, that they (individually) should show forth the praises of him who hath called them out of nature's darkness into his marvellous light," — which is just what Peter said Christians ought to be.

Congregationalism — to use the words of one of its most eminent living transatlantic writers — " covets most earnestly popular intelligence, as the soil from which extraordinary minds may be expected most naturally to spring up, and from which alone they can derive permanent sustenance and power. It aims to form intelligent churches; it *must*, in consequence, have an intelligent ministry; and it must, as a further consequence, have its seminaries of learning to realize that intelligence. It rests nothing upon privilege, or prescription, but everything upon truth and reason. It leans not on extraneous support of any kind, but upon its own intrinsic merits. It knows that the learning and science of the world may be arrayed against it, and it is prepared to do battle with the learning and science of the world in its own cause, and to abide single-handed the issues of that conflict. This is the spirit of our system, and if so, where is the department of knowledge with which it may not be expected to sympathize and intermeddle? It may content itself with average attainments for average purposes; but it does not rest at that point. Its argument depends on a wide range of philosophy and history, and embraces a multitude of subtle questions relating to social polity and the nature of man; — can these things be wisely dealt with by the ignorant, or by only the moderately informed? It contemplates changes which will affect the whole complexion of modern society; and its reasons for these changes must be shewn, or its pretensions be mockery."[1]

Not without some honest pride may the Congregationalist point to New England, with its world-conceded unusual average of general

---

has some corresponding evil very near it — and may lead him to imagine, that he is far more learned than he really is. But this folly is not one of the most dangerous kind; and, for ourselves, we would much rather fall in with a poor and industrious peasant, though elated perhaps a little too much with his stock of ecclesiastical, and theological, and metaphysical words and knowledge, than with the most quiet and passive drudge which the country can furnish. The former, whatever be his imperfections, is more of a human being than the latter." — Ballantyne's *Comparison of Established and Dissenting Churches*, p. 200.

[1] Dr. Vaughan's *Congregationalism Viewed in Relation to Modern Society, &c.*, p. 17.

popular intelligence, as the demonstration of what that free religious system, which founded her social as well as religious institutions, and — with all dilutions and alien admixtures — has substantially made her what she is, can do for the general culture of mankind. As long ago as the colonial times, when the influence of Congregationalism in this particular was here almost unmixed, Governor Hutchinson remarked that "men took sides in New England upon mere speculative points in government, when there was nothing in practice which could give any ground for forming parties;"[1] and Edmund Burke declared in Parliament, that the American "mode of professing" religion was a "main cause" of their "fierce spirit of liberty." He characterised our Congregationalism as "the dissidence of dissent, and the Protestantism of the Protestant religion — of that kind most adverse to all implicit submission of mind and opinion," and in remarking upon the position of the people with regard to intelligence, he quotes Governor Gage to the effect, that "all the people in his government are lawyers, or smatterers in law," and proceeds himself to characterise them as "acute, inquisitive, dexterous, prompt in attack, ready in defence, full of resources. In other countries, the people more simple, and of a less mercurial cast, judge of an ill principle in government only by an actual grievance; here they anticipate the evil, and judge of the pressure of the grievance by the baseness of the principle."[2]

The inevitableness of popular intelligence as the result of a living Congregationalism is well set forth by one of our own lay writers — "the *priest* gave way to the *preacher*, and the gospel was *preached*. The ministers were now to instruct the people, to reason before them and with them, to appeal to them; and so by their very position and relation, the people were constituted the judges. They were called upon to decide; they also reasoned."[3] Like its counterpart in civil order — Republicanism — our religious system cannot be true to itself without favoring, both directly and indirectly, the fullest diffusion of knowledge among all the people. It is the friend of the masses. Free schools are among its means of grace.[4]

---

[1] Quoted in the *The Pulpit of the American Revolution*, p. xxvii.
[2] *Burke's Works*, (Bohn's Ed.) 1 : 466, 468.
[3] J. Wingate Thornton, Esq. *The Pulpit of the American Revolution*, xxvii.
[4] "Our fathers acted out the real feelings which their ecclesiastical system inspired, when they sent preachers to the red men, as soon as they had built churches for themselves and

SECTION 4. *Congregationalism is superior to any other form of Church government, because it naturally tends, more than any other, to promote piety in its membership.*

There are four accessories of the highest form of piety in the Church. It is needful that each individual Christian be thoroughly aroused to his duty of personal responsibility, and then that he be thrown earnestly upon the Bible, and the Spirit, and the Saviour, for their aid and guidance, to the end that he be aroused to the full comprehension of what he ought to be and to do, and what he can be and do, for God; and that, in the full understanding of this, he may grow up to the measure of the stature of the fullness of Christ. Our system especially favors the success of each of these preliminary works.

(1.) *Congregationalism develops, as no other system naturally does, the sense of individual responsibility in private Christians.*

Christ left the command to his followers to disciple all nations, and preach the gospel to every creature. That command was addressed to those who loved him, as individuals. And the only reason which can be given why it has not been obeyed; why the earth is not now the Lord's, and the fullness thereof; is that enough Christians have not yet felt their *individual responsibility* to that command, and obeyed it; by giving their prayers, their alms, and themselves, to missionary labor. No man will dare to say — since Christ has been eighteen centuries waiting to see of the travail of his soul, and help the work — that there has not yet been money enough, and knowledge enough, and everything enough in the world to have converted the whole of it long ago; provided individual Christians enough had left money-getting, and politics, and all sorts of secularities, and devoted themselves, with all their hearts, to this preaching the gospel to every creature. The great demand of Christianity, it is confessed on all hands, now is, to arouse and deepen and quicken that feeling in every Christian heart, which says; " Christ died for

---

had scarcely reared their own cottages, at the time of their beginning to erect a university for the defence and dissemination of the Gospel; and they established a system of collegiate instruction better fitted for their times than the present system is for our times." Prof. Park's *Fitness of the Church, &c.*, p. 45. The Synod of 1697, urged, "the interests of Religion and good Literature have been wont to rise and fall together." — Elliott's *New England*, i : 428.

me, and I must do something for him. That great command binds *me.* Lord, what wilt thou have *me* to do?"

But when we desire to awaken a sense of personal responsibility in our children, we make them do responsible things. Give a child a sum of money, and require him to expend it according to his best judgment for the poor; or let him make such purchases as he thinks wisest for the family — and you begin, at once, to develop the feeling of personal responsibility. He is "somebody," and he is always more man-like thereafter. Trust him to go a journey, and carry a message of consequence, and no wealth of words, no abundance of books on journeying, will do half so much to train him, in that direction, as this *trusting him to do it.* This is common sense in everything to which it applies. And Congregationalism, by trusting everything to her private members, trains them to a sense of individual responsibility, which must be unknown to the subjects of an Ecclesiastical hierarchy. Every member of a Congregational Church has as real a responsibility as any Cardinal who sat in the Council of Trent; for his vote says yea or nay to every doctrine which that Council had under discussion. Does the Church languish, our membership cannot turn to each other, and say, " I wish our Bishops, or our General Assembly, would see what is the matter, and tell us what is to be done." Each one is compelled to sit down for himself to devise what is to be done; feeling that no mitre, nor surplice, nor convocation comes between him and blame, if things go wrong. Congregationalism places its members, in regard to all Ecclesiastical responsibility, precisely where they are in the matter of their personal salvation. To know what to do to be saved, they go to no Bishop, and to no Body, and to no book, but the Word of God'; and bringing the naked truth of revelation to bear upon their necessity, they get an answer to their question. So, to know what to do in the Church — what is Orthodox, what is orderly — they go, as before, to no manual, and to no man, but to the self-same truth of God — and bringing, as before, its light to bear upon their duty, they decide and do. All this is simple, self-consistent, successful. It makes intelligent, earnest, growing, useful Christians. It makes them, consistently with all the principles of its system; and not in spite of them, as other systems must. Hence Congregationalism is marked by its missionary spirit and success, not merely in its work in heathen lands, and in the waste places of the West, — but at its own doors — in mission schools and tract distribution, and the general home work.

(2.) *Congregationalism throws its membership more directly upon the Bible, and the Holy Spirit, and the Saviour, than any other system.*

Nothing comes between the Congregationalist and these original and celestial sources of light and love. No question of doctrine or practice can be put to him which he may not, and must not, naturally, take to them for answer. We, of course, would be far from intimating that good men of other systems do not ask God for wisdom, and open the Bible for light, but we do say that their systems not only do not so much favor this, but do not even permit them to do it simply and purely. They have always a double question; "is this in accordance with the Book of Discipline — with the established order of our Church?" as well as, "does it accord with the Word of God, and the promptings of the Spirit, and the example of Christ?"

Now, to any man who remembers how strong is the tendency of poor human nature toward that which is material and visible, instead of that which is unseen and eternal, it will be clear that any system which propounds such double questions, will be apt to get its best answers to its easiest inquiries, and that its tendency will be very strong to incline the mind to rest in the lower authority — as to be assumed to be, as a matter of course, in accordance with the higher. It takes more faith to get an answer from God than it does from a hierarchy, and therefore, when hierarchies are accessible to answer questions, and assume the responsibility, faith in God grows dull.

Congregationalism has no ritual, no ceremonies, no book of discipline — nothing but the Bible in the hand, the Spirit in the heart, and Christ overhead. That is all. Its prayers, its songs, its sermons, all get their vitality from the Bible, as the seed out of which they grow; from the Holy Spirit, as the influence that makes them grow; from the Saviour as the Good Master, under whose eye, and to please whose heart, and promote whose cause, all is done.

Its methods of operation, also, all throw it directly upon the naked truth, with nothing between it and the soul. If a Pastor is to be chosen or removed; if a member is to be admitted or disciplined — whatever is to be done affecting, in any way, the interests of the Church or the general cause, no Pope nor Bishop settles it; no organism sits in solemn conclave upon it, and decrees how it shall be, — thrusting themselves and their *dictum* between the Church and the truth; no Book of Discipline, or Chapter of Canons interposes the fossil judgment of the dead; but each Church-member is called upon (before God, and in the love of Christ, and out of the Bible, as interpreted to him by the Holy Ghost,) to say how it shall be.

All this magnifies the truth and makes it honorable. It forms the habit of reliance upon the Bible in all things — the custom of submitting *every* concern of life to the same truth for decision. It makes independent thinkers, who are almost necessarily the most efficient laborers. It accustoms its subjects to the most constant practical communion with God, through his Word, and his Spirit, and his Son; because it so places them that they must daily do many things which they necessarily feel that they cannot do suitably — not even safely — except by the results of such communion. *They* navigate the ship which carries them — they can lean upon no captain or mate — and the urgency of their own interest in its fortunes, as well as their desire, for Christ's sake, that it should safely reach its desired haven, drives them daily to the quadrant and the sun, and hourly to the log, and momently to the compass; that they may work out their own salvation with fear and trembling.

It is agreed that the Scripture theory of the most perfect Christian life, is of one united to Christ "as the branch is to the vine;" living in him; going directly to him with all perplexities, and getting from him a resolution of all doubts. Now we maintain that our system falls in with this theory of life, and works directly toward its realization throughout the length and breadth of the Church, training its membership to do that very thing — to lean upon God, without any hierarchal inventions, which are interventions — putting nothing between the visible Church and its invisible Head, and distracting the mind with no side issues, confusing it with no jar and din of machinery. As in the old-fashioned saw-mills, where one shaft went directly from the crank on the end of the water-wheel to the saw — so here, the motive power is geared directly to the work that is to be done. There is the least possible friction, and if anything is out of order, there is but one place to be visited to discover what it is. Whereas these great affiliated hierarchies are like huge cotton-mills, where thousands of looms and tens of thousands of spindles are belted together — there is story piled on story; there is confusion and clatter, and enormous friction, and, when something breaks, hundreds of places may need to be visited before it can be determined what it is that needs repair.

We do not claim that every, or even any, Congregational Church is, — few things are what they might be — but we do claim that any and every one ought to be, and could be, and would be, if it did justice to its own peculiar principles, such a nursery of the highest, purest, clearest, holiest, most blessed and beneficent communion with God, and walk with him, as the earth can see nowhere else, and as heaven would look upon with strange joy.

SECTION 5. *Congregationalism is superior in that it more favors true Gospel discipline, and so especially tends to promote the purity of the Church of Christ.*

This has been hinted already,[1] but it demands further exposition.

If a member of a Congregational Church — be he officer or private member — becomes guilty of faith or practices contrary to Godliness, and inconsistent with Christian purity; the directions of the Saviour in the eighteenth of Matthew are literally followed. He is labored with, in the intent to bring him to repentance and reformation, by some suitable fellow member, who tells him of his fault " alone," seeking to " gain " his brother. But if the effort be unsuccessful, and he will not "hear," the affectionate endeavor is repeated, in the presence of " one or two more, that in the mouth of two or three witnesses, every word may be established."[2] If he remain incorrigible, the matter is brought to the notice of the Church, in its collective capacity; who labor with him. Should he deny his guilt, a fair trial is granted, in which his rights are scrupulously guarded, and if its result prove him in the wrong, they suspend him from all privileges of communion, until his day of penitence, or cut him off from membership, and make him to them " as a heathen man, and a publican."

---

[1] See pp. 41, 188 et seq., and p. 241.   [2] Matt. xviii: 16.

If he feels that he has been misunderstood and hardly used, he can ask them to call with him a council of the delegates of sister churches to review the case, and give advice. If they decline to aid him in such a review, he can call such a council, by himself, which council, examining the case, would advise all parties to adhere to, or suitably to modify, the former decision. And then the Church, and the offender, follow this advice, or not, as in their judgment, duty, and the will of Christ, demand.

This way of discipline commits the custody of the rectitude of the Church to the Church itself, and so stimulates the individual conscience, and promotes fidelity and purity. As every member of the brotherhood is charged before God with his own share of the responsibility of maintaining a conscience and a life void of offence, not only for himself, but for the whole body of which he is a member, a degree of watchfulness and care is secured which is highly favorable to the ends of Church discipline, and which almost necessarily goes beyond what is easily attainable in other communions.

With them, the trial of offences is removed from the people into the hands of the hierarchy. The Presbyterians provide that the "judicatory" shall initiate and carry forward all Church discipline.[1] By consequence, until the oligarchy of the session is ready to proceed in the matter, nothing can be done. If — through prejudice, or indifference, or the fear to offend important men — it is never ready, the process of discipline is made impossible, since the complainant has no right of appeal to the Church as a body, and the higher Church courts, if requested, may decline to interfere.[2] In the Prot-

---

[1] Directory for Worship, &c., Chap. x., Sect. 2.

[2] A case in point, not long ago occurred in the Madison Square Presbyterian Church, in New York city. In the course of business transactions, difficulties arose between Mr. George D. Phelps and Mr. William E. Dodge, which involved grave charges of moral delinquency — of "gross misrepresentation," "malignancy," "false and wicked insinuations," "vindictiveness," &c., &c. — by the latter against the former. This led to a correspondence, continued at intervals for three years, or more, in which the offender declined either to confess the wrong, or to refer the whole matter to mutual friends for advice and settlement. Failing in all such efforts to right himself, Mr. Phelps, in April, 1862, brought the matter to the notice of the Session of the Madison Square Church. A committee was appointed to confer with the parties and endeavor to bring about a settlement, but Mr. Dodge persistently refused to see either the committee, or Mr. Phelps. On the 20th October, the committee reported to the Session that they "had been unable to accomplish the objects for which they were appointed." The Session, 4th November, adjourned consideration of the subject to allow another effort at pacification, and 8th December, an agreement was signed by the parties to submit all matters to five mutual friends; but Mr. Dodge the next day erased his name and repudiated the contract.

estant Episcopal Church' the duty of purifying the Church from scandal and offense, seems to rest primarily on its rector. The first two rubrics of the Communion service require the minister to prevent (1) "open and notorious evil livers," &c., and (2) those "betwixt whom he perceiveth malice and hated to reign," from coming "to be partakers of the Holy Communion;" and to give account of the same "to the Ordinary [that is, the Bishop] as soon as conven-

---

On the 18th December, the Session, to whose hands the matter now reverted, voted, "that, in view of all the circumstances of the case, and in the exercise of the discretion enjoined upon the Session by our Book of Discipline, it is inexpedient for the Session to entertain the charges and specifications of Mr. Phelps against Mr. Dodge, and that the same are hereby dismissed." Mr. Phelps carried his case up, by appeal and complaint, to the Fourth Presbytery of New York. The Presbytery met 19th January, 1863, specially to hear the case. It immediately adopted the "General Rules for Judicatories" in the appendix of "the Book" for the government of its business, and by Rule XI., of that code, appointed a "Judicial Committee" of five ministers and one Elder. The papers containing the appeal and complaint were placed in the hands of this committee. Mr. Phelps attempted to address the Presbytery, but was ruled out of order by the moderator. He appealed, but the Presbytery sustained the decision of the moderator. The Judicial Committee reported that " the matter be dismissed," because an appeal or complaint presupposes a trial with a result, and in this case there had been no trial in the court below [the Session] and so no appeal could hold. The Presbytery then heard Mr. Phelps and the Session, after which they sustained the report dismissing the case. Mr. Phelps gave notice of appeal from the Presbytery to the Synod, but despairing of obtaining justice by the Presbyterian Church courts in face of an opposition so determined and violent as he had already encountered, he desisted from all further attempts in that direction. The case, however, came indirectly before the Synod at its next meeting, in their review of the records of the Fourth Presbytery of New York; when the Synod approved the record, with the exception of the principle on which the Presbytery acted, viz: that there could be no appeal except after trial of a cause with a result, on which state of the case, however, they took no action, inasmuch as they said "the assumption of the false principle has led to no result which makes it the duty of the Synod to require the Presbytery to revise and correct its proceedings."

This case, then, sums up thus: One Christian brother receives gross and repeated injury — as he thinks — from another; he labors for years in vain personally, and through mutual friends, to have the difficulty settled; he brings the matter on complaint before the Session of his Church; they dismiss his case — as he feels, most injuriously, and through the predominant influence over its small number, of relatives and special friends of the offender; he carries the case up to Presbytery, who coolly tell him that nothing can be appealed but a judgment, after trial, so that his grievance (which has been specially aggravated by the fact that he has not been able to get any judgment upon it in the lower court,) can receive no attention there; discouraged, the injured man gives up all hope of receiving a reasonable settlement of his case by the vaunted Church courts of Presbyterianism, but — as if to clinch the nail, and prove beyond the possibility of a doubt, the essential weakness of their system in this respect — the Synod, having the matter subsequently indirectly before them, condemn the principle on which the Presbytery dismissed the case, and yet approve that dismission!

For the facts in the case, see *The Polity of Presbyterianism, in a review of proceedings of a Session, Presbytery, and Synod in a recent case of discipline*, by J. Holmes Agnew, D. D., New York, 1864, 8vo., pp. 40; *A New Phase in Ecclesiastical Law and Presbyterian Church Government, &c., &c.* New York: 1863, 8vo. pp. 64; *Supplement to a New Phase, &c., &c.* New York: 1864, 8vo., pp. 30; *Review of the Report of the Committee of Investigation into the Affairs of the Delaware, Lackawana, and Western R. R. Co., &c.* New York: 1858, 8vo., pp. 64; *Railroad Mismanagement; the dangers of exposing it, and the difficulty of correcting it, illustrated, &c., &c.* New York: 1859, 8vo., pp. 61, &c., &c.

iently may be."[1] But the Canons provide that it shall not be the duty of the Bishop to act in the case, unless there be a complaint made to him in writing by the injured party. If such complaint be made, the Bishop may restore him if he think fit, or institute an inquiry into the case according to the rules of the diocese; when in case "of great heinousness of offence" offenders may be proceeded against, to the depriving them of all privileges of Church-membership, according to such rules of court procedure as the General Convention may provide.[2] Thus, the whole matter is taken even more entirely out of the hands of the local body of believers than in the Presbyterian Church, where it first goes to the session. The Methodist Episcopal method, ordains that discipline shall be conducted by the local preacher before the local society, or a select number of them, at his pleasure. If found guilty by a majority vote, the offender is to be expelled by the preacher having charge of the circuit, appeal being allowed the accused to the next Quarterly Conference; the preacher himself having the same right of appeal — if, in his judgment, the majority vote has not been right.[3] It will be necessary to bear in mind, however, that in its practical working, this rule is modified by the fact that the offender may *always* be tried by a small committee selected by the preacher in charge — if he please to have it so [4] — while the lay members of the Quarterly Conference are either directly or indirectly made such by the same preacher;[5] so that the accused is practically tried, in the first instance, by a court appointed solely by the preacher, and, on appeal, by a court in which the preacher's power is still controlling, so far as the representatives from his own locality is concerned; and to which neither the accused, nor the people, have so much as the right of nomination — involving possibilities of monstrous injustice.[6]

---

[1] *Prayer Book.* Order of Communion. Preliminary note.
[2] Canon XLII., Sect. 2. *Wilmer's Episcopal Manual,* p. 286.
[3] *Book of Discipline,* Part I., Chap. 10, Sect 4.
[4] "The expulsion of Church-members *by a vote of the society* is as absurd in theory, as it would be ruinous in practice." — *Christian Advocate and Journal,* Nov. 25, 1840. "I never knew *one case* conducted by the society. This committee is constituted by the sole will of the preacher in charge." *Polity of the M E. Church,* by D. Plumbe, p. 26.
[5] "Nearly every member of the Quarterly Conference is appointed to that body by the preacher himself, or holds his seat at the preacher's will." Hawley's *Congregationalism and Methodism,* p. 219.
[6] A few years since, a member of the M. E. Church having failed in business, was charged with dishonesty. A committee was appointed to try the case; the accused pleading not guilty.

How different are all these schemes from the simple, Scriptural, salubrious Congregational way. How can such appeals, in various forms, to an aristocracy, be made consistent with Christ's command to tell it to *the Church?* And how infinitely more kind and fair and Christ-like, is our method of friendly consideration of the matter, as among family friends, and, if it be needful to go to formal trial, of trial by the whole body of neighbor believers; whose undue bias or prejudice would seem to be well-nigh an impossibility, and by whose good sense the whole difficulty may be settled without troubling remote years or dignitaries.

SECTION 6.—*Congregationalism claims preëminence over all other systems of Church government, in virtue of its favorable influence upon its ministry.*

It divorces them at once from all official pride. The distinguishing idea of their office is that they are servants and not masters of the Church. They owe their pastorship to the will of Christ, but as expressed by the vote of the membership of the Church; they are liable, at any moment, to owe their removal from it, to the same cause. They can have, from the nature of the case, little or no factitious influence. If they deserve to be honored and loved, they usually will be loved and honored. If not, their official position furnishes them no shield. They stand, and must stand, upon their actual merits. If they show themselves approved unto God, workmen that need not to be ashamed, rightly dividing the word of truth;

The evidence was "common fame." The committee finally decided that "they *believed* the accused had acted dishonestly, though there was no positive evidence of the fact." On this result the preacher in charge excommunicated the accused. The defendant appealed to the Quarterly Conference. The Presiding Elder ruled that " the opinion of the brethren expressed in the above case was a sufficient verdict, and was actually finding a person guilty according to the Book of Discipline;" whereupon the decision already made was confirmed. A petition was next sent up to the New York Conference, asking a decision on this judgment. No answer was returned the first year. But the second year the matter was referred to a committee who made a report justifying the course which had been pursued; which report was adopted without discussion — the report being afterwards withheld from the baffled seeker after justice, on the ground, " you might make a bad use of it! " [See *Thoughts on some parts of the Discipline of the M. E. Church*, by John W. Barber.] See also in the *True Wesleyan*, 18 Oct. 1845, the statement of a case, like this: While a certain appeal to a Quarterly Conference was pending, one of the preachers, discovering " that a majority of the members of the Conference differed in opinion from himself, removed a sufficient number of class-leaders from office, and placed others in their stead, who he knew had the same view with himself," and thus gained a majority vote, — all of which, by Methodist rules, was perfectly legal !

they will, ordinarily, be approved of man, and be esteemed very highly in love for their work's sake. But if not, they can take shelter behind no vote of Presbytery, nor act of Conference, nor Bishop's mandate. Moreover, they are freed from much temptation which inevitably, though often doubtless unconsciously, assails the ministers of the hierarchal churches. When once Pastor of a Congregational Church, such an one is essentially as high in office as he ever can be; for each Congregational Church is on a par of essential dignity with every other. There is no ascending grade of ecclesiastical promotion stretching before him up toward a Bishop's lawn, or an Archbishop's crosier, admonishing him not so much to 'take heed to the ministry which he has received in the Lord, that he fulfil it,' as to take heed to that moderate, and conservative, and conciliatory course towards those parties in whose hand it is to make great and to make small in the Church, which may be likely to result in the gratification of that ambition which the hierarchal systems create. Many of the noblest and most truly memorable Divines whose ministrations have adorned the annals of Congregationalism, have been, through life, the pastors of some of the quietest and most unassuming of her country churches.[1]

Congregationalism favors its Pastors, also, by the independence of position which it secures to them. Albert Barnes could not preach the truth of God as he understood it, and as his people rejoiced to hear it, without being intermeddled with by the Presbytery, on a charge of heresy, and being driven out of the pulpit, and silenced for weary months. An Episcopalian Rector cannot expound the thirty-nine Articles, though his conscience demand it, and his parish desire it never so much, essentially above or below the grade of Churchmanship of his Bishop, without risk of trial, and perhaps suspension and deposition. In the Book of Discipline of the Methodist Episcopal Church, we read, "remember! a Methodist Preacher is to mind every point, great and small, in the Methodist Discipline!"[2] and, on the following page, his seven Bishops, in

---

[1] William Hubbard and Joseph Dana, lived and died at Ipswich; Joseph Bellamy, at Bethlem, Conn.; Samuel Hopkins, at Newport; Moses Hemmenway, at Wells, Me ; Stephen West, at Stockbridge ; Nathaniel Emmons, at Franklin ; Samuel Niles, at Abington ; Charles Backus, at Somers, Conn.; Alonzo Hyde, at Lee; and John Hubbard Church, at Pelham, N. H. Nor should it be forgotten that Richard Salter Storrs still abides at Braintree, Leonard Withington at Newbury, Jacob Ide at Medway, Noah Porter at Farmington, Conn., &c., &c.

[2] *Book of Discipline*, Part I., Chap. 4, Sect. 9.

whose hand his ecclesiastical breath is; who can send him to Siberia or Ethiopia, to exercise his ministry, as they please — say to him, as the condensation and consummation of all their counsel in regard to his duties as a minister — "Above all, if you labor with us in the Lord's vineyard, it is needful you should do that part of the work which WE advise — at those times and places which WE judge most for his glory!" This is "a yoke upon the neck of the disciples, which neither our fathers nor we were able to bear."[1]

So, also, Congregationalism favors her ministry, above other forms of Church order, in the facilities which she afford them for usefulness. It is an old maxim that the less the harness chafes, the better the beast will draw; and our ministers are left to judge for themselves what field of labor will most befit their abilities. Each knows himself, and when a Church invites his service, *he* can tell, much better than any remote or stranger Bishop, or Presbytery, whether it is the place for him to work to the best advantage or not. And when his decision is made, there is a freshness and affection about it which peculiarly open the way for usefulness. They have chosen him, and he has chosen them — both of free will. He is their Pastor. They are his flock. They support him. He serves them in Christ's name. Here is no outward interference to awaken jealousies, and confuse the mind. All is natural, and favors the fullest working of the Gospel. If he is faithful to them, and they to him, this affection, so largely facilitating usefulness, may grow stronger through many delightful years. He can say, as did the good Shunamite, "I dwell among mine own people;"[2] or as Ruth said to Naomi, "thy people shall be my people, and thy God my God; where thou diest will I die, and there will I be buried, the Lord do so to me and more also, if aught but death part thee and me."[3] Friendships of years are formed. They know him, and he learns to know them; and they trust each other, and do each other good all the days of their life. Such a life-union, which accords with the genius of our system, is like the marriage relation, which makes home — and that is heaven on earth; as much better for the real interests of all than the best itinerant ministry, as marriage is always better than concubinage. Having in the passage of the years followed them, one by one, to the grave, he goes, at last, to lie down by their side. No sight is more

---
[1] Acts xv: 10. [2] 2 Kings iv: 13. [3] Ruth 1: 16, 17.

touching than some of the grave-yards of New England, where, before its Congregationalism became polluted by the invasion of the itinerant element, from another communion, under the shadow of the meeting-house, where all worshiped together, the bodies of Pastor and flock sleep sweetly, side by side, waiting for the resurrection trump.

Moreover, Congregationalism is fitted to stimulate its ministry, as no other system can naturally do, toward the highest intellectual and spiritual attainments, and the noblest and broadest influence. The very facts — that they are not honored because of their office merely; that they are free from Ecclesiastical temptations; that they are left independent of all external advice or control, to be and to do for their people all which they *can* be and do, tend to stimulate them to the highest possible usefulness. They are thrown, by this very peculiarity of their position, directly upon God and Christ, and the Holy Spirit, for the supply of all their wants, of counsel and sympathy and strength; and, living thus near to God, and accustomed to ask wisdom directly from Him, they get wiser and kindlier answers to their daily inquiries, than ever naturally fall from Prelatical or Presbyterial lips. So, also, the independence of thought which prevails in our churches, and the general intelligence which is stimulated by it, compel the Pastor to wider research and deeper thought, and a higher level of general attainment, in order to retain his position as a servant of the Church, in teaching it, and guiding it, under Christ, in the green pastures and by the still waters of prosperity and piety.

SECTION 7. *Congregationalism has preëminence over all opposing systems in that its fundamental principles are more favorable than theirs to the promotion of the general cause of Christ.*

The advancement of that cause unfolds itself especially in three departments; the growth of individual Christians in grace, and the promotion of associated Christian activity by every Church upon the community around it — developing in revivals of religion, and in missionary labors reaching out of itself toward the distant heathen.

We have already urged that our system has special fitness under the first of these heads.[1] We have alluded also to the second.[2]

---

[1] See page 255.   [2] See page 237.

But we desire to say a few words more upon it. We do not deny that God has greatly blessed other denominations of Christians with the outpourings of his Spirit; — he will always reward all true faith and honest labor, however imperfect in its processes. We do not affirm that the special advantages of Congregationalism in this regard have ever had justice done them among ourselves by a full application of their power. But we do claim that its fundamental principles give it special adaptation to the promotion of revivals of religion.[1]

(1.) We claim that they do so in virtue of its special freeness of action, and flexibility of adaptation to varying circumstances that may surround it. That state of high devotional feeling, and eager interest in the great truths of the Gospel, which is commonly called a Revival of Religion, is — we are not discussing now, whether it ought to be, or not — exceptional to the ordinary conditions of the Church and the world. It makes special claims upon the officers and membership of the churches. Pastors are called upon, by it, to a different presentation of truth; to warmer and more solemn appeals; often to a multiplication of services undesirable before; and especially to an amount of personal labor with inquirers, for which opportunity is not given in the ordinary experiences of their office. And individual Christians are often constrained by it to intermit, for a time, the duties of their ordinary vocations, and give themselves to the sweet work of persuading those to be reconciled to God, who meet them half way in interest, and whose eager souls are asking them, 'what must we do to be saved?'

If, now, our religion is to imitate that laborious adaptation of itself to all classes and every condition of society, which is suggested by the example of the great Apostle, who made himself a servant to all that he might gain the more: — unto the Jews, becoming as a

---

[1] The Episcopalians, as a body, disbelieve in revivals of religion, and denounce them. Their system has no place for them — although individual members of that communion, labor for them. One chapter in a late work, written in the interest of that sect, is devoted to the exhibition of the "fanaticism and pernicious influence" of the great revival of 1857, when "all sorts of profane places were opened for 'special prayer,' and preaching day by day." A number of the hymns then sung (such as "Just now," &c., &c.) are referred to and ridiculed; several sermons preached against the revival by eminent Episcopalian divines are quoted with approval; and it is declared that "The Church is able to repel the assaults of fanaticism and does not fail to stand unshaken by them when they rage around her." [*Recent Recollections of the Anglo-American Church*, ii: 179-195.]

Jew, that he might gain the Jews; to them that were under the law, as under the law, that he might gain them that were under the law; to them that were without law, as without law (being not without law to God, but under the law to Christ,) that he might gain them that were without law; to the weak, becoming as weak, that he might gain the weak; and being made all things to all men, that he might by all means save some; — it must, not merely in its essential spirit, but in all its forms and methods, possess that flexibility and power of instant adaptation to every possible exigency of time, place, and circumstance, which will enable it always, and at the shortest notice, to do the right thing, at the right time, and in the right manner. Congregationalism — as has been aptly and beautifully said, by one of the brightest ornaments of the New England pulpit — is nothing else than common sense applied to the matters of religion; and common sense applied to matters of religion is just the thing, and the only thing which is, or can be, equal to the peculiar exigencies of a revival of religion. When the Spirit of the Lord has come down in great power — as it did so wonderfully through all our borders in the Winter and Spring of 1857-8, — and crowds daily throng unusual places of prayer, as well as fill the churches at the time of Sabbath worship; bringing special requests to be offered to the Lord; bringing peculiar difficulties to be solved by the ministration of the Word, as a medium of the teaching of the Spirit; bringing unwonted states of mind to the hearing of the Gospel; bringing spirits burdened, and even crushed, by the heavy anxieties of sin, to be lightened by the manifestation of the truth; then what is needed is not a Prayer Book, not a volume of Homilies, nor any service that is foreordained to meet the chronology of the ecclesiastical year — beginning at Advent, and proceeding duly through Septuagesima, Sexigesima, and Quinquagesima Sundays, Easter, Ascension, Whit-Sunday, Trinity, and the twenty-seven Sundays after it; the circumcision of our Lord, the Epiphany, the conversion of St. Paul, the Purification of the Blessed Virgin, St. Matthias the Apostle, the Annunciation of the Blessed Virgin, and so on in the order prescribed in the Prayer Book, which no minister has any right, for himself, to alter — no matter what the exigency that presents itself: — but prayer that will be prayer for them because it will go up to the throne of grace in simple, apt language, pouring their actual requests into the infinite ear, and calling down upon them the very blessings of which at that moment they feel themselves to stand in perishing need ; and preaching that will array before them those motives, and burnish before them those appeals, and press upon them those doctrines, which to them, *as they are*, may helpfully and therefore hopefully, become the wisdom of God and the power of God unto salvation.

Other preachers may break over the formal obstacles that hem them in at such a time, and may preach truth, and *the* truth which is called for by the condition of the people ; but we claim that Congregationalism especially favors that freeness and flexibility of religious movement which may always easiest adapt itself to the exact phase of the work which Providence appoints to be done. It has no system which claims particular Sabbaths for particular subjects and services ; it is left to be guided always, in its selection of topics, by its study of the need of the people for instruction, or reproof, or comfort — just as the physician never dreams of giving calomel to all his patients on Mondays, and quinine on Tuesdays, and so on — with the days and with the drugs — but rather feels the pulse of his patient, and notes all the symptoms of his malady, and shapes his prescriptions by the contemporaneous demands of the disease. It is perfectly easy to see, at a glance, that the Rubrical system of the English and American Episcopal churches never contemplates revivals — never presupposes any particular exigencies of spiritual need — but lays out its work on the theory of dispensing, in an orderly and progressive manner, about so much Gospel in each year — just as in material things, it anticipates the usual fall of rain, and the ordinary visitations of the sunshine. In case of fearful drought, or appalling pestilence, or sudden invasion, the Archbishop of Canterbury — or the Bishop, or Bench of Bishops here — must write a prayer, which may then be circulated among the clergy, and not until that time can the Lord be called upon, in a lawful manner, by the great congregation, to be merciful and to spare his people, and bless his heritage, in the particular manner which their particular exigency requires.

It is over Episcopacy in all its forms that Congregationalism has special advantage in this particular. In like manner we claim that it has advantage,

(2.) In its want of reliance upon anything formal, or ritual, for salvation. The first necessity of right teaching in a revival of religion, or, in the aim to produce one, is to impress upon the soul the indispensable and immediate necessity of penitently believing on the Lord Jesus Christ unto salvation. Every other reliance must be swept out of the way. All confidence in good works must be destroyed. All idea that the being baptized, or the partaking of the sacrament, or the regular attendance upon the means of grace, or a scrupulous morality, with the ability to "say the Creed, the Lord's Prayer, and the Ten Commandments, and also to answer such other Questions as in the short Catechism are contained;"[1] or *anything* that can be done by a man, or can be done to him, that is not repentance and faith in the crucified Redeemer, will save him, must be renounced, at once and forever. Only when the sinner is convinced that his sins are many, and great, and grievous to be borne, and fatal in their tendency; that left to himself, he has no power at all, because he will never have any effectual desire, to work out his own salvation; that all his sufficiency must be of God's grace; that that grace is only promised to him who makes *now* the accepted time, and the day of salvation; that there is, therefore, no reasonable hope that he will ever be cleansed by the washing of regeneration, and renewing of the Holy Ghost, shed on him abundantly, through Jesus Christ the Saviour, unless, without the delay of a moment, he becomes reconciled to God, by the death of his Son; only then is he brought into that position of soul into which he can be saved.

Such teachings then must be considered essential to a Revival of Religion. He who teaches sinners this, may rightfully be said to be laboring to produce a Revival. And that system of church order which especially favors such teaching may, without impropriety, be claimed to be specially congenial toward that coöperative energy of the Holy Spirit, which, in that teaching, it constantly invites.

Far be it from us to claim that such teaching as this is confined to Congregationalism. Still, those creeds and methods of labor which are most often found in connection with it, and with which it is popularly identified, do specially renounce and condemn all reliance upon rites, and forms, and do press upon the sinner the duty of immediate repentance and faith, as the absolute condition of being saved; and

---

[1] See "Order of Confirmation," Prayer Book of Protestant Episcopal Church.

hold that Church membership, and the reception of the sacraments, require them as indispensable preliminaries; in opposition alike to the Episcopal theory before noted, and the Methodist idea of admitting to *quasi* membership in the Church (and hence, by inevitable popular inference, admitting to heaven also,) those who merely have a "desire of salvation."[1] So that, however nearly some other denominations of Christians may share this advantage with it, it is nevertheless true that Congregationalism, more than some other systems, and at least, equally with any, is in this particular specially adapted to promote revivals of religion, by the point and practicalness and fervor of its public and private ordinary method of appeals. Consider, again in immediate connection with this : —

(3.) The high character of its spiritual demands. We are confident that no other form of Church order is naturally led to be so vivid and constant in its appeals from the higher motives of the gospel, to those who are under its influence. The creed usually associated with it is thoroughly and earnestly evangelical; the preaching of its ministry is nearly always direct and pointed — giving no quarter to sin, and demanding for God the instant and entire surrender of the soul; while the preponderating influence of its working, as a system, is calculated to heighten the popular conception of the importance of religious verities over all other things. Truth — the truth of God, sublime, eternal, saving or condemning — furnishes the root and heart of its chief interest and influence; so that if it have not that, it has nothing with which to grapple itself to the affections of men. Its unadorned and often unimpressive sanctuaries, the plainness and simplicity of its methods of worship, the absence from its public services of æsthetic beauty and ritual splendor, and of almost every such thing which, in connection with other forms of worship, attracts and delights the multitude, throw it back with hightened necessity upon its underlying doctrines, for its practical hold upon men; and this is the main reason why it is nearly impossible for the Congregational polity to work well in the hands of those who ignore or deny the essential doctrines of the Cross; and why it sets them to complaining of its barrenness, and coldness, and lack of interest, and

---

[1] "There is only one condition previously required of those who desire admission into these Societies [Methodists call their churches *United Societies*,] viz: 'a desire to flee from the wrath to come, and to be saved from their sins.'" — *Methodist Discipline*, Part I., chap. ii., sec. 1, (4).

puts them to inventing new elements of variety, and to hankering after some liturgical additions to its worship, and some "Broad Church" method of working up toward it the sympathy of the masses.

Being that system of religious working which we believe was divinely intended to put the least machinery of ceremony and office between divine truth and human hearts — which all will at any rate probably admit actually does so — it must follow, on the one hand, that Congregationalism will fail powerfully to affect men unless the truth which is in it affects them, and, on the other, that when it is true to itself — and so to its Divine Author — it must specially press upon all who come under its influence, the vast import of the plan of salvation, and the glorious realities of the government of God.

But, in so far as it does this, it works specially and directly toward that state of things which we call a Revival of Religion — which never can exist until men are brought face to face with truth, and which God's promises make sure, whenever and wherever that truth is pressed upon the soul, with no disturbing or beclouding medium between; and when, in all its length and breadth, and hight and depth, its claims are crowded into direct contact with human consciousness.

(4.) Furthermore, we submit that Congregationalism is specially adapted to promote Revivals of Religion, in virtue of its constant training toward dependence upon Divine aid. Revivals are, in a special manner, God's work. It must be the Lord of Hosts who opens the windows of heaven to pour upon the ministry of his word, and the individual labor of his professed followers, a blessing, that there shall not be room enough to receive it. No dependence upon an arm of flesh will avail anything for this end. The Divine sovereignty, while merciful in its intimations of willingness to bless on prescribed conditions, is yet jealous of the honor of the great work of saving men; and where attention is diverted from God, as the sole as well as supreme source of spiritual healing, by the intervention of any ecclesiasticism, there is, by so much, a lessened likelihood of Divine interposition, for it is " not by might, nor by power, but by my Spirit, saith the Lord." Accordingly, that system of religious faith and order which trains it adherents to look most directly to God as its guide and strength ; which rests most entirely and lovingly upon his Word for constant direction in little things and great things;

which most appeals to his Spirit for light upon all its ordinary works and ways, will — so far as it is faithful to its principles — permanently abide in that condition of special nearness of access to the Great Head of the Church, which will most favor and promote his intervention in the form of Revivals of Religion.

Now it is the distinguishing characteristic of Congregationalism, that it puts nothing between the individual soul and God — as a friend, counsellor, and guide. In the matter of personal salvation, it prescribes no baptismal purification, no atoning life of penance or good works, no ecclesiastical grace of any kind, but remits the inquiring soul directly to the Lamb of God, which taketh away the sins of the world. And when that soul has believed, and hopefully been washed and sanctified, and justified in the name of the Lord Jesus, and by the Spirit of our God, and has come into the covenant relations of the Church, it puts it under the tutelage of no Priest nor Bishop nor Council nor Articles nor Canons; it relieves it in no one particular of the entire responsibility of all its relations to God and to man; and sends it directly to God and to Christ, in the Word, and in the teaching of the Spirit, for all light — for its own conduct, and for its share of the responsibilities of the organization. If a question of import arises — as whether such or such a doctrine is to be taught or suffered in the Church; or whether such or such conduct in a brother is consistent with Christian principle and covenant obligations, every individual member of the Church is directly charged, as before God, with the responsibility of the decision; and must go to God, in prayer and faith, to find the answer which pleases Him. No rubric fetters it; no decree of General Assembly, or Presbytery, or Bench of Bishops, or Council, or of any other Church; no judgment of the past; not even any suggestions of the present, can come in to take off, hardly to lighten, this load of direct responsibility to God, and absolute dependence upon Him, which Congregationalism, in its very essence, fastens upon every believer. And by this training, we hold that this system proves itself specially congenial to Revivals of Religion, by pressing the Church to ask for and receive them.

(5.) But that peculiarity in Congregationalism as a system of Church order and labor, which, in contrast with all other systems, most clearly gives it an advantage in the matter under consideration, is its intense development of individualism in all its Church membership. It is the only form of Church working in which the responsibility of activity and success, or of sluggishness and failure is thrown directly, always, and fully, upon each one of those who are associated under it; in which the duty and the privilege of every Church act, as well as of all individual Christian acts, are lodged with the individuals who compose the Church. In the monarchic forms of Church government, the responsibility and the power are with the hierarchy, in whatever guise it appears, and each private member is taught that for him obedience is the first duty, so that if things go right, or go wrong, no immediate responsibility rests upon him, unless he has failed to do something which *it* has commanded him to do. In other words, the hierarchy steps in between the individual Christian and his God, adjusting his relations, assuming his responsibility, and claiming his submission. In the aristocratic form of Church government the same thing, for substance, is done by the "Session," or the "Council," who receive members and dismiss them, and discipline them, and so, in like manner, step in between the individual and the Great Head; and train all the membership practically to feel that the responsibility is with the Church, as a body, or with its judicatories, and not upon them, and each of them, as before God bound to give answer for all. But Congregationalism rests all upon each. Every member of its churches it holds responsible, in his measure, for the soundness of its creed, the wisdom and energy of its management, the success or failure of its endeavors to do good. It trains each one to feel that if things go wrong, he cannot reasonably throw off the blame upon the shoulders of "the Church" as a body, nor upon the pastor and officers, nor upon any person or persons other than himself. It teaches each one that there is a responsible sense in which he may use Paul's words: "Who is weak and I am not weak? Who is offended and I burn not?" It hightens all motives to individual activity, not merely by pressing them upon the souls of its members with all the force of the Word of God, but by arranging all its processes so as to favor their development, and further their working. It is always repeating the last command of Christ in the ear of each of its faithful ones; "Go *ye* into all the world and preach the Gospel to every creature." It stimulates its laity to work in Sabbath Schools, and Mission Schools; in tract distribution, and visiting from house to house, among the poor and the abandoned; to fill their pockets with appeals and their mouths with arguments, that they may sow the seed of Divine truth beside all waters, and in all way-side paths. "BY ALL MEANS SAVE SOME," is the motto which it embroiders, from the lips of Paul, upon the pennon waving from the lance which it puts into the hand of every one of its private soldiers, as it sends them forth to the battle of the most high God. We do not deny that other forms of Church government do often seek to stimulate their membership to these same individual toils and triumphs, but what we claim is that no other system does, or can, *logically* do so. It is only by deserting, and in some cases, by doing violence to, its own first principles, that any other system can appeal, as ours always and inevitably does, to the individual force of its communion. Most others are afraid to trust the people. A prayer meeting, even, that should not be presided over by the "proper authorities," — likely enough, then, so programmed beforehand as to prevent all but persons previously invited from taking part in its services — would seriously alarm them. They cannot understand how there can be freedom without misrule and misfortune; any more than the old subjects of the European despotisms can understand how we can be safe in this country without bayoneted sentinels on every corner. But Congregationalism trusts the people; educates them; leans upon them and each of them; trains them to understand that God has left the work of reconciling the world to himself through the death of his Son — so far as human agency goes — for them to do, and commands them to do it in his name, and for his sake, and in personal dependence upon him; tells them, however ignorant and weak they may be, to remember that God hath "chosen the foolish things of the world to confound the wise, and the weak things of the world to confound the things which are mighty;" tells them that a Church is not a mysterious galvanic battery of spiritual power, but rather a regimental organization, by means of which the individual soldiers can best be trained for, and marched into the fight; that pastors are captains under the "Great Captain" of salvation, whose function is rather to lead and guide the masses in their work, than to do the work in their stead.

Thus teaching, we claim that Congregationalism equally fits its membership for that individual labor with the impénitent, and that individual faithfulness in prayer and every good work, which the Holy Spirit demands as the great requisite of human coöperation in its redeeming work in revivals of religion. The great revival of 1857, was peculiarly marked in this direction. The Congregational churches every where fell in at once and entirely with its claims for, individual work, while other systems were obliged to desert their own peculiarities, and, in a manner, Congregationalize themselves, before they could become largely the channels of its power of spiritual healing. Daily noon-day prayer meetings, in unconsecrated rooms, presided over by Christian laymen, and open to the speech even of the young, were strictly *Congregational* means of grace;[1] and all remember how vast and vital was their connection with the glorious result. Nor will it be forgotten that such Congregational churches as departed most widely from the democratic freedom of their own system, and most assimilated their methods of labor and worship to those of the hierarchal systems, shared least in the blessing that then descended.

While, then, Congregationalists have never in one single instance done full justice to the capabilities of their simple and Scriptural system in the direction now indicated, and while God will bless all who truly love him, and sincerely try, at whatever disadvantage, to advance the coming of his kingdom; these considerations urge, that no form of polity so invites, or can so readily and naturally coöperate with the Holy Spirit in its copious descents of mercy, as that which, reproducing here the Apostolic pattern, first planted itself, in this hemisphere, on Plymouth Rock.

A similar especial fitness, as might be anticipated from the fact that it worked so well in the Apostolic times, has been developed by our system for the foreign missionary field. The Congregational

---

[1] It is only a few years since so much, and so bitter, objection was made in the Episcopalian Church in this country against prayer meetings (as being of evil tendency and subversive of the principles of "the Church;" that lay exhortation is unlawful, and extempore prayer schismatic, &c., &c,) that Bishop Griswold was moved to write a pamphlet on the subject, [*Remarks on Social Prayer-Meetings*, by Rt. Rev. A. V. Griswold. Boston, 1858, pp. 99]; and the "High" portion of that Church remains of the same mind still.

An eminent and catholic Englishman wrote, not longer ago than 1848, "the Anglican churches have sunk into a low religious state. *In a great majority of parishes*, as we have too much reason to fear, the Gospel is not preached, and the people are indifferent to religion." — Hon. and Rev. Baptist Noel's *Essay on the Union of Church and State*, p. 420.

churches were the first in this country to move in that direction, and experience has settled it, that in remote missionary work the system of local Church organization, unhampered by vital connections with other, distant, and uncongenial fields and central organizations, is the best [2] — nay, that something like it, is almost the only one practicable.[3]

SECTION 8. *Congregationalism is better than any other form of government for the Church, because it furnishes a more effective barrier than any other, against heresy and false doctrine.*

(1.) It favors less than any other the *development* of doctrinal error. The history of the Church teaches that the sources of heresy have been mainly four, viz: corrupt tendencies in human nature; paganism; unchristian philosophy; and ambition, with other motives connected with and growing out of hierarchal influence. To the first of these, the Congregational churches — if they are true to themselves — are less exposed than any others, because their system, in throwing them upon God, and Christ, and the Spirit, more practically

---

[1] The "American Board of Commissioners for Foreign Missions" was formed by the General Association of the Congregational Churches of Massachusetts, at Bradford, 29 June, 1810.

[2] See *Report of the Special Committee on the Deputation to India.* 1856, pp. 43–47.

[3] The members of the Ceylon Mission say, in 1855, "In regard to the form of organization and the officers most proper for native churches, we stand on higher than sectarian ground. Our commission is not to proselyte, but to preach the Gospel; and whatever preferences we individually cherish for specific forms of Church government and discipline, however desirable or necessary they may be considered in those lands that have been long favored with the light and influence of the Gospel and its ordinances, we are convinced that the *most plain and simple organizations* are, by far, the best for the training and discipline of the native converts in this field." [*Minutes of the Special M·eting of the Ceylon Mission*, May, 1855, p. 84.] So the Madura Mission say, "Mission churches obviously require the utmost simplicity of structure; and all that they require, and all that is good for them, may be learned from the New Testament. A local Church is God's institution. . . . . . No improvement can be made on the simplicity and the efficacy of the New Testament plan for propagating the Gospel among the heathen; whatever may be thought of the application of it to the old Christian communities of Europe and America." [*Minutes of the Special Meeting of the Madura Mission, held at Madura*, March, 1855, pp. 112, 113.] A Conference of Missionaries held at Constantinople in November, 1855, said, "when, in 1846, the Armenian Mission was called to propose a basis of Church organization, there were brethren of several different Ecclesiastical connections engaged in the discussion and charged with the responsibility of this great work; yet no one sought to have his denominational peculiarities transferred to the infant churches of this land. It was agreed, without a single dissenting voice, to propose for the adoption of our Armenian brethren, a simple, Scriptural organization, without any reference to the particular constitutions or rules of our respective organizations." [*Report*, p. 13.] Something a little different and more Presbyterian was tried in the Sandwich Islands, but worked badly and had to be modified into something much nearer Congregationalism. [*The Hawaiian Islands*, pp. 307–314.]

and continually than any other, and promoting revivals and a high tone of piety among their members, antidotes those tendencies of human nature, and tends to save their piety from losing its savor through them. To the second, Congregationalism opposes special resistance in the fact that its peculiarities are exactly antipodal to those peculiarities of paganism by which it most tends to corrupt the faith, and so make it less in danger from them than if it lay more within the range of their probable influence. The three most dangerous elements of paganism have proved to be its fondness for gorgeous and pompous ceremonials, its multiplicity of objects of worship, and its absolute reliance upon things done (*opus operatum*) at appointed times — rather than motives behind them, and states of mind revealed by them — for acceptance. So long as the simplicity of early Congregationalism remained, it was able to resist these tendencies, and to keep itself pure. But so soon as the churches began to lose their original peculiarities, and to take on a hierarchal form, they fell into these temptations, and became corrupted by them, until in a little time it was not always easy to distinguish between a pagan and a "Christian" assembly and service.[1] When, in the days of the Reformation, and after, the spirit of original Congregationalism reasserted itself, its urgency was especially manifest in casting all this paganism out of the churches, and recovering them to the old-fashioned simple, and simply-administered doctrines of grace. And it is a fact to-day, that no churches on the earth are so pure from all taint of the old leaven of paganism, as the Congregational churches of England and America.[2] To the third source of false doctrine,

---

[1] "In these times [the times of early hierarchal corruption] the religion of the Greeks and Romans differed very little in its external appearance from that of the Christians. They had both a most pompous and splendid ritual, gorgeous robes, miters, tiaras, wax tapers, crosiers, processions, lustrations, images, gold and silver vases; and many such circumstances of pageantry were equally to be seen in the heathen temples, and the Christian churches." — Mosheim, *Eccles. Hist.* i, 393, 394.

"The sublime and simple theology of the primitive Christians was gradually corrupted: and the monarchy of Heaven, already clouded by metaphysical subtleties, was degraded by the introduction of a popular mythology [of saints and martyrs,] which tended to restore the reign of polytheism. . . . . . If in the beginning of the fifth century Tertullian or Lactantius, had been suddenly raised from the dead, to assist at the festival of some popular saint or martyr, they would have gazed with astonishment and indignation on the profane spectacle which had succeeded to the pure and spiritual worship of a Christian congregation. . . . . . The religion of Constantine achieved, in less than a century, the final conquest of the Roman Empire: but the victors themselves were insensibly subdued by the arts of their vanquished rivals." — Gibbon. *Roman Empire*, iii., 432.

[2] The hierarchal churches need not be specified as redolent of the taint of heathenism at

the speculations of an unchristian philosophy, Congregationalism opposes the influential fact that she rests the purity of the faith of her churches upon the masses who compose their membership, and not upon the few cultivated and ambitious — and likely to be erratic — who set themselves up as a hierarchy over them. The philosophy of the subject, and the history of the past combine together to give equal and abundant proof that there is no security so absolute, under God, for a pure faith, as the Christian common sense of the great mass of believers enlightened and purified by the constant influence of the Holy Spirit; when it is allowed to do its proper work. In point of fact it is almost impossible to get a vote for any invasion upon the old creed of orthodoxy from a Congregational Church, that has remained true to Congregational principles, after never so long and labored endeavor on the part of the few of learning and influence who desire the change.[1] The Unitarian heresy came into New England only through the fact that many of the Congregational churches had, for years previous, departed from one of their fundamental principles, and received unregenerate members to their communion; so that here and there the body of the Church had thus become corrupt, and in that manner the way was prepared for corruption in the creed. From all hierarchal corruptions, our churches are radically free. Their purity of faith is not endangered by a latitudinarian pastor forced upon them whether they will or no; nor by a creed modified without their consent, by " the Church;" nor by the ambition of a few leaders of some new movement for power, which can be most craftily accomplished by a new rendering of the old dogma; nor by the calmer and more natural corruption of a great corporation settled upon its lees, conservative of all its past peculiarities however unsuited to the genius of the present, and nothing if

---

every pore. The Presbyterian Churches still retain in their semi-hierarchal government the impress of that grasping for power on the part of the few, and that distrust and contempt of " the people," which characterized the old paganism.

[1] "Laymen, when our polity has its normal influence upon them, are not so easily pushed into sidelong measures. They must perceive some broad tangible good to be gained, or they will not rally around a turbulent dogmatist. If a false doctrine, or a clannish scheme begin to fascinate the community, every distinct Church is a new obstacle, and in the Church itself, every distinct member is a new impediment to the proposal, unless the proposal have some palpable and sterling merit. Hence, it is notorious, that when false doctrine has inundated the Church, it has flowed from the clergy and not from the people, and when the people have been trusted with power commensurate with their spiritual culture, they have stimulated their pastors to a maintenance of the simple truth." — Prof. Park. *Fitness of the Church, &c.*, 38.

not consistent. The Congregational system offers little field for great discoverers of "new light" which invariably turns out to be old darkness. They may publish their books, and ring out their rallying cries long and loud, and gather their little "schools" of disciples, but the great mass of the lay believers will still go "to the law and the testimony" to test their pretensions, and are very sure in the end to reach the prophet's decision — "if they speak not according to this word, it is because there is no light in them." New England Congregationalism has been supposed by many, who have taken the *dictum* of interested opponents of her system for truth, without investigation, to have been the hot-bed of heresies. But the truth is, as all who really know the facts must concede, that there is no harder soil on earth in which to germinate successfully the seeds of a religious error, than the membership of her Orthodox Churches. It may be said, indeed, that they are conservative almost to a fault. And however much they may admire the intellectual ability, and enjoy the eloquence, and respect the life of the proposers of new theories of the Gospel, they are apt to remain essentially unmoved by them.[1]

(2.) Congregationalism furnishes a much less favorable *shelter* for religious error than any other system. Grant that, by some method, some unsound view of truth has gained a lodgment in each of the main systems of Church government, our assertion is that it is less safe under Congregationalism than anywhere else. It is always open to review there. Any member of the Church, who is grieved by it, has the right of bringing it at once to the test of the prayerful and labored investigation of his entire co-membership. Nay, if it exists in any other Church than his own, he has the right of indirectly procuring the same result, through the principle of the communion of churches. So that such a heresy is at once exposed to attack from the widest possible range. Moreover, the process of assault is so simple, and feasible, that the man whose conscience is disturbed in the matter, has no excuse for not bringing it immediately to trial. There is no certainty of vast trouble, and uncertain expense, and incalculable delay, discouraging him, in the outset, from any such duty.

---

[1] I mention in this connection, without design of opprobium toward an honored brother, whose general faith I respect as much as I admire his pure and faithful life, the fact, that while thousands of copies of the *Conflict of Ages* — one of the ablest books of the century — were bought, and read, in New England and elsewhere, there are not, probably, three scores of converts to its hypothesis in all the Congregational churches of the land.

There are no forms of trial to be gone through with, so elaborate that nothing short of a life devoted to their study can make entirely safe any intermeddling with them.[1] If a Church member becomes a heretic, the others deal with him and cast him out. If a Pastor becomes a heretic, the Church terminates his relation, and that very fact warns other churches against him. Each Church being self-complete, there is very little danger of any taint — if there be such — in one, spreading from one to another. So far as other churches are concerned, it affects them only as another is added to the many bad examples that already exist around; to stand for warning before them. Whereas, in an affiliated hierarchy, so many steps are to be taken, and so many trials had; there is so much inter-dependence and so many chances for contagion to spread, that the case becomes as much more difficult to manage than it is among us, as *scarlatina* in a crowded school is worse than in an isolated dwelling. So that in its antagonist forms of Church government, difficulties such as we have hinted hedge the way, and often render the securing of a really just result the exception more than the rule — after the intervening years of constitutional delay.[2]

(3.) Congregationalism has actually proved itself a safer barrier against heresy than its competing systems. We have referred to the fact — which no well-informed person will be likely to deny — that it was only as the hierarchy superseded the primitive Con-

---

[1] "The practice of law in the Presbyterian Church has become so much a science and profession, that long ago reports of cases and precedents began to be published by the General Assembly, which have now grown to a large volume of cases, precedents, and commentaries constantly swelling in its dimensions with every new edition, under the title of the *Assembly's Digest*. It is manifest that none but a lawyer can now understand the law of the Presbyterian Church." Colton's *Thoughts on the Religious Sta'e of the Country*, 61.

[2] Bishop Eastburn tried, in vain, for long, to stem the tide of Puseyism which was flowing into Boston through the "Church of the Advent," but was at last compelled to succumb, and, after years of refusal to visit the Church and perform confirmation there, to do so, as if in approval of what he himself had characterized as a "pointed and offensive resemblance to the usages of the idolatrous papal communion," as "superstitious puerilities," and irregularities degrading to the character of the church and perilous to the souls of the people." [See *Correspondence between the Rt. Rev. the Bishop of Massachusetts, and the Rectors of the Parish of the Advent, &c.*, 1856, pp. 123] And the issue of the Colenso case, in England, is well known. In regard to the burdensome formalities which under the English Church it is needful to go through in order to settle the question of heresy, the *London Times*, of 21 December, 1864, said: — "Considerations so abstruse and subtle, even when divested of their legal guise, are more within the province of lawyers than clergymen. Unless they were all taken into account by the Bishop of Cape Town and his two Episcopal assessors, a most serious responsibility was undertaken without adequate information; yet to suppose that they were taken into account would be absurd."

gregationalism, that those doctrinal corruptions came on which resulted in the "dark ages."[1] It is the avowed principle of the hierarchal churches that it belongs to the clergy, and to the clergy alone, to settle "questions of doctrine, or such as in any way involve decisions upon doctrine."[2] The American Episcopal Church has been declared by Dr. Pusey to have "abandoned a bulwark of the faith," in admitting laymen to her counsels.[3] So that the issue is directly joined as between those who trust everything to the membership, under Christ, and those who trust nothing to them. And we claim that our own system has uniformly favored a purer doctrine than that of our opponents.

The Roman Catholic body has so far departed from the "faith once delivered to the saints," toward actual paganism and practical idolatry, that it can only by stretch of courtesy be called a Christian Church at all. The Church of England was never more than half reformed, and to-day undeniably includes within its pale all forms of error,[4] from the lowest rationalism of the Broad Churchmen to the

---

[1] "The entire perversion of the original view of the Christian Church was itself the origin of the whole system of the Roman Catholic religion, — the germ from which sprang the popery of the dark ages." [Dr. Neander. — Introduction to Coleman's *Apostolical and Primitive Church*, 22.] "It is remarkable that the lax penitential discipline had its chief support from the end of the second century, in the Roman Church. . . . . . Callistus, whom a later age stamped a saint, because it knew little of him, admitted *bigami* and *trigami* to ordination, maintained that a bishop could not be deposed, even though he had committed a mortal sin, ... In short, he considered no sin too great to be loosed by the power of the keys in the Church. And this continued to be the view of his successors. . . . . . Here we perceive also, how the looser practice in regard to penance was connected with the interest of the hierarchy. It favored the power of the priesthood, which claimed for itself the right of absolution; it promoted the external spread of the Church, though at the expense of the moral integrity of her membership, and facilitated both her subsequent union with the state and her hopeless confusion with the world." — Schaff's *Hist. Christ. Church*, 447.

[2] See *The Councils of the Church*, p. 17.

[3] "It must be said plainly, that the precedent set in the United States is radically wrong, and in fact, is so far, the adoption of a principle belonging to bodies who reject the Apostolic succession, and the whole principle of a deposit of faith," &c. *Ibid*. 25.

[4] "There is no church in the world that has, in fact, so great a diversity of opinion in her own bosom, as the Church of England, and not a little of downright infidelity." [Colton's *Religious State of the Country*, 200.] "Lord Chatham said, in his time, that the English Church had Calvinistic articles, a Papistical service, and an Arminian clergy. The saying has become a general opinion, but the designation of the dogmatic sentiments of the clergy, is only now in so far correct, that the great majority of the clergy agree with the Arminians in rejecting the favorite doctrines of the Reformation age, 'justification by imputed righteousness,' and 'Calvinistic Predestination.' The fact, however, that the Established Church has not so much as the semblance of unity of doctrine and character, is well known to every educated Englishman, and appears as something quite natural, and as a matter of course." Dollinger's *The Church and the Churches*, 169. "The pulpit is as little trusted for sincerity, as that appointed resort of hired advocacy — the bar." *Westminster Review*, liv., 485.

straitest Romanism of Dr. Pusey, and John Henry Newman, and Father Ignatius.[1] The Lutheran churches on the Continent have a strong government, but have become almost entirely corrupt in doctrine and practice,[2] more especially in Sweden and Norway. In Switzerland, Calvin's pulpit is occupied by Rationalists,[3] while in Geneva, few care for the great Reformer, and nobody knows where his body molders; but Jean Jacques Rousseau lies in the Pantheon, and his bronze statue on the Isle of Poplars is one of the principal attractions of that beautiful city.

And this reminds us of the general fact that Presbyterianism has proved itself in the old world especially powerless as a conservator of purity of doctrine. In the Presbyterian Church of Scotland, the "Moderates" — many of whom ranged from Arminianism down to bald Deism — were long in the ascendant.[4] Essentially the same has been true of a large part of the Presbyterian Church in Ireland.[5] The Presbyterian Church in England has become, and remains, almost wholly Unitarian;[6] while the Congregational churches of Scotland

---

[1] Nor is the presence of doctrinal error the only rotten symptom in the Church of England. It is notorious, that many of her clergy are men giving no evidence of piety, not merely, but sometimes of questionable morality. Says a faithful witness, "it is neither truth nor piety that gives clergymen their livings. Numbers of them preach a gospel neither more pure nor more evangelical than was done by Socrates and Plato, and other heathen moralists; and some of the most deserving of their brethren, who ought to know, are continually bringing against them the most pointed accusations."—Ballantyne's *Comparison, &c.*, 171.

[2] In Germany the strongest infidels have been in the Church, and accredited teachers of its formulæ. While so totally has Christian discipline been disregarded there, that according to the declaration of a devout minister of the Lutheran Church persons known to be of abandoned character, and the most notorious slaves of lust, are publicly and indiscriminately received to the Lord's Supper.—See Liebetrut. *Tag des Herrn*, s. 331.

[3] "Protestant to the back-bone, even to Unitarianism, and very proud of its Protestantism." [Rev. E. E. Hale's *Ninety Days' worth of Europe*, 162.] "Confessions of faith are abolished, and the Church grounds its belief on the Bible, and allows to every one the right of free inquiry; among the clergy prevails the most absolute confusion with respect to doctrine."— Genf's "Kirkliche und Christliche Zustande" in *Der Deutschen Zeitschrift*, i., 248, 253.

[4] "The tone of their theology was moral, mitigating the strictness of the old Confessions." [Smith's *Hagenbach*, ii., 430.] "For the last half century, the leading clergy and laity have departed from the simplicity that is in Christ, having been spoiled through philosophy and vain deceit. The General Assembly has presented a considerable majority approving sentiments and practices in opposition to which the ancient Covenanters would have laid down their lives. Ministers selected by patrons have been placed over many of the churches against their consent, driving most of their pious members into the churches of the Seceders."—Marsh's *Eccles. Hist.*, 343.

[5] See Alexander's *Hist. Pres. Church in Ireland*, pp. 301–342.

[6] "During the life and popularity of Dr. Priestly, who abhorred a middle course, the Presbyterians generally renounced their ancient discipline. From Arianism they have descended to Socinianism, and now choose to be known as Unitarians." [Marsh, 350.] "The old Presbyterian

and England,[1] have been models of unity and purity in their Evangelical belief.[2]

Looking at our own country, we find the same causes producing the same results; though not always in a manner so obvious, and even striking. It has been the fashion among the opponents of our system to denounce it as responsible for the "great Unitarian apostacy" in New England.[3] But the father of Unitarianism in this

---

community, once the most powerful and influential among non-Episcopal connections, has, in the course of the last century fallen completely into decay in England. The cause of this is to be found chiefly in the change of doctrine. The most distinguished Theologians of the party — Richard Baxter and Daniel Williams — had demonstrated so clearly and convincingly the contradictions in the Calvinistic doctrine of justification, and its inevitable moral consequences, that most of the congregations renounced this doctrine, and became, according to the customary mode of expression, Arminian." [Dollinger's *The Church and the Churches*, 178.] "Scores of Presbyterian congregations admitted heretical assistants to their orthodox pastors, and heretical successors too In most of their principal congregations it became the order of the day. . . . . Arianism was the grave of the Presbyterian congregations." — Bogue & Bennett's *History of the Dissenters*, ii., 303, 313.

[1] An Aberdeen Presbyterian writing to the *Presbyterian Banner*, bears the following testimony to the relative purity and soundness of Congregationalism and Presbyterianism in Scotland, — "*Scottish Congregationalism*, in connection with the resurrection of the old Gospel which Knox had preached, was for years a light in a dark land. It supplemented what was wanting elsewhere. More than this, while many did not join it, and were Presbyterians still, its Sabbath evening services were largely attended by them, and there they found refreshment, consolation, and blessing to their souls. Many of the parish [Presbyterian] ministers were then ungodly men, without unction or earnestness, and Congregationalism, setting up its small meeting-places in the different parishes, led many formalists to the Saviour's feet, and was a living witness within the region of a holy and unselfish Christianity. Even now, although there are not more than one hundred Congregational churches in Scotland, and except two at Edinburgh, one or two at Glasgow, and a considerable body in Dundee, they are comparatively weak as to numbers; yet they present noble specimens of healthy piety, and of zeal in every good work. The name of Wardlaw is still fragrant, and others there are who, having sat at his feet as students, perpetuate his spirit, and his message, and his influence. I have been providentially brought into contact, this week, with Congregationalists, both ministers and people, and, as a Presbyterian, I give you my honest impressions, and pay to them such a tribute, which truth and love demand."

[2] "It is doubtful whether a *single strictly Congregational Church* passed over into heresy." [*MS. Letter* from Joshua Wilson, Esq., Tunbridge Wells, Eng.] "Instead of the diversity of sentiments which prevailed among the Presbyterians, the religious principles of the Non-Conformists were maintained by the Independents, in all their purity; it may be questioned whether an Arian, or even an Arminian, was to be found in the whole body. There was no denomination in England which could boast of so much unanimity as to doctrine."— Bogue & Bennett, ii. 313.

[3] "Congregationalism is constantly charged with the *Unitarian defection in Massachusetts*. Episcopalians, Presbyterians, and even the advocates of that singular mixture of ecclesiastical ideas which in Connecticut is called 'Consociationism,' all cry out in chorus — 'Look at the fruits of Congregationalism in Massachusetts!' This is like charging upon Bowditch's Navigator, the wreck of a ship set out of her course by an unknown tideway or a deep ocean-current. The current opinion, among those who know little or nothing of the facts, that the Congregationalism of Massachusetts is responsible for the Unitarian defection, is of a piece with the idea which prevails through the benighted South, that Democracy is responsible for a slimy brood of infidelities and heresies and immoral philosophies, from 'socialism' to 'free love,' with which

country, was the rector of the first *Episcopalian* Church that was ever founded in New England, who, in 1785, succeeded in transforming his Church into the first Unitarian Church in America;[1] while that Church which, in 1803, ordained Dr. Channing — the great heresiarch of his day — as its pastor, was the first Scotch-Irish *Presbyterian* Church ever founded in the State.[2] It is true, that of

its tropical imagination has peopled our Yankee land. It is well to remember that people may be neighbors who are not relations, and that contiguity is not necessarily causation." — Rev. J. P. Gulliver. *Independent*, March, 1865.

[1] "This important change is to be attributed mainly to the judicious and learned expositions of Mr. Freeman, who preached a series of doctrinal sermons to his people, and by the aid and influence of the word of God, moved them to respond to his sentiments. *The first Episcopal Church in New England, became the first Unitarian Church in America*, and our venerated senior minister, though not absolutely the first who held or even avowed Unitarian opinions, still on many accounts deserves to be considered as *the father of Unitarian Christianity in this country*." [Greenwood's *History of King's Chapel, in Boston*, p. 139.] There appears to have been, at this time, a decided Unitarian tendency in many of the Episcopalian churches of this country. A convention for three New England States met in Boston, in September, 1785, which resolved that the Athanasian and Nicene creeds, and one article of the Apostle's creed ought to be omitted; that several amendments should be made in the liturgy, and that the Offices of baptism, matrimony, visitation of the sick, and burial of the dead, should be altered. A convention assembled at Philadelphia, in October, 1785, resolved to reduce the 39 articles to 21 The feeling then prevalent expressed itself in a pamphlet published the following year, which said, "There are many parts of the Liturgy, 39 Articles, &c., which were by the bigotry of the age, conformed to Papistical and Calvinistical errors, and other doubtful systems, which are not well understood. They have occasioned many well disposed Christians to dissent from the Church of England; and they are esteemed great obstacles to its increase."—[*Remarks on the proceedings of the Episcopal Conventions, &c., by a Layman*. Boston: J. Hall. 1785.] But all this was corrected, as the regulating influence of the mother Church of England was brought to bear upon the Colony, and it became understood that it was a much better plan to ignore all inconvenient clauses in the Articles, or the Liturgy, or the Offices, than to change them, and so, with the exception of King's Chapel, which had been hasty in its honesty, the Episcopalian body here relapsed into quietude under its accredited forms, with the single exception of the Athanasian creed, which it omitted in deference especially to Connecticut, where, it was said, the insisting on it "would hazard the reception" of the prayer-book. [Hook's *Church Dictionary*, 39.] This reference to Connecticut, finds explanation in the fact mentioned by Dr. McEwen [*Contributions to the Eccl. Hist. of Connecticut*, 274,] that "that class of the population which in Massachusetts became Unitarians, have in our commonwealth [Connecticut] chosen to be Episcopalians." And Anderson says that great numbers of the people of Connecticut "thankfully repaired" to the Episcopal Church "as the ark which could alone carry them in safety over the raging floods" of the great revival of Whitfield's time.—*Hist. Colonial Church*, iii., 399.

[2] The Scotch-Irish founded a Presbyterian Church in "Long Lane," Boston, soon after 1727, under Rev. John Moorhead. Rev. David Annan succeeded him, after whom were Rev. Jeremy Belknap, D. D., and Rev. John S. Popkin, D. D., whose successor Dr. Channing became, in 1803. The Church now worship, under the pastorate of Dr. Gannett, in Arlington street. The Rev. Alexander Blaikie organized a Presbyterian Church in this city, in 1846. which he assumed to be this original Church, and entitled to the property of the "Federal Street Parish," and sued for the same before the Supreme Court in 1849. 6 March, 1855, Chief Justice Shaw decided adversely to the claim. Mr. Blaikie, with characteristic pertinacity, appealed to the Supreme Court of the United States, whence, in 1862, he was dismissed "for the want of jurisdiction." — See Judge Davis's *Memoir of the Federal Street Church and Society*, 33–36, and *Boston Recorder*, 2 April, 1863.

the three hundred and sixty-one Congregational churches in Massachusetts, in 1810,[1] ninety-six — or a little more than one in four — passed over to Unitarianism. But the Socinian tendency came to them from the mother-country of "strong" Church government, and they had first exposed themselves to its contagion by departing from fundamental Congregationalism in imitation of the "strong" governments, in admitting those who were not believers to their communion; while their system, as such, showed its vitality and self-purgative power by very soon sloughing off these new converts to a lax faith, and rendering itself pure;—which is more than Presbyterianism has done in England, Scotland, or Ireland;[2] more than Episcopacy ever did or can do anywhere.[3] It may, indeed, well be doubted whether any other form of Church government in Massachusetts, at that time, would have saved the State from being delivered over bound hand and foot to Socinianism. It was the fact that God's faithful ones in the local churches had power there, and were not, in a manner, compelled to follow their eminent leaders, which stayed the defection.[4] "The gracefulness of Buckminster, the amenity of Green-

---

[1] The *Presbyterian* Church in Peterborough, N. H., having got rid of two ministers — the first as a sceptic and profligate, and the second for immorality — were now preparing to follow the third into Unitarianism. [Lawrence's *New Hampshire Churches*, 240] A portion of the First Presbyterian Church in New York City, in 1754, objected to Dr. Bellamy's becoming their pastor, because he did not "preach so free and generous a Gospel" as they had been used to, and as was agreeable to them. — Bellamy, *Memoir*, xvii.

[2] Of the two hundred and twenty-nine Unitarian chapels which existed in England in the year 1851, one hundred and seventy had been originally Presbyterian. — Mann's *Census of Religious Worship*, pp. 1-lxviii.

[3] "The Church [of England] has no fixed doctrine; its formulas contradict each other; and what one part of its servants teach is rejected by the other as a soul-destroying error." [Dollinger's *The Church and the Churches*, p. 72.] Its "Articles" are no defence against any kind of teaching which its rectors may be pleased to use. "There is nothing," says the London *Times*, "to prevent any one from going into the market, and buying a living for any silly, fanatical, extravagant, or incapable booby of a son, and installing him forthwith as the spiritual mediator between the Almighty and one or two thousand of his creatures." [See *Weekly Register*, 11 May, 1861]. To understand the utter helplessness of the American Episcopal Church to the work of any self-purification from the gravest doctrinal errors, it will be quite sufficient to read the facts in regard to the "Smith and Anthon" controversy, in New York city in 1843; where it was distinctly avowed that the issue was "between the Church and Romanism," and where "Romanism" triumphed. — See *The True Issue for the True Churchman, &c., &c.* New York, 1843.

[4] "Unitarianism has not flourished so vigorously in this Puritan Commonwealth as Deism has flourished under a more concentrated Church government; not- so extensively as — in the opinion of wise observers — it would have prevailed under any other than our free polity; for if the churches of Massachusetts had been amalgamated into one State confederation, it is supposed that nearly all of them would have gone, where the few dominant spirits had led the way. and the Congregationalism of that venerable commonwealth would probably have been — what the Presbyterianism of England now is — penetrated with Socinianism." — Prof. Parke's *Fitness of the Church, &c.*, 39.

wood, the sober sense of Ware, the wit of Kirkland, the genius of Channing, the strength of Theophilus Parsons — himself a host — the fame of the University, the princely fortunes of the metropolis, would have carried the churches headlong, unless every Church had been trained to stand on its own foothold, and feel its responsibility to God rather than to the dignitaries of the State. The life of the churches in Massachusetts, after the irruption of Unitarianism, when contrasted with the death-like torpor of the Prussian churches after the irruption of Rationalism, affords an indisputable argument for the policy which trusts the conservation of the truth to a free people. It is a noteworthy fact, that those churches of New England, whose Congregationalism was the most unshackled, remained the firmest against the Unitarian onset. While ecclesiastics who had a centralized government, were oscillating or yielding, the Baptists,[1] who stretched Congregationalism into Independency, stood erect in the faith." [2]

It is, moreover true, that the Congregational way has proved itself especially efficient in dealing with individual cases of defection. Its churches are enabled to let heresy alone — which is a great blessing. If a pastor becomes tainted in doctrine, he is either sustained or condemned, as a matter of course, by the majority of his Church. If the former, the minority protest; if the latter, the majority proceed; and the question comes to a Council, who throw the moral weight of their opinion upon the side of truth. If the majority of the Church sustain the heresiarch, surrounding churches withdraw from him and them, as by instinct, and the spread of contagion is checked. If the majority of his Church renounce him, he is thrown off, and is no longer a Congregational minister in good and regular standing, so that, in that way, the contagion is arrested. Possibly one or two more councils may be called; but beyond that there is no opportunity for "persecution," and the generation of "sympathy," and the formation of a party to follow the thing for years on its travels through the upper courts.[3] There can be little doubt, in any rea-

---

[1] "In general our churches appear to stand steadfast in the doctrines of grace; and indeed, the Baptist churches are almost left alone in defending them against Arminians and Universalists, as our brethren of other denominations, who are sound, appear much discouraged."— Letter of Pres. Manning to Dr. John Rippon, 8 Aug. 1784. Guild's *Life, Times, &c.*, of *Manning*, p. 328.

[2] Prof. Park's *Fitness of the Church, &c.*, 39, 40.

[3] The benefit of this "letting alone" process is clearly seen in the recent case of the Rev. L.

sonable mind, that the Presbyterian standards honestly do justify the claim of the old school branch of the Presbyterian Church, that their new school brethren are "lax" and "heretical;" but the efforts of the constitutional party to maintain those standards and to try and condemn prominent doctrinal offenders against them, and so purify their Church, have nearly always signally failed;[1] and in the

---

A. Sawyer, the new translator of the Bible; who seems to have gone over to the extreme ranks of Rationalism, but who, not being enabled to make any fuss about it, except in a civil form by libel suits against those who have called him an Infidel, has carried nobody with him, and relapsed into insignificance. If we had been compelled to make a Colenso case of it; the end would not be by and by.

[1] A fair illustration of the spirit, wearisomeness, and ineffectiveness of the Presbyterian way of dealing with heresy may be found in its process in the case of Rev. Albert Barnes, for holding and teaching "New School" errors. In 1830, Mr. Barnes was called from Morristown to Philadelphia, by vote of 54 to 1 in the First Presbyterian Church in that City. The Presbytery of Philadelphia, after four days of discussion — by vote of 21 to 2 — gave the Church leave to present the call. Mr. Barnes, on 22 June, after protracted debate, was received to the Presbytery, by vote of 30 to 16. Charges were then presented there against him with a view to prevent his installation; which the Presbytery decided out of order, 32 to 17. The minority appealed to Synod, which sustained the complaint, 30 to 8, and enjoined the Presbytery to hear and decide the complaint. Presbytery met 30 November, and adjourned to hear objections. Great confusion followed, and the whole matter was appealed to the Assembly. That body appears to have been slightly "packed" — at any rate Dr. Green so complained — and it recognized the "conscientious zeal" of Mr. Barnes's opponents, but recommended a division of the Presbytery "in such a way as to promote the peace of its ministers and churches," i. e., to get round the difficulty by throwing Mr. Barnes and his friends into one Presbytery, and his opponents into another. The Synod, however, refused to coöperate in this neat arrangement, and the Presbytery remained undivided. Whereupon Mr. Barnes's friends complained to the Assembly of 1832, which "passed over the contumacy of the Synod as lightly as possible," but ordered the division. The Synod checkmated the Assembly, however, by dividing, but not in the way proposed — which made a bad matter worse. The next Assembly (1833) heard from all parties by complaint and appeal. It referred the whole matter to a Committee who, after most patient incubation, recommended a withdrawal of the complaints, and a general smoothing over of the whole business, for which "amicable adjustment" God was publicly thanked. The inveterate Synod, however, proceeded to "re-arrange" the Presbyteries so as still to harass Mr. Barnes. Of course appeal was made to the Assembly of 1834, which declared the action of the Synod void, but "as a peace measure" did not disturb its result; a course against which 38 members of Assembly protested. The Assembly further made a new Synod, in which the troubled Presbytery could be at peace. The next Assembly — packed again, the other way — (1835) dissolved the new Synod, and carried Mr. Barnes back to the jurisdiction of his own enemies — he, meanwhile having been tried before his own Presbytery and acquitted. Dr. Junkin appealed from this decision to the Synod (now once more all right for him — by the late reconstructive act). But the past records of the Presbytery, covering the date of this trial, were subject only to the revision of the Synod then existing, but now dissolved, and not to the Synod now having jurisdiction; and the Presbytery refused to furnish them to the Synod. The Synod was not to be so bluffed off, but censured the Presbytery, and attempted to try Dr. Junkin's appeal; but Mr. Barnes refused to appear. The Synod suspended him from the ministry, on the ground of holding fundamental errors, by a vote of 116 to 31, and proceeded to extirpate the offensive Presbytery by requiring its members to seek admission to other Presbyteries in six months, or be declared *ipso facto* cut off from the Presbyterian communion. Whereupon Mr. Barnes demitted his ministry and appealed to the next Assembly, and the Presbytery appealed also. That As-

efforts now making to procure a reunion of the long separated portions of that Church, the permanent dilution of the high orthodoxy of those standards is imminently threatened, while the machinery by which heresy is sought to be purged excites the criticism of many of the best friends of the system in which it has its place.[1]

SECTION 9. *Congregationalism is better than any other form of Church polity, because it has a kindlier bearing than any other, toward a republican form of civil government.*

We believe such a form of government is the best; and, with the gradual advance of general intelligence, will be seen to be the best, for *all* men. But whether this be so or not, it is *our* form of Government, and our national prosperity and happiness are so bound up

sembly (1836) — accused of being packed once more, on the " new side,"— spent a week on the case, and by 134 to 96, sustained Mr. Barnes's appeal, and by 145 to 78, restored him to the ministry. Further action followed, including a protest signed by 101 members; but Mr. Barnes resumed his ministry, and has gone on to the present time, preaching and printing things not according to the strict standard of the Presbyterian faith; denying our responsibility for Adam's sin, and our inability to obey God, and teaching, generally, " New School " views. So that, after six years of turmoil in the attempt to cast him out, the Church by its courts only succeeded in fastening him, and his (by *its* creed) erroneous views, the more firmly upon itself, and in exciting toward him and them more widely the notice and sympathy of the Christian world. [See Gillett's *Hist. Presbyterianism*, ii : 400 - 480 ; Stansbury's *Report of the Trial of Rev. A. Barnes.* New York: 1836. 12mo. pp. 416 ; Barnes's *Defence, and other Documents*. New York : 1836, 12mo. pp. 266 ; *The facts in the case of the Rev. A. Barnes, &c.* Philadelphia: 1836. pp. 20, &c., &c. *Assembly's Digest*, Ed. 1858, pp. 661 - 705 ; *Address of First Pres. Church in Philadelphia to the Presbyterian Churches of the United States*, pp. 11.] Similar facts occurred in the case of Dr. Duffield and Dr. Beecher. In regard to " packing " Church Courts, some queer developments might be made. Dr. Beecher states that on his trial, " the Old School had raked and scraped all the old dead churches where they could get an Elder, and thought they might carry the day ; it looked squally." [*Autobiography*, ii : 357.] — See for further facts on this general subject, *Beecher's Works*, vol. iii : 82 - 413 ; *Trial of Lyman Beecher on the charge of Heresy*. New York : 1835. 4to. pp. 83 ; *Trial of Rev. Alex. Bullions*. New York : 1831. 8vo. pp. 45 ; *Official documents of Presbytery of Albany in Trials of John Chester, Mack Tucker*, and *Hooper Cumming*. Schenectady : 1818. 8vo. pp. 255 ; *Narrative of Proceedings of the Judicatories relative to Rev. D. Graham.* Pittsburgh : 1811. 8vo. pp. 200 ; *Trial of N. S. S. Beman, before the Troy Presbytery.* Troy : 1827. 8vo. pp. 47 ; *The several Trials of Rev. D. Barclay before the Presbytery of New Brunswick, &c.* Elizabethtown : 1814. 12mo. pp. 405.

1 " Upon any fair calculation of probabilities, how likely is it that a promiscuous assembly [General Assembly] at Indianapolis will decide a question aright for the whole Church ? I have long looked in vain for any Scripture or rational foundation for supreme ' courts ' having half a continent for their scope." [Dr. J. W. Alexander's *Forty Years' Familiar Letters*, ii : 288.] The same excellent man said, " I see but one plan — *Reduce the Church to its constituent Presbyteries.* These are all that are essential to the notion of a Presbyterian Church." — [*Ibid*, i : 251. See, in this connection, *The Constitution of Courts of Appeal in the Presbyterian Church*, by a Pastor. 8vo. pp. 16.]

with it, as to make it of no small consequence that the prevalent religious faith should work kindly with it, and promote it.

Congregationalism was, historically, the mother of our civil liberties. It was so first at Plymouth, and in the Massachusetts Colony.[1] It was so, later, in the days of the Revolution.[2] And it would seem

---

[1] Bancroft says, speaking of the compact executed 11 November, 1620, "This instrument was signed by the whole body of men, forty-one in number, who, with their families, constituted the one hundred and one, the whole colony, ' the proper democracy,' that arrived in New England. This was the birth of popular constitutional liberty. . . . . . In the cabin of the Mayflower humanity renewed its rights, and instituted government on the basis of 'equal laws' for 'the general government.'"—[*History United States*, i : 310.] So he adds, "For more than eighteen years, ' the whole body of the male inhabitants' constituted the legislature ; the State was governed like our towns,"—he might have added, ' like the churches whose principles, expounded by John Robinson, had led to the adoption of this method of civil government'—"as a strict democracy."—*History United States*, i : 322.

The historical truth on this subject has been very happily stated by a late able writer, who says, "There is a connection between the Church Polity of the Pilgrim Fathers and the civil polity which they adopted, and also between their civil polity and that which the nation subsequently accepted, which has not been sufficiently traced and pondered. The purely democratic form of Government in the Church at Leyden, already entrenched in the warm affections of the Pilgrims, led to the adoption of a corresponding form of civil government on board the Mayflower for the Colony at Plymouth. It has been said, and it is true, that it was a Congregational Church meeting that first suggested the idea of a New England town-meeting ; and a New England town-meeting embodies all the germinal principles of our State and national government."—[Wellman's *Church Polity of the Pilgrims*, pp. 68, 69.] It was the opinion of Mr. Pitt, that if the Church of England had been efficiently established in the North American Colonies, they would never have refused allegiance to the British crown.—Park's *Address before American Cong. Union*, Jan. 1854, p. 13.

One of the bitterest of all the bitter enemies of the Pilgrims has been compelled to concede, "our country, reaching from sea to sea, received its first impulse in the homely meeting-houses of Puritanism. Each little band of Pilgrims under its chosen shepherd, was a free and independent State. There was assembled the future caucus-loving nation. There preached the future patriot, and there listened the war-worn army of liberty. In a century, behold the meeting-house has swelled into the capitol, and the Church members have become citizens of a stupendous empire."—[Oliver's *Puritan Commonwealth*, 493.] So De Tocqueville says our fathers "brought with them to the New World a form of Christianity, which I cannot better describe than by styling it a democratic and republican religion. This contributed powerfully to the establishment of a republic and a democracy in public affairs."—[*Democracy in America* (Bowen's Ed.) i : 384.] And John Adams always named the Congregational churches of New England as chief among the causes of their civil progress.—[*Works*, iii : 400 ; v : 495.] David Hale said, "If Congregationalism does not unavoidably lead to the establishment of a democracy, it certainly favors that form of government."—*Life and Writings*, 276.

[2] "The late Dr. Fishback, of Lexington, Ky., a few years since, made the following statement, which he received from the late Rev. Andrew Tribble, who died at the age of about 93 years. Mr. Tribble was pastor of a small Baptist Church, near Mr. Jefferson's residence, in the State of Virginia, eight or ten years before the American Revolution. Mr. Jefferson attended the meetings of the Church for several months, in succession, and after one of them, asked the worthy pastor to go home and dine with him, with which request he complied.

Mr. Tribble asked Mr. Jefferson how he was pleased with their Church government? Mr Jefferson replied, that its propriety had struck him with great force, and had greatly interested him ; adding that he considered it the only form of pure democracy which then existed in the

a natural inference that the same polity which gave us a Republic would be most favorable, in all its workings, to the permanent welfare of the State.

And if we look into the structure of the system, we shall see that being itself a democracy, training all its members to individual responsibility and labor — under the highest and purest pressure of motive — its natural tendencies and influences will be as much better for a Republic than those of its antagonist systems, as the training of a merchant-man is kindlier than that of a cotton-mill to fit sailors for a man-of-war.

It has, indeed, been urged that the Presbyterian system is more nearly allied to the American civil government than our own; it being claimed that in its graded courts of Sessions, Presbyteries, Synods, and General Assembly, it resembles our civil ranks of towns, counties, States, and the Federal Union.[1] It is well nigh incredible, however, how such a remark can be honestly made, by any person in the remotest degree in possession of the facts in the case. The fundamental principle of our Republicanism is, that every man is equal in the eye of the law, and that every citizen shall contribute his share of sagacity, influence, power, and force, to the common task of governing the nation. So long as it was possible, the republic met *en masse*;[2] and then, as a concession to necessity, a local community deputed some one of their number to go and cast their votes and utter their voice, coming back continually — through fresh election — to receive anew their deputized will. As the States grew to a nation, this system of deputed power and responsibility gradually expanded

---

world, and *had concluded that it would be the best plan of government for the American Colonies.*" — Belcher's *Religious Denominations in the United States,* 184.

So John Wise's famous *Vindication of the Government of the Churches of New England,* was twice re-printed a short time before the Revolutionary war, and its list of subscribers shows that it was called for by a large number of men then prominent in civil life. This contains [pp. 22-43, Ed. of 1772,] a thorough discussion of forms of government, and an earnest plea for a democracy in the State, in connection with its consideration of democracy in the Church.

"I regard the Revolution as the legitimate fruit of Congregationalism...... The principle of the independence of churches or congregations ..... is, in fact, the republican principle." — Dr. Lamson's *Congregationalism,* pp. 16, 17.

[1] "The Presbyterian Church possesses more analogies with our excellent confederated Republic than can be found elsewhere, and moves on with our political government *pari passu*; two free federative republics, one spiritual, the other temporal; neither infringing on the rights, nor curtailing the privileges of the other." — *The Presbyterian's Handbook of the Church,* p. 17.

[2] Bancroft's *History United States,* 1: 322.

and framed and balanced itself into our present town, State, and Federal system. But it never has been severed from its original stock, and to-day every member of every State Legislature and every Senator in Congress, gets the sap which keeps him in official life from this old root of free, and frequently renewed, delegation from the votes of the masses of individual citizens. This is in exact accord of principle with the working of Congregationalism, which indeed deputes no legislatures nor senates, because all its republics are local, and can meet and do all their work at first hand; and so it is not compelled to that concession to necessity which has been referred to. Its working, therefore, is identical with that of our government in its initial, and purest form, being even more republican than it is possible for the huge Republic to be.

The system of Presbyterianism, on the contrary, is in essence a purely aristocratic system. When one of its churches is formed, its membership do indeed, elect their Elders by ballot; but subsequently whenever the office — which is of life tenure — becomes in any one case vacant, the Elders still in office nominate the new incumbent, or he is nominated by a committee, appointed half by the Church, half by the Session, and the Church confirm.[1] Years may thus pass during which the membership of the Church are never appealed to for their judgment on any question whatsoever. They have no voice in the admission of new members to their own body. They have no voice in the discipline of members of their own body. They have no voice in regard to any Church concerns. All is done for them by the Session, which carries its judgments up to the Presbytery, Synod, and Assembly.

To say that this is like our republicanism is as much as to say that it would be no change in our civil system, if, instead of frequent town-meetings, in which every voter expresses his preference for his representatives in the Legislature, and in Congress; for Governor and President, &c.; and — directly or remotely — in regard to all matters of town, county, State, and National concerns (e. g., like the Slavery amendment to the National Constitution,) &c.; the "Selectmen" of our towns, and the Mayors and Aldermen of our cities should — once chosen — hold for life, and take into their own hands the election of all superior officials, and run the nation; the

---

[1] *Handbook of the Church*, 34, 118.

people merely doing the drudgery and paying the bills! Possibly some man may be so astute as to suppose that a proposition to make such a little change as this, would meet with no opposition in this land as a radically anti-republican measure; if so, let him with all his might assert the "more analogies" which Presbyterianism has than Congregationalism, to "our excellent confederated Republic!"[1]

As to the hierarchal forms of Church government, they can, of course, make no pretense to any sympathy, as such, with our civic system. They — as such — would prefer a regulated monarchy; and should the question ever be left to them for settlement, they would doubtless make such preference manifest.

SECTION 10. *Finally, we urge that Congregationalism has preëminence over other Church polities, in the fact that its obvious advantages are organic and peculiar to itself, while what may seem to be its disadvantages, in contrast with opposing systems, are merely incidental to the imperfections with which it has been worked, and will be removed by a more faithful application of its principles.*

We have claimed, as its inherent advantages over other systems, its superior practicability, simplicity, and spirituality; its remarkable development of general intelligence, and the sense of individual responsibility; its readier conservation of a just and faithful discipline; its influence in making its ministry studious, devout, independent, useful, permanent; its easier adaptation to the works of pious benevolence; its safeguards against heresy; and its peculiar fitness to American society, in its kindlier bearing toward our form of civil government. All these advantages are structural, and not accidental; growing naturally out of the peculiarities of the system, and therefore to be found, except as exotic, in none of its opposites.

On the other hand, those features in which other systems sometimes seem to excel us, put us at a disadvantage, in the comparison, only because of our own unfaithfulness to the capabilities of our system. Thus, it is an apparent advantage, which our Methodist brethren sometimes have over us, that — by means of their compact and powerful organization, with its central treasury — they can send a

---

[1] I have referred to Jefferson's estimate of Congregationalism, and to his conviction of its salubrity for a Republic. It is not unfair, in this connection, to add a word of his judgment of Presbyterianism, where, writing to Dr. Cooper, 14 Aug. 1820, he refers to "the ambitious sect of Presbyterians, indeed the Loyalists of our country."— *Works*, vii : 70.

preacher to a place that cannot sustain him, and keep him there until he can develop strength enough to build up a permanent Church upon the spot. But when the sisterhood of Congregational churches becomes fully awake to its missionary responsibilities, and ready to perform all its Church Extension duties, its hand will be stretched out toward all such remote places; and churches will be established there, more in sympathy with the *genius loci* than the despotic Wesleyan system will permit. Nothing needs to be added to our system, nor anything taken from it, to give it this new efficiency; we only need to live better up to its fraternal capabilities. So, if we mistake not, it will be found to be, in every other particular in which any other system may have us at a temporary disadvantage. The superior 'order' of the stately hierarchies, so far as it really is any better than our own, is only supplemental, and not antagonist to it, and will be superinduced upon ours, as we grow in grace, and in the knowledge and practice of Godliness.

It is curious, indeed, to see how the systems that oppose us are compelled, when in stress of difficulty, to forsake their own first principles and appeal to ours. Thus, it is a first principle with us, that the last appeal is to the people. It is a first principle in the English Church, on the contrary, that the last appeal is to "the Church," meaning a hierarchal organism, headed by the Queen, and officered by Archbishops, Bishops, &c. But, let some Churchman be censured and degraded — as he thinks, unjustly — by the proper tribunal, and you will at once see him appealing *to the people*, through the press, and pleading his cause with them, in the hope of so stirring up a popular commotion, as to convince his judges that their own safety requires the reversal of his sentence. And, if he succeed well in his effort, you will see his judges pleading their cause before the same people in defence of what they have done, both parties thus committing a solecism to their first principles, coming over to our position, practically confessing that the ultimate power and right of judging, after all, are with the people; and seeking to do indirectly by public sentiment, what we do directly by vote. So, in the great Presbyterian division, when the exscinding acts of the General Assembly of 1837, 'cut off, at one blow, " nearly one-fifth of the entire membership of the Church;"[1] declaring — without trial, or even citation

---

[1] Gillett's *History Presbyterian Church*, p. 517.

— by snap-judgment, a number of Synods and Presbyteries which had made themselves obnoxious, for various causes, to the Old School majority of that Assembly, to be "out of the Ecclesiastical connection of the Presbyterian Church in the United States, and no longer in form or fact, an integral portion of said Church;"[1] that Church was compelled to desert its own principles and appeal to ours; to go before the tribunal of its own private membership for its last appeal, and as the result of that appeal, great efforts are now making, year by year, to undo all that was then done, and relieve the good sense of the world of the absurdity of the one indivisible Presbyterian Church of the United States, showing itself in the shape of "two denominations, each claiming the same title, adopting the same standards, and, to a considerable extent, occupying the same field, and represented by its *General* Assembly."[2]

The Old School Assembly, which insists that the "standards" shall be especially interpreted as teaching the "innate, hereditary, sinful corruption of nature; the sinner's inability to repent and believe without the supernatural aid of the spirit, and the sovereignty of God in election,"[3] is dependent upon the faith of its constituent Church members in the strict construction of those doctrines; and in that moment when the masses of those Church members favor the milder interpretations of the "New School," the Old School ceases to be, as inevitably, as if, like Congregationalists, they assumed that the power is in the hands of Christ's people, under him.

In the matter of discipline, as well, the hierarchal sects are, in the last result, driven to stand on essentially Congregational ground. If a Church functionary, or Church Court, deposes or disciplines a man, unjustly — in the judgment of the masses of its communion — the pressure of public sentiment will be almost certain soon to compel a reversal of the act.

We shall doubtless be reminded in this connection of the fact, stated by us early in this volume,[4] that there are some thirteen or

---

[1] Gillett's *History Presbyterian Church*, p. 513.
[2] *Ibid*, p. 553. This is not the worst of the matter, however. There are eight or ten distinct Presbyterian organisms — each of which is "The Church" in this country, involving, according to the *Princeton Review*, (which ought to know,) "not only the evils of sectarian jealousy and rivalry, but the enormous waste of men, labor, and money." — *Princeton Review*, xxxvii: 272.
[3] *Princeton Review*, xxxvii: 309.   [4] See page 5.

fourteen hundred churches in this country which are, in substance, Congregationally governed, and which are yet avowedly and fatally heretical in their creed — so far as they have any; and shall be asked to reconcile that fact with the argument of this chapter.

Nothing is easier than to do so. While their existence, and what measure of thrift they possess, are a continued demonstration of the needlessness of hierarchal institutions, and a proof that Congregationalism, even in its most imperfect and erroneous development, has important advantages over all other forms of Church Polity; it is enough to say that by ignoring two of its fundamental principles (that the Bible is to be taken in its uttermost exactness of honest literal meaning as our guide, and that hopeful piety be an indispensable condition of Church membership) they have hindered our system from working its spiritually purgative work upon them, and made themselves thus exceptional to its beneficent tendencies, without, in any degree, impairing the proof that they exist.

CHAPTER V.

WHAT OUGHT TO BE DONE ABOUT IT?

This is the practical question which sums up all. We do not propose to go into any answer in full detail, but merely to throw out a few suggestions as the seeds of thought, and, so far as God please, of action.

We have seen that Congregationalism is that democratic form of Ecclesiastical order and government, which Christ and the Apostles established in the earliest days of the Christian Church, and which emerged from the hierarchal eclipse of fourteen hundred years into which it was speedily thrown, in immediate connection with the blessing of God upon the pious studies, labors, and sufferings of our Pilgrim fathers. We have seen that it is grounded upon the teachings of Christ, and the testimony of the Apostles; that all its essential principles are immutably founded upon the rock of Scriptural precept, and example, and buttressed on every side by the clearest deductions of pure reason. We have seen how its system works in general, and in detail. And we have seen how and why it is better than any other form of Church polity:—in its nearer accordance with the mind of Christ; its superior practicableness of working; its especial stimulation of general intelligence; its eminent furtherance of piety in its membership; its peculiar promotion of that discipline on which purity depends in the Church; its extraordinary kindliness toward its ministry, and their work; its singular adaptation to those revivals, which are the life of the Church, and the hope of the world; its inapproachable facilities for the Gospel treatment of false doctrine and heresy; and its unique congeniality with the working of those republican institutions, which are indeed its own gift to the world. We have further seen how all these considerations are heightened by the fact that these advantages of Congregationalism are innate and organic, while what sometimes seem to be its disadvantages in contrast with the working of other and hostile systems, are incidental to present imperfections in its development, and will disappear of themselves, as it grows to do its perfect work.

In view of these considerations, and such as these, which will crowd upon every reflecting mind having due cognizance of the facts, it becomes an inquiry of special interest, what duty rests upon the believers in this system of polity.

We suggest: —

1. Congregationalists should recognize the fact that Congregationalism is a polity. They have been too apt to esteem it as rather the negation of a system. They ought to see that it is an orderly, self-consistent, compact, and singularly perfect plan of Christian working; more nearly adapted than any other to the needs of individual human nature and the necessities of the advancing intelligence of the world; and quite as sharply defined in its qualities, and as imperative in its duties growing out of them, as any polity with which it competes among men. Like our form of civil government, it sits loosely upon loyal shoulders, and seldom forces itself upon the thought of the obedient and the faithful; but it has as distinct an entity as that government itself, and, like that, will not fail to make itself felt as a corrective upon the offender. So far from being nowhere as a philosophy and a doctrine; not Rome herself with her canons and decretals has a position for her devotees, and a demand upon them, any more thoroughly self-consistent, or distinctly defined, than Congregationalism has for her disciples.

2. Congregationalists ought to comprehend the fact not only that they have a polity, but that they have that polity which Christ especially loves and would promote. His own directions for Church life, as we have seen, cannot be applied to any other system without violence; while our simple, unostentatious, and spiritual methods are such as most entirely comport with what he was, and what he loved, and what he did, and what he desires. It must be that it is a part of that "travail of his soul," which is the Millenium he shall be satisfied with seeing, that his cause here should be brought back from all false and formal and worldly ways, to that simplicity that is in him; until we all do this in remembrance of him, in that way in which he did it, and in which it was done, and caused to be done, by those who saw him oftenest, and loved him most, and knew him best, and followed him nearest.

3. Congregationalists ought to master their polity in its grand general scope, and in all its minutest details. The fact that it has no " Book " in which is a written code; that it has no authoritative exposition of what the Bible teaches, and the churches should practice; makes this duty of especial importance. The two foci of our ellipse are, on the one side, the independence of the local Church, and on the other, the mutual friendship and helpful co-working of all local churches. Around and from these two centres, the circumference of duty is drawn, and it is for each man's conscience, enlightened by the word of God and by prayer, to sweep that including line for himself, and decide what things fall of necessity within it, and what things lie inexorably outside of it. The fact that others have gone over the ground before, and have left more or less record of their solution of the question at issue, may help him — must help him — but cannot supersede his duty of working out the problem for himself. Common sense, guided by a devout spirit, can hardly fail to lead the honest inquirer into essential truth in all his deductions from the first principles of our system; while the circumstance that a great diversity sometimes exists in Congregational practices of minor import, is much more an illustration of the historical fact that we have heedlessly borrowed our usages from surrounding polities in some points incongruous with our own, than an argument against the safety of the deductions of individual research.

It is a disgrace to our denomination, that, in so many instances, its members are so helplessly ignorant of its plainest requisitions. But the disgrace attaches to the weak concessions of the past to the influences of Presbyterianism, and the so great commingling of the two polities in the broad field of the West, rather than to the system itself; as if its natural tendency were to make its disciples unaware what manner of spirit they are of. They owe it to themselves to know. They owe it to their Master, and to the world for whom he died, to know, and to know assuredly.

4. Congregationalists ought to appreciate the fact that no other polity can be so helpful as their own to this land in its immense, and now immensely augmenting need. The days when American Congregationalism was impudently assumed by those who did not desire it at the West, and weakly conceded by those who did not understand it at the East, to be constitutionally ineffective, irrelevant, and

exotic beyond Byram river, have passed a long way into history. *Fourteen hundred and forty-six* — more than half — of her 2,863 churches; 1,149 of her 2,719 ministers; and 89,020 of her 268,015 Church members, are now catalogued in "the regions beyond." Congregational churches have demonstrated to a not overwilling world, that they can live and thrive anywhere and everywhere, where Christ has redeemed people whom he desires should be banded together to serve him, and where it is his purpose to have his kingdom come. The purity of the republicanism of our system, and the stimulus which it affords to popular education, make it directly subservient to the cause of sound civil government in this nation, as no other system can be; while, at the present time, when all the forms of hierarchy are hampered by their unyielding organism, or by something in their past record, which stands in the way of their meeting the new demands of the opening free South for Christian aid, guidance, and reconstruction, it offers itself, as, on the one hand, actually fitted by all its peculiarities, and on the other hand, passively prepared by all that it is not, and has not been, and done, as no other can be for the great and glorious work. Its professors ought to enlarge their minds to the fullest comprehension of all that the Lord is now making possible for them to do, that they may justify the Master's hope for them by fulfilling that Master's purpose of blessing for the world through them.

5. Congregationalists ought to feel that their polity is preëminently the polity of revivals, and so the best hope of the kingdom of God on earth; and feeling this they ought to work it in that aim, and to that end. The watchword of glorious old Lyman Beecher, "revivals are the hope of the Church," ought to be their battle cry. They believe in revivals. They are not afraid of them. Their whole system is congruous with them, and trains all whom it fitly influences, just as they need to be trained, to promote them. And the history of the Congregationalism of New England, almost for the last one hundred years, has been such a history of revivals as it is believed no other churches on earth could ever show. And now that the world, and our nation, need revivals of pure and undefiled religion as they were never needed before, and as God is throwing open avenues to human hearts as they were never opened before, Congregationalists will be the most ungrateful, as well as faithless,

of all people of God, if they do not awake to righteousness, and develop to the utmost the beneficent powers with which God has entrusted them.

6. Congregationalists, understanding that they have a polity — that polity which Christ founded and loves, and comprehending it in all its breadth of detail, and appreciating the significance of its healthy extension to the civil welfare of the nation, and to the religious welfare of the world; ought to determine, by the grace of God, to use all honorable means to secure its prevalence through the land and over the world. They need no longer be afraid of the cry of "Congregational Puseyism."[1] They need no longer shrink before the Presbyterian sneer at the sectarian propagation of their distinctive principles, as if for Congregationalists to do anything to promote Congregationalism, were to commit one of those blunders which are worse than a crime. And why, forsooth, in the name of all goodness, may not Congregationalists propagate their distinctive principles — so be that they do it in an honorable and Christian manner — with as much self-respect and as much other respect, as the believers in any less Scriptural form of faith? Why ought they not to do it? What is there "funny" in the idea, that they should have "distinctive" principles — except it may be that their own impotence for so long in setting them forth, has prepared the world to believe that they are without them? Is not the Gospel principle of the independence and self-completeness of the local Church as really a "distinctive" principle, as its corrupt hierarchal opposite; and, being taught of God that it is the truth, and that all other theories of the Church are grounded in error and fraught with harm, are Congregationalists to be despised, because they contend manfully for the faith once delivered to the saints?

By no means. The world always respects earnest men, even when it cannot agree with them. And it is because so many nominal Congregationalists have dilly-dallied and shilly-shallied over their polity, so long and so apologetically, and proved themselves so

---

[1] Dr. Rice came in this evening from his mission to the Massachusetts General Association at Pepperell. He says the Congregationalists are blowing up the sectarian flame very hard, and laboring to propagate their 'distinctive' principles. Congregational Puseyism is funny enough!"—Letter, of date, 29 June, 1840.— *Forty Years' Familiar Letters, of J. W. Alexander, D. D.*, ii: 54.

ready to leave it on the slightest occasion,[1] and so anxious to have it understood that it unites the maximum of agreement with everybody else, to the minimum of self-coherence and self-consistence, that they have excited toward it — or toward this wretched caricature of it — the pity of some, the contempt of others, and the misapprehension of all.

It is high time for every member of the denomination to awake out of sleep, to study its system until he discovers that it has 'distinctive' principles, and to become so steeped in them, and possessed by the thought of the good that is in them for a clamoring country and a waiting world, as to feel that nothing will suit his utterance short of those energetic words of Peter and John, and he ' cannot not speak'[2] the things which he has seen and heard. When he is thus aroused, and has made himself intelligent in his own faith, appreciative of it, and enthusiastic for it, several things will be likely to occur to him as desirable to be done to promote it — such as some of these: —

(1.) It should be preached as a system which Christ and the Apostles shaped, and which ought to be made clear in what it is, what it is not, and what it demands, to all true believers. As it is a system especially for the lay masses — one which peculiarly honors, blesses, and leans upon them — it should be made especially familiar to them, until a public sentiment is created which esteems the quasi boast not now infrequently heard from the lips of Congregational ministers — " I believe I have never preached on the distinctive principles of Congregationalism, in my life, so that I surely cannot be called very sectarian," to be, rather, a humiliating confession of professional malfeasance, and personal cowardice. Without ringing changes upon it, without tiring people with it, and making a hobby of it, Congregationalism ought to be expounded from its own pulpits with sufficient frequency to indoctrinate the people thoroughly in its essence and excellence, and to save the young, especially, from those snares which the systems of more hierarchal pomp and splendor will be very likely to set for their giddy feet.

(2.) Distinctively Congregational Missions, home and foreign, should be supported by all Congregational churches, in preference to

---

[1] Of a Presbyterian call, provided it be reasonably "loud."
[2] Acts, iv: 20. "οὐ δυνάμεθα μὴ λαλεῖν."

all others. In regard to foreign missions, it is not indeed needful that there be any pledge that mission churches should take the Congregational form — that, Providence, through the inherent necessities of the case, will sufficiently secure.[1] All that is needed is that the missions be not distinctively pledged to any hierarchy.

As to home missions, the case is different. Believing, as we do, that no Church but a Congregational Church can be fully Scriptural, reasonable, or preferable in this land, it is natural that we should demand that, in the matter of a Society whose work is to found churches in the distant West and South, there should be some security that our money does not go to pull down what we believe to be truth, in the interest of that which we believe to be error. Of course *any* Evangelical Church is better than none, and where the question must be (for any reason) between no Church at all, or one of Evangelical faith of some other polity, we could not hesitate to authorize such a concession to Providence. But the cases must be very few where, when the especial fitness of Congregationalism for "fresh woods and pastures new" is understood, it will not seem best to all concerned to let the new organism begin with the Scripture, and not with the traditions of the Elders. The West is no longer preëmpted to Presbyterianism. And in some parts of the South, they have had quite Presbyterianism enough — such as it was — to last them until the rebellion shall be forgotten, and its blood-stains fade. There is no reason why — in due comity to all less Scriptural competitors, and with no enmity toward anybody, — the Congregational churches should not take the blessing of Napthali, and 'possess the West and the South.'[2]

(3.) Congregationalists — since their system more than any other, both promotes intelligence and depends upon it — should abundantly endow, and then thoroughly use, their existing (and all needed additional) Colleges and Theological Seminaries. It is deplorable that they have so long neglected their own interests in this regard. If the Seminary at Andover had always been (as it now is, and is to be) a thoroughly Congregational institution, with a trumpet uttering a certain and a Scriptural sound upon the question of Church polity; it may well be doubted whether our Congregationalism at the West might not now have been of double its present strength. Men for

---

[1] See page 277.   [2] Deut. xxxiii : 23.

many years went forth thence instructed that the Congregationalism of New England lacked some of the very elements which Presbyterianism offered,[1] and that, at any rate, " it was best for Congregationalists to become Presbyterians when they moved to the West."[2] That folly is now outgrown,[3] and yet it may well be questioned whether there is not room for improvement in the tone of all our New England Seminaries upon this question. Congregationalists, whom God has blessed with abundant wealth, should endow these Seminaries so amply, that there shall no longer be inducement for our young men to seek an education within their slender means in other Seminaries out of New England, and become Presbyterianized in the process.[4]

Every Pastor, and indeed every Church officer, ought to be inquiring now for young men of piety and talents, who may be, as soon as possible, put in training in these institutions for the great need of the churches and the world. There is danger of a speedy famine of ministers, unless the ranks of preparation are quickly and amply filled.

(4.) Congregationalists should purify the practical working of their system from those inconsistencies which now, on the one hand, detract from its usefulness and acceptance within, and, on the other, impair its good name, and so hinder its progress, without. We here refer, more particularly, to those not very unusual crude, ill-judged, and hasty procedures in which some simple fundamental principle of our polity is violated, in the endeavor to right some felt wrong;—as where a Council, called for some specific purpose, and for that only, being in session, and becoming cognizant of some apparent evil which it thinks it possible to cure, makes an uncalled for deliverance in regard to it—to the alienation of those who may be aggrieved by their procedure, and who have sense enough to perceive its unconstitutionality; or where a Conference of Churches, (by its very funda-

---

[1] Dr. Woods's *Works*, iii : 577-583.   [2] *Congregationalist*, 15 Mar. 1861.

[3] Dr. Woods repented of his judgment in this respect before his death. In July, 1844, he said, "I have altered my opinion. I think the Congregationalists ought to remain such, at the West. The house is not large enough for two families, and each family ought to have its own separate tenement."—*Ibid.*

[4] It is greatly to be hoped not only that the new plans at Andover may be carried out, but that the East Windsor Seminary may receive an ample endowment on its contemplated removal to Hartford, so that those young men of Old School preferences, who would not be happy — or think they would not — at Andover, or Bangor, or New Haven, need not be driven to Princeton, as so many of them now seem to be.

mental constitution, to the last degree, destitute of the faintest shadow of power over the churches) with a good motive in a particular case, practically decides, by some indirect yet effectual vote, that a given Church is not a Church in good and regular standing; or where an association of ministers (which is as purely a voluntary association as a sewing circle or a debating club,) on what it thinks to be due cause, and because it judges that the thing ought to be done, and does not instantly discern in what other, and regular way, the end desired may be reached, professes to depose from the ministry some erring brother whose name may happen to be on its list of membership.

It is humiliating that the doctors of our law are not sometimes better instructed in its principles than they prove themselves to be, but so it is. And some of them are in great danger of thinking that because our system is not a very rigid one, therefore almost anything, which it seems desirable to have done, may be rightly done, in almost any manner. Any end which God in his Providence sets before it may indeed be reached through it, — there is no doubt of that. But there is a right way, and a wrong way of procedure toward every end, and it is of very great consequence that our system be sufficiently understood by its professors, to secure the right doing always of all that needs to be done in the churches.

Our great danger is from a distrust of our own first principles. We are afraid to do right and trust God, and wait. Some among us often long for a "strong government" by which a heretic could be at once compelled to renounce our name, and his Church compelled to accept some other teacher. They do not see that the only force that is "strong" enough to deal successfully with such a case, is that of truth and time which, under God, will bring all right, and quicker under the moral appliances of our system than under the sharper force of any other.

(5.) Congregationalists ought to cultivate a spirit of unity and concord and co-working, that shall do such justice as has never yet been done to their great fundamental principle of the communion of the churches. They do not need a General Assembly, nor a General Convention, nor any great overshadowing all-engulfing hierarchy. But they do need to understand each other, to love each other, to trust each other, and to plan to work with each other.

The good old Synodic way of meeting together for general counsel upon matters of common concernment, is fragrant in our history, and, as we experienced it a few years since, in the "Albany Convention," it did great good, and little or no harm. And it may be hoped, and confidently expected, that that new Synod of Boston — under the more appreciable and appropriate modern name of Council — which is soon to be held, may make suggestions in this, and other directions, which shall be of incalculable benefit; as the result of which the world shall see that a denomination of churches, simply affiliated by sisterhood in Christ, is more homogeneous, more strong, beneficent and practical, than any hierarchy that the world ever saw.

The Lord our God be with us as He was with our fathers, — let Him not leave us nor forsake us; that He may incline our hearts unto him; to walk in all His ways, and to keep His commandments, and His statutes, and His judgments, which He commanded our fathers. AMEN.

THE END.

www.ingramcontent.com/pod-product-compliance
Lightning Source LLC
Chambersburg PA
CBHW030004240426
43672CB00007B/826